THE DOLSON FAMILY HERITAGE:

A RESEARCH-BASED NARRATIVE

David P. Dolson III

Table of Contents

Preface

This sketch of the Dolson family history follows a specific branch of the family from its assumed origins in the village of Dalsen, Overijssel Province, in the Netherlands to Sacramento, California, USA. The time span covered is approximately1600 to 2018. The narrative describes the family's sojourns in the Dutch North American colony of Nieuw Netherlandts, the British colonial province of New York, as well as its migration to Westchester, Dutchess, and Orange counties in New York before reaching the Sierra Nevada Mountains and the Sacramento Valley in California. Specifically, this volume provides a detailed description of each male forebear in this line of the Dolson family, commencing with the immigrant ancestor, Jan Gerritsen de Vries van Dalsen, and ending with David Pelton Dolson II.

As a general tenet, this manuscript is based on documentary evidence obtained from primary sources such as government, business, and church records. Secondary sources such as historical and genealogical works as well as newspapers and other periodicals were also tapped. In some cases, tertiary information garnered from a variety of sources, including family history narratives, both professional and amateur, and local history manuscripts, is reported. In relation to the data concerning collateral families, the author readily acknowledges considerable reliance on the work of other genealogists, who thankfully published their efforts or otherwise made their narratives available in family history repositories or online.

Regardless of source, when the documentation for statements is omitted, ignored, or claimed to be nonexistent, the author attempts to categorize and label such information as undocumented, theoretical, or even speculative, depending on the context.

Each chapter of this volume focuses on the biography of a single male ancestor in this particular branch of the Dolson family. In addition to a description of the life of the ancestor himself, details are provided regarding his spouse, the spouse's family, the ancestor's children, his siblings, and other contemporary relatives and noteworthy associates. In an effort to be as unbiased and as discreet as possible, the author has decided not to include a detailed description of any living Dolson or to write an autobiographical chapter. Prudence suggests that the inclusion of such information should be left to the future when another writer can more objectively describe the life events of these contemporary Dolsons.

Not uncommonly, some researchers of the Dolson family have made conjectures about individuals and events without sufficient evidence, disclaimers, or justification. Even more problematic, some family historians mistakenly have reported inaccurate information, and these erroneous accounts have been passed along haphazardly by others. This type of carelessness has become exceedingly recurrent and far reaching in the age of the Internet.

The writer has discovered blunders by amateur genealogists as well as imprecise work by recognized historians. Inaccuracies and mistakes can even be encountered in the primary source materials themselves. Church records in particular, but also government and business archives are not perfect. Transcriptions and translations of original documents occasionally are problematic. There are also some instances when the Dolson ancestors themselves may have provided, for whatever reasons, vague or inaccurate information to census takers, tax collectors, and other officials.

Documenting and interpreting family history can be a complicated, confusing, and frustrating endeavor. The writer attempts to advise the reader when the evidence is non-existent, weak, confusing or open to multiple interpretations. Also, as necessary, the writer purposefully points out errors, omissions, and irregularities encountered in the family literature. This is done for several reasons. First, the writer wishes to provide readers with an account of the Dolsons that is as complete as possible. Rigorous research combined with thorough analyses and, when appropriate, theoretical hypotheses provide a comprehensive representation of the family's past. Secondly, readers who venture beyond this volume are likely to encounter contradictions from other sources. Whenever this occurs, the writer would like to assure readers that he was aware of prevailing conflicts and, to the best of his ability, has suitably addressed such issues in this volume. Finally, in an effort to provide a straightforward portrayal of the various Dolson ancestors, the writer avoids outright conjecture while still permitting some level of inference when confronting gaps in the family's story. Unless readers are warned otherwise, the writer has narrowed his formulations to logical contextual suppositions and congruent theoretical hypotheses.

This is not to say that this manuscript does not contain errors of its own, both of commission and omission. The Dolson family history is a monumental puzzle. There are many missing pieces. Mysteries from collateral family genealogies have become entangled with those of the Dolsons. Perhaps the most formidable challenge however is the fact that the exact number of pieces which make up the whole of the Dolson narrative is unknown. It is implausible that family historians will ever be able to reconstruct an exhaustive and precise account. Additionally, the reader should be aware that this volume contains a significant number of quotations from many works. In a number of cases the spelling and word choices are antiquated and no longer meet the norms of standard usage. In fact by modern standards, some of the language used is downright offensive, sexist, and racist. Still, the quotes have been left as encountered in the historical literature. The readers will be able to judge for themselves the original intent and meaning.

The reader should be aware that additional Dolson data are discovered on an ongoing basis. Old Dutch colonial manuscripts are encountered and then translated. Historical and genealogical information stored in private and public archives is released, transcribed, and published regularly. Copies of rare and newly-discovered manuscripts are posted online. Facts about the Dolsons hidden in other family genealogies come to light as these works are shared. Difficult to locate and access information continues to be catalogued in family history repositories such as libraries and genealogical societies. For these reasons, this manuscript should be viewed as a work-in-progress. Undoubtedly, future Dolson researchers will clarify, correct, and add to the information contained in this volume. As mentioned earlier, the writer hopes that they will expand on this work to include chapters on the present and future generations of the Dolson family.

In the end, it is the writer's wish that Dolson family members, friends, individuals associated with the collateral families, and anyone interested in the genealogies contained herein will find this volume interesting and informative. Supplementary input on Dolson family history is welcome. Readers are encouraged to send corrections and additions to the author at d_dolson@yahoo.com. The writer also invites refutations. Differing interpretations and analyses will make the sketch more interesting. The entire project has been a great adventure and additional interaction with Dolson cousins and other interested parties will surely enhance the documented history of the Dolson family.

Acknowledgements

The writer began this project in 2003. At that time, he expected to complete a brief manuscript of approximately twenty-five pages in a matter of weeks. Well, weeks turned into months, and months into years. Twenty-five pages turned into more than 250. In all, the completion of a preliminary edition took nearly a decade of research and writing. Another six years were dedicated to the development of this final manuscript. Many corrections, additions, and other revisions were needed. Along the way, many persons have assisted, but the writer wishes to acknowledge a few special individuals and institutions which made inestimable contributions.

First, the writer thanks his cousin, Patricia Loverde Heinrich, who kindled his initial interest in the project. In the 1990s, Pat began the family history research that has led to the development of this volume. She initiated study on parents, grandparents, and great grandparents in California. As part of that work, she discovered the link to the Dolson family in Orange County, New York.

Secondly, the writer is indebted to another cousin, albeit distant, Ron Plimley of Wappinger's Falls, New York, whose seminal work entitled *Dalfsens to Van Dolsons: A Collection of Dolson Genealogy Records* (2003; Revised 2011), provided a framework for this volume. Ron's opus allowed the writer to not only confirm the connection of the California Dolson branch to the Dolsons of Orange County, New York, but also to Dolson ancestors from other areas of New York such as Dutchess and Westchester counties as well as to the family's roots in New Harlem, New Amsterdam, and in the Netherlands.

Of note has been the genealogical research and analyses of James Downey of Burlington, New York. James shared with the writer his extensive analysis of existing Vermilyea family literature, including a review of several generations of the Dolsons. James has exceptional skills in detecting inaccuracies in research, identifying more reliable sources, and advancing plausible theories whenever there are gaps in documentation. James' adherence to rigorous research standards caused this writer to re-examine thoroughly the contents of the preliminary edition and to address research shortcomings when developing this final edition.

The writer also acknowledges the Orange County Genealogical Society (OCGS) of New York. Over many years, the members of that organization have provided the writer with valuable assistance. The research library at the Old Goshen Court House has been a particularly valuable resource. Additionally, the writer benefitted greatly from attendance at several "Research Seminars" sponsored each fall by the OCGS and held at the Warwick Center. It was during these trips to New York that Sue Gardiner, Local History Librarian at the Albert Wisner Library in Warwick, was not only helpful in identifying relevant family sources but also in providing corresponding, contextual information to promote fuller understanding.

Others that deserve mention include the staff and volunteers at the Family History Library in Salt Lake City as well as that organization's branch in Sacramento. Additional institutions that were particularly helpful include the Orange County Historical Society, the Adriance Library in Poughkeepsie, the Thrall Library in Middletown, the Middletown-Wallkill Historical Association, the Minisink Museum (particularly Teresa Weeden Gurdineer, Historian for the Town of Minisink), the Blodgett Memorial Library in Fishkill, and the Dutchess County Historical and Genealogical Societies.

Thanks are due to the Holland Society of New York City, The New York Historical Society, and the New York Public Library. All three of these institutions arranged customized appointments for the writer.

Online and print resources accessed through organizations such as the New York Genealogical and Biographical Society and the New England Historic Genealogical Society, as well as several commercial providers of online data and print books have proven to be immeasurably valuable.

Finally, special thanks to Gerald Ward, Librarian, of the I Street Press at the Sacramento Public Library. Gerry not only walked the author through the publication process but assisted in editing the volume, preparing the cover, and formatting the manuscript for printing. Without Gerald Ward's contributions, this volume would not have been published.

This volume is dedicated to (1) the writer's father, David Pelton Dolson II, who more than anyone else, would have been amazed at the many incredibly interesting stories and details associated with the nine generations of the Dolson family depicted herein and (2) to the writer's solitary grandchild, Penelope Riley Dolson, who alone must carry on the name of the family with the dignity collectively contributed by all of the ancestors who preceded her.

Prologue

As far as it is known at this time, the earliest, unquestionable documentation of a Dolson ancestor is found in the following marriage record dated 18 December 1660 from the Dutch Reformed Church in what was then the city of Nieuw Amsterdam in the Dutch colony of Nieuw Netherlandts:

> **18 dicto. <u>Jan Gerritszen</u>, Van Worcum, in Vrieslant, en Grietje Theunis, Van Amsterd. in N. Nederlt.**[1]

In the early annals of Nieuw Amsterdam, our ancestor, Jan Gerritsen, is referred to with the patronymic of *Gerritsen* and the suffix of *de Vries*, and combinations of the two. The suffix *de Vries* denotes "the Frieslander" or a person from the province of Friesland (*Vrieslant*) in the Netherlands. This type of attribution was common among the Dutch of that period and fortunately for family historians, assists to distinguish persons of similar names by indicating a place of origin.

The Dolson Surname

Jan Gerritsen de Vries is the name found commonly in the church, court, and tax records of Nieuw Amsterdam (later renamed as New York under the British) and Nieuw Haarlem (New Harlem); the latter at that time, simply a small village located a short distance north of Nieuw Amsterdam on the Island of Manhattan. Riker (1904) suggests that to distinguish himself from other contemporary Jan Gerritsens, our Jan eventually recycled another suffix, *van Dalsen*, to show lineage from the village of Dalsen (presently referred to as Dalfsen), apparently the origin of the Dolson family. Literally *van Dalsen* means "from" or "of" Dalsen in Dutch. Theunis, Jan's son, was referred to as a *Dalsen* during his lifetime. Jan's daughters alternatively used *Jans, Janszen, Gerrits,* and *Dalsen*. Beginning with the third generation of the family, *Jans, Janszen, Gerrits, Gerritsen,* and *de Vries* were dropped and members of this line of the family, from that period forward, used one spelling variation or another of *Dolson* (or less frequently, *van Dolson*) as their surname.

E Pluribus Unum

Based on a review of Dutch records from Nieuw Amsterdam, there appear to be more than a dozen contemporary colonists referred to as Jan Gerritsen (along with alternative spellings such as *Gerritiszen, Gerrits, Garreson,* and *Garrison*) during the mid-1600s. Examples include Jan Gerritsen Brouwer, Jan Gerritsen Decker, Jan Gerritsen Van Buytenhuysen, Jan Gerritsen Van Marken, Jan Gerritsen Groll, and Jan Gerritsen Van Boxel to name just a few (Riker, 1904). Yet other Jan Gerritsens were referred to according to their corresponding

---

[1] Translation: *18th of this same month, Jan Gerritszen, from Workum, in Friesland, and Grietje Theunis, from Amsterdam in New Netherlands.*

occupations such as Jan Gerritsen Smith or Jan Gerritsen Mason. This occurred in both English and Dutch renditions of the names. Although none of the records associated with our Jan indicate Jan Gerritsen Scheepsmaker (Ship's Carpenter), there are instances when our ancestor is referred to as Captain, primarily in church records and family history accounts.

During these times, there were far fewer colonists who used de Vries as part of their name. The most notable and most thoroughly studied is the famous Captain David Peterszen de Vries, an important colonial official, who upon his return to the Netherlands, published extensive chronicles. Another interesting de Vries family is that of Captain Jan de Vries and his son, Jan Jacob de Vries (sometimes written as *de Fries*, *de Frees* or *de Vrees*). The younger de Vries was born in Nieuw Amsterdam in 1647 and married in the colony (Gordon, 2001). The Dutch Reformed Church records report on the baptisms of several of Jan de Vries children. In none of these records are the names Gerritsen or Dalsen associated with this de Vries family. Additional information on the elder Captain de Vries is provided in Chapter I.

According to Riker (1904), and supported in a variety of other sources, there were several other "Dolson" families in Nieuw Netherlandts. The most notable is a Van Dalssen or Van Dalsem clan originally from Haarlem, Netherlands that located first in New Jersey and subsequently in Rockland County, New York. The immigrant of this family was Jan van Dalssen who married Anna van Raesveldt. The family arrived in New York as early as 1702 but removed to New Jersey. To confuse matters further, there were coincidently, descendants among the members of this family named Jan, Theunis, and Aaltje. Apparently, this Jan was a *voorleser*, a lay clergyman who visited and provided comfort to the sick. A five generational history of the Van Dalssen family is found in two chapters written by George O. Zabriskie and contained in a collection entitled *New Jersey Genealogies* (2005). There is no known ancestral link between the Van Dalssen and Dolson families.

By coincidence a *voorleser* named Jan van Dalsen is recorded as a witness to the signing of the will of Aeltje Waldron Vermilyea (Theunis Dalsen's mother-in-law) on 23 May 1730 in Yonkers. Yet another *voorleser* named Jan Gerritsen is reported to be administering to the sick in Orange County between 1680 and 1699. There are also several references to individuals with the surnames Gerritsen and Dolson at Fort Orange (now Albany) and in other locations in Nieuw Netherlandts during the Dutch period.

None of the persons mentioned in this section appears to be related to our Dolson branch. In addition, in an article for the *Record* (Vol. 116, Nos. 3 and 4, 1985), the journal of the New York Genealogical and Biological Society, the noted genealogist, Harry Macy Jr., conducted a comprehensive study on the Gerritsen and Garrison families of the time. No link was detected to our Gerritsen ancestors. Out of the many individuals researched as our possible immigrant ancestor, the available evidence consistently supports the conclusion that Jan Gerritsen de Vries van Dalsen is the single progenitor of our line of the Dolson family.

From Dalsen to Dolson

How then did our surname end up being spelled as *Dolson*? There are many factors that contributed to the shift from *van Dalsen* to the present *Dolson*:

- The official and modern name of the Dutch village is Dalfsen; however, until the Middle Ages, the village was known as Dalsen and is still referred to as Dalsen in the Lower Saxon dialect of Dutch.

- Until the nineteenth century, many languages had not been codified academically. There was no standardization of grammar and spelling. For instance, a Dutch dictionary was not available until around 1800.

- During the colonial period and even into the late 1800s, relatively few individuals were fully literate. Additionally, often the British and later American officials in charge of recording names on tax lists, deeds, military rolls, and the like were not acquainted with Dutch names. As a result, the family name has been spelled phonetically in at least the following ways:

Dalfsen	*Dolsen*	*Dollson*	*Dollsen*	*Dalsin*
Dalsen	*Dolson*	*Dalson*	*Dalcin*	*Doolsen*

- In the mid-1660s, the Dutch colony of Nieuw Netherlandts was ceded by Holland to Britain and the English language and associated British social customs gradually replaced those of the Dutch, including the structuring of surnames. Overtime, the use of the Dutch *van* remained as part of the surname of some Dolson branches but in most instances, such as our family line, the *van* was dropped.

- Some aberrations in spelling may be attributed to misunderstandings between individuals, errors in transcription, inability to decipher handwriting, or simply typographical errors. Some examples of errors found in Dolson records include *Dalce, Dalse, Dalee, Dalsing, Dollison, and Dollen*.

- Later, family members may have been involved in spelling variations. Until the mid-1800s, it appears that both *Dolsen* and *Dolson* were used interchangeably. Such orthography is noted on the family grave stones in Pine Hill Cemetery in Wawayanda near Middletown, New York in what was originally called the Dolsen Burying Ground. Not until John Carpenter Dolson migrates to California around 1850 was there an exclusive reliance on the spelling of *Dolson* in this line of the family.

More on Names

Until the early 1800s, the Dutch in America used a system of naming called patronymics. Unlike contemporary surnames, a child's patronymic (customarily) would be generated from the father's given name. Several examples are noted below:

Father	Son or Daughter
Hendrick Jansen	Altje *Hendrickse*
Jan Gerritsen	Jannetje *Jansen*
Dirk Cortlandt	Martinus *Dirksen*
Kiers Wolter	Jan *Kiersen*

In the Dutch language a number of suffixes attached to the end of a patronymic were used to indicate "son or daughter of" and included: *sen, zen, s, sz, se, ena,* and *a.* The suffix *sdr* was reserved for females.

By the time children belonging to the second generation of Dolsons were born in America, the family members, in most instances, adopted the British system of surnames. However, patronymics lingered capriciously among some of the Dutch families that were linked to the Dolsons through marriage, as sponsors and witnesses at baptisms, and among business associates. Of particular interest, the writer notes that Jan Gerritsen's wife is identified as *Grietje Theunis* (daughter of Theunis Cray) and one of Jan's daughters, as *Annetje Jans* in some records. Note that in the early generations of the family, women were often referred to by their maiden and not necessarily by their married names.

In addition to the use of patronymics, the Dutch followed the tradition of naming children after their ancestors in the following pattern: (1) First-born male named after the paternal grandfather, (2) Second-born male named after the maternal grandfather, (3) Third male child named after the father or an uncle. Females would follow a parallel pattern. That is, the first-born female would be named after the paternal grandmother, and so forth.

Nevertheless, there were numerous variations in the practice of this tradition, some practical and others quixotic. For example, if a child died young, the next child born of the same gender might receive the same name as the deceased child (Stryker-Rodda, 1969). Also, if a wife held sway in a marriage, naming in a particular generation might heavily favor the collateral family. For example, in the second generation, virtually all of Theunis Dalsen's children were named after members of his wife's (Sarah Vermilyea's) family.

Eventually, by the third generation of Dolsons in America, Dutch naming traditions gave way to British and later American cultural practices. As few of the Dolson spouses of later generations were of Dutch heritage, there was little incentive to maintain the Dutch naming patterns.

There were also inconsistencies between the use of Dutch and English versions of first names as well as the common use of nicknames and diminutives. For example, in the third generation, Johannes Dolsen (son of Theunis and grandson of Jan) was alternatively referred to by his formal baptismal name and in other instances as *Jan, Johan, John,* and even *Hans.*

Following are examples of Dutch given names that appear in the Dolson line or among members of collateral families. In some cases, only the English versions of the name are found in family history documents, but the Dutch rendering is listed here because in most circumstances, the English names were probably selected in honor of Dutch ancestors. The reader is advised that, whenever possible, the spelling of first names used in this manuscript follows the standard or most commonplace Dutch spelling of the time as suggested in the *Dutch Family Heritage Society Newsletter* (Vol. 5, No. 1, 1991).

Dutch Name	**English Equivalent**
Aaltje (Aeltje, Altje)	*Adeline, Alida*
Abraham (Abram)	*Abraham*
Aarie (Ari)	*Aaron*
Aeltje	*Eve*
Andries (Andres)	*Andrew*
Annetje (Antje, Anna, Anneken)	*Ann, Anna*
Catrijnte	*Catharine*
Dirk (Derck, Dirck)	*Theodore, Hendrik, Richard*
Elisabet (Lisbetji, Betji)	*Elizabeth*
Femmetje	*Phoebe*
Fredreck (Fredrick)	*Frederick*
Gerrit (Gerret)	*Gerard*
Gerritje (Feminine of *Gerrit*)	*Gertrude*
Grietje or *Grietie* (Diminutives)	*Margaret*
Izaak	*Isaac, Isac*
Jacobes (Jacobus)	*Jacob*
Jan (Jans, Johannes)	*John, Hans*
Jannetje or *Jannetie* (Feminine of *Jan*)	*Jane, Jennie, Jeanette*
Lijsbetje (Diminutive of *Elisabet*)	*Elizabeth*
Margrietje or *Margrietie*	*Margaret*
Marya (Marytje, Marytjen or *Mallie)*	*Mary*
Maarten or *Martinus*	*Martin*
Mathijs or *Mathias*	*Matthew*
Pieter	*Peter*
Reinert, Reynier	*Reinhard*
Sara	*Sarah*
Theunis (Teunis or *Tunis)*	*Anthony* or *Tony*

Theuntje (Feminine of *Theunis*)	*Antonia*
Tryntje (Diminutive of *Catrijnte*)	*Catharine*

Name Entanglements

A challenge in doing Dolson family history has been the fact that during most generations, the same given name of our ancestors was held simultaneously by more than one Dolson. For example, this was the case with the men named Theunis, Isaac, Abraham, James, John, Frederick, Theophilus, and several others. Some repeatedly-used female names include Aeltje, Maritje, Sarah, and Phoebe.

There were also anomalies in the use of Senior (Sr.) and Junior (Jr.) for individuals with the same given name. In some cases, the suffixes are noted in records and in other instances, they are omitted. On some occasions an incorrect suffix may have been ascribed. Apparently, the use of Senior and Junior was not limited to fathers and their sons but also to uncles, nephews, and even to cousins. In addition, it appears that the suffixes of Senior and Junior were time specific. A nephew living near an uncle with the same given name might use Junior during the lifetime of his uncle but once the uncle died, the nephew summarily dropped the suffix. For example, while Abraham Sr. [*Theunis, Jan*] was alive, his nephew/son, Abraham Jr. [*Undetermined, Theunis, Jan*] carried the suffix Junior but after his uncle's/father's decease, Abraham Jr. became simply Abraham. To complicate matters further, a former Abraham or an Abraham Jr. might carry these titles as younger men but eventually might have switched to Abraham Sr. in later life. This would occur in instances where subsequently another, younger Dolson, by the name of Abraham would be born in or relocate to the same vicinity. In these uncommon cases, a man named Abraham might be referred to over his life span in three distinct ways: Abraham Jr., Abraham, and Abraham Sr.

In early records such as tax lists, land documents, and military rolls, often names were chronicled without any additional identifying or corroborative descriptions. For example, on the lists of signers of the Articles of Association at the commencement of the Revolutionary War, it is perplexing to recognize which specific Isaac or Abraham is referenced on these rolls. In the Orange County tax assessment of 1775, two Isaacs and two Abrahams are listed. These are probably references to four different men but there is an outside chance that they may be references to solely two men who each may have owned more than one property. Several Dolsons with the same names (e.g., Abraham, Isaac, Jacob, James, John, and Matthew) lived during the Revolutionary period and several would have been of sufficient age to sign the Articles and participate in military, legal and, financial matters. Given the existing evidence, it is often problematical to distinguish between and among these men.

Chapter I – First Generation

Jan Gerritsen de Vries

Virtually no documentation regarding Jan Gerritsen de Vries and his ancestors while in the Netherlands has been discovered[2]. The date of his birth is unknown. Based on his 1660 marriage date, a judicious estimate is that this Jan was born sometime during the period of 1630 to 1640. Some family researchers pin his birth date at 1638 which seems reasonable, even if it means a fairly young groom for the time. This assumption would mean that Jan was merely twenty-two years of age at the time of his marriage. Given some of the earliest possible sightings of Jan, this author speculates that our Dolson ancestor was born ca. 1630.

Jan in the Netherlands
Jan most likely was born in Workum in the province of Friesland or lived in this seaport village immediately previous to immigrating to Nieuw Amsterdam. It was the custom in Dutch Reformed Church marriage registers to list the birthplace of the bride and groom. Jan is reported in his marriage record as from Workum, which is a village located on an inlet along the Frisian seacoast.

Since by tradition, Jan Gerritsen eventually referred to himself as "van Dalsen" (from Dalsen), there is a supposition that his family had its roots in this village located the province of Overijssel, Netherlands (Riker, 1904). It is not known if Jan's father was the most recent Dolson in this line to be born in Dalsen or if the link to that village stemmed from ancestors in the more distant past.

James Riker and the History of Harlem
More than any other single source, James Riker provides the bulk of information regarding Jan Gerritsen de Vries van Dalsen. In 1881, Riker published his work with the impressively long title of *Revised History of Harlem (City of New York): Its Origin and Early Annals Prefaced by Home Scenes in the Fatherlands; or, Notices of Its Founders before Emigration - Also Sketches of Numerous Families, and the Recovered History of the Land-Titles*. A mini-biography of James Riker, including the titles of his other works, can be found in *The New York Genealogical and Biographical Record* (Gibson, Vol. 20, No. 4, 1889).

Riker's volume on Harlem is available in the original (1881) and revised versions (1904). The longest is more than 635 pages in length. His work is factual and for the most part, based on

---

[2] Perhaps no information has been discovered because no extensive research has been conducted. In networking with other Dolson family historians, the writer is not aware of any serious attempts to do research in the Netherlands. Clearly, problems of language, customs, bureaucracies, and distance make such study difficult. Eventually, some energetic Dolson researcher may take on this task.

documentary evidence. Still, with so many details at hand, occasional dependency on unconfirmed accounts, imprecise translations, ambiguity regarding names, and conflicting iterations, it is clear that Riker's work, on occasion, includes inexact information garnered from others as well as inaccuracies of his own making. The writer also notices that in some instances, Riker is lax in identifying his sources. In addition, not having the benefit of computers, Riker was unable to systematically tap many important sources of information and technologically process the enormous corpus of data encountered. Clearly Riker (1904) was confronted with information gaps and sometimes filled in these gaps with his own creative, albeit educated, constructs.

For example, other family researchers have criticized Riker (1904) for suggesting that Jan Gerritsen de Vries came to use "van Dalsen" as part of his name since it was a "*childhood pet name and because the Dutch were addicted to such practices.*" The latter claim is a sweeping generality and might not apply to our Jan and the former assertion about a name having "clung" since childhood is pure conjecture and would be impossible to confirm unless Jan stated such and his statement had been recorded. In this instance, Riker (1904) fails to provide corroborating evidence of what he probably considered at the time to be an inconsequential detail.

Riker (1904) also states that Jan Gerritsen removes from Nieuw Amsterdam on account of the British takeover in the fall of 1664 and does not return to the area until 1673 for the "inducement" (administering his brother's inheritance). Yet, there are a number of records showing that Jan returned to Nieuw Haarlem as early as 1667, several years before Lubbert Gerritsen's death. Perhaps, in an attempt to pinpoint the rationale for Jan's return, Riker (1904) mistakenly links it to Lubbert's passing, not realizing the disparity in dates.

Riker is to be commended for an excellent body of work and this writer is grateful to him for collecting and preserving so much information regarding early Harlem and its residents, including the Dolsons to whom Riker is distantly related through marriage. Still, readers should be cognizant that errors can exist, even in works of this prominence.

Following the norms of Dutch patronymics, Jan Gerritsen's father's given name was *Gerrit* and if Jan were the first-born son in his family, it is possible that Jan was named after his paternal grandfather. If that were the case, then Jan's paternal grandfather also carried the name *Jan Gerritsen* and Jan's father would have been named *Gerrit Jansen*. On the other hand, Jan may not have been the first-born son and therefore his grandfather's and father's patronymics could be associated to one of Jan's other alleged brothers: Lubbert Gerritsen and Reynier Gerritsen. In these particular cases, Jan's father then, possibly was named alternatively *Gerrit Lubbertsen* or *Gerrit Reynierson*. Of course, there is at least one other possibility. Jan may have had one or more older brothers whose names remain unknown. Further information regarding Jan's male siblings is provided later in this chapter.

This writer is not certain of Jan's mother's first name. Plimley (2011) logically surmises that her name may have been Lysbetje based on the name given to Jan's first female child. This assumption is supported by the fact that Lubbert Gerritsen also named his first daughter Lysbetje. However, the author notes that the name Lysbetje is found concurrently among the family of Jan's wife, Grietje Theunis Cray.

Even though the birth records of Jan's parents have not been located, the writer estimates that his parents were predictably between the ages of 20 to 40 when Jan was born ca. 1630. This suggests that his parents were born sometime between the years 1590 and 1610.

The Dutch Colony of Nieuw Netherlandts

As far as European exploration, the Vikings are thought to have established the earliest outposts in North America----in Greenland and as far south as Canada. Some of the first explorers in the northeast coast of North America were the Portuguese. In the late 1400s, Gaspar Corte Real visited Labrador and is reported to have reached as far south as New England. Later, in 1524, the Italian navigator Giovanni da Verrazano, in the service of the French crown, reached Manhattan Island. In 1609, Henry Hudson, a British captain, working for the Dutch West Indies Company, sailed the *Halve Maen* up the river named after him, thinking it might be the Inland Passage to the Far East.

The Dutch West India Company spearheaded the Dutch colony in North America. Beginning in 1624, settlements were established and were concentrated in Manhattan, Long Island, New Jersey, and throughout the Hudson Valley, reaching as far north as Albany. Some of the Dutch place names were replaced when the British took over the colony in 1664; but there are many notable exceptions such as the Bronx, Hoboken, Yonkers, Brooklyn, Tappan, and the Bowery. Other place names were influenced by Dutch but are practically unrecognizable today. For example, the name Poughkeepsie, derived from a Lenape Indian word (roughly *Upukuipising*), meaning "the reed covered lodge by the little-water place" was Dutchified as *Poughkeepsink* (meaning the region of Poughkeepsie) and finally Anglicized as it is spelled today. Another example is Fishkill coming from the Dutch *Vischkill* or Fish Creek. These two localities in New York were important to Dolson family history in the 1700s.

In 1660, around the time of the first sightings of our Dolsons in the New World, the capital of Nieuw Netherlandts, Nieuw Amsterdam, had a population of approximately 1,500 persons. The settlement served as a seaport for the colony and a trading center for the Dutch West India Company. The majority of the inhabitants were Dutch and their cousins (the Flemish, Huguenots, and Walloons) but there were also substantial numbers of British, French, German, and Scandinavian settlers. There was also a significant population of African slaves and a few free Negros, many originating from Angola and other areas of Africa controlled by the Portuguese. The majority of colonists were Protestant, but there were some Roman Catholics and after 1654, a modest number of Jews, mostly Portuguese Sephardim, who made their way from Europe via Brazil.

Nieuw Netherlandts grew in size and prospered throughout the period of Dutch rule. The British took over the colony for the first time in 1664 and renamed it New York. In 1673, the Dutch recaptured the area but held it only for one additional year, after which it was returned to the British who ruled the colony until the independence of the United States.

Coming to America

One of the major gaps in Jan's history relates to his arrival in Nieuw Amsterdam. The writer has reviewed ship passenger lists of voyages from Holland to the Nieuw Netherlandts during the period of 1630 to 1660 without any sightings. This is not unusual however since, on some voyages, only a handful of passengers have been identified, even though it may be assumed that, commonly, dozens of colonists were onboard a vessel.

Given the lack of evidence, the writer surmises that Jan came to America as a young man, perhaps between the ages of eighteen and twenty-five, a short time before his marriage in December of 1660. After his marriage, there is a more consistent paper trail (court, land, and church records for instance) obviously identifying this man, but previous to 1660, there are only a few contentious sightings of Jan Gerritsen in Nieuw Amsterdam.

It is improbable that Jan journeyed to America as a child with his parents. There isn't any evidence that either parent came to Nieuw Amsterdam, nor are there any records in the colony of financial or legal dealings with any persons who might have been his parents. There is an outside chance that Jan came to America with another relative (brother, cousin, or uncle) or as an indentured servant. If any of these situations was the case, researchers might expect to uncover additional records of social, legal, financial, or church entanglements between such persons and Jan.

In 1645, Grietje Theunis Cray, Jan's future wife, was baptized at the Dutch Reformed Church in Nieuw Amsterdam:

> **1645 Jan 08; Teunis Cray; <u>Griete</u>; Capiteyn de Vries, Marten Cregier, Jan Huybert, Belitje Cornelis**

Even though our ancestor was infrequently referred to simply as *Jan de Vries* and because he was a ship's carpenter and occasional skipper of sloops, he was from time to time addressed as captain. Nevertheless, it is doubtful that the person listed as a sponsor in Grietje's baptism is our ancestor. Even if our Jan were as old as thirty at the time of his marriage, he would have been only fifteen years of age at the time of Grietje's baptism. It seems questionable that a teenager would be referred to as captain and that an adolescent would be selected as a sponsor for the baptism of the daughter of a prominent Nieuw Amsterdam burgher. Grietje's father, Theunis Cray, would be expected to invite distinguished, mature, and financially-secure persons to serve as sponsors (godparents).

For example, another sponsor on the list, Martin Cregier, later became the first Burgomaster of Nieuw Amsterdam. The Captain de Vries listed in Grietje's baptismal record is probably the Dutch colonial military figure who died in 1647 in a shipwreck upon a return voyage to the Netherlands.

The Genealogical and Biographical Directory of Persons in Nieuw Netherlandts from 1613 to 1674 (Riker, 1999), contains an entry for the surname Dolson that records the arrival of a *Jan Gerritzsen de Vries* in 1648. Unfortunately, David Riker, editor of the directory, does not cite the source of this information nor provide additional details.

There is a 1654 court record of a property lease between a *Teunis Kraey* and a *Jan Gerritsen Vries*:

> **On 12/19/54 Teunis Kraey leased it [a property] to Jan Gerritsen Vries & Geurt Teunisen Kraey** (Holland Society, p. 69).

The land is described as a lot of thirty-seven *morgens* (approximately seventy-four acres) near Hellegat, Long Island. Theunis Cray purchased this property on 25 October 1653 (O'Callaghan, 1890). The facts that *Jan Gerritsen Vries* is listed as one of the lessors and that the primary party (owner of the property) on the lease was Theunis Cray, suggest that this is our Jan. If Jan Gerritsen de Vries were in Nieuw Amsterdam as early as 1654, perhaps additional illuminating records will be discovered eventually. The other lessor on this lease, *Geurt Teunisen Kraey*, was, no doubt, Theunis Cray's son, born ca. 1634 (Hoff, 2006).

In 1656, the following court entry was published:

> **Jan Gerritsen, pltf. vs Solomon La Scheer, deft. Deft. In default for payment of his monthly wages on deft's yacht. And whereas he, deft., being absent, requests delay until his return from Fort Orange (Albany), the matter was postponed to deft's arrival.**

Jan Gerritsen is referred to in this record as working on a yacht. Our Jan Gerritsen is reported by Riker (1904) and other historians to be a ship's carpenter and on occasion, skippering boats in the local water ways and even out into the open sea. It should be noted that other court records show that around this time period, Jan's father-in-law, Theunis Cray, also had business dealings and legal entanglements with Solomon La Scheer. Solomon La Scheer (also on occasion spelled La Chair) was a lawyer and a government scribe.

Plimley (2011) quotes a 1657 notice (no source given) which indicates that Grietje Theunis "*to be wife of Capt. Jan Van Dalsen of Harlem*". This notice was issued three years before the marriage. What is curious about this entry is that it implies that Jan Gerritsen was in Nieuw Harlem as early as 1657 and was referred to as Van Dalsen by that early date.

If the above sightings are associated to our Jan, it shows that he may have been present in Nieuw Netherlandts from six to twelve years previous to his marriage in 1660.

<u>Jan's Early Years in Nieuw Amsterdam</u>
From the time of their marriage in December 1660 until September 1664, some historians believe that Jan and his wife, Grietje, lived in Nieuw Amsterdam. Winslow (1955) says that Jan was a builder of boats and a mariner aboard the sloops and ketches that were commonly used for commercial purposes on Long Island sound in those days. This assertion is supported by the various appearances of Jan Gerritsen's name in the court minutes of Nieuw Amsterdam as recorded by Fernow (1976) and others.

One possible sighting of Jan concerns the famous map, the Castello Plan, which shows the layout of Nieuw Amsterdam in 1660. The map highlights individual buildings including residences of the colonists. A Jan Gerritsen is listed as a renter of a house at No. 18 on Block A of the Castello Plan. This list has been abstracted from Volume II, pages 215-341 of *The Iconography of Manhattan Island, 1498-1909* by I. N. Phelps Stokes (1967). If this is our Jan, it may record his place of residence while still a bachelor since he did not marry until mid-December of 1660. Theunis Cray's house is also identified on the Castello Plan.

A 1660 court proceeding is recorded as follows:

Styntje Pieters, pltf., lodges a complaint against Jan and Reinier de Vries, deft., both in default.

This court proceeding does not divulge the reason why the two de Vries men were in debt to Styntje Pieters; the interesting aspect here is the possible relationship between Jan and Reynier. The way their names are listed in the court record suggests that they might be related. They clearly had some mutual financial dealing with Styntje Pieters, probably involving rent. Additional information shall be provided regarding Reynier de Vries later in this chapter.

On 8 July 1660, *Schout* Resolved Waldron, whose son, Johannes, in 1690, would marry Annetje, one of Jan's daughters, sanctioned Arien Janzen Visser, Symon Fransen, Joghim Andriesen, and a *Jan Gerrizen* for being on board ships recently arrived from Holland without permission. The men were fined according to their degree of misconduct. According to the record, Arien de Visser and *Jan Gerrizen* did not actually go on board any ship, but stood in the "chains". For this infraction they were to pay a fine of twelve guilders and ten stivers.

On 29 November 1661, Jan Gerritsen appeared in court as a witness concerning a claim against Andres Joghanson for tapping and drinking. The next year, 14 November 1662, Cornelis Janzen Van Horn took Jan to court to collect a debt of twelve florins. The amount

6

was owed by Jan's brother who had requested payment via Jacob Wolfertsen. In another 1662 incident, on 5 December Lysbet Tysen filed a claim for 164 guilders and ten stivers against Jan Gerritsen. The defendant admitted the debt and said that he would give the plaintiff a hog and other payment as soon as obtaining money for his boat.

The year 1663 did not start out well for our Jan. He was arrested and charged with a major offense. The following court record (Fernow, 1976) provides details:

> **Wednesday, 3rd January 1663. In the City Hall. Present the Heeren Pieter Tonneman, Olof Stevensen van Cortlant, Paulus Leendertsen van de Grift, Joannes van Brugh, Joannes de Piester, Jacob Strycker, Jacobus Backer, Isaack Greveraat.**
>
> **Officer Pieter Tonneman, pltf. v/s Jan Gerrisen de Vries, deft. and prisoner. Pltf. concludes that the deft. shall be condemned for his perpetrated theft, to be fixed to a stake at the place of justice and be there scourged and further banished for the term of four consecutive years out this City's jurisdiction: moreover for his blow, in a fine of one hundred guilders as the blood flowed; all with costs---producing certain declaration taken to that effect. The declaration being read to deft., he denied having stolen the meat, saying the mate gave it to him, when he had done work on board----and moreover said---come, carpenter, you are done, let us drink together; and that he gave him the meat he brought and laid it behind the cabin and was not on shore with the meat----that the mate was drunk, when he enquired for the meat, but sober when he gave him the meat, and that the boy knew nothing of the sack, as he was going with the skipper of the ship, the Gilded Fox, when he was brought ashore and was altogether drunk when it happened. The W. Court decree, whereas there is no right explanation of the matter; also the ketch, where the crime is committed is not present, that the deft. shall be released on bail to appear in Court and defend himself, whenever he shall be summoned. Pursuant to the foregoing judgment Teunis Cray father in law of the above named Jan Gerrisen de Vries appears in Court, who enters himself bail, that his son in law Jan Gerrisen above named shall appear in Court, whenever he shall be summoned touching the above written matter.**

Despite the shortcomings in the translation, it is clear that this was considered to be a serious crime but the Court's observation that *"there is no right explanation of the matter"* seems to be an accurate characterization of the event. The transcript indicates that Jan was working on the *Gilded Fox,* a ship noted in the records as making the voyage between Holland and Nieuw Amsterdam on many occasions. Secondly, the court record identifies this Jan as the son-in-law of Theunis Cray, providing corroboration that this is our ancestor.

Tuesday, 23 January 1663. In the city hall, Present the Heeren Pieter Tonneman, Olof Stevensen van Cortlant, Paulus Leendersen van der Grift, Joannes Van Brugh, Joannes de Peister, Jacob Strycker and Jacobus Backer.

Schout Pieter Tonneman, pltf. v/s Jan Gerrisen de Vries, deft. appearing with Jan Barfort, Abraham Darby and Jan Torner, sailors, navigating the bark named Nicolas and Sara and by them accused of having stolen two pieces of meat, are asked, who gave it to him? Where upon the persons present being designated, who deny it, saying he has taken it; all fully declaring it, whereupon Burgomasters and Schepens having called them in one by one and examined each apart, they answer conformably to their rendered declaration. The Officer persists in his previous demand and rendered conclusion; requesting that deft. shall go into closed confinement. The Officer's demand being read to the deft. he says he is innocently accused. The W. Court orders the Officer to place the deft. in prison.

On Saturday, 27 January 1663, the Court announced its ruling which appears to resolve the *Gilded Fox* incident:

The prisoner Jan Gerrisen de Vries entering is asked, if he does not recollect anything of the matter, of which he is accused? Answers No. Burgomasters and Schepens having considered the demand and conclusion of the Officer on and against the prisoner have ex gratia and not for his merits, reprimanded him for his committed fault and delict; and condemn him for his mutiny, perpetrated on ship board, in the fine of fifty guilders with costs incurred herein and order him to remain in prison, until the aforesaid fine and costs be paid. Tryntie van Campen, mother in law of the aforesaid Jan Gerrisen de Vries, appears in Court, who declares herself bail for the payment of the above entered fine; in case her son in law aforesaid do not pay the same within two or three weeks, that she shall then give, satisfy and pay it. In witness hereof she has signed the blotter.

Thus Jan Gerritsen's so called "mutiny" draws to a conclusion. His mother-in-law, Tryntie van Campen, comes to his rescue just as his father-in-law, Theunis Cray, did at the initial hearing; an indication that our Jan had the support of his wife's family (Winslow, 1955).

During the same month, on 15 January 1663, a Tuesday, it appears that our Jan was involved in another, but unrelated, legal dispute:

Cornelis Pluyvier, pltf. v/s Jan Gerrisen de Vries, deft. Pltf. Demands delivery of a boat agreed for and made by deft. payment of which has been almost received, producing the a/c thereof. Deft. says that the boat is attached and he

***cannot therefore deliver it. The W. Court orders the deft. to take the attachment
from the boat and to deliver it to the pltf.***

The British captured Nieuw Amsterdam on 5 September 1664 and renamed it New York.
Riker (1904) claims that Jan, along with his family, left the city immediately after the takeover
for a destination somewhere in New England. There are no further sightings of the Dolson
family until 1667 when Jan reappears in New York and New Harlem records.

During Jan's alleged absence from New York, in December, 1665, Lysbetje Tysen lodges a
complaint in the court against Martin Jan Smit regarding rent for a house in Nieuw
Amsterdam. As part of the testimony, a *Jan de Vries* is identified as the previous lessee.
According to the landlord, this *Jan de Vries* occupied the house until all Saints Day
(November 1) of the same year. This is an interesting incident since Lysbetje Tysen had
previously, on 21 November 1662, sued a *Jan Gerrisen de Vries* for default. This certainly
sounds like our Jan yet there are two points that create doubt. First, according to Riker
(1904), Jan was not supposed to be in Nieuw Amsterdam in 1665, but rather somewhere in
New England and second, the court record implies that Jan occupied the back room of the
house during most of 1665, not something you would expect from a married man with
children.

Possible Siblings
In his comprehensive genealogical work, *Dalfsens to van Dolsons* (2003; revised in 2011),
Plimley speculates that one or more of the following individuals may be a sibling of our Jan:
Jacob Gerretsen, Jacob Wolfertsen, Wolfert Gerretsen, Reynier de Vries, Lubbert Gerretsen,
and Zeegert Gerretsen.

This writer has researched the backgrounds of these and several other potential siblings with
the patronymic Gerritsen or the suffix de Vries. In the end, the evidence suggests that only
Reynier de Vries and Lubbert Gerretsen may be brothers of Jan Gerritsen de Vries.

Reynier de Vries is a compelling candidate. He appears to have been in Nieuw Amsterdam
early and was classified as a "Small Burgher" in the *Register of Nieuw Netherlandts* posted
on 18 April 1657 (O'Callaghan, 1865). His name was written as *Reynier Gerritzen Vries*. In a
similar reference by Fernow (1897), a *Reynick Garritsen Vriesin* was noted on an April 1657
list of men with Burgher Rights. A third researcher, Nash, notes in an article published in the
New York Genealogical and Biographical Record (Vol. 141, No. 1, 2010), that this individual
was alternatively recorded as a Burgher and Freeman as *Reindert Gerrisen Vrisin* and
Reynier Gerritzen de Vries. Nash claims to have reviewed all of the known documents which
contain information on the names of Burghers in Nieuw Amsterdam.

On 20 November 1657, Reynier de Vries name appears in a letter from Jacob Alrichs to
Director-General Petrus Stuyvesant. The section of the letter pertaining to Reynier is difficult

to decipher however it does mention that Reynier was a *"skipper now with the galliot."* The letter goes on to list a number of provisions such as butter, bricks, planks and other materials, possibly items transported on the boat (*Delaware Papers: Dutch*, 18:37).

There are sightings of Reynier de Vries in the following New Amsterdam Court records:

>Friday, 11 Oct. 1655: **Reynder de Vries, bercquier [boatman] is listed as owing 12 florins in back taxes.**

>21 Oct. 1659: **Lucas Dirckzen, pltf. v/s Reinick Gerrisen, deft. Pltf. Demands from deft. 8 whole and two half beavers for tobacco pipes and a cap; also fl. 15:16 zeawant according to obligation. Deft. acknowledges the debt but says he has not wherewith to pay. The Court orders deft. to pay the pltf.**

>Monday, 3 Jul. 1660: **Johannes Withart vs. Reynder de Vries for debt concerning 16 beaver skins worth 712 florins. Record indicates that Reynder is trading in the "south."**

>24 Aug 1660: **Styntie Pieters sues Jan and Renier de Vries for a debt owed.**

>Tuesday, 7 Nov. 1662: **Arien Janzen Visser sues Reinik Gerriz de Vries for a debt.**

The similarities of name and place of origin of the Reynier mentioned in these records suggest a familial relationship. Also, Reynier is referred to as a boatman, a similar profession as Jan. Furthermore, Arien Janzen Visser, who in 1662 sued *Reinik de Vries* for a debt was previously involved with our Jan in a 1660 incident regarding the alleged boarding of a ship without permission. Of course, none of this evidence conclusively proves that the men were related, let alone brothers. There are no sightings of a *Reinik, Reynder, Renier,* or *Reynier* involved in any marriages, baptisms, or business matters associated with Jan or his immediate family.

Another thought-provoking case is that of Lubbert Gerritsen, who Riker (1904) reports to be forty years of age in 1663, the year in which Lubbert was drafted for standby military duty as a result of the Esopus Indian massacre. Lubbert therefore was born ca. 1623, which would make him approximately seven to fifteen years older than Jan. Lubbert passed away on 21 November 1673, at the age of fifty, the same day during which the Dutch recaptured New York from the British.

Importantly, according to Riker (1904), Lubbert nominated in his will, our Jan, and Adrian Dircksen Coen from Maasen in Utrecht, a brother-in-law from Lubbert's first marriage, to be co-guardians of his children. After Lubbert's first wife and mother of his four children, Grietje

Dircks, died, he remarried Femmetje Coenrats from Goningen, Netherlands on 7 July 1669 at the Nieuw Amsterdam Dutch Reformed Church. She was the widow of Hendrick Karstens. On 4 August 1670, Lubbert sold a New Harlem home with garden to Joost Van Ohlinus for tho oum of 400 guilders. The monies were placed in a trust fund for Lubbert's step sons, Conraet and Jan Karstens (Riker, 1904). Two months later, on 23 October 1669, Lubbert Gerritsen executed a power of attorney to his brother-in-law, Phillip Weckman (Wakeman) of Leyden, Netherlands, to enable the latter to collect from the Orphan Masters of that City a legacy of 800 guilders left to his second wife, Femmetje Coenrats, by her maternal aunt, Tryntie Gerrits, who had died in Leyden on 7 October 1669.

Interestingly, in 1665 Lubbert Gerritsen and Jan Peterson Slot approached the court with a request for arbitration regarding a sale of livestock. Assur Levy and John Montagne were chosen as arbitrators. The question at hand was the price for eight head of goats (O'Callaghan and Fernow, 1897). Jan Peterson Slot was an ancestor of Marytjen Slot, who would later marry Abraham Dolsen [*Theunis, Jan*] at Fishkill, Dutchess County.

Lubbert was wealthy and held several important posts in Nieuw Netherlandts, first in Gravesend, Long Island and then in Nieuw Haarlem. Lubbert is consistently listed as one of the original titleholders and a founder of the village of Nieuw Harlem. Of particular note is a description of Lubbert's property as reported in Riker (1904):

But for an inside view of the domestic life and home comforts of these villagers, let us visit the worthy and well-to-do Lubbert Gerritsen, late one of the magistrates living near the west end. We enter. No carpet hides the well-scrubbed floor, and in vain, we glance around the room for many articles which in our day imperious fashion and even comfort demand. The furniture goes but little beyond the practical and useful. A gilded mirror indeed adorns the whitewashed wall. The two beds have pillows and striped curtains. Two chests very convenient contain the clothing, one of the wife and the other of the daughter, fair Eva, who five years later married the Bussing ancestor. On one side is a small octagon table; and here a brass candlestick and a warming-pan. Upon hooks on the wall hang a musket and firelock. No stove is there but in the ample fireplace the wood crackles and blazes cheerfully above the huge backlog and around the two iron dinner pots hung to the trammel by hooks and chain. On the table or shelves, and in the pantry, we notice exactly 1 pewter bowl, 2 small pewter platters, 4 pewter trenchers, 6 pewter spoons, a pewter cup with a lid, and another without, 2 white earthen jars, a copper cake pan, a small copper pot, a small brass kettle, 2 water pails, and 2 churns for butter making. There is still place for 2 siths [sic], 2 sickles, and 2 augurs.

We ascend to the "loft". Here are 4 milk pans, 2 iron hand-basins, 2 tubs, a lye barrel, a cask filled with buckwheat, 2 ploughshares, a plough-chain and rope, a coulter, a yoke with a hook, 2 old sickles, an adze, and a sail mast, perhaps belonging to the "canoe at the strand".

Invited out to the barn: here is the garnered harvest, stores of rye, peas, and buckwheat in the sheaf, and 10 or 12 bundles of unswingled flax; also a fan harrow, and 2 iron forks. On the premises, fat and sleek in their sheds and stalls, are the livestock: 2 yoke of oxen, 2 cows, one black, and the other red; 1 steer and 2 calves. Four young hogs are running upon Little Barent's Island. Other farming implements are at hand: 2 ox-yokes, 2 iron plough-rings, a wood axe, 3 iron wedges, 2 hand-saws, and a draw-saw, 2 iron-bound buckets, and an iron lamp. Ah! Here stands the ox-cart, and here are 2 new cart-wheels. The plough is missing; left where Lubbert's last ploughing was done, out on one of the bouwlots [farm field], of which he has the Nos. 4 and 9 on Jochem Pieters [Flats], with salt meadow, and out-garden No. 11 beside. Busy bees still hum about, sucking sweets from the fall flowers, with which to sore the seven hives in the garden, and hens as busily scratch and cluck about the barnyard. Not an item of Lubbert's effects has escaped our notice; all as enjoyed by him at the time of his decease soon after, affording us a reliable index to the average style of living observed here at that period (pp. 298-299).

Jan Gerritsen de Vries was, by all appearances, a person of relatively modest note in the colony. Without some familial tie, it is difficult to believe that Lubbert would appoint him as a custodian of his children and as an executor of his estate. After all, Lubbert rubbed elbows with many important individuals in New Amsterdam and could have selected any one of his friends to act as a custodian and executor. According to one study, Lubbert may have been from Wesel, a town that is located in Germany (Ludington, 1925). But that report probably was inaccurate. Still, there is no documentation that Lubbert was a Frieslander nor from Overijssel. Except for the fact that Lubbert named Jan as co-guardian of his children's inheritance, the writer is not aware of any direct interactions between these two Gerritsens.

Until 1661, Lubbert was in Gravesend, Long Island. Then he relocated to Nieuw Haarlem until his death in 1673. Lubbert became a prominent resident of Nieuw Haarlem where he served as a magistrate. He owned home lots numbers four and nine in Jochem Pieters Flat and several lots (seven to nine) in Van Keulen's Hook. Jan was in nearby Nieuw Amsterdam according to Riker (1904), until he self-exiled to "somewhere in New England" when the British first took over New York in 1664. Based on some reports, Jan returned to Nieuw Haarlem about 1667---six years before Lubbert's death. In the 1650s if Jan had arrived in America by then; during the first half of the 1660s when it is reported that Jan was in Nieuw Amsterdam; and finally, between 1667 and 1673 when Jan resided in Nieuw Harlem; there are no sightings in any records to indicate that Jan and Lubbert interacted with each other on any familial, social, or business matters. This despite the fact, that during most of these years, the two men lived within close proximity of each other.

Lubbert Gerritsen and Grietje Dircks' first child, Lysbeth, was born in 1651. Next there were baptisms for twin boys in 1653 and then for mixed gender twins, Grietie and Gerrit, born in 1655. All of these baptisms were recorded at the Dutch Reformed Church in Nieuw Amsterdam:

1651 Apr 09; Lubbert Gerritszen; <u>Lysbeth</u>; Capt. Nuyting, Marritie and Engel.

16 Mar 1653; Lubbert Gerritszen; <u>Gerrit</u> and <u>Dirck,</u> two children; Laurens de Noorman, Coenraedt ten Eyck, Thomas Hall, Michiel Janszen, Tryntie Van Campen, Tryntie Greveracts.

25 Apr 1655; Lubbert Gerritszen, <u>Grietie</u>; <u>Gerrit</u>; Albert Leendertszen, Dirck de Noorman, Ariaentie.

1657: <u>Eva</u>. No baptismal record located (Hall, No Date).

All of these children were the product of Lubbert's first marriage with Grietje Dircks. Apparently Gerrit, one of the twins died before 1655, since a second son was baptized that year and also was given the name Gerrit. Among the sponsors at one of the baptisms is a recognizable individual, Tryntie van Campen, Jan's future mother-in-law. The writer wonders if there was a link between these families. However, Jan himself does not appear as a sponsor or witness at any of these baptisms.

At least one of Lubbert's two boys, Gerrit, later appears to have migrated to Albany and married Alida Everts there in 1684 (Riker, 1904). Lubbert's eldest daughter, Lysbeth, is noted as a sponsor at a New York Dutch Reformed Church baptism in 1672:

Mar 14; Jean de Lamontagne, Marritie Waldron; <u>Petronella</u>; Jacob Kip, Lysbeth Lubberts

Lysbeth Lubberts, married first Dirck Evertszen Fluyt and second in 1689, Joris Burgher, both in New York. She and her first husband baptized a child at the New York Dutch Reformed Church in 1672:

May 05; Dirck Evertszen, Lysbeth Lubberts; <u>Grietie</u>; Geertruyd Jans.

Another child of this marriage was baptized in 1676:

Nov 22; Dirck Evertszen, Lysbeth Lubberts; <u>Fytie</u>; Gerrit Lubbertszen, Evertie Lubberts.

Lysbeth bore a child with her second husband Joris Burgher. The baptism took place at the New York Dutch Reformed Church in 1692:

Jul 31; Joris Burger, Elisabeth Lubberts; Elisabeth; Arent Harmenszen, Ewis [Eva] Lubberts.

As noted, Lysbeth's brother, Gerrit, and her sister, *Evertie*, were the sponsors of Fytie in 1676. Lubbert Gerritsen appears to have had a younger daughter born ca. 1657 (no baptismal record found) named Eva. This Eva appears at the baptism of Elisabeth in 1692 along with husband, Arrent Harmenszen. On 31 March 1676, she married Arent Harmanszen Bussing (widower of Susannah Delamater) at the Dutch Reformed Church in New York. Arent Hermanszen was from Bentheim, Netherlands, a town near the boundary of Westphalia and Overijssel provinces. The couple had the following children. All but the last two listed are found on the baptismal register of the New York Dutch Reformed Church:

1678 31 Mar; Arent Hermanszen, wid Susanna La Maistre; Divertje Lubberts, jd van N. Haerlem.

1680: Jan 24; Arent Gerbrantszen [Harmanszen?], Eva Lubberts; Dirck; Pieter Van Oblinus, Hester de La Maistre. Dirck died young (Hall, No Date).

1681: Mar 15; Arent Hermanszen, Eva Lubberts; Margariet; Pieter Van Oblinus, Hester Lamaistre. Margariet married Lawrence Kortright.

1684: Feb 23; Arent Harmenszen, Eva Lubberts; Susanna; Isaac de Lamaistre, Magdalena Terneur. Susanna never married (Hall, No Date).

1686: Oct 27; Arent Hermanszen, Eva Lubberts; Engel; Jan Dyckman, Lysbeth Lubberts. Engeltje married Abraham Meyer, brother of Johannes Meyer, husband of Tryntje Van Dalsen.

1692: Apr 24; Arent Hermanszen, Eva Lubberts; Elisabeth; Samuel Waldron, Maria Ver Veelen. Elisabeth married Matthew Benson.

1694: Sep 02; Arent Harmensz, Eva Lubberts; Geesje; Otto Van Thuyl, Jannetje Fruyt. Geesje (Gertrude) married Teunis de la Montanye.

1697: John. John was a weaver. He married Metje Kortright (Hall, No Date).

1700: Maria. Maria married John Martinus Van Harlingen, a clerk at New Harlem (Hall, No Date).

Generally, the sponsors/witnesses at these baptisms appear to be residents of New Harlem. Still, neither Jan Gerritsen nor his spouse nor any of the couple's offspring appear in the baptismal records of the children of Eva Lubberts and Elizabeth Lubberts.

In addition to the significant fact that Lubbert named Jan as a custodian of his children, another, equally compelling argument that Lubbert and Jan may have been brothers is the fact that both men named their first-born male and female children Gerrit and Lysbetje respectively, an action congruent with the Dutch tradition of naming the first-born children of each gender after their paternal grandparents.

To conclude, while there is no definitive documentation, the writer believes that Reynier Gerritsen and Lubbert Gerritsen were likely Jan's brothers. As far as the other contemporary individuals living in Nieuw Netherlandts are concerned, there is no convincing evidence that any of them is related to our Jan Gerritsen de Vries.

Jan's Spouse - Grietje Theunis
Limited information is available about Jan's wife who is referred to as Grietje Theunis. In the Nieuw Amsterdam Dutch Reformed Church register, she is noted as baptized on 8 January 1645. Her parents were Theunis Geurtszen Cray and Catrintje (also referred to as Tryntie and Catalina) van Campen (van Kampen).

Grietje Theunis' Parents
Grietje's father, Theunis Cray (Kray, Crey, Krey, Craey, and *Kraey*) was a Dutchman from Venlo, who along with his wife and children living at the time, immigrated to Nieuw Amsterdam before 1639. Also present in Nieuw Amsterdam were at least two of Theunis' sisters: Wyntje Theunis, married to Herrick Syboutszen, and Geertje Theunis, married to Kersten Luurzen. There are baptismal records for the children of both couples archived at the Dutch Reformed Church of Nieuw Amsterdam.

Theunis Cray purchased and sold lands during the early years of the Dutch colony on a recurrent basis. He had properties on Long Island, a farm in mid-Manhattan near Peter Stuyvesant's bowery, and a house lot within the Wall (now Wall Street) in Nieuw Amsterdam (Stokes, 1918). His very first home was located outside the village at a locality that in modern times corresponds to Twenty-first Avenue and Forty-fifth Street, near the East River in downtown Manhattan (Winslow, 1955). The history of Cray's residences is detailed in the volume, *Nieuw Amsterdam and Its People* (1902) by John H. Innes. Theunis Cray was a Burgher in good standing in Nieuw Amsterdam and involved in many business matters and held minor government posts. He also was involved in ship building and appears to have been an owner of a sloop (Winslow, 1955). Perhaps it was his activities in shipping that brought him into contact with Jan Gerritsen de Vries.

Henry Hoff (2006), a noted New York genealogical scholar, provides the following details regarding the children of Theunis Cray and his spouse, Tryntje van Campen:

1. <u>Geurt Teuniszen Cray</u> was born ca. 1634 in the Netherlands and immigrated to Nieuw Amsterdam with his family.

2. <u>Jacob Teuniszen Cray</u> was born ca. 1638, either in Nieuw Amsterdam, or perhaps on board a Dutch schooner in transit between Holland and the New World, or in the Netherlands itself. This Jacob was captured by the Turks in 1662 and held for ransom (Riker, 1904). There is a list of Nieuw Amsterdam residents who donated funds for his rescue. Apparently, Jacob was freed within two years. He is listed in court and church records in Nieuw Amsterdam in 1664. Jacob Teuniszen Cray returned to Holland where Gemeentearchief records show that he married, 23 February 1669, Giertje Franse, in a civil ceremony in Amsterdam. Giertje was baptized at the Oude Kerk in Amsterdam on 13 May 1640, the daughter of Frans Pietersz, a farmer, and Barbara Elbers. Giertje was the widow of Hendrick Jacobse (Hoff, 2006). This couple had four children baptized in Amsterdam: Lysbet in 1669, Jannetie in 1673, and Teunis and Barbara (twins) in 1675.

3. <u>Jannetje Teunis Cray</u> was baptized 4 May 1642 at the Dutch Reformed Church in Nieuw Amsterdam:

    4 May; Theunis Cray; <u>Janneken</u>; Silbol Caleszen, Huyck Aertszen, Hendrick Pieterszen Metseir, Lybeth Dircks, Anneken Lookermans.

    Jannetje's marriage bans were announced at the same church on 26 July 1658 to Philippus Jacobus Schoof from Antwerp. This couple did not have any children in Nieuw Amsterdam and relocated to Europe by 9 May 1662.

4. <u>Grietje Teunis Cray</u> was baptized 8 January 1645 at Nieuw Amsterdam and in 1660 became the wife of our ancestor, Jan Gerritsen de Vries.

5. <u>Lysbeth Teunis Cray</u> was baptized 29 July 1646:

    29 Jul; Theunis Cray; <u>Lysbeth</u>. Gerrt Doyman-Sergt., Ariaen Janszen, Hester Simons

    This Lysbeth must have died young since in 1653, Theunis Cray and Tryntje van Campen baptized a second daughter with the same name.

6. <u>Gerrit Teuniszen Cray</u> was baptized 10 May 1648 at Nieuw Amsterdam:

> ***10 May; Theunis Cray; <u>Gerrit</u>; Jan Snedeker-Shoemaker, Thomas Hall, Jan Van Ditmarsen, Lucas Tamboer, Pietje de Ruyterinne, Marie Lievens.***

This Gerrit entered into the service of the Dutch West India Company in 1672.

7. <u>Metje Teunis Cray</u> was baptized 12 June 1650:

> ***12 Jun; Anthonis Cray; <u>Metje</u>; Willem Beekman, Albert Swart, Marie Swart, Elisabeth Cregiers.***

Metje married Jan Corsen (Corszen) of Recife, Brazil on 25 October 1673 at the Dutch Reformed Church, Nieuw Amsterdam. The marriage record noted that Metje was born in N. Orangien. In May of 1676, a *Jan de Vries* and a *Tryn Van Campen* were sponsors for Kors, a child of Jan Corsen and Metje Teunis Cray.

8. <u>Lysbeth Teunis Cray</u> was baptized 17 August 1653:

> ***17 Aug; Theunis Geurtszen Cray; <u>Lysbeth</u>, Mr. Gysbert, Phillip Gerritszen, Maria Lubberts, Maria Gerards.***

This Lysbeth, the second daughter by this name, also appears to have died young.

Tryntje van Campen not only assumed the roles of mother and homemaker, but according to court records, she was often involved in various social and business matters in Nieuw Amsterdam. Apparently she and her husband, Theunis, provided boarding for workers and guests associated with the Dutch West Indies Company. This activity is recorded in court minutes dated April 1661:

> ***Tryntje van Campen appearing, a contract is made with her to lodge and board the widow of Hendrick Pietersen van Hasselt and provide her with all she needs for which she is to have 36 florins every month from March 22 last. Tryntje Ruyters is informed that the widow of Henrick Pieterson van Hasselt is to live with Tryntje van Campen and says that she is satisfied with it but complains that she has broken a looking glass worth 5 to 6 florins, also a fine comb, and torn a cover for which she demands payment which is promised her. She says further that according to notice of the estate she must have something besides boarding and lodging said widow whereupon she was told she should be satisfied for it. As some property of said widow is at her house, Jan Jellissen Koeck is ordered to fetch it with Tryntje van Campen taking the widow along*** (Minutes of the Orphan Masters).

While Theunis was reportedly a tavern keeper and tapster (purveyor of beer and other spirits), Tryntje was appointed by the Dutch government to serve meals to prisoners (Niebrugge Hults, 1963). Tryntje may have served as a midwife as she was a witness or sponsor at many baptisms. In several instances, she represented her family's business interests at court proceedings (Fernow, 1976). Even though Dutch women in the mid-1600s appear, as a group, to have been more socially-assertive when compared to counterparts from many other national origins, Tryntje appears to be an exception even among the dames of Nieuw Amsterdam.

On 13 November 1665, Theunis Cray and two of his children were involved in an interesting court appearance:

> *William Barker 12 yrs. was on the vessel of John Bradley at 8-9 pm. Teunis Cray and Sunn and daughter measured several scippels of appels. Gave boy 3 styvers to remain quiet. The boy was whipped with rods until truth because his testimony was contradictory* (O'Callaghan and Fernow, 1897).

Theunis Cray died after 22 March 1675 when he reported a stolen boat, but prior to 1677 when his widow signed a conveyance deeding her house to the deacons of the Dutch Reformed Church in return for support and maintenance. Tryntie van Campen died around 1682. In that same year, the deacons sold her property (Hoff, 2006).

A chronicle of Theunis Cray's life entitled, *Teunis Cray, Our Earliest Ancestor in Nieuw Amsterdam* (2009) by O. Keith Hallam, is available in print. Documented details regarding the family of Theunis and his wife, Tryntje van Campen, are contained in *Nieuw Netherlandts Connections* (Vol. 11, No. 3, 2006) by Henry Hoff.

The first documentation of Grietje Teunis is her baptismal record at the Nieuw Amsterdam Dutch Reformed Church in 1645. In the mid-1650s, Grietje made a trip to Holland with her parents and returned with the family to Nieuw Amsterdam in 1657. She was a passenger on the ship *Draetvat*. The family is registered on the passenger list as follows:

> *Teunis Craey from Venlo, and wife and four children and two servants, 2 of the children were under 10 years.*

The next mention of Grietje is her wedding in December of 1660 to Jan Gerritsen. Calculating that Grietje was born within a few months of her baptism in January 1645, she appears to have married at the young age of sixteen years. Subsequently, between the years of 1661 and 1682, Grietje is listed as a parent, along with a *Jan Gerritzen* or a *Jan de Vries*, on the Nieuw Amsterdam Dutch Reformed Church baptismal registers.

Grietje Teunis was a baptismal sponsor at the Dutch Reformed Church in New York for at least two grandchildren: first Jannetje, daughter of Jan Kiersen and *Gerritje Janszen Dolsen* on 13 March 1687 and secondly, Annetje, child of Johannes Waldron and *Annetje Gerrits Dolsen* on 17 April 1692. It is interesting to note the inconsistencies in the presentation of the Dolson women's surnames. Gerritje was referred to as *Janszen*, following traditional patronymics, while Annetje is referred to as *Gerrits*, referenced according to her father's patronymic.

The 1692 baptism is the very last documentation found on both Jan and Grietje; thus it can be assumed that they may have died soon after this date. However, the tax records of New Harlem for the years 1695 and 1696 include the *Widow of John Gerrits*, assessed at £5, a similar rate as an earlier assessment for *Jan Gerritsen Dalsen* and the same rate as Grietje's son, Theunis Dalsen, who is on the New Harlem tax lists in the years 1697 and 1698. This levy appears to be the standard tax assessment in New Harlem for an *erven*, a house lot containing a small garden. If Grietje died ca. 1697, she would have been approximately fifty-two years of age at the time.

Jan Gerritsen's and Grietje Teunis' Children
Based on the available evidence, Jan Gerritsen de Vries and Grietje Teunis Cray may have had as many as eleven children. The children tended to be referred to by the surname *Dalsen* (various spellings), although, as mentioned previously, the patronymics Jans, Janszen, and Gerrits were used also, albeit temporarily.

One of the most thorough accounts, but not necessarily the most accurate, of the Dolson children of this generation is contained in the *Genealogical and Biographical Directory to Persons in New Netherland from 1613 to 1674* by David Riker (1999).

The children of Jan Gerritsen and Grietje Teunis Cray are listed in Riker's volume in chronological order according to their birth/baptismal dates. All of the baptisms were recorded at the Nieuw Amsterdam/New York Dutch Reformed Church:

1. ***Baptized: 4 dec 1661; Jan Gerritszen, Grietie Theunis; <u>Lysbetje</u>; Tryn Van Kampen, Annetie Adriens.***

   Most family historians believe that Lysbetje died young. There is no further record of this person. According to traditional Dutch naming patterns, Lysbetje would have been named after her paternal grandmother, suggesting that Jan's mother was named Lysbetje or Elisabet. The child's maternal grandmother, Tryntje van Campen, was noted as a sponsor at the baptism.

2. **Baptized: 6 dec 1662; Jan Gerritszen, Grietie Theunis; _Gerrit_; Theunis Geurtszen, Marritie Pieters.**

The sponsor, here referred to as Theunis Geurtszen, was almost certainly Grietje Theunis' brother. There is no further trace of this child. As in the case of Lysbetje, among family historians there seems to be a consensus that Gerrit died young. Again, according to Dutch patronymics, this child may have been named after his paternal grandfather. In this case, confirming that Jan's father's given name was Gerrit. Interestingly, unlike many other families who had children die young, Jan and Grietje never re-applied the names Lysbetje nor Gerrit to any of their subsequent offspring.

3. **Born: 5 Sept 1664; _Theunis_** [Birth date according to obituary; no baptismal record located].

According to Riker (1904), Jan Gerritsen and his family left Nieuw Amsterdam immediately after Theunis was born as this child's birth coincided with the first British takeover of Nieuw Netherlandts. This may mean that Theunis Dalsen was not baptized or, more likely, that he was baptized somewhere in New England. At the time of Theunis Dalsen's death, several major colonial newspapers (e.g., _New Hampshire Gazette_) ran an obituary notice which reported his date of birth as 5 September 1664.

4. **Baptized: 19 Oct 1667; Jan Gerritszen, Grietie Theunis; _Gerritje_; Theunis Kray, Hester.**

Plimley (2011) reports that Gerritje Dalsen was born on 12 October 1667 in New England, but the writer has found her baptism recorded as 19 October 1667 at the Dutch Reformed Church in New York. Gerritje's marriage record states that she was born in New England. Perhaps Gerritje was born before the family returned to New Harlem and her parents had her baptized at the Dutch Reformed Church in New York after resettling in the village of New Harlem.

As in the case of two of her sisters, Gerritje married into a prominent New Harlem family---in this instance, Jan Kiersen. This Jan was involved in land transactions in New Harlem and in one particular case, obtained an important lease of the Great Maize Land in conjunction with his father-in-law; Jan Gerritsen de Vries van Dalsen. Kiersen also purchased a lot on which, in later years, the famous Morris-Jumel Mansion was constructed. This mansion is the oldest existing house in New York City (Bolton, 2016).

5. ***Born: ca. 1669; <u>Annetje</u>*** [birth date according to Riker (1904), no baptismal record located].

Annetje Dalsen's existence and reported birthdate ca. 1669 are fairly well established. She married into the well-respected Waldron family of Nieuw Amsterdam and Neiuw Harlem. The Waldrons were one of the most prominent families in the Dutch colony and the history of this family is well-documented.

6. ***Baptized: 20 Oct 1671; Jan de Vries, Maria Kray; <u>Pieter</u>; Evert Pels, Cuiertie Hendricxs.***

It is possible that this Pieter was not a Dalsen child. First, the *Jan de Vries* in this record may not be our Jan. In addition, the mother is not reported as Grietje Theunis or Grietje Cray. This of course, could be a simple error made at the time of entering the record or in the subsequent transcription. The identity of a person named Maria Kray is not known. The sponsors and witnesses do not include any known relatives or associates. If however, *Cuiertie Hendricxs* is actually Grietie Hendricx, this woman could be the same person as the sponsor who appears in Tryntie Dalsen's baptismal record which follows. There is no further trace of this Pieter in the records.

7. ***Baptized: 23 Sept 1674; Jan de Vries, Gritie Theunis; <u>Tryntie</u>; Jan Corszen, Grietie Hendricx.***

The names of the sponsors for this child ring familiar. Jan Corsen was the husband of Metje Theunis Cray, Tryntje's maternal aunt. Grietie Hendricx name is found in other family baptisms as well as those of children whose parents are associated with the Dolson and Kray families. On 30 January 1702, Tryntje married Johannes Meyer, a grandson of a very prosperous German immigrant to Nieuw Harlem. The Meyer family is featured in Riker's (1904) work. This Tryntje is referred to as a Dalsen in many records.

8. ***Born ca. 1677; <u>Margrietje</u>*** [date according to Riker (1904), no baptismal record located].

While no baptismal record has been located for Margrietje, her 29 July 1702 marriage to Martinus Cregier, a grandson of the renowned military commander and first *Burghermeister* of Nieuw Amsterdam, is well documented. Her grandfather-in-law, Martin Cregier, was an immigrant from Borcken, Germany. Margrietje served as a sponsor at several baptisms held at the Dutch Reformed Church in New York City during the first decade of the 1700s. On each of these occasions she is referred to as a Dalsen. More information regarding the Cregier family genealogy is available in Cregier (1959).

9. *Baptized: 8 Oct 1679; Jan de Vries, Grietie Theunis; <u>Jacob</u>; Kasten Luurzen, Geertie Theunis.*

The sponsors at this baptism are Grietje Theunis' paternal aunt and uncle. Nothing is known about the life of this Jacob. This person may have died young or he may have used another patronymic or surname. The name Jacob does appear in Grietje's family line and was subsequently applied to men belonging to several later generations of the Dolsons.

10. *Baptized: 27 Sept 1682; Jan de Vries, Grietie Theunis; <u>Elisabeth</u>; Joost Van Harlingen, Mayken Vlamings.*

The witnesses/sponsors have no known link to Jan or Grietje and besides this birth record, there is no other mention of an Elisabeth Dalsen, Jansen or Gerritsen connected to the family. The fact that this daughter is named Elisabeth may be a further indication that Jan's and Grietje's child named Lysbetje died after Magarietje's baptism in 1677. As in the case of Jacob, nothing more is known about Elisabeth. She may have died young, used another surname, or never married.

11. *Baptized 8 Dec 1685; Jan Gerritszen, Grietie Jans; <u>Jannetie</u>; Jan Kierszen, Annetie Jans.*

Grietje Theunis is shown in this record as *Griete Jans*, an example of one way in which Jan Gerritsen's patronymic could be formulated to refer to a spouse in the transitional, bicultural, and bilingual context of early New York. The witnesses were clearly Jan Gerritsen's son-in-law (married to daughter, Gerritje) and Jan's sixteen year old daughter, Annetje. Nothing more is known about this Jannetje. This Jannetje may have died young.

The Dutch Reformed Church in Manhattan

There were several Dutch Reformed Church parishes in Nieuw Amsterdam. In fact, to determine the exact location of Dalsen family marriages and baptisms, one has to match up the dates of the specific events with dates of the establishment of the various congregations which constituted the Reformed Collegiate Churches of New York. The records of the various congregations were collectively maintained as the Collegiate Churches were administered as a single entity.

Religious services were offered as early as the 1620s in the Fort and at near-by barn lofts. Around 1638 the first church edifice, the tallest structure of Nieuw Amsterdam, was built inside the fortified wall, now known as Wall Street. Within another decade, a second congregation was established at Peter Stuyvesant's bowery near the location of the present

St. Marks Church (Eleventh Street and Second Avenue). A third congregation of the Dutch Reformed Church in Manhattan became operational at New Harlem in 1667.

The marriage of Jan and Grietje and the early baptisms of their children took place at the very southern tip of Manhattan. Later, other family marriages and baptisms may have taken place either within the Wall or at the bowery congregation, depending on the location of residences or the choice of the particular Dalsen and collateral family members involved. After 1667, any three of the church sites might have been used, but certainly New Harlem would have been favored by the families living in the northern part of Manhattan. For example, Jan Kiersen's and Grietje Dalsen's 1667 marriage probably took place in New Harlem because both the Dalsens and the Kiersens were residing there at the time. On the other hand, Margrietje's wedding might have taken place at the lower Manhattan Dutch Reformed Church since the homestead of the prominent Cregier family was located inside the Wall.

Later Years in New Harlem
Riker (1904) writes that in January 1667, the village of Harlem was expanding. Farm and house lots were being allocated to new settlers based on petition. According to Riker (1904), our Jan took advantage of this opportunity to apply:

> *The vacant land to the south of the village, north of lots 1, 2, 3, Van Keulen's Hook, and reserved to the town uses, was also encroached upon and a triangular piece in the northwest corner opposite the erven of Karstens and Cresson (taking its form from the course of the creek), was sold at the above price [25 gl.] to Jan Gerritsen De Vries, who built upon and fenced it.*

Two months later, on 10 March 1667, Tho. Wandel requested that the New Amsterdam Court order *John de Vries* to deliver the boat promised to the complainant.

On 29 October 1667, the New Amsterdam Court summoned a number of individuals to inquire why they had not paid their quota for the ministers' salaries. A *Jan Vrees* is recorded as answering, "*If I be forced, I must pay, otherwise I cannot.*" This might not be our Jan since in 1667 he is thought to be residing in New Harlem, but if it is our ancestor, it certainly sounds like a Dalsen lament. And there is another 1667 entry from the New Amsterdam Court that most certainly relates to our Jan Gerritsen de Vries:

> *Tho. Wandel, plt: v/s John de Vries, deft. Uppon hearinge off both parties, this Court did order that the def: should deliver up the plt's boat to this plt: besides the £0:6s:8d which this plt: paid to this deft with costs of the Court.*

In January 1668 Riker (1904) reports that:

> *The first vessel of size put upon the stocks here, of which any notice is taken, was a sloop built this year, under a contract, by Jan Gerritsen De Vries, for Capt. Thomas Bradley, who before this had sailed a market yacht between New York and "Stafford". On November 17th, the parties discharged each from their contract, Bradley giving De Vries a bond for the balance due him, 122 gl. in sewant, to which Verveelen and William Sandford were witnesses.*

In another court entry, the jurors ruled in favor of Jan regarding a debt owed:

> *19 March, did Thomas Maria of New Towne confess a judgment to the use of Jan Gerrisen d'Vries to the summe of fl. 111 Wampum and court charges.*

Apparently, from January 1667 to March 1670, Jan and his family lived on a house lot in the southern section of New Harlem. Riker (1904) indicates that:

> *Jan Gerritsen De Vries obtained from the overseers on March 2nd [1670] a formal grant of the house lot set off to him some years before at the south side of the village, on condition of his paying as other such small house lots (erfjes), and also the same servitudes. He is charged for it in the town book, under 1667, 25 gl. De Vries had sold this lot, with its house and improvement to Resolved Waldron, to whom he conveyed it the next day, March 3rd. Here Waldron took up his residence.*

Based on the purchase price, Jan probably acquired a house lot of less than one *morgen* (two acres); nevertheless, he must have built a rather substantial home and made other significant improvements to the property. After all, Resolved Waldron was quite wealthy and, given his prominence in the community, he would not have taken up residence in 1670 in just any dwelling.

In the spring of 1670, Warnaer Wessells complained to the Court that Humphry Davenpoort did not pay for rum that he had Jochem De Shoemaker delivere to *Jan de Vries'* residence. This Court record is poorly translated and it is difficult to understand the case; however, it appears that our Jan may have been accused of being a recipient of unpaid goods.

Scott and Stryker-Rodda (2009, p. 85) note that a *Jan Gerritsen* was among the persons who signed an allegiance to the Dutch at either Fordham or Yonkers on 10 October 1673.

Although none too clear about the date of this occurrence, Riker (1904) states that New Harlem land records show that Jan petitioned for another lot. The Council noted that he had previously been given a lot, but Jan insisted that the lot was not given to him but rather that he had purchased the lot, but did not have the means to prove it. In the end, the Council decided to give him another parcel provided that Jan should not sell it, *"but for want of heirs it should relapse to the township"* (Riker, 1904).

In 1682, Jan Gerritsen de Vries, footnoted by Riker (1904) as *Dolsen*, is shown on the Harlem tax list as the owner of a small *erven* or house lot. The list is dated 14 February 1682 and the tax rate is shown as £7:0. Unfortunately, Jan's is the only *erven* on the list without a designation linking it to one of the Harlem neighborhoods such as Jochem Pieters Flat, Van Keulen's Hook, Spuyten Duyvel, Horn's Hook, or Moertje David's Fly.

Thomas Hedding from Amsterdam had leased a farm in New Harlem. When he died in 1683, his livestock and the other possessions within his estate were sold at auction. On 12 May and 2 June 1683, buyers included a *Jan Gerrits de Vries* along with Johannes Vermielje, Jan Dyckman, William Bickley, Barent Waldron, Reyer Michielsen, and Lourens Jansen.

While residing in Harlem, Riker (1904) says that Jan Gerritsen van Dalsen appears among the erf-holders from 1681 to 1683. In 1685 and 1686, Jan subscribes to Dominie Selyn's salary, which means that he contributed funds to support the clergy of the Dutch Reformed Church. Around this time, he built one or more vessels and sailed an "open boat" out of New York (Riker, 1904).

Jan dedicated most of his working years to a career as a ships' carpenter. However, in 1686, his last recorded commercial venture involved real estate. Riker (1904) is quoted on this matter as follows:

> *Coeval with the church enterprise was another looking to the opening of a new section of the township to the plough and husbandman, and to the ultimate increase of the town revenues. Midway on the long range of heights stretching from Moertje Davids Fly to Sherman's Creek and not far below Fort Washington, was an Indian clearing known as the Great Maize Land. This was now leased to Capt. Jan Gerritsen van Dalsen and his son-in-law, Jan Kiersen, upon the following curious terms:*

> *On this date [31 March 1686], We the Constable and Magistrates hereby acknowledge to have consented and agree in a manner hereafter written. Jan Gerritse van Dalsen and Jan Kiersen own and declare to have received from the aforesaid Constable and Magistrates, a piece of land named The Great Maize Land, belonging under the jurisdiction of New Harlem; which aforesaid piece of land the before written Jan Gerritse van Dalsen has been given and Jan Kiersen shall use, build and live upon, for the time of twelve successive years, to commence in the month of August of this years, 1686, and ending in the month of August, after the harvest is off; and the hirers shall be permitted the last*

years to sow two schepels of buckwheat and to plan a piece of maize (corn); also the lessees, for the first several years, shall occupy it free, only each giving to the lessors a fat capon yearly, as an acknowledgement and shall be obligated for the last five years to pay each year two hundred guilders in good wheat, rye, peas, or barely, at the market price; from each parcel the just fourth part to be given to God the Lord. The lessees shall be allowed to make an orchard, and at the end of their years, shall have the right of taking up half of the same from the large fruit trees or the nursery; and the lessees shall be required to clear fourteen morgen of land in the first years, which will be two morgen yearly and if the lessees shall; have need of more land, the lessors shall be required to assign more land to the lessees, at the most convenient time; also is leased with the land a piece of meadow lying at the farthest point at the North River. So also the lessees are required to deliver up the building in good condition at the end of the years, as also to deliver the fencing of the land tight and sufficient. To the extent of fourteen morgen, the lessees shall be obligated to bear the ordinary town charges, but no extraordinary. The lessees shall be allowed to continue living on the aforesaid land till May of the last year being the year 1699. The lessees shall have the liberty of removing, upon condition that they signify one year before, their intention to give up the lease. All thus performed and agreed to, and with our usual hand undersigned, Done at Nieuw Haerlem this 30th day of March 1686. [Signed by Jan Delamater, as Constable, Daniel Tourneur, Jan Nagel, Jan Kiersen, and Jan Gerritsen van Dalsen, in the presence of Jan Tibout, Clerk.]

According to James Renner (2003), the Great Maize Land was bounded by present-day 179th Street to 181st Street and Broadway to Pinehurst Avenue (Retrieved 3 April 2010 from *Native American Life in Washington Heights and Inwood,* No longer posted). Another description of this property is contained in Bolton (1916):

When the decision was reached in 1691 to allot among the freeholders the common lands of Jochem Pieters Hills, now Washington Heights… one of the first allotments made was that in favor of Van Oblienis, being number 19, comprising 22 and three fourths Dutch acres upon the south end of the Hill which eminence later became known as Mount Washington. This, the northerly boundary of the tract, was the present 181st Street and further acquisitions of the family brought its southerly line to 170th Street, where it extended from the Post Road to the Hudson River. Within this area had existed, long prior to these divisions, the "Great Maize Land" or planting ground of the local Indians which had been temporarily occupied on a dubious sort of town lease by Jan Kiersen and his father-in-law, Captain Van Dalsen, on an agreement to "be allowed to make an orchard" and for rental to give a fat capon yearly and "a fourth part of two hundred guilders in good wheat, rye, peas, or barley to be given to God the Lord" (p. 64).

Bolton goes on to say that the Native American group, "Weck-quas-keeks", had originally farmed this land. He provides several additional details regarding research on this property associated with excavations conducted in the early 1900s:

The opening of 176th Street across vacant property between Broadway and Fort Washington Avenue brought to light evidence of the one-time dwelling of the Van Oblienis family, pioneer settlers of the Heights. The discovery became of special interest because of the prominence of that family in the affairs of the township of Nieuw Haerlem in its early days and because the Oblienis farm was a direct successor of the aboriginal cultivation of the same area known to the settlers as the "Indian field".

When the decision was reached in 1691, to allot among the freeholders the common lands of Jochem Peters Hills, now Washington Heights, and the Round Meadow, now the Dyckman tract, one of the first allotments made was in favor of van Oblienis, being number 19, comprising 22 Dutch acres upon the south end of the Hill, which eminence later became known as Mount Washington. This, the northerly boundary of this tract was the present 181st Street and the further acquisition of the family brought its southerly line to 179th Street where it extended from the Post road to the Hudson. Within this area there had existed long prior to these divisions the Great Maize Land or planting ground of the local Indians, which had been temporarily occupied on a dubious sort of town lease by Jan Kiersen and his father-in-law, Captain van Dalsen, on an agreement to be allowed to make an orchard and for rental to give a fat capon yearly and a fourth part of two hundred guilders in good wheat, rye, peas, or barley, to be given to God the Lord (p. 64).

Albeit unusual, the lease of the Great Maize Land was a major event for both the village and the leaseholders. It is also interesting to note that the record shows that a *Jan van Dalsen* signed his name to the lease document instead of simply making his mark----perhaps an indication that he was literate. Jan Gerritsen de Vries van Dalsen probably did not live to see the end of the contract period. His partner, Jan Kiersen, may have modified or cancelled the lease upon or after Jan's death. As mentioned, the next owner of this property was Joost Van Oblienis (Bolton, 1916).

Riker (1904) suggests that Jan Gerritsen de Vries van Dalsen was still living in 1692. This appears to be accurate as the last documented sighting of Jan was at the baptism of his granddaughter, Annetje, in the same year:

27

17 Apr; Johannes Waldron, Annetje Gerrits; <u>Annetie</u>; Jan Gerritszen, Grietie Theunis.

After this occasion, nothing more is heard from Captain Jan Gerritsen de Vries van Dalsen and most researchers presume that he died in 1692 or soon thereafter. It is not known where Jan was buried. Potential locations include the original New Harlem Dutch Reformed Church Burying Ground and the Nagle-Dyckman-Vermilye Cemetery at the time located between West 212th and 214th Streets and 9th and 10th Avenues in Kingsbridge. Unfortunately, neither of these cemeteries now exists. In the latter many graves were disturbed over the years and 417 plots were relocated to Woodlawn Cemetery (Lincoln, 1910). The family names associated with this burying ground are known contemporaries of Jan and his son, Theunis, during their time in New Harlem. The Nagle-Dyckman-Vermilye Cemetery and adjoining Old Slaves Graveyard are reported to have been the oldest resting places in the northern section of Manhattan.

Chapter II – Second Generation

Theunis Dalsen

[Jan]

According to his obituary notice published in various newspapers of New England, Theunis Dalsen was born on 5 September 1664, immediately after the British took over Nieuw Amsterdam from the Dutch and changed the name of the city to New York. No baptismal record has been located. Theunis is reported to have spent his infancy somewhere in New England, but by 1667, his family had returned to New Harlem (present-day Harlem), where it appears that he grew into manhood.

Theunis in New Harlem

There were several interesting sightings of Theunis in New Harlem. He was a witness to the baptism of his sister Annetje's child named Cornelia in 1696:

> **22 Mar; Johannes Waldron, Annetje Dalson; <u>Cornelia</u>; Theunis Dalson, Catharina Dalson.**

Catharina, the other sponsor, is a formal reference to another of Theunis' sisters, Tryntje, which was also the nickname of his maternal grandmother, Tryntje van Kampen.

On 21 May 1696, Theunis purchased house lot number eight in Harlem from Joost Van Oblinus (Riker, 1904). Theunis was still single at the time. His marriage to Sara Vermilyea would not take place for several months. Theunis' house lot was on the tax rolls of New Harlem during the period of 1697-1698. On 29 September 1697, Theunis was appointed as a constable for the Village of Harlem.

A Theunis Dalsen is shown on the list of "Freemen" (resident citizens) of New York City on 6 September 1698. Some family historians assume that this indicates that Theunis and his family moved to a location outside of New Harlem around this time and that his relocation accounts for his inclusion on the list of Freemen of New York City. However, a review of tax records for the period shows that New Harlem was considered the "Outward" of New York City and thus, the residents of New Harlem were concurrently Freemen of New York City. It is almost certain that Theunis' family remained at the home on lot number eight in New Harlem until moving to Westchester County sometime in late 1698.

In 1701, Theunis sold his house lot in Harlem to his brothers-in-law, Barent and Johannes Waldron, for 1,070 Guilders. As far as the writer knows, this is Theunis' final act on the

Island of Manhattan. Records show that by this time, Theunis already had relocated to Westchester County and would reside there for a span of twenty-eight years, from 1698 to 1726, after which time he moved north to Dutchess County.

Theunis' Wife, Sarah Vermilyea, and Her Family
On 28 August 1696, wedding banns for Theunis and his bride, Sarah Vermilyea, were announced at the Dutch Reformed Church in New York:

Eodem. Theunis Dalee, J.m. van N. Yorck en Sara Vermelje, J.d. als boven, beyde woonende op N. Haerlem. getrouwt tot Haerlem.[3]

This wedding most likely took place in the following month, September 1696, at the Harlem Congregation of the Dutch Reformed Church, since both the Dalsen and Vermilyea families resided in Harlem at the time. Sarah Vermilyea was nearly twenty-three years of age on the day of her wedding while Theunis Dalsen was just shy of thirty-two.

Sarah Vermilyea was baptized at the New Amsterdam Dutch Reformed Church on 4 October 1673:

4 Oct; Johannes Vermelje; Aeltie Waldron; Sara; Willem Waldron, Rachel Vermelje.

The sponsors were William Waldron, the child's maternal uncle and Rachel Vermilyea, the child's paternal aunt and future wife of Jan Ter Bos.

Sarah's father was Johannes Vermilyea (*Vermelje, Vermeille, Vermilye, Vermilyer*), an immigrant from Leyden, Holland. He was baptized at Leyden on 4 November 1632, the son of Isaac Vermilyea and his first wife, Jacomina Jacobs. The family left the Netherlands for America on board the *Plumerland Kerk* on 12 October 1662. Johannes died after 1693, but before 1696, probably in New Harlem (Downey, 2013). Surprisingly, although he was a prominent land owner in Lower Yonkers (now part of Brooklyn), according to The Vermilyea Family Genealogy (Vermilyea Todd, 2016), Johannes never lived in Yonkers. Instead he lived in New Harlem for most, if not all of his life. He was one of the original patentees of Manhattan and an important but controversial magistrate in Nieuw Netherlandts and later in the British Colony of New York. The Vermilyea Family Reunion website (*vermilyeafamilyreunion.com*), developed and maintained by Sandra Vermilyea Todd, contains an extensive and well-documented genealogical history of many generations of the Vermilyea family. Downey (2013) has contributed an excellent addendum and analysis.

---

[3] Translation of the Dutch Reformed Church record: *On the same date, Theunis Dalee, a young single man from New York and Sara Vermilje, a young, single woman from the same place were wed and are living in N. Harlem.*

On 27 August 1670, Johannes Vermilyea married Aeltje Waldron. The wedding was recorded at the New Amsterdam Dutch Reformed Church, but according to La Coste (1992), the ceremony took place at the Stadt Huys (government house or city hall) of New Amsterdam.

27 dicto. Johannes Vernelje, en Aeltje Waldron. Eodem Jan Nagel, en Rebecca Waldron.

The records show that this was a double wedding. Not only did Johannes marry Aeltje, but Jan Nagel married Rebecca Waldron, Aeltje's sister, on the same day.

Aeltje Waldron was born in 1651 in Amsterdam, Netherlands and baptized on 2 January 1652 at the Nieuw Kerk of that city. The sponsor was *Alioch Hendrix*. Altje was the daughter of Resolved Waldron and Rebecca Hendricks, both of Amsterdam. Waldron is an English surname but the family had immigrated to Holland in the early 1500s.

Resolved Waldron was born in the Netherlands ca. 1620 and died at New Harlem on 17 May 1690. He was a printer by trade. Arriving in America between 1647 and 1650, Resolved continued to work as a printer in Nieuw Amsterdam. He and his brother, Joseph, purchased a home at the corner of Broadway and Wall Street. Resolved Waldron soon became a well-respected magistrate. He was held in high esteem by Governor Peter Stuyvesant. He was one of the original patentees of Nieuw Harlem.

Resolved Waldron married Rebecca Kochs Hendricks on 29 July 1645 at the Nieuw Kerk in Amsterdam. Rebecca was the daughter of Hendricks Melcherts and Clarsje Lamberts. She died ca. 1654 in Amsterdam and Resolved Waldron married second, Tanneke Barents Nagel on 23 April 1654 at the Nieuw Kerk. Tanneke was born ca. 1624 in Goningen, Netherlands, the daughter of Barent Nagel and his wife, Janeke. Riker's (1904) comprehensive history of New Harlem contains a sketch of the Waldron family. Resolved's son, Johannes Waldron, was the man who eventually married Annetje Dalsen, Theunis' sister.

Aeltje Waldron Vermilyea lived most of her life in New Harlem with her husband Johannes. After her husband's death, Aeltje is shown on the Harlem Ward tax rolls of 1695-1698, paying an assessment, depending on the year, of £3 to £5 for a house lot. In later years and until her death, she probably lived in Lower Yonkers, most likely at Kingsbridge (Downey, 2013). Aeltje died shortly before 23 April 1734 when her will was proved as follows:

In the name of God, Amen, May 23, 1730.
I, Altie Vermillie, of Yonkers, in Westchester County, widow, being in health. I leave to my eldest son Abraham £25, and one bed and furniture; "which said bed is my own proper lodging bed." I leave all the rest of my estate to my

children, Abraham, Isaac, Johannes, Rebecca, wife of Peter Bussing, Rachel, wife of Charles Vincent, Hannah, wife of Johannes Odell, and to the children of my daughter, Sarah, deceased wife of Tunis Dolsen. I appoint my sons, Isaac and Johannes, and my son-in-law, Peter Bussing, executors. Witnesses, Charles Warner, Edward Smith, Roger Barton.

Aeltje Waldron Vermilyea's last testament not only reveals the names of her children with Johannes Vermilyea, but indicates that her daughter, Sarah, wife of Theunis' Dalsen, had died previous to Aeltje's will dated May 1730. What is not clear however is the manner in which Sarah's inheritance was to be divided. It's most likely that the Dalsen children received, as a group, one seventh of the funds----division of the total estate among seven Vermilyea beneficiaries----with the Dalsen children getting a single share; that portion of the estate which had been designated for their mother, Sarah. According to Benton (1906) and Downey (2013), Aeltje Waldron Vermilyea and Johannes Vermilyea had the following children:

1. Rebecca, baptized 1671; married Peter Bussing.
2. Sarah, baptized 1673; married Theunis Dalsen.
3. Rachel, baptized 1675; married Charles Vincent.
4. Abraham, baptized 1677; died as infant.
5. Isaac, baptized 1682; married Josyntie Oblinus widow of Teunis Corsa.
6. Maria, baptized ca. 1691; married Peter Kierse.
7. Jacob, baptized 1686; died young.
8. Johannes, born ca. 1688; married Sarah Odell and second, Maria De Bruin.
9. Hannah, born ca. 1693; married Johannes Odell.

Clearly, the given names of Sarah, Abraham, Isaac, Jacob, and John, names which became common for future generations of Dolsons, originated primarily with the Vermilyea family.

Children of Theunis and Sarah

Records support the notion that Theunis Dalsen and Sarah Vermilyea Dalsen had at least six children. Amazingly, it seems that none of their known children died young. All appear to have lived into adulthood, migrating together as a family from Westchester to Dutchess County in 1726.

Except for the eldest daughter, Aeltje, who was baptized at a Dutch Reformed Church in New York, all of the other children are assumed to have been born at various hamlets in Westchester County. The writer has not located the baptismal records of any of these children. The dates of birth of these individuals have been garnered from several sources, most notably Plimley (2011) and Downey (2013). Places of birth are noted when possible.

1. <u>Aeltje Dolsen</u> was baptized at the Dutch Reformed Church in New York City in 1699, probably at the New Harlem congregation:

   16 Jul; Theunis Dalsen, Sara Farmielje; <u>Aaltje</u>; Jan Kierse, Aaltje Waldron widow of Joh. Farmielje

   At this baptism, Jan Kiersen, Theunis' brother-in-law, and Aeltje Waldron Vermilyea, his mother-in-law, were sponsors. The Aeltje baptized on this date was named after her maternal grandmother, who also became her god mother on this occasion. After moving to the Fishkill area of Dutchess County with her family, Aeltje married Dirk Hegeman of Fishkill.

2. <u>Johannes Dolsen</u> was born ca. 1702, perhaps at Fordham Manor. Johannes birth year has been calculated according to a self-report of his age as eighty-one in a census taken at Niagara in 1783 (Downey, 2013). Johannes' maternal grandfather was Johannes Vermilyea and of course, his paternal grandfather was Jan Gerritsen de Vries van Dalsen. By naming their eldest son Johannes, Theunis and Sarah selected a name that honored both grandfathers. Johannes married at the Fishkill Dutch Reformed Church, Elizabeth Buys, from the Oswego area of the Beekman Patent.

3. <u>Jacob Dolsen</u> was born ca. 1704 (Downey, 2013) in Westchester County, perhaps in the hamlet of Throggs Neck (Hamlin, 1905). Jacob's marriage record simply indicates that he was born in Westchester. This Jacob had a maternal uncle named Jacob Vermilyea. Jacob married at the Fishkill Dutch Reformed Church, Maritje Buys, a younger sister of Elizabeth Buys.

4. <u>Isaac Dolsen</u> was born ca. 1707 in Yonkers (Downey, 2013). The location of his birth was garnered from Isaac's Fishkill Dutch Reformed Church marriage record. The life story of Isaac will be presented in the next chapter. Isaac was named after his maternal uncle, Isaac Vermilyea. Isaac married Maritje Hussey at the Fishkill Dutch Reformed Church.

5. <u>Abraham Dolsen</u> was born ca. 1710 in Westchester County (Downey, 2013). Again Hamlin (1905) identifies the birthplace as Throggs Neck, but Abraham's marriage record simply notes that he was born in Westchester County. Abraham was named after an uncle on the Vermilyea side of the family. Abraham married, at the Fishkill Dutch Reformed Church, Maritje Slot of Poughkeepsie.

6. <u>Johanna Dolsen</u> was born ca. 1712 (Downey, 2013), perchance in the vicinity of Eastchester Town. Johanna was named after her grandfathers or perhaps after an Aunt Hanna/Johanna on her mother's side of the family. Hanna Vermilyea was married to

Johannes Odell. Johanna married, at the Poughkeepsie Dutch Reformed Church, Nicholas DeLang from the Beekman Patent.

Substantial genealogical documentation is available to support the existence of the six individuals listed above. It is possible that Theunis and his wife, Sarah Vermilyea, had additional children. The following three paragraphs contain suppositions regarding this matter which have been advanced by Downey (2013) and Dougherty (1990).

As Theunis Dalsen and Sarah Vermilyea were married in 1696, it is possible that they bore a child in 1697. Since we know that a daughter Aeltje (named after her maternal grandmother) was baptized in 1699 and a son named Johannes, named after his grandfathers, was born ca. 1702, then it is plausible to assume that if a female child were born in 1697, she might have been named Grietje, following the Dutch custom of naming the firstborn girl after the paternal grandmother----in this case, after Grietje Theunis Cray. There is no further record of a Grietje Dalsen from this family, suggesting that, if she existed, she may have died young or married before the rest of the family relocated to Dutchess County. If however a male child were born to this family in 1697, he almost certainly would have been named Johannes and if this were the case, this child must have died before 1702 when the couple named a subsequent son Johannes. As in the case of Grietje, it is possible that the first Johannes never existed.

In addition, there may have been a Sarah Dalsen or a Theunis Dalsen II born ca. 1715 (Downey, 2013; Dougherty, 1990). If either a Sarah or Theunis existed they may have been born in the vicinity of Eastchester Town or less likely in Mamaroneck, places where the Dalsen family was living during that period. Sarah would have been named after her mother and Theunis after his father. There is a Montgomery, Orange County Dutch Reformed Church record showing that a Sarah *Dalson* and her husband, Israel Rotsiker, baptized a son Daniel on 25 May 1736; however, no additional information on this Sarah has been uncovered and with the existing evidence, it is impossible to identify this Sarah conclusively as a daughter of Theunis Dalsen and Sarah Vermilyea Dalsen. In a similar manner, there is no compelling evidence of the existence of a Theunis Dalsen II in Westchester, Dutchess, nor Orange County which can be attributed to a man of this name from this generation of the Dalsen family.

More information is provided on the adult lives of the children of Theunis Dalsen and Sarah Vermilyea Dalsen in the next chapter. As an ancestor of this writer's line of Dolsons, that chapter will be dedicated to the narrative of the couple's fourth child, Isaac.

Theunis' Sisters
Unfortunately, as mentioned earlier in this chapter, no information is available on any of Theunis' brothers. All appear to have died young. Several of his sisters also died young;

however, noteworthy information is available regarding the lives of four of Theunis' sisters: Gerritje, Annetje, Tryntje, and Margrietje.

1. Gerritje Jans Dalson. Gerritje married Jan Kiersen, one of the early patentees of New Harlem on 9 October 1685:

> **9 dicto. _Jan Kiersen_, j. m. Van Aenhout, gelegen in Drenthe en _Gerritje Jans_ [Dalsen], j. d. Van N. Engelandt, beyde woonende tot N. Haerlem. Getrouwt tot N. Haerlem.**

This marriage record indicates that Jan Kiersen (Kere, Keres, Ciersen) was born in Drenthe, Holland and Gerritje was born in New England. At the time of the marriage, they were both living in New Harlem. One genealogist has posted information indicating that Gerritje lived until 1754 and died at the age of 87; however, no documentation is provided. Jan Kiersen is said to have lived to a very old age.

La Coste (2003) provides a detailed account of Jan Kiersen and the family he made with Gerritje Dalsen Kiersen. This Jan came to New Amsterdam from Delaware in 1657 and eventually settled in New Harlem. By 1682 Jan Kiersen had joined the Dutch Reformed Church in Harlem and later became a deacon. He was involved in the lease of the Great Maize Land in Harlem in 1686 with his father-in-law, Jan Gerritsen de Vries van Dalsen. Jan Kiersen held various governmental posts in Harlem such as assessor, tax collector, and constable between 1695 and 1701. In 1694 Jan Kiersen purchased lots sixteen and eighteen in New Harlem from Thomas Tourneur (La Coste, 2003).

Of special note according to Riker (1904):
> **In March of 1696 Kiersen obtained the signatures of every inhabitant of the town [Harlem] granting him a half morgen of land from the common woods, lying at the southeast hook of the land that Samuel Waldron had drawn out of the common woods, which half morgen of land he may build upon, thereon setting a house, barn, and extensive gardens. The King's Way ran through his property, and Samuel Waldron's. On 7 March 1700 he received a deed for this property. This was the first known settlement in Harlem Heights. Jan then purchased the lands and patent rights of Wiliam Haldron. This was lot number 17 of the original Harlem Patent. In 1712 these lots were listed as number 18 and comprised 40 acres of land. Meanwhile in 1712 he enlarged his house and lot holdings near Harlem to 8 acres on the King's Way. To this in 1720 he again added another 4 acres of land (New York Land Records). Afterwards he added lot number 6 known as the Vermilyea lot. This added another 20 acres to his growing estate.**

Bolton (1916) describes the family's early years on the property:

The pioneer settler had long before transferred his operations from the Indian clearing [Great Maize Land] to a property on the east side of the post-road, extending between 158th and 163rd Streets, and having built thereon a humble dwelling of the usual cottage farmhouse type … The attractive position of this little farm, above the bold bluffs overhanging the winding Harlem, invited the attention of travelers … (p. 49)

Pumpelly (1903) indicates a similar location for the mansion while providing a few additional details:

Situated at the northern extremity of Manhattan Island on a plot of ground almost opposite to the intersection of Tenth Avenue and 160th Street with the Old King's Bridge Road is the Roger Morris house or "Jumel Mansion." The first house built on Harlem Heights was erected upon this spot by Jan Kiersen. In March, 1695, he obtained the signatures of every inhabitant of the town [Harlem] … granting him … land from the common woods on which to have a house, barn, and garden. Kiersen received his deed March 7, 1700. (pp. 80-81)

Jan Kiersen's former estate is presently known as the Morris-Jumel Mansion; as of 2018, the oldest existing residence in New York. The present mansion was built in 1765; the same year in which Jan Kiersen's sons sold the land to James Caroll, who afterward sold this property to Colonel Roger Morris (Pumpelly, 1903). The lands of the estate not only contain the mansion itself, but also gardens. When the Kiersen descendants sold the property on 29 January 1765, the deed read as follows (Romer and Hartman, 1981):

… Together with all and singular the orchards, gardens, fences, trees, woods, underwood's, fields, feedings, pastures, meadows, marshes, swamps, ponds, pools, lakes, streams, rivulets, runs, and streams of water, fishing fowling, hunting, hawking, and all other profits, privileges, advantages, emoluments, hereditaments, right of commonage, and appurtenances, to the same belonging …

A general history of the mansion may be found at: *www.morrisjumel.org*.

The children of Jan Kiersen and Gerritje Dalsen Kiersen were (Clark, 2015):

a. <u>Jannetje Kiersen I</u> was baptized 13 March 1687 at the New York Dutch Reformed Church. Witnesses to her baptism were Hendrick Kiersen, her paternal uncle, and

Grietje Theunis, her maternal grandmother. Since the couple named their fourth child Jannetje, this first Jannetje must have died before May of 1693.

b. Grietje Kieroon was baptized 25 November 1688 at the New York Dutch Reformed Church.

c. John Kiersen was born ca. 1690 at Harlem, New York. He is often referred to as John Kiersen Jr. and his name appears on several of his father's warrants and deeds. John Jr.'s name was also listed on the role of Captain Stuyvesant's company of militia in 1738. This man appears in some Harlem documents in 1767 as John Kere.

d. Jannetje Kiersen II was baptized on 25 May 1693 at the New York Dutch Reformed Church:

> *… den 25 ditto. Jan Kiersen, Grietje Van Daelsen, <u>Jannetij</u>. Theunis Van Daelsen, Tryntie Van Daelsen.*

Theunis Dalsen and sister, Tryntje Dalsen, were sponsors for this child. Jannetje Kiersen II married Jacob Dyckman on 16 May 1716. Dyckman was a prominent resident of New Harlem and Westchester County. Information on the life of this Jacob is contained in a manuscript by Romer and Hartman (1981, pp. 12-14).

e. Abraham Kiersen was baptized 6 October 1695 at the Dutch Reformed Church in New York. He appears on the list of Captain Stuyvesant's New York Militia in 1738, along with his brother, John Jr. He followed the trade of animal husbandry. Abraham was a Constable of Harlem in 1728. He signed many documents as an unmarried freeholder in New Harlem. He appears in Jacob Dyckman's will on 10 August 1767 as *Abraham Kere*. Abraham and his brother, John Jr., sold property inherited from their father to the Carroll family, which in turn sold the same property to Colonel Roger Morris, whose stately mansion is, in modern times, referred to as the Jumel-Morris House, the oldest existing home in New York City (La Coste, 2003).

f. Sarah, date of birth unknown; married Barent Nagel.

2. Annetje Jans Dalsen. Annetje, also referred to as Anneken and Ana, married Johannes Waldron on 25 April 1690:

> *den 25 dict. <u>Johannes Waldron</u>, j. m. Van N. Haerlem, en <u>Anneken Jans</u>, j. d. Van N. Haerlem. d' Eerste wonende tot Haerlem, en twede alhier. getrouwt tot Haerlem.*

Riker (1881, p. 554) describes the Waldrons as the most notable family in New Harlem. Johannes was the son of Resolved Waldron and his second wife, Tanneke Nagel. Waldron family researchers report that Johannes was born on 12 September 1665 in New Harlem (La Coste, 1992). Johannes' residence was located adjacent to Jochem Pieters Hills at what is now approximately 133rd Street between 8th and 9th Avenues (Riker, 1904). During the time he lived in New Harlem, La Coste (1992) reports that Johannes held a variety of posts such as surveyor of highways (1700, 1704, and 1709), overseer (1701), constable (1703-1706) and town assessor (1705). Johannes, along with his brother, Barent, bought lot number eight of the New Lots from his brother-in-law, Theunis Dalsen, on New Year's Day, 1701. Johannes died in 1753 having survived his wife, Annetje, and all of his children with the exception of his son, Resolved (Bergen, 1915).

Johannes Waldron and Annetje Dalsen Waldron baptized the following children at the New Amsterdam Dutch Reformed Church (Clark, 2015):

a. Anneken was born in early 1691 and died within months.
b. Annetje was born on 17 April 1692. She married John Delamater.
c. Margaret was born on 22 October 1693. She married Adolph Myer.
d. Cornelia was born on 22 March 1696. She married Ryck Lent (1699-1732) on 26 December 1722.
e. Johannes Jr. was born on 22 May 1698 and married Elizabeth Benson.
f. Resolved was born ca. 1702 and married Metje Quackenbosch.
g. Samuel was born ca. 1705 and married Engletje Meyer.

3. Tryntje Dalsen. New York Dutch Reformed Church records indicate that Tryntie married Johannes Meyer (*Myer*) of New Harlem:

den 30 January 1702; Johannes Meyer *j.m. Van N. Haarlem met* Tryntje Van Dalse [Dalsen], ***j.d. Van Haarlem;***

According to Riker (1904), Johannes Meyer was baptized on 13 August 1671. The couple had the following children, some of whom were baptized at the New Amsterdam Dutch Reformed Church (Clark, 2015):

a. Jannetje was born ca. 1705. She married Resolved Waldron.
b. Jacob was baptized on 8 May 1709. He married Aeltje Meyer.
c. Maria was baptized on 6 May 1711. She married Aaron Bussing.
d. Elizabeth was born ca. 1714. She married Peter Waldron.
e. John was born ca. 1716. He married Cornelia Delamater.

Johannes' parents were Adolph Meyer, an immigrant from Ulsen, in the parish of Bentheim in Westphalia, Germany and Marritje (Maria) Verveelen, daughter of Johannes Verveelen and Anna Jarsvelt, both of Amsterdam. The Verveelen family was originally from Cologne, Germany.

Johannes Meyer's first purchase of land was a share of Harlem lot number four in partnership with his father. He eventually became a large landholder. In 1748 Johannes inherited part of his father's estate, including the old homestead located on another portion of lot number four. Johannes died at the age of eighty-four in 1755. He left his estate to his widow, Tryntje, until she remarried or died. Subsequently the property was to pass to their sons, Jacob and John.

4. Margrietje Dalsen. Margrietje married Martinus Cregier (Kregier, Krieger) III on 29 August 1702 (Munsell, 1865). Martinus III was the son of Martin Cregier Jr. and Hendrickse van Doesburg. Martinus III was the grandson of the famous Captain Martin Cregier, an important magistrate of New Amsterdam. Martinus was a vintner and the couple relocated to Albany for a time. In 1741, the couple and their adult children---John (vintner), Anne, Henry (vintner), Martinus IV (mariner), Jane (single), and Margaret (widow of Bordet Fleetwood, who was a mariner), were living in New York City (Munsell, 1865).

    Captain Martin Cregier (1617–1713) was an early French Huguenot settler of Nieuw Netherlandts. Although he started out as a fur trader, he became a prominent citizen of Nieuw Amsterdam and served three terms as Burgomaster of the settlement. Cregier was also a military officer and led several battles against the Munsee Band of Native Americans during the Esopus Wars. Cregier's house and lot stood on Broadway, just north of Battery Park.

    In 1643, the elder Cregier oversaw the construction of the first public building on Broadway in Manhattan, a tavern located at present-day Ground Zero. The tavern was later known as Atlantic Gardens and survived until 1860. In 1648, Cregier was one of four men appointed as the city's first fire wardens. Toward the end of his life, Cregier retired to a plantation at Niskayuna, New York, reported to be a tranquil spot on the banks of the Mohawk River (Munsell, 1865).

The Dalsen Family in Westchester County
In Liber C, p. 5 of the Westchester County Deeds, as reported by Hall-Bristol in the *New York Genealogical and Biographical Record* (Vol. 59, No. 1, 1928, p. 66), the inhabitants of Westchester were asked by a proclamation dated 31 January 1698, to sign an allegiance to King William of Great Britain as follows:

I ____, do sincerely promise and sweare that I will be faithful and beare true allegiance unto his Majestie King William, so help me God. I do swear that I do from my heart abhor, detest, and abjure impious and heretical that damnable doctrine and position that princes excommunicated or deprived by the pope or any authority of the see of Roome may be deposed or murdered by their subjects or any other whatsoever. And I do declare that noe forreigne prince, person, prelate, state or potentate hath or ought to have any power, jurisdiction, superiority, preheminence or authority ecclesiasticall or spirituall within the realm of England or his province, so help me God.

A *Teunus Van Dolson* is recorded as signing this allegiance under a list of residents from Eastchester Towne.

In Liber C, p. 21 of Westchester County, referring to the year 1699, a *Tunis Dolson* is reported to have sold a parcel of forty acres to W. H. Harden of Eastchester (Hamlin, 1905). In the same Liber, a *Tennis Van Dolsen* purchases a property from William Acidea on 7 July 1699.

In the records of the Town of Eastchester there are three entries related to a *Tunisse* (*Tunis, Tunys*) *Vandals* (*Vandalls*) during the period of 1699 to 1700. First, this Theunis is assessed eight shillings for the purchase of common property for the town. Secondly, during November 1700, he is involved in a purchase of a tract of land. On 26 March 1700, his mark (brand) for livestock is recorded. Curiously, this last entry refers to *Tunis Vandals* as an "Indian". Such identification and the spelling of the surname cast doubts regarding the identity of the individual involved in these three incidents.

There is a notice of a property transaction in Westchester County regarding the purchase of a parcel of eight and one-half acres in the Town of Eastchester on 20 April 1700. Theunis Dalsen obtained this property from Jacob and Laddea Larrance who made their marks on the deed. Another purchase of land from Jacob Larrance is recorded in Liber C, p. 114 on 16 October 1701.

On 26 July 1701, a *Tuinnis Dolson* was one of two witnesses to the sale of land from Jeremiah Fowler to Edmund Ward. On 22 September of the same year, a *Tunis Dolsen* sells, "for a valuable consideration" to Edmund Ward of the Manor of Fordham, a property thusly described:

All that my forty acres of land be it more or less with a lott of fresh meddow scituate, lying and being within the Towne of Eastchester, aforesaid and is butted and bounded as is hereafter exprest; that is to say, Southwest beginning at a red oak tree marked and from thence running north west one hundred rood to a double walnut straddle and from thence easterly sixty-four rod to a red oak *tree, marked; and so from thence southerly one hundred rood to a leaning white oake tree marked, and so from thence sixty-four rod to the first marked red oake tree. Which land & meadow I bought of William Hayden, as also contains piece of land lying near the fresh meadow commonly called the first meadow, which is the second division scituate, lying and being within the limits and bounds of the Towne of Eastchester, being eight acres and a halfe, be it more or less, and is butted and bounded… by the highway, … by a piece of land formerly belonging to Richard Hadley, and... by land formerly belonging to William Hayden… IN WITTNESS WHEREOF, I THE SAID Tunis Dolsen, have hereunto putt to my hand and seale this six and 20th day of July in the thirteenth yeare of his Majesties raigne one thousand seven hundred and one.* (*Westchester Deeds*, Liber C, p. 103).

Theunis' wife, Sarah Vermilyea, also signed the codicil related to this transaction:

I, SARAH DOLSEN, wife of Tunis Dalsen, do give my consent to the above sale as witness my hand and seale this eighth day of September 1701.

Then appeared before me the person of TUNIS DALSEN and SARAH his wife, and did acknowledge this instrument to be there real act and deed this eighth day of September 1701. THO. PINCKNEY, Justice of the Peace for the County of Westchester.

On 8 January 1712, a *Tuniss Dalson* purchases a home lot near the bridge at the *Brunkes* [Bronx] River from Elizabeth Dikeman, single, and Samuel Hadley and his spouse, Sarah (*New York Genealogical and Biographical Record*, October 1929, p. 309). Later in the same year, on 7 February, a *Tunis Dolson* bought thirty-four acres of land from Joseph Taylor, cordwainer (shoemaker), of Eastchester. The next year, on 30 May 1713, Jonathan Huestis of Eversham, West Jersey sells to *Tunis Dalson* of Westchester, six acres *"near the highway that goes from the passage to William Smith's at Brunkses."* Davis (1988), reports that a *Theunis Dolson* purchased several parcels of land in Westchester through May 1713 according to the Town Records of Eastchester.

The sale of a property from Theunis Dalsen to Edmund Ward was done apparently as part of an exchange by Edward Ward to Theunis and his brother-in-law, Peter Bussing (husband of Rebecca Vermilyea), of another parcel. According to the deed of record, on 26 July 1701, for the sum of £280, Edmund Ward transferred title of 103 acres of land within the Manor of Fordham to *Tunis Dalsen* of Eastchester and Peter Bussing of Harlem. The land is described as lying by the *Brunkes* [Bronx] River in an area commonly called Little Plains. Downey (2013) suggests that this property was located just east of the Bronx River on the border of Eastchester and Westchester towns. The property contained a dwelling house, barn, and several other buildings, as well as an orchard, with all fencing, fencing stuff, timber woods, trees, runs, spring, and a sixteenth lot of salt meadow and a sixteenth lot of fresh meadow, and access to the common lands within the patent (Liber C, p. 417). Theunis is referred to as *Tunis Dalsen* in this particular transaction.

When Peter Bussing wrote his will on 19 February 1733, he mentioned the "farm or plantation" in the Manor of Fordham, which he had purchased from Edmund Ward and *Thomas Dollsen*. Apparently after initially purchasing the property located in the northeastern part of Fordham manor, in partnership, subsequently Peter Bussing bought out Theunis' interest in the farm. Peter Bussing was Theunis' brother-in-law, having married Sarah Vermilyea's sister, Rebecca.

By all appearances, Theunis Dalsen and Sarah Vermilyea signed the various deeds in their own hand indicating that they were literate. Based on the various documents recorded in Westchester County between 1698 and 1701, it appears that Theunis and his growing family transitioned to Westchester County ca. 1698, approximately three years before the sale of the house lot in Harlem.

Towns, Manors, and Hamlets of Westchester County
One has to take a close look at both current and historical maps of Westchester County, New York to appreciate the various locations and proximities of points of interest in this area as they pertain to Dalsen family history. First of all, Westchester County lies just northeast of Harlem across the Harlem River. During the Dutch period there was a ferry service, but by the first decade of the 1700s, a bridge connected the two regions. Particular Westchester locations associated with Dalsen family history include the following:

Eastchester Town
Many of Theunis' property transactions refer to this town located in the south central part of the county. Records indicate that Theunis was very active in this area between 1698 and 1714. The family's principal residence during this time period may have been located in or very near Eastchester Town.

Fordham Manor
Fordham lies directly across the river from Harlem. The Dalsen family had two connections to this manor. First, Theunis held property here and secondly, the Vermilyea family apparently came to Fordham from New Harlem. In land transaction documents, Johannes Vermilyea of "Fordham" is recorded as purchasing property in Yonkers and other locations in Westchester County. Readers are advised that Fordham and Fordham Manor represented different and separate localities. Fordham Manor lay adjacent to what was then called Lower Yonkers.

Mamaroneck

There are several reports from Riker (1904) and others that Theunis was a farmer in Mamaroneck as early as 1721. It is likely that he continued to hold property in this area until the time of his removal to Dutchess County ca. 1727.

Throggs Neck

Hamlin (1905) reports that the births of Abraham [*Theunis, Jan*] and Jacob [*Theunis, Jan*] Dolson took place in Throggs Neck, which is located on the southern shore of the county, not too distant from the Town of Eastchester. There is no documentation to support Hamlin's claims.

Westchester

Westchester is the name of the county, as well as, of the town that serves as the administrative seat of the same county.

Yonkers

According to various land records and wills, the Vermilyea family held tracts of land in Yonkers as well as in Fordham Manor and of course, Harlem. In his marriage record, Isaac Dolsen's [*Theunis, Jan*] birthplace is identified as Yonkers. Downey (2013) points out that historically, there was a Lower Yonkers and well as a Yonkers proper. The majority of the real estate activities associated with the Vermilyea family took place in Lower Yonkers.

After residing but a few years in Westchester County, a *Teunis Daltson* was elected as an assessor in May of 1704 of the Town of Westchester, a jurisdiction which included Fordham Manor (*New York Genealogical and Biographical* Record (Vol. 60, No. 3, 1929, p. 304).

In the *Records of the Combined Parish of Westchester, Eastchester, New Rochelle, Yonkers, Pelham and Morrisana 1702-1720* (Eastchester Historical Society, 1975), there are a number of references to a *Tunis Dalton*. Evidently Theunis was a vestryman, a position on the regional council of the Church of England. This position carried with it responsibilities of civil government. Tasks included oversight of the poor and monitoring resolutions regarding land ownership. Our Theunis is listed as present at vestry meetings between 1717 and 1720 (pp. 47-51).

A *Tunnis Daltson* is noted in Westchester County as a member of the Grand Jury on 3 October 1717 and then again on 3 June 1718. He was a panel member for the Court of Common Pleas on 7 June 1722.

On the 14th of April in 1717, *Tunis Dalston* for the price of £145 purchased fifty-nine acres of farm land plus two acres of salt meadow from Joseph Jennings and his wife, Mary (Liber E, p. 188). This same property was sold just four days later, on the 18th of April 1717, to John Ferris (Liber E, p. 195) for the same amount of money. This property was located in Throggs Neck.

Perhaps Theunis Dalsen's most expensive land transaction was that of 5 October 1718 between a *Thomas Dalton* (also written as *Thennis Dalton* and *Tuinnis Dalsen* in the same document) of Westchester and Colonel Jacobus Van Cortlandt of New York, a merchant. For the impressive sum of £700, Theunis purchased a home adjoining the *Brunxes* River with just eight acres of farm land and six acres of salt meadow in Westchester. The sale also included a separate lot of twenty acres and privileges to other rights. The statement of indenture is complicated and appears to include several exchanges of land previously purchased by Theunis.

In 1721, Henry Fowler of Mamaroneck and his brother, Moses Fowler of Eastchester, loaned money on land in Westchester to a *Teunis Dalson* of Mamaroneck (Hall-Bristol, 1927). In Volumes LVIII and LIX of the 1927 edition of the *New York Genealogical and Biographical Record*, Theresa Hall-Bristol published an outline in two parts concerning the descendants of Henry Fowler of Roxbury, Massachusetts and Mamaroneck, New York. In this article Hall-Bristol quotes a 1721 manuscript:

> **Moses Fowler, a carpenter, … with his brother, Henry Fowler Jr. of Mamaroneck advanced money by mortgage, on a large tract of land in Westchester, owned by Teunis Dalson of Mamaroneck.**

This transaction is recorded in the Westchester County Deeds (Liber E, pp. 306-308). Later, on 28 November 1721, a *Tunnis Daltson* sells, for the sum of £200, several tracts and parcels of land to Henry and Moses Fowler in the Town of Westchester, which Theunis had previously purchased from Isaac Dickermans, Joseph Talors, Richard Garreetson, Howard Haddens, David Huesties, Erasmus Hortons, John Quiby, and Nathanal Underhill Jr.

On 2 September 1721, a *Tunnis Daltson of Mamaroneck* sold three acres of salt meadow in the town of Eastchester to Lewis Guion Jr. for the sum of £27. Also, in 1721, Theunis Dalsen transacts a deed with Tunnis Jacobus Van Courtlandt (Liber E, p. 296). Other grantors of property to Theunis were Edward Smith in 1721 (E-309) and Lewis Guion Jr. in 1723 (E-368).

In the first three decades of the eighteen century, Theunis was involved in what seems to be an extraordinary number of land dealings in Westchester County. The writer believes that there may be additional transactions that have yet to be uncovered----especially for the period between 1723 and 1726. For example, when Theunis removed to Dutchess County in 1726, he must have liquidated his remaining holdings in Westchester County; however, the writer has not located any records of such transactions.

Most family historians assume that Theunis was a farmer and there is little reason to question that portrayal. However, given the large number of properties that he bought and sold, Theunis also appears to have speculated in real estate. Note that an early property which he purchased in 1700 in Eastchester Town was a parcel of just eight acres in size while a purchase recorded in 1721 involved a "large tract" of land. It seems that Theunis did well in his real estate dealings and perhaps he was also successful at farming. In addition, he may have come into some money through other means. Theunis' financial standing will be analyzed later in this chapter.

Dutchess County Sojourn

In 1726, Theunis, with his children, now between the ages of twenty-seven and fourteen, left Westchester County and relocated to an area in the Rombout Patent known as Fishkill in Dutchess County. It is not known for certain what motivated Theunis to take this dramatic step.

Sarah Vermilyea Dalsen may have died shortly before the family moved to Dutchess County. When Sarah's mother, Aeltje Waldron Vermilyea, wrote her will in 1730, she referred to her "deceased" daughter. There are no recorded sightings of Sarah Vermilyea Dalsen in Dutchess County. After Sarah's death, Theunis may have felt the need for a fresh start of life for himself and family.

The decision to relocate to Fishkill area may be associated with family ties. There were members of several past and contemporary collateral families from Nieuw Amsterdam, New York City, New Harlem, and Westchester County who had resettled in the Rombout and Beekman Precincts of Dutchess County. Examples include individuals from the Bussing, Buys, Slot, Vermilyea, and Waldron families. Perhaps Theunis was influenced by one or more of these individuals. In particular Maritje Ter Bos Hussey, the daughter of Rachel Vermilyea Ter Bos, born in 1672, was a very close first cousin to Sarah Vermilyea Dalsen. Rachel Vermilyea Ter Bos, was not only Sarah's aunt, but also her godmother. Maritje married James Hussey, a wealthy farmer in the South Ward of the Rombout Patent. In 1733, Maritje Hussey, a daughter of James Hussey and Maritje Ter Bos Hussey, would marry Isaac Dolsen [*Theunis, Jan*] (Downey, 2013).

As far as financial assets are concerned, there are multiple explanations for the manner in which Theunis and his sons acquired sufficient funds to purchase leases in the Rombout and Beekman Patents in Dutchess County. It is possible that Theunis inherited some monies after the death of his parents, Jan Gerritsen de Vries van Dalsen and Grietje Theunis Dalsen. It is also possible that as a result of his many real estate transactions, a few in Harlem and a greater number in Westchester County, Theunis made substantial profits. He similarly may have been successful at farming. Additionally, there is the possibility that he received assistance from in-laws, either from one or more of his sisters' well-off families (e.g. Waldron, Cregier, Kiersen, or Meyer) or from Sarah Vermilyea's family. For example, it is clear that his mother-in-law, Aeltje Waldron Vermilyea, who earlier was the beneficiary of her husband Johannes Vermilyea's estate, subsequently made provision for the Dalsen grandchildren in her will. A combination of these assets is likely to have given Theunis and his band the financial resources that they needed to establish farms in Fishkill and beyond.

The first sighting of the Dolson family in Dutchess County is the inclusion of Theunis [*Jan*] on the tax assessments of the South Ward for the year 1727 (*Old Miscellaneous Records of Dutchess County—Second Book of the Supervisors and Assessors*, 1909). Our Dolson ancestor is listed as *Tunnys Doolson* and over the next several years, alternatively as *Tunnys Dolson* and *Tunnys Dollson* as well as *Thomas Dolson, Thunas Dalson, Thunis Dollson,* and *Tunis Dolson*. He first paid a tax assessment of £6 which in the second year increased to £7. Theunis is listed between *Roulouff Ostrom* [Oosterum] and Johannes Mettlar. He is just two properties distant from James Hussey (*The Dutchess,* Vol. 26, No. 3 and No. 4, 1999; Buck, Kelly, and Reese, 1900). In the next chapter of this volume, there is an explanation of the relationship between the Oosterum and Hussey families and the Dalsens. Besides the Oosterums and Husseys, other collateral families that appear on the Rombout and Beekman tax lists during these years are the Buys, Delongs, Hegemans, and Slots.

Eventually all of Theunis' sons establish farms in Dutchess County. Johannes, Jacob, and Isaac registered ear marks (livestock brands) as early as 1729. Soon afterward, all four sons, now including Abraham, appear on Dutchess tax assessments. Records indicate that Isaac remained in the South Ward or Rombout Patent of Dutchess County until the mid-1750s at which time he relocates to Minisink in Orange County. Johannes, Jacob and Abraham, after relatively brief stays in the South Ward, relocated to the Oswego and Clove areas of the Middle Ward for a lengthier period of time. As early as 1736, the neighborhood was referred to as Oswego in the assessment lists of the county. Oswego Village was once part of LaGrange, now Union Vale. Oswego is an indigenous word meaning a place in the high country which gives way to the low country. Around 1760, Abraham may have moved to Orange County, probably to the Florida area north of Warwick. About the same time, Johannes and Jacob ventured to Poughkeepsie and New Marlborough respectively. While Jacob ultimately settles in New Marlborough, Johannes and his family would move on to the Wyoming Valley of Pennsylvania ca. 1769 and, at the end of the Revolutionary War, move north to Canada because of maintaining loyalty to the British. Details regarding the sojourns of all four brothers will be provided in the next chapter.

Theunis' last documented activity is found in a 28 February 1738 Dutchess County court record which contains the following language:

> ***Know all men… that Leonard Reed of Westchester County and of this Province of New York and Cornelles Bogardes of the Fish Kills in the County of Dutchess Province aforesaid… are held and firmly bound unto Teunis Dollson of Oswego in the said County of Dutchess… in the sum of ten pounds current money of the Colony of New York… 28th day of February in the twentieth year of his Majesty's Reign Anno Domini 1738.***

The fact that the Court identified Theunis' place of residence in 1738 as Oswego suggests that the man in question may have been living at the home of Johannes, Jacob, or Abraham

One of the baffling questions concerning the elder Theunis [*Jan*] relates to his whereabouts and activities during the period from 1738 until his death in 1766. After 1738, this writer has not found a single additional sighting feasibly attributable to this Theunis.

By 1738, Theunis would have been seventy-four years of age. He was certainly old enough to retire, even for the times in question. Yet, based on records in New Harlem and Westchester County, Theunis was an extremely active individual and it is hard to believe that there would not be additional records of his activities in Dutchess. One would expect to see his name on land transactions or loans. He should have been recorded as a participant at weddings and baptisms. Why didn't he hold public office or become involved with the Dutch Reformed Church or any other organization? If illness curtailed his activities, how then did he live to the incredible age of 101? There is no convincing explanation for the sparse documentation on this man during the last twenty-eight years of his life. And it is thought-provoking that the writer hasn't been able to locate a will nor a grave site for such a remarkable individual.

To add to the mystery, there is the following puzzling entry in the *Ancient Documents of Dutchess County* (1909). Doherty, the author of the historical series entitled *The Settlers of the Beekman Patent* (1990), references the said entry in Volume 5 that a constable by the name of *Thunas Dalson* was assaulted in 1751 by a band of hooligans. Specifically, the Dutchess County Court records (Items 2392, 2397 and 2415) note that:

> **Thunas Dalson in Batemans Precinct Constable and William Humphrey Esquire on the twenty ninth of November in the year of our Lord 1751 were bound in appearance bonds to ensure that Thunas Dalson do at the next general sessions to be held in the County of Dutchess prefer or cause to be preferred to give in evidence against Lewis Hunt, Chiliab Bemis, and Robert Morey, and Edward Hunt for assaulting and beating bruising of him the said Thunas Dalson in the execution of his duties.**

Theunis is also referred to as *Thomas* in these court proceedings. The incident was adjudicated on 29 November 1751 by John Brinkerhoff and Cornelius Wiltsie. It appears that each of the defendants was fined £20.

Analysis of the Assault

Doherty (1997) correctly calculates Theunis' age at the time of the assault to be near ninety, eighty-seven to be exact. This is exceedingly old for a constable. On the other hand, the only other Theunis known to be living at the time was Theunis [*Jacob, Theunis, Jan,*], who was born in 1735. The younger Theunis would have been just sixteen in 1751. This seems exceedingly young to hold a post such as constable. The extreme ages of the two men named Theunis lead Doherty (1997) to speculate on the possible existence of a third man by that name.

Doherty suggests that Theunis I, son of Jan, may have had a son of the same name, who was born sometime around 1715. The evidence to support this claim however is thin. There is no corroborating evidence to identify a son named Theunis Dalsen Jr. as belonging to the family of Theunis Dalsen and Sarah Vermilyea Dalsen. No baptisms or marriages are noted for this man as was the case for all of the other children of this family. While this writer doesn't find Doherty's argument regarding a third Theunis to be conclusive, there is no denying that the identity of the Theunis involved in the assault incident is bewildering.

The 1751 court record mentions that the assault took place in Beekman's Precinct. This writer has looked into the backgrounds of the five perpetrators, Lewis Hunt, Chiliab Bemis, Roger Morey, Edward Hunt, and William Humphry (Doherty, 1990). All are noted as settlers in the Middle Ward of the Beekman Patent lending some support to the idea that the constable with whom these men were involved probably also resided in or near the Middle Ward. Perhaps Theunis I was living at the time with one of his sons at Oswego or perhaps, the Theunis referred to as the participant in the 1751 episode was the speculated son of Johannes [*Theunis, Jan*] or more likely the son of Jacob [*Theunis, Jan*].

There is a sighting of a *Teunis Dolson* on the tax lists of the Poughkeepsie Precinct for the period of February 1757 to June 1760 (Reese and Reynolds, No date). This is undoubtedly a reference to Theunis II [*Jacob, Theunis, Jan*].

Moving on to Orange County
Many family historians believe that Theunis relocated to Orange County with his son Isaac or less likely, his son Abraham. The move is reported to have taken place ca. 1756. The idea that Theunis accompanied Isaac to Orange County around 1756 seems to be accepted by many family researchers. This belief stems from the facts that Theunis and Isaac are known to have lived together or in close proximity in the South Ward of the Rombout Patent near Fishkill. The three other sons subsequently relocated to the Oswego section of the Beekman Patent. Consequently, it is logical to assume that when Isaac migrates to Orange County, that Theunis, in his old age, might follow. Theunis' death in 1766 is reported to have occurred in Goshen, a township in Orange County which had jurisdiction at the time over not only Dolsentown, but also Minisink. Theunis left no will, most likely an indication that he no longer possessed any property, but instead lived with one of his sons such as Isaac. From a family history perspective, it is quite comforting to believe that the Dolsentown area was named in honor of Theunis, but in reality, the evidence points more towards Isaac as the

founder. Isaac purchased and settled the land and is frequently noted in the records of Orange County. In fact, Theunis' 1766 obituary represents the singular, documented mention of this ancestor as an Orange County resident.

There is also a theory, likewise problematic to substantiate, that Theunis may have relocated to Orange County with his son Abraham or with a grandson of the same name (Abraham Jr.). Some historians believe that Abraham Sr. may have moved from Dutchess to the Warwick area of Orange County before the Revolutionary War. As in the case of Minisink, Warwick at the time fell under the jurisdiction of Goshen.

Theunis died on 30 August 1766. During the month of September 1766 his death was reported in various newspapers throughout New England such as the *Boston Evening Post* (September 22), *The Connecticut Gazette* (September 19), *The Newport Rhode Island Mercury* (September 22), and the *New Hampshire Gazette* (September 26), the oldest newspaper in the United States. All of the death notices were similarly brief. Following is a copy of the announcement published in the *New York Mercury*:

> *(9/15/1766) Dolson, Tunis, first male born in NYC after it was ceded to the English by the Dutch---died Aug. 30 at Goshen, NY, in his 102nd year.*

As mentioned previously, it is not known where Theunis is buried. Although no grave site has been located, the writer has some confidence that he may have been interred at the old Dolsen burying ground, now called Pine Hill Cemetery, located just off Bradley's Corners on Route 6 in Wawayanda, New York. The cemetery is situated adjacent to the southern boundary of Middletown. Many generations of the Dolsen line are buried in Pine Hill including Isaac, James I, James II, Frederick, Theophilus I, Theophilus II, as well as most of the corresponding spouses of these men. Ruttenber and Clark (1881) describe the cemetery in the following manner:

> *The summit is a beautiful, symmetrically-shaped elevation, commanding an expansive view of the surrounding country. Twelve pine-trees lift their dark green foliage above the resting place of the dead, memorials of the ancient forest that crowned the height. Stretching away in every direction is a magnificent rolling landscape of unsurpassed beauty, comprising rich fertile farms, substantial, elegant dwellings, all indicating homes of wealth and abundant resources. This ground has evidently been used for burial from the earliest settlement. Here are the common field stones that mark the earliest attempt at preserving the place of burial, but with neither name nor date. Then follow the old red stones, sometimes with quite elaborate carving, and with well-preserved inscriptions. Next are found the early plain slabs of marble, while to represent the later years, these are the costly monuments which wealth delights to erect over the remains of the loved and the lost (p. 688).*

If Theunis' resting place is in Pine Hill Cemetery, his now unmarked grave may very well be near that of his son Isaac or perhaps, in the vicinity where in 1889, James F. Dolson [*Frederick, James II, James I, Isaac, Theunis, Jan*] underwrote the construction of the only mausoleum in the cemetery. Following the theory that Theunis may have accompanied one of the Abrahams to Warwick near the end of his life, the likely burying ground in that town would have been the cemetery at the Old School Baptist Church.

Highlights in the Life of Theunis Dalsen

His obituary notices claimed that Theunis was the first child born in the city of New York. As far as this writer can discern, this distinction has no other claimants and so, by default, the entitlement belongs exclusively to Theunis Dalsen. However, there are caveats. First of all, the city was known as Nieuw Amsterdam until the Dutch relinquished possession to the British who renamed it New York around 4 September 1664. So technically, Theunis was the first person born after the name was changed. Secondly, distinctions of this sort were reserved for European men with full citizenship, freeholders as they were called. Women, slaves, and Native Americans were not considered.

There is little doubt that Theunis lived into his 102nd year. This is an extraordinary feat even in modern times, but in the 1700s, such a long life would have been astonishing. Theunis' wife, Sarah Vermilyea Dolsen, died before 1730. Theunis would have been in his mid-sixties at the time and there is no record that he remarried. This means that Theunis not only raised his children as a single parent, but that he spent roughly thirty-five years of his life as a widower.

Theunis grew up in a New Harlem home that was dominant in the Dutch language and culture. He almost certainly spoke Dutch as did his wife, Sarah, and most other family members. Based on Theunis' business dealings, he was also conversant in English. As far as the Dolson family history is concerned, Theunis represents the transition from a mostly Dutch way of life to a mostly "American" way of life---even if Americans at the time often spoke English with a British accent and practiced cultural traditions heavily influenced by the mother country.

By all indications, Theunis provided more than satisfactory financial support for his family. All of his children for which information is available appear to have done very well through marriage, farming, a profession, business, real estate ventures, or combinations of these activities. In particular, Theunis' son, Isaac, seems to have been exceptionally successful from an economic perspective. The next chapter is dedicated to a description of the life of Isaac Dolsen, from his birth at Yonkers to his young adulthood in Fishkill, and then on to the founding of Dolsentown in Orange County.

Chapter III - Third Generation

Isaac Dolsen

[Theunis, Jan]

Although no baptismal certificate has been discovered for Isaac, other evidence informs us of the place and date of his birth. According to his marriage record, Isaac was born in Yonkers, Westchester County, New York. From the age given on his grave marker, the writer calculates the date of his birth to be 24 March 1707[4]. Analyses, such as those of Downey (2013), support this date by suggesting that Isaac must have been at least twenty-one years of age by 1729, when records show that he not only owned property but also held a public office.

Nothing is known of Isaac's childhood in Westchester. It is clear that he migrated to the area just north of Fishkill in Dutchess County, with his father and the rest of his family ca. 1726. He would have been nineteen years of age at this time.

Beginnings in Dutchess County

Not long after Isaac's arrival in Dutchess, there are accounts of his activities in the old records of the county. Isaac appears to have lived with or near his father, Theunis, on a farm in the South Ward of the Rombout Patent. As suggested on tax assessments, road records, deeds, and other documents, Isaac and Theunis located in an area along Sprout Creek northeast of the town of Fishkill. When the Dolsons first arrived in Dutchess, the farm may have been leased by Theunis who later turned over the lease to Isaac. It is also possible that Isaac obtained a property of his own nearby. By 1756 at the latest, Isaac, perhaps with the financial assistance of his father, accumulated sufficient wealth to purchase 700 acres of land in neighboring Orange County.

Theunis' name appears on the Dutchess County tax rolls (Reese, 1938) during the period of 1726-1729 as:

Tunnys Doolson	*1726-1729*	*£ 7.0*
Tunnys (Tamus) Dalson	*1727-1728*	*£ 6.0*
Tunnes Dollson	*1728-1729*	*£ 7.0*

---

[4] Isaac's gravestone is located in Pine Hill Cemetery, Wawayanda, New York. The monument likely built in the late 1800s to replace the original marker, indicates that at the time of his death on 20 May 1794, Isaac was eighty-two years and fifty-seven days old.

A *Teunis Dolson* is also on Poughkeepsie tax records for the period of February 1757 to June 1760, but the writer assumes that these records refer to a younger man named Theunis [*Jacob, Theunis, Jan*].

On 1 April 1729 *Isaac Dollson*, along with *Arrye Du Longe* and *Frances Drack*, was elected as an "*overseer of ye common high ways out of ye woods to ye naighbourhood*" in the South Ward. In the same election, James Hussey was chosen as one of the "*surveyors of ye fences*" (*Book of Supervisors and Old Miscellaneous Records of Dutchess County,* Vol. 2, p. 142). Also in 1729, Isaac's ear mark (livestock brand) was recorded as:

> *... a half moon at the underside of the right ear and a slit on the top of the left ear--his brand is thus to be affixed on the left buttock: I-D...* (p. 194).

Isaac appears on the Rombout tax lists in the following manner:

> **Isaac Dollson   1735 until 1753**

On 20 January 1739, Isaac was sworn as a juror for the Dutchess County Court of Sessions (*Ancient Documents of Dutchess County*, No. 288). On the 15 of May 1739, the names of both Isaac and his brother, Jacob, appear in the court record. The nature of the matter is not known because the text is now indecipherable (*Ancient Documents of Dutchess County*, No. 568A).

In 1740, James Wilson, Sheriff, certified a list of freeholders in Dutchess County which totaled 235 souls (Hasbrouck, 1909). Names on this certification included a *Jacob Drom* (perhaps Jacob Dolson), a *Johannis Dollson*, and an *Isaac Dollson* (p. 50). Other heads of families noted as freeholders included Hegeman, *Ostrom*, and Ter Bos.

In 1740, the location of Isaac's property is mentioned in a county road survey. The report indicates that a road had been laid out in the following manner:

> *... and so along as we have it now marked on the South Side of the Fishkills on the North Side of the Hill... and so along as wee have it marked... till Robbert Britt Land which he now posest; and Allow him Swingin Gates; and if he don't keep no gates so he may let the Road so near the Crick as it for him and other People good is... thill the Kings Bridge... and so along the Way goes by Robbert Bretts door... and so along as the Road goes now by Henry Ter Bos... and So along as the Road now goes by Isaack Dollsen... and so Along as the Road goes now by Johannes Ter Bos... and so along as the Road goes by John Losies... and Francis Bretts... and so along as the Road goes till a White Oak Tree marked... and then betwixt the Land which belongs to the Mill and Francis Brett... and So Along as we have marked it... till by Matthew Du Boys and so as*

the way goes to Low Water Mark... this allow we for a Generall Landing for our Ward for Wagons, Slays, Carts, and Horses (*Book of Supervisors and Old Miscellaneous Records of Dutchess County, p. 169*).

This road passed near or through Isaac's farm. Based on this account, the writer infers that Isaac's farm was situated along the main road, not far from the "crick" [Sprout Creek], between Henry Ter Bos and Johannes Ter Bos. The distances between the various points mentioned in the survey are unknown but the Brett Mill was situated east of Beacon on the western outskirts of the Town of Fishkill.

A road report dated 26 May 1741 indicates that an *Isaack Dollsen* was situated along a road with the following neighbors:

... the Kings Bridge... Robbert Britts... Henry TerBos... Isaack Dollsen... Johannes TerBos... John Lossee... (*Old Miscellaneous Records of Dutchess County – The Second Book of Supervisors*, 1909, p. 170)

Isaih Dalsen was included on a list of freeholders submitting a 1 August 1739 petition to have a road constructed from *Weccopee* along the south side of the Fishkill Creek and crossing the creek at Judge *Ter Boshe's* [Ter Bos'] land. Other names on the petition include John Montross, Dirck Hegeman, Isaac Lossing, Peter Monfort, Theodore van Wyck, Cornelius Wiltsie, and Robert Brett (Smith, 1882; Brinkerhoff, 1866).

After 1753, Isaac's farm was taxed under Peter I. Monfort through 1779 (Reese, 1938). Possibly, Monfort bought out Isaac's lease on the farm through a multiyear payment plan. Peter I. Monfort was in Dutchess by 1730. His first wife was Cathryntje Ditmar and his second, Magdalena Pieterse. It is reported that he had eleven children. Peter Montfort purchased 370 acres from William Verplanck in Fishkill Plains in 1735. There he built a stone house with a chimney imported from Holland. Around 1753 he obtained an additional 100 acres (probably Isaac's farm). Peter died 25 September 1791 and is interred in the Montfort Burying Ground. His will was filed in Poughkeepsie (*Monfoort, Monfort, Montfort Family*, No Date).

On 21 April 1795, Susannah Monfort, maiden of Fishkill, in consideration of £583, transferred a ninety-nine-acre parcel of land to Stephen Monfort (Liber XIV, p. 224). That deed contains the following information:

Parcel... on the west side of the highway to Fishkill town and on Sprout Creek and adjoining lands of Richard Jackson and George Bloom. Whereas Peter I. Monfort died interstate, seized of certain land in Fishkill town and his heirs partitioned the land; and lot number 5 to Susannah Monfort. The land having

formerly been purchased of Isaac Dolston. Witnesses Marya Monfoort and Peter Monfort.

This deed confirms that the location of Isaac's farm was at a point near where the highway to Fishkill in those days crossed Sprout Creek. Present-day Monfort Road may be the modern version of that highway. On each side of the Monfort Road Bridge, at Sprout Creek, there is a boundary marker. Going north the sign says Wappingers and in the southerly direction another indicates Fishkill (observed by this writer, September 2010). Monfort Road is near Robinson Lane which is located in the same vicinity. There was once a "Dutch Cemetery" on this lane known as the Monfort Burying Grounds. Local historians noted the location and condition of the cemetery in 1913:

> *... near Fishkill Plains, on the original Monfort farm. In an orchard with no underbrush or small growth; some stones fallen, some broken, some in good order. Peter Monfort (1711-1791) of Long Island settled on this farm about 1735 and built a stone house, still standing* (Poucher, 1924).

In a Dutchess County deed dated 11 April 1786 (Liber IX, p. 328), a description of a farm adjoining the lands of Isaac Dolsen is noted as located in the rear part of Lot No. 2.

Maritje Hussey and Her Family

Marriage bans were announced in March 1733 and less than a month later, on 23 April 1733, a twenty-six-year-old Isaac Dolsen married a twenty-one-year-old *Marytje Hoosie* at the Fishkill Dutch Reformed Church. The marriage record (Kelly, 2005) divulges the couple's places of birth and the location where each was living at the time:

> **Isaac Dolts, YM – born Yonkers: living in Vischkill**
> **Marytje Hoosie, YD – born and living in Vischkill**

YM means young, single man and YD means young, single dame or maiden. *Vischkill* of course is the Dutch version of Fishkill. The notations indicate that the marriage was the first for both the bride and the groom. Transcribers of the church records further note that the couple was married by a Justice of the Peace during an absence of the minister.

Marytje Hussey's baptism is recorded at the Sleepy Hollow (Tarrytown) Dutch Reformed Church in the following manner:

> **1712 Mar 25; Jacobus Hoszy, Maritje; <u>Marytje</u>; Bastiaen Michgielze and wife [Gelante or Jolante].**

Her father's name was James (*Jeems, Jacobus*) Hussey and that of her mother was Marytje Ter Bos Hussey. Maritje was the widow of Jan Schut who died ca. 1702. One of the sponsors, Jolante, wife of Michael Bastiaens, was a daughter of Mary Vermilyea [*Isaac*], and thus a cousin to both Sarah Vermilyea and Maritje Ter Bos Hussey (Downey, 2013). James Hussey was in Dutchess County as early as 1714. The Fishkill Dutch Reformed Church membership list dated 29 December 1731 contains the name of *ter Bos, Maria* and indicates that she was the wife of *Jeems Horsie*. On 24 October 1731, a *St. Jeems Hossie* and a *Maria Ter Bos* were sponsors at the Fishkill Dutch Reformed Church baptism of Sara, daughter of Jacobus *Ter Bos* and Catharyna *Beely*. A year and a half later, on 21 March 1734, Isaac Dolsen and *Malli* Hussey served as godparents for Arreantje, another daughter of Jacobus *Ter Bos* and *Kaetje Balle.*

Most references to Maritje Hussey are associated with Dutch Reformed Church records and this may account for the fact that most spellings of her first and maiden name reflect Dutch renderings. For example, Mary is written alternatively as *Marytje, Maritje, Mollie, Mallie,* and *Marya.* Hussey is represented as *Hoosie, Hossie, Hoosey, Hossey, Hussie, Horsie,* and *Huzzy.*

Maritje's father, James Hussey, was one of the earliest farmers in Dutchess County. James was born in 1681. He is listed as James *Husey* in the 1714 Dutchess County census between Arret Masten and Roger Brett. Roger Brett was the spouse of Catherine Rombout Brett and the son-in-law of Frances Rombout, the original co-patentee of the Rombout Patent. The 1714 Dutchess Census indicates that there was a total of 445 souls in the county in that year (O'Callaghan, 1850). While this count included slaves, it did not enumerate Native Americans.

James Hussey held several government posts in Dutchess such as supervisor, surveyor, and assessor during the period between 1714 and 1737. He lived in Fishkill in a log house that afterward was replaced by a stone house on the road to Beacon. Besides James, a John and a Joseph Hussey are found on Dutchess County tax lists between 1718 and 1738. The writer is not certain of the relationship between these men.

Some historians, such as Eager (1846) and Doherty (1990), claim that the Hussey family was of English heritage and migrated to Dutchess County from New Jersey. In fact, Hussey does seem to be a Norman surname common to Great Britain. Another account suggests that the family came to Fishkill from Long Island. James Hussey may be a descendent of Frederick Hussey who was a British soldier stationed at Kingston in 1664 and subsequently given land at Marbletown, Ulster County along with his wife, Margaret, in 1668.

The first deed recorded in Dutchess County (Liber I, No. 1) is a grant from Cathryna Brett to James Hussey, yeoman of Fishkill, on 23 May 1720. For the amount of £75 and the quit-rent of one half bushel of winter wheat annually, Hussey obtained 100 acres of land on the north side of Fishkill Creek and on the south side of the road leading from Fishkill to the mill of Madame Brett. He concurrently garnered the privileges of *"mowing grass, cutting hay in the meadow, using pastures and ranges for cattle and horses, and cutting timber in the woods."* Witnesses to this transaction were A. D. Peyster, John Jones, and Henry Van Derburg.

Around 1736 or 1737, near the time of James Hussey's death, the ownership of his property was transferred to Hendrick Kip, a descendent of a well-known and prosperous family that had been in Nieuw Netherlandts as early as 1639. The Kip House[5] is located on Old Glenham Road just south of Route 52 in the Village of Fishkill. When James Hussey purchased the property, there was already a house, barn, and other structures on the land. Hussey is said to have remodeled and expanded the home. Later Hendrick Kip purchased the property in 1736 and would enlarge the house and make additional improvements in 1756 (Eberlein and Hubbard, 1990). Most likely, in the early 1730s, Isaac Dolsen made numerous visits to this house during his courtship of Mary Hussey.

James Hussey is buried in the Fishkill Dutch Reformed Church cemetery. According to Wolf (2000), Van Voorhis (1900), and Roosa (1906), his grave stone is the oldest in this cemetery. The following inscription has been transcribed:

> *James Husy / Borned AD 1680 / Dyed Augustus ye 16th dye /1737/age 57 years.*
> *Mr. Husy was one of the founders of this church.* (*New York Genealogical and*
> *Biographical Record*, 1892, Vol. 23, No. 4, p. 212)

The date of James Hussey's death is recorded by Van Voorhis (1900) along with some additional details regarding this man:

> *James Hussy dyed August 22, 1737. Aged 56 years. Born 1681. James Hussy*
> *the oldest stone in the yard. His name is attached to the petition to Gov.*
> *General Montgomerie (sic) for the erection of the First Reformed Dutch Church*
> *of Fishkill. He lived probably in a log house which was afterwards replaced by*
> *the present stone house. Lived in stone house on road to Beacon, now (1920)*
> *occupied by John Knapp.*

The last sentence, although included as part of the quote attributed to Van Voorhis, is not actually original. The notation was inserted by an unknown docent from the Fishkill

---

[5] The Kip House, part of the original structure built by James Hussey, is recognized as an historical landmark. See Plate 47 in Eberlien and Hubbard (1990). The core of the present house was built by James Hussey ca. 1720. The second owner of the home, Henrick Kip, acquired the property in 1736 and subsequently enlarged the home and made other improvements. The present 2000-square foot, ten-room, stone-and-brick house has been maintained in virtually its original form. During the Revolutionary War, the house served as the headquarters for Baron Frederick William von Steuben and was visited on a number of occasions by Generals Casimir Pulaski and George Washington. The Kip House is located at 155 Old Glenham Road in Fishkill. A historical marker stands in the front yard.

congregation, who in 1920, compiled transcriptions of the tombstones located in the yard of the Dutch Reformed Church.

The maiden surname of Maritje Hussey's mother was Ter Bos. Maritje Ter Bos was the daughter of Rachel Vermilyea [*Isaac, Johannes*] and Jan Ter Bos (Ter Bosch). Rachel was Sarah Vermilyea Dolsen's sister. Jan Ter Bos came to New Netherlandts on the ship *Fox* which sailed from Amsterdam on 31 August 1662. Jan was recorded on the ship's passenger list as *Jan Bosch, Westphalia.* Westphalia is in Germany and may be his place of birth or simply his last residence previous to immigration to America (Downey, 2013). He died in 1678.

A Tale of Two Wives

According to the available Fishkill and Poughkeepsie Dutch Reformed Church records and a Hussey family bible, Maritje Hussey is the mother of all of Isaac Dolsen's children. She is also listed as his spouse and as a co-sponsor at the Dutch Reformed Church of baptisms of several of Isaac's nieces and nephews and also of several children of family friends or neighbors from the period of the early 1730s to 1750.

The last documented sighting of Maritje Hussey Dolsen is the baptism of her daughter, Altje, at the Rombout Presbyterian Church on 25 August 1750 (*New York Genealogical and Biographical Record*, 1937, Vol. 68, No. 3, p. 291). Curiously, this child was not baptized at a Dutch Reformed Church and the name of Isaac Dolsen does not appear on the baptismal record. Maritje Hussey Dolsen is not mentioned in Isaac Dolsen's will which was probated in 1794. There is no record of Maritje in Orange County and no grave marker has been found for her at Pine Hill Cemetery. These circumstances may indicate that she died sometime in the early 1750s, perhaps before Isaac's family relocated from Dutchess County to Orange County ca. 1756 but certainly before 1765 with Isaac Dolsen's name appears on an indenture to James Dolsen with the name, Sarah Dolsen, who is identified as Isaac's wife.

Although a marriage record has not been located, it is certain that Isaac Dolsen married a second time. In his will, he refers to his current wife as Sarah. He shares a tombstone in Pine Hill Cemetery with a woman by this name. There is some evidence that a woman of majority age, named Sarah, carried the Dolsen surname as early as 1765. Later in this chapter, the writer shall look into some of the sightings of this Sarah and delimit, to the extent known, her identity.

The Children of Isaac and Maritje

The most reliable record of births in this family comes from notations in a family Bible ostensibly recorded by Maritje Hussey Dolsen herself. The Bible, printed in 1630 in London, contains the names and birthdates of six Dolsen children in this family: James, Sarah, Mary, Isaac, Margaret, and Altje (Alcha). Also noted are three grandchildren: Sarah, Ana, and Isaac Harding. The first entry is for Maritje's eldest son, James, dated 1 February 1734 and the last, for a grandson named Isaac Harding born on 20 February 1777. In the decade of the 1920s, this Bible was in the possession of Emma Caunce of Patterson, New Jersey. During the same time period, excerpts containing the names and birthdates of these children were transcribed by Marion Kenna Jones for D. Stanton Hammond (Town of Minisink Heritage Center, No Date).

Of Isaac's and Maritje's presumed six or seven children, baptismal records have been found for only two, Abraham and Altje. During the time period that these baptisms took place, the Dutch Reformed Churches in Fishkill and Poughkeepsie operated as a joint congregation. A single clergyman, referred to as a *dominie*, administered to both communities. It is likely that, on occasion, baptisms that took place at Fishkill were serendipitously recorded under Poughkeepsie and vice versa. It is conceivable that some of the children of Isaac Dolsen and Maritje Hussey Dolsen were baptized but the proceedings were not recorded or that the Dutch Reformed Church and Rombout Presbyterian Church records of some of these baptisms are missing or incorrectly entered. Fishkill records do show that between the years of 1734 and 1741, Isaac and Maritje were present at the church to serve as sponsors for several children of Isaac's siblings, other family members, and neighbors.

Based on the available evidence, this writer is confident that Isaac Dolsen and Maritje Hussey Dolsen had the following children:

1 James Dolsen Sr. was born on 1 February 1734. No baptismal record has been located. In Maritje Hussey Dolsen's family Bible, James is referred to as "my eldest son". James is the ancestor in this branch of the Dolson family and his life events are described in detail in Chapter IV. Since this James had a son named James, he is consistently referred to as James Sr. in the remainder of this volume. James Sr. was named after his maternal grandfather, James Hussey.

2 Sarah Dolsen was born on 20 August 1735, according to her mother's bible notation. She is probably the child baptized at Fishkill on 6 October 1735. No definitive documentation has been found regarding the adult life of this daughter. Sarah would have been named after her paternal grandmother, Sarah Vermilyea. She may have died young. Sarah is not mentioned in her father's will. Possible sightings of this Sarah in Orange County during this time period may be confused with those of Isaac's sister or even Isaac's second wife, both of whom were named Sarah. On 6 October 1735 at the Fishkill Dutch Reformed Church, Jacob Dolsen and *Marya* Buys baptized a child named *Thunes*. No sponsors are listed. On the lines immediately below this entry, in the column set aside for the names of parents, we see Isaac *Dalson* and *Marya Hussif* listed. No corresponding child's name is given. In place of a name, three dashes are marked in the corresponding column. This is obviously an error of omission in the church registry. Maritje Hussey clearly records in her bible that less than two months previous, her daughter Sarah was

born and the incomplete entry found in the Fishkill Dutch Reformed Church records most certainly refers to this Sarah.

3   <u>Mary Dolsen</u> was born on 17 December 1738. Mary is not mentioned in her father's will. There is no additional information on this individual. She may have died young. Mary would have been named after her paternal grandmother, Marytje Ter Bos, wife of James Hussey.

4   <u>Isaac Dolsen Jr.</u> was born 27 November 1743. Isaac Jr. is characterized in his father's will as *non-compos mentes* and he is reported to never have married (Eager, 1846). Isaac Sr. also included in his will a provision for Isaac Jr.'s care. This man may have died before 1802, as Isaac Jr. is not mentioned in his step mother's, Sarah Dolsen's, will. Since Isaac Jr.'s mental disability is documented as late as 1794, when he was fifty-one years of age, this writer concludes that this man was mentally disabled during his entire lifetime and that none of the contemporary sightings (e.g. legal, military, and church documents) of an Isaac Dolsen or Isaac Dolsen Jr. refer to this man.

5   <u>Margaret Dolsen</u> was born on 23 February 1745. Margaret is referred to in her father's will as *Margret* Gardner. Her husband was James Gardner of Minisink.

6   <u>Altje Dolsen</u> was born on 14 May 1750, and baptized on 24 August 1750 at the Rombout Presbyterian Church. *Mary* Dolsen is listed as the parent. Altje is referred to alternatively as *Alche, Aliha, Alina,* and *Alcha*. She is mentioned in her father's will. Altje was the wife of Abraham Harding of Minisink. Around 1773, Abraham Harding took up residence in the area between the Shawangunk Mountains and Dolsentown. Altje's husband, Abraham, as well as two children, Isaac (born 20 February 1777), and Sarah (born 11 April 1773), are mentioned in Isaac Sr.'s will. A third child from this family, Ana, according to Mary Hussey's bible, apparently had died previous to the writing of Issac Sr.'s will.

An interesting note regarding the Rombout Presbyterian Church: The church was built in 1747 on land donated by Jacobus Ter Bos, an uncle of Mary Hussey Dolsen. Jacobus also was instrumental in supporting the development of the congregation financially and administratively in the early years. During this time, Henry TerBos, Jacobus' brother, after a controversy at the Dutch Reformed Church, left that congregation to attend the Rombout Presbyterian Church. One Sunday morning he brought all of his slaves in a large lumber wagon to attend services. Henry seated himself along with the Negroes in his designated pew. This caused great excitement in the congregation. Some were incensed and others amused. Subsequently, Henry was instructed to seat the Blacks in a portion of the church gallery that was allotted to slaves.

7   Although an <u>Abraham Dolsen</u> was baptized on 4 October 1741, at the Fishkill Dutch Reformed Church and his parents were identified as Isaac *Dolson* and *Marytje Hosse*, the

include the name of Abraham in her family bible. Also, there is no mention of an Abraham in Isaac Dolsen's will dated 1794. Because of these anomalies, this writer posits that Isaac Dolsen and Maritje Hussey Dolsen did not parent a son named Abraham, despite the existing baptismal record at the Fishkill Dutch Reformed Churc Although several other researchers have placed a man by this name in this family, th writer has decided to the contrary. Amplifications regarding this decision are contain the Appendix to this volume.

This writer notes that this Isaac and Maritje had a male child named Isaac Jr. in 1743. T suggests that by this date, at least according to Dutch naming traditions, that Maritje Hus Dolsen may have previously given birth to a son named Theunis. If a Theunis were pres in this family, he may have died young or remained in Dutchess County. There are no sightings of a Theunis in and around Minisink or Warwick in Orange County nor was a m this name recorded in his father's will. Most importantly, Maritje Hussey Dolsen did not include the name of Thuenis in her family bible. In this writer's opinion, the available evi does not support the theory of some family historians that a son named Theunis belongs this family.

Settlers of the Beekman Patent

From roughly 1726 to 1770, the Dolsons resided in several locations in Dutchess Count They first settled in the Rombout Patent located mid-way between Fishkill and Wapping Falls. Within a few years, Thuenis' sons Johannes, Jacob, and Abraham relocated to th Oswego community of the Clove area of the Beekman Patent situated near present-day Union Vale. It appears that Isaac and his father, Thuenis, remained along Sprout Creel Fishkill, Rombout Patent.

James Doherty's Historical Volumes

James Doherty has developed an authoritative history of the region in a multi-volume tre entitled *The Settlers of the Beekman Patent* (1990). Doherty's work presents genealogi and biographies of the members of the various families that settled early in Dutchess Co The volumes, each consisting of approximately 1,200 pages, are organized alphabetica according to surnames with each volume addressing a range of families. For example, Dolsons are found in Volume IV (1997), which contains information on families with surr from Barbyshire to Everitt. The first volume was produced in 1990 and as of 2018, Doh had reached the surname Swift in Volume XIII. Several volumes remain unfinished unti Doherty concludes addressing all surnames through the letter Z.

Doherty has done an outstanding job of compiling genealogical and biographical inform often in great detail. His work is especially helpful in identifying the various geographica locations where the Dolsons settled. There is however, a failing in Doherty's work rega the Dolsons. Frankly, he frequently errs in attributing the life events of the various Dolson men who carried the same given names. In the case of Theunis, he speculates on the existence of a third man by this name and fortunately, on this occasion, Doherty makes readers aware of his assumptions. However, in other instances, and without provisos, he confuses various Dolson men, particularly those named Isaac, Matthew, Jacob, Abraham, and James. There is no denying the complexity of the puzzle and the difficulties faced in distinguishing between and among Dolson men with the same given name; nevertheless, Doherty's work unfortunately missteps here. Readers should be alert to the fact that when Doherty attributes a particular event, endeavor, or lineage to a certain Isaac, Abraham, or other Dolson, in several cases he suffers from mistaken identity.

Isaac's Siblings

Isaac had seven siblings, all of whom lived into adulthood. Much is known about his three brothers: Johannes, Jacob, and Abraham. Each of these men led an intriguing life. Less information is available regarding Isaac's sisters. Following are condensed versions of the information that the author has collected regarding each of Isaac's siblings, their spouses, and their children to the extent known:

1. <u>Johannes Dolsen</u> was born in the vicinity of Fordham Manor (Downey 2013). No baptismal certificate has been located. Johannes' year of birth, ca. 1702 in Westchester County, has been calculated from a self-report of age eighty-one in response to the second Census of Loyalists taken at Fort Niagara, Ontario, Canada on 1 December 1783 by Coronel John Butler, commander of Butler's Rangers.

   Johannes went first to Dutchess as a young man with his family. He is shown on the Rombout tax records between 1730 and 1735. On 6 April 1731, a Johannes *Dollsin* along with *Jan De Lange*, Jan Brinckerhooff, John Mills, Johannes Middellar, and Francis Drack were elected as "*survayors of the Common Ways*" (*Book of Supervisors and Old Miscellaneous Records of Dutchess County,* Vol. 2, p. 150) in the South Ward.

   In 1735 Johannes was in the Beekman Patent in the area known as New Oswego and the Clove. According to Doherty (1997), Johannes and his brothers, Jacob, and Abraham, located on Lot Seventeen of the Beekman Patent. Johannes obtained, in 1735, a lease to a 180-acre farm in the Clove Valley adjacent to the family of Matthew Buys. Johannes Buys, the brother of Johannes Dolsen's wife, Elizabeth, led the settlement of this region. The word clove is derived from the Dutch *klove* which means a rocky cleft or fissure, a gap or a ravine. Johannes Dolsen's farm (Number Ten) was located just off the present-day County Road 89, one-half mile south of Hoxsie Corners on land which presently is occupied by the Mid-County Rod and Gun Club (Doherty, 1997).

In September 2010, the writer of this sketch visited the Club and was shown an old cabin in the woods with notched (tongue and grove) ceiling beams which Club members reported as "very old", perhaps a remnant from the early Dolson dwelling. This structure is called the "Boomer House" by the Club members. Doherty (1997), states that Johannes sold his lease to this farm to Nathaniel Yeomans in May of 1751.

According to the *Ancient Records of Dutchess County* (No. 250), a John *Dollson* signed a 1737 declaration recognizing the authority of the King of England. The earliest report of a Dolson family member in the military is that of Johannes, who, in 1739, is listed as a lieutenant in the Room (small military unit) of John Montross under Captain Frans de Lange's Company of the Colonial Regiment of Beekman Precinct in Dutchess County. Later, in 1744, Johannes was a captain in the Beekman Militia (Plimley, 2011). None of Johannes' brothers are found on Dutchess County military rolls. Members of the colonial militia from collateral families in Dutchess during this time include Hendrick and Roelef Oosterum, Jonas *Slodt*, Johannes and Abraham Buys, and Johannes *Hussie*.

On 10 August 1739, Francis Filkin, one of his majesties justices, codified a complaint against Johannes Dollson at the Dutchess County court. Johannes was in debt to the crown in the amount of £10 for taxes owed.

In 1751 Johannes Dolsen sold the lease to his farm to Nathaniel Yeomans and for a time relocated across the Hudson River to New Marlborough, Ulster County (Downey, 2013). Afterwards he is found on the Poughkeepsie Precinct tax rolls from 1757 to 1763. Soon after the French and Indian War, ca. 1765, Johannes and most of his family moved on to the Wyoming Valley where the family is reported to have resettled on a 150-acre farm at Lot 23 in the Manor of Sunbury, Northumberland County, Pennsylvania by 1769 (Plimley 2011, Downey 2013).

The Buys and Brouwer Families

Johannes Dolsen married Elisabeth Buys ca. 1730, most likely at the Fishkill or Poughkeepsie Dutch Reformed Church. Elisabeth was baptized at the Sleepy Hollow (Tarrytown) Dutch Reformed Church on 1 June 1708:

1708: Jun 01: Johannes Buys, Maritje; <u>Elisabeth</u>; Jan Buys and wife

Elisabeth was the daughter of Johannes Buys and Maritje Brouwer. Johannes Buys and Maritje Brouwer were married ca. 1707. Johannes Buys was born in Albany on 1 November 1685, the son of Jan Janise Buys and Elizabeth de Groot. The immigrant ancestor of the family was Arien Pieterse Buys from Thiel, Gelderland, Netherlands (New Netherlands Settlers Project at *WikiTree.com*, retrieved on 25 March 2014), who married Tryntje Oosterum, baptized at Bergen, NJ on 2 April, 1689.

Johannes Buys is shown on Beekman tax records as early as 1718. On 29 December 1731 Johannes Buys and *Maria* Brouwer were listed as members of the Fishkill Dutch Reformed Church. Johannes eventually settled on a 160-acre farm about one fourth of a mile east of the present location of the Oswego Quaker Meeting House. The old family house on this farm still exists and today is owned by Trade Land Investors. The house sits back a considerable distance from the road (Barnes, 2016).

Maritje Brouwer was baptized on 21 November 1686, at the Dutch Reformed Church in New York. She was the daughter of Matthys Adamsz Brouwer and Marietje Peterse Wyckoff, both born in Nieuw Amsterdam. Marriage bans for the couple were announced on 26 January 1673 at the Dutch Reformed Church in Nieuw Amsterdam. The immigrant ancestor of Maritje Brouwer was Adam Brouwer (AKA Berkhoven), a native of Cologne, Germany. It is likely that Adam came to Nieuw Amsterdam on 14 July 1644 aboard *De Blauwen Haen*, *The Blue Cock*. Adam Brouwer married Magdalena Verdon at the Dutch Reformed Church in Nieuw Amsterdam on 21 March 1645. Magdalena's father was Jacob Verdon from La Rochelle, France and her mother was Marie Badie, from Liege, Belgium (Brouwer Genealogy Database, retrieved 11 April 2016).

The Buys family is featured in the multi-volume series, *The Settlers of the Beekman Patent* (Doherty, 1990). A more thorough family history is posted online at *buicefamilyreunion.com* developed by Cyrene Buys Barnes. One of the most detailed versions of the Buys family genealogy is an article in the *Record* of the New York Genealogical and Biographical Society (1935, Vol. 66, No. 3). The surname has alternately been spelled Brice, Buys, Bice, Bryce, Beuys and Buys. The first recorded ancestor of this family was Hendrick Beuys who was born in 1480 in Holland (*buicefamilyreunion.com*, retrieved on 11 April, 2016).

Dolson (1932) has developed a comprehensive synopsis of the Brouwer family's connections to the Dolsons. An excellent resource on this family is The Brouwer Genealogy Database compiled by Chris Chester and posted at *Ancestry.com*.

In May of 1760, court records show that John *Dollson* was late on a debt of more than £39 to Charles LeRoux. The debt was incurred on the last day of March 1758. The matter appears to involve a failure to deliver goods and merchandise on Johannes' part (*Ancient Documents of Dutchess County*, No. 3871). Later, in 1765, another complaint is filed against John *Dalson Sr.* for failure to pay a debt on a loan incurred on 1 June 1756 from Jacob Westervelt (*Ancient Documents of Dutchess County*, No. 1164).

Documentation exists to substantiate that Johannes Dolsen and Elisabeth Buys Dolsen had the following children:

a. Maria (Maritje, Mary) was baptized at the Fishkill Dutch Reformed Church on 2 April 1732. Her maternal grandparents, Johannes Buys and *Maria* Brouwer, were sponsors. She married Annanias Valentine and lived in New Marlborough until at least 1801 (Downey, 2013; Tharp, 1801). Annanias was noted as a Captain of a bark that delivered supplies to the militia during the Revolution. In 1801, local newspapers carried the following article regarding Annanias' death:

> *An Elegy on the death of Capt. Annanias Valentine, Thomas Pinkney, Isaac Elliot, Jacamiah Cropsey and Leonard Merrit, all respectable citizens of the town of Marlborough, who were unfortunately drowned on the Flatts, in front of the town attempting to go on shore, on Friday morning, the 12th of December, 1800 in a violent storm of wind and rain--- by Peter Tharp, 1801.*

> *These unfortunate men arrived from New York, and came to anchor on the Flatts a little before day, and about sunrise, they, together with Henry Cropsey and Charles Merrit, descended into their boat, and the instant that they… their sloop, the boat overset and turned them all in the water-- -fortunately Henry Cropsey and Charles Merrit were saved, the other five perished amid the waves---the bodies of four of them were found the same day at evening and the other early next morning---On the day following, which was the Lord's Day, their remains were placed in the Meeting House in Marlborough when (in the midst of a crowded and solemn audience) a discourse suited for the occasion was delivered by the Rev. Lavi Hall from Eccl. IX chapter, XII verse---after which they were decently interred in the burying ground adjoining the meeting house--- They have left many friends in morning their untimely deaths.*

> *Capt. Valentine, age 56 years, has left a widow and one child---…*

The full elegy, penned on 4 January 1801, consists of eighteen verses. Interestingly, Annanias son, Annanias Jr. married Elizabeth Meeker, sister of Phoebe Meeker, wife of James Dolsen Sr. [*Isaac, Theunis, Jan*] (Heidgerd, 1977). Annanias Jr. is noted as a veteran of the Revolutionary War.

b. A son, Johannes was baptized at the Fishkill Dutch Reformed Church on 5 April 1735. Only a single sponsor is shown on the baptismal record, a maternal uncle named *Mattheus* [Buys]. This Johannes Jr. is said to have married ca. 1762 Elizabeth Simpson (Downey, 2013).

c. Observed from private family records, Downey (2013), notes the birth of a son named Jacob on 2 November 1736. No baptismal record has been discovered. The full name of this individual may be Jacob Meir (Meyer) Dolsen. Remember, Meyer was the name of a collateral family from New Harlem. Johannes Meyer married Tryntje Dalsen [*Jan*]. A *Jacob Dolfsen* was a sponsor at a baptism at the Zion Lutheran Church in Loononburg on 27 May 1758. A man named Jacob Mier Dolsen is recorded as serving in a Revolutionary War unit originating in Newburgh, New York. This Jacob married Mary Cook on 23 March 1763.

d. A son named <u>Isaac</u> (Isaak) was baptized at the Poughkeepsie Dutch Reformed Church on 27 May 1739 with sponsors Steven Kriger and Margriete De Duyster, probably neighbors in Oswego. By coincidence, a cousin named Isaac [*Jacob, Theunis, Jan*] also was baptized at the Poughkeepsie Dutch Reformed Church on the same date. An *Isaac Dolfsen* served along with his sister, Catharina, as a sponsor at the baptism of Jane Koek at the Zion Lutheran Church on 26 August 1760. This Isaac could also be the man who was a sponsor with Sarah Lassing, for Sara, daughter of John Sanders and his wife Gertruyt on 17 March 1763 at the same church. Later in life, this Isaac became a well-known Loyalist and his Tory exploits in Orange County, the Wyoming Valley of Pennsylvania, Detroit, and Canada are well documented.

e. <u>Abraham</u> was baptized at the Poughkeepsie Dutch Reformed Church on 27 May 1741. Sponsors were his paternal uncle and aunt, Abraham *Dalson* and Marytje Slot. No additional, definitive record is available for this man. He may have died young. Additional analyses regarding the many men named Abraham Dolsen of this period are contained in the Appendix to this volume.

f. Another daughter, <u>Catherine</u> was born ca. 1743. She would have been named after a maternal aunt, Catherine Buys, wife of Thomas Vorse. This Catherine married first, Peter Andrew Lassing (1739-1787) ca. 1763, perhaps at the New Hackensack Dutch Reformed Church, and second, Nazareth Brower at the Fishkill Dutch Reformed Church on 12 April 1795. The former couple is thought to have had at least eleven children (Ewins, 1999). The latter couple lived in Poughkeepsie.

g. <u>Samuel</u> was baptized at the Fishkill Dutch Reformed Church on 2 September 1744. Sponsors were his maternal uncle and aunt, Samuel and *Rebekker* Buys. According to Hamlin (1905), this man died in Marlborough in 1769. Samuel [*Johannes, Theunis, Jan*] had a son, born ca. 1763, also named Samuel.

h. A son named <u>Matthew</u> was born ca. 1750, but no baptismal record has been located. Matthew, as his brother Isaac, was also a famous Loyalist and participated in many of the same Tory activities as his older brother. Matthew became a well-known pioneer in the Ontario Province of Canada.

In addition to the eight individuals listed above, Johannes Dolsen and Elizabeth Buys Dolsen may have had several other children. Downey (2013) hypothesizes the existence of the following offspring based on various Dutchess and Orange County records as well as traditions associated with Dutch family naming patterns:

i.   A son named <u>Theunis</u> may have born to this family in late 1730 or early 1731. No baptismal certificate has been located. Perhaps there is no record of this baptism for the same reason that Johannes' marriage record to Elisabeth Buys has not been found. During this time period, some entries of the Fishkill and Poughkeepsie Dutch Reformed Churches may not have been recorded or are missing. Later events at the Pougkeepsie Dutch Reformed Church were recorded. On 22 January 1756, a *Hans Dolfsen* and his wife *Liesabeth* served as sponsors for a daughter, named *Liesabeth*, of *Thonis Dolfsen* and his wife *Rahel* at the Zion Lutheran Church in Loonenburg. A Hans Dolsen was a sponsor for another child, Catharina, of Thonis Dolfsen and Rahel at the same church on 27 November 1757. The co-sponsor is listed as Hester Kranckied, perhaps an indication that Johannes Dolsen's wife, Elizabeth Buys Dolsen, had died by this date.

James Downey (2013) theorizes that a man named Thuenis found in Dutchess County records beginning in 1751 may have been the eldest son of Johannes Dolson and Elizabeth Buys Dolsen. This conveniently would resolve the mystery concerning the assault on the Beekman constable. Subsequent to that assault however; other sightings of a Thuenis Dolson on Revolutionary War rosters and on land records in and around Newburgh and Marlborough, as well as even later sightings in Big Flats, Tioga County may be confused between this alleged Theunis [*Johannes, Theunis, Jan*] and a son of Jacob [*Theunis, Jan*], and Martyje Buys by the same name, who was baptized on 6 October 1735, at the Fishkill Dutch Reformed Church.

j.   A daughter <u>Sarah</u>, named after her paternal grandmother, Sarah Vermilyea, may have been born ca. 1742. Doherty (1997) indicates that a Sarah from this family may have married James Knapp of Marlborough, a Loyalist who relocated to Canada after the Revolution.

k.   Undoubtedly, a son named <u>Peter</u>, born in 1748 or within a few years of that time, belongs in this family. Peter would have been named for his maternal uncle, Peter Buys. In the period of March and April of 1778, a Peter Dolsen, a known Tory, was being held with several other Loyalists at the jail in Goshen, Orange County. Peter's brother Matthew, aided by a Dolsen cousin of the same name, instigated a jail break. While Peter escaped, he was apprehended later the next day near Blooming Grove, Orange County and was killed in the ensuing gun battle (Downey, 2013 citing the Public *Papers of George Clinton*). Incredibly, there is a remote possibility that this Peter may also be the same man who served in the Third New York Regiment of

Colonel Rudolphus Ritzma in 1776 as a sergeant. An Orderly Book, written by a Peter Dolson is on file in Washington, DC (*Guide to the Archives of the Government of the United States in Washington*, 1907).

Downey (2013) also mentions the possibility that Johannes Dolsen and Elizabeth Buys Dolsen had a daughter named <u>Elizabeth</u> (named after her mother). An Elizabeth Dolsen is said to have married a man named Lewis Kniffen (Doherty, 1997). The writer has not seen this record and has not located any additional compelling evidence for the placement of an individual named Elizabeth in this family.

As early as 1769, Johannes and several of his sons had resettled in the Manor of Sunbury in Northumberland County, Pennsylvania (Reaman, 1993). Much has been written about Johannes' family, particularly his sons Isaac and Matthew. The family were Loyalist during the Revolutionary War. Their colonial property in the Wyoming Valley, situated between Sunbury and Wilkes-Barre, was confiscated and in 1783 the family moved to Niagara, then to Detroit, and finally to Ontario, Canada in the late 1780s (Dolsen, 1992). The last sighting of Johannes Dolsen [*Theunis, Jan*] was on 20 July 1784 when his name appeared on a list of Loyalists who subscribed their names in order to settle and cultivate the crown lands opposite Niagara and who were qualified to receive rations. Johannes' privileges were subsequently reassigned to another family member, an almost certain sign that Johannes died shortly after this date.

A Loyalist Branch of the Family
As far as is known, the family of Johannes Dolsen is the only branch of the Dolsons to remain loyal to the British Crown during the Revolution; however the Loyalist entanglements of Johannes and particularly his sons, Isaac, Matthew, and Peter, would, at least in one occasion, compel the involvement of other Dolson cousins, specifically one or more sons of Jacob Dolsen [*Theunis, Jan*].

Before the Revolutionary War (ca. 1769), Johannes and several of his children, relocated to the Wyoming Valley of Pennsylvania, along the Susquehanna River. There, the Dolsons were neighbors of the family of George Field, who became a Loyalist activist. Isaac eventually married Mary Field and Matthew married Hannah Field, daughters of George Field. While in the Wyoming Valley, the Dolson brothers obtained sizeable farms and were involved in numerous civic, political, and local military events. By 22 August 1771, Isaac *Dalson* was wounded in a skirmish when migrants from Connecticut were "*firing with ball at the Block House*" (Colonial Records of Pennsylvania, 1852). Matthew Dolsen is noted as living in the vicinity of Luzerne County, Pennsylvania in 1776 (Bradsby, 1893). However, as a result of their Loyalist ties and primarily their Tory activities (e.g., becoming members of Butler's Rangers), Isaac and Matthew were avowed to be "traitors" and their farms were confiscated by the Continental Congress. By 1777, the brothers are included on the Black List---a list of those Tories who took part with Great Britain in the

Revolutionary War and were attainted of High Treason (Saterfield, 2002). On one list of Loyalists, a *John Dalton* is enumerated immediately following the name of his son, *Matthew Dalson* (Van Deusen, 1900).

At some point early in the Revolution, Matthew Dolsen [*Johannes, Theunis, Jan*] became a member of the notorious gang called the "Cowboys", led by the infamous Claudius Smith. This gang took part in various raids alongside the famous Mohawk Indian Chief, Joseph Brandt. In 1778, Peter Dolson [*Johannes, Thuenis, Jan*] was confined with other Tories, such as Daniel Field, in Goshen for stealing public stores and private property and other felonies. On the night of 29 March 1778, these men were freed from jail by Peter's brother, Matthew Dolsen, of Susquehanna [*Johannes, Theunis, Jan*], his cousin, Matthew Dolsen of Orange County [most likely *Jacob, Theunis, Jan*], and three additional Cowboy associates (*Public Papers of George Clinton, First Governor of New York*, 1973).

Peter was killed the day following the escape and the Matthew of Orange County was captured. Subsequently, this Matthew was found guilty and sentenced to be hung in January 1779 alongside Claudius Smith and several of the other "Cowboys". However, notwithstanding conflicting reports (Ruttenber and Clark, 1881), the available evidence suggests that the sentence was not carried out. Sheriff Nicolls of Orange County interceded on Matthew's behalf and requested clemency from Governor Clinton on 19 January 1779. The Governor replied two days later that a pardon for Dolson was "likely" but not certain. Subsequently a petition from Orange County for the pardon of *Mathew* Dolson was submitted around 14 February 1779. Nicolls' rational was that Matthew turned himself in when he could have fled to the enemy; he was convicted by his own confession; "*he heartily repents the Evil he has Don*"; and "*he has a wife and one Child a woman of good Charactor and a very honast Family*". Fully a year after the jail break, on 13 April 1779, the sheriff, Colonel Nicolls, notes that Matthew Dolson has been confined in a house and not in jail. He informs Governor Clinton that his order regarding Matthew Dolson will be forthcoming at the next Court of Oyer and Terminer. Newspaper reports notwithstanding, other evidence indicates that the Matthew of Orange County was never executed. Much of the information regarding Matthew Dolson [*Johannes, Theunis, Jan*] was collected from the *Public Papers of George Clinton, First Governor of New York* (1973, Vols. II, III, IV and VI).

The Matthew of Susquehanna made good his escape and he, along with his brother, Isaac, and his father, Johannes, eventually made his way to Niagara in Canada by 1782. Matthew and Isaac then moved on to Detroit until it was surrendered by the British. Ultimately the two brothers settled in and around what is now Chatham-Kent, Ontario, Canada. Isaac and Matthew became well-known pioneers of the area. They were involved in many events of the time, of particular note, the War of 1812. The skirmish, in which the legendary Native American leader, Tecumseh, lost his life in 1813, was fought at Isaac's farm along the Themes River. Matthew in turn, was the founder and proprietor of an important trading post and tavern.

The author of this volume notes that several researchers have confused several Dolsen men associated with this family. Often Isaac Dolsen [*Johannes, Theunis, Jan*] is confused with his son named Isaac Jr. [*Isaac, Johannes, Theunis, Jan*] and Matthew; son of Johannes [*Theunis, Jan*] is sometimes mistaken for Matthew, son of Jacob [*Theunis, Jan*].

The fascinating details regarding the adventures and achievements of Johannes and his sons Isaac and Matthew are well documented. Noteworthy sources include: *The Valley of the Lower Thames* by Fred Coyne Hamil, 1951; *Loyalist Mosaic* by Joan Magee, 1984; the *Trail of the Black Walnut* by G. Elmore Reaman, 1993; *Names Only But Much More* by Janet Carnochan, No Date; and Early Ontario Settlers, A Source Book by Norman K Crowder, 1993.

2. <u>Aeltje Dolsen</u>, likely born in Westchester County, was baptized at the Dutch Reformed Church in New York in 1699. She was married on 3 December 1738 at the Fishkill Dutch Reformed Church. The wedding record provides the following details:

> **Dirck Hegeman, ym born Langeyland** [Long Island]
> **Aeltje Dolsen, yd born Westchester Co.**

The couple is not known to have had children; most likely a result of Aeltje's relatively advanced age of thirty-nine at the time of her marriage. Dirck Hegeman and Aeltje Dolsen Hegeman are reported to have lived in Hopewell and Stormville (Hamlin, 1905). On 23 March 1759, a Dutchess County deed (Liber III, p. 253) indicates that a *Dirck* Hegeman, blacksmith of Rombout Precinct, purchased, for the amount of £151, a tract of 108 acres from Catheryna Rombout Brett in what is now East Fishkill on the north side of Fishkill Creek. Here the couple built the core structure of a home that would become known as the Storm-Adriance-Brinckerhoff House (named after several, subsequent, prominent owners). A kitchen fireplace with a beehive, Dutch oven, strap hinges, and box locks are some of the intriguing features of the house (Dutchess County Historical Society, 2004). In the west wing of the house, the hand-hewn beams with which Dirck Hegeman constructed a stout ceiling are still visible (Town of East Fishkill New York's Year of History, 1959). On 1 May 1760, the couple sold the aforesaid property to Thomas Storm for the amount of £660 (Liber V, p. 256). *Dirck* Hegeman signed the deed and *Aelyte*, his wife, made her mark. This house is still standing and is a registered historical landmark [See Plate 54 in Eberlien and Hubbard (1990)]. By tradition, there is a story connected to the house regarding a visit by George Washington during the Revolutionary War:

...It is a tradition handed down from Revolutionary times that Washington and his staff remained at this house one night on their way to Boston and that the next morning as the neighboring farmers gathered on the green at these crossroads to greet him, raising their hats with the old-time deference, he said to them, `Gentlemen, put your hats on; I am but a man like yourselves and wish no such deference shown. (Daughters of the American Revolution: Touring Southern Dutchess County. Posted *at* http://melzingah.awardspace.com/id8.htm; Retrieved on 1 March 2011).

Hegeman Family

Dirck Hegeman was baptized in 1714 at Flatbush, Long Island. Between 1753 and 1789, a Dirck *Hagaman* was involved in several Dutchess County court proceedings in Poughkeepsie. Dirck was a blacksmith, but was required to keep school at Hopewell (located in the eastern part of Rombout) in 1760. Dirck was also a customer at the Sleight Store in Greenhaven, Beekman Patent in 1770 (Doherty, 1997). The last sighting of this man was in the 1790 census when he is shown on a property in Fishkill between John Philips and John Adriance.

Dirck Hegeman's father was most likely Adrian Hegeman, born ca. 1683 in Maine of a Dutch immigrant family; his parents being Denuyse Hegeman and Grace Lucretia Dollen. Adrian's will, dated 11 August 1762, reads as follows:

> *In the name of God, Amen, August 11, 1862. I Adrian Hegman, of the Ferry in the Township of Brookland* [Brooklyn], *in Kings County, baker, desiring that all persons concerned may be fully contented and satisfied, and raise no contention. All debts to be paid. My executors are to sell all estate with 6 weeks at Publick Venue, and all my estate in New Jersey or elsewhere. The proceeds and all the rest of my money I leave to my wife Sarah, and my children, Cornelius, Dirck, Adrian, Elizabeth, wife of Jacobus Simonse, Sarah, wife of Richard Morret, Lucretia, wife of Alexander Forbus, Petrus, Joseph, and the children of my eldest son, Denys Hegeman, deceased, who are to have their fathers' part, except that Adrian Hegeman, the eldest son of my said son Denys, deceased, shall have my silver watch and my Dutch Bible before any division is made. I make my son Dirck, and my brother, Denys Hegeman, and my grandson, Adrian Hegeman, executors.*

3. Jacob Dolsen was born ca. 1704 at Throggsneck, Westchester County (Hamlin, 1905). There is a Jacob *Dollson* on the Rombout tax lists from 1729 to 1736, 1737 to June 1748 in the Middle Ward of the Beekman Patent, 1762 to 1763 in Poughkeepsie Precinct, and again in Rombout from 1765 to 1766. Afterwards, we find that this Jacob settled across the Hudson River in New Marlborough, Ulster County where he died in 1775.

In Oswego, Jacob's farm was located adjacent to that of his brother, Johannes, just south of present day Hoxsie Corners. Beekman Precinct road records contain mention of the two brothers:

> ***Also, a road from Matthew Buis his house at Oswego to the run along the road that now is to and along the houses of Johannis Dalson, Jacob Dalson, and John Buyses and further westward until it comes on the road lad out from George Elsworth's Mill leading toward Poghkeepsinck*** (p. 176, *Old Miscellaneous Records of Dutchess County – The Second Book of the Supervisors and Assessors*, 1909).

Replicas and descriptions of the earmarks (livestock brands) of both Jacob and his brother, Johannes, were registered in 1729 in Dutchess County[6].

Jacob married Maritje Buys on 12 January 1734 at the Fishkill Dutch Reformed Church. Maritje was the younger sister of Elisabeth Buys, who previously married Jacob's older brother, Johannes. The church recorded the wedding of Jacob Dolsen and *Marya* Buys in the following manner:

> ***12 Jan 1735 <u>Jacob Dolsen</u>, ym, b. Westchester Co, <u>Marya Buys</u>, yd, Vischkill***

Maritje Buys was born at present-day Fishkill and baptized at the Sleepy Hollow Dutch Reformed Church on 25 March 1712. Sponsors were Johannes Brouwer and his wife, Altje.

Jacob Dolsen and Maritje Buys Dolsen baptized the following children:

   a. Thunes, 6 October 1735. Isaac Dalson and Marya Hussif.
   b. Johannes, 15 May 1737. Isaak Dolsen and Mallie Hussie.
   c. Isaac, 26 May 1739. Johannes *Dolsin* and Elizabeth Buys.
   d. Aeltje, 28 April 1745. Dirck Hegeman and Aeltje Dolsen.

The children were baptized alternately at the Fishkill and Poughkeepsie Dutch Reformed Churches. The sponsors were paternal aunts and uncles of the children. Johannes is noted as living in Marlborough as early as 1769 (Woolsley, 1908). In that year he buried

---

[6] ***Johannes Dolson; his ear mark apleyed to his horses and cattel & sheep is a half moon under each ear and a sleet at the top of the right ear and his brand is thus which he brands his horses with IxD. Jacob Dolson his ear mark apleyed to his horses and cattel & sheep is a half moon on the top side of the right ear and half moon on the upper side of the left ear and his brand on the right buttock is thus P*** (p. 194, *Old Miscellaneous Records of Dutchess County–The Second Book of the Supervisors and Assessors*, 1909)

his son Samuel on 28 August. This writer believes that the brothers named Thunes and Johannes, listed above, participated in the Revolutionary War in various Newburgh units. Thunes was residing in Marlborough as late as 1776 when he had a daughter named Mary baptized on 12 July (Woolsley, 1908). In addition, a son of this Thunes [*Jacob, Theunis, Jan*] named Johannes, also participated in the Revolutionary War (probably initially as a drummer). As a result of military service, Thunes and his son were granted land in Big Flats (Newtown), Tioga County. They were some of the earliest settlers in the region. In August of 1795; Thunes was noted as the first "white man" to die in the community. Often sightings of Thunis' son, Johannes, and Thunis' brother, Johannes, are confused in the records. One of the most cogent clarifications regarding these two men is found in a manuscript by Samuel D. Dolson (1932, pp. 159-160). Samuel Deyo Dolson, a member of the Holland Society, was the son of George Dolson [*Hachaliah Purdy, John, Jacob, Theunis, Jan*].

Although no additional baptismal records have been located for this family, there is a significant possibility that Jacob Dolsen and Maritje Buys Dolsen had several additional children such as:

e. <u>Sarah</u>, ca. 1741, named for her paternal grandmother, Sarah Vermilyea.
f. <u>Maritje</u> or <u>Mary</u>, ca. 1743, named for her maternal grandmother, Maritje Brower.
g. <u>Matthew</u>, ca. 1747, named for his maternal uncle, Matthew Buys.
h. <u>Jacob</u>, ca. 1749, named for his father. A child named Yoris was baptized on 13 September 1767 at the Dutch Reformed Church in Shawangunk. Parents are listed as Jacob Dolson and his wife, *Maryte Kock*. The Dolson and Kock families may have known each other previously. On 9 May 1740, Abraham Dolsen and his wife, Martyje Slot, served as sponsors for the baptism of Femmetje, daughter of Jan Kock and his wife, Rebekka Elsewart.
i. A son named <u>Peter</u> may have been born ca. 1751. The author speculates on the existence of a man of this name in this family. See the Appendix for elaborations regarding this matter.

This line of the family contains some very remarkable individuals. Perhaps the most famous was Jacob Dolson Cox (1828-1900), who became an author, abolitionist, lawyer, and a Union Army General. After the Civil War, he served as the Governor of Ohio and subsequently, Secretary of the Interior under President Ulysses S. Grant. Also from this branch was George M. Dolson (1811-after 1836), a Texas military officer, who served as an interpreter at a prisoner-of-war camp for Mexican soldiers at Galveston Island. On 18 July 1846, George was asked to translate a statement of a Mexican officer who had witnessed several executions at the Alamo, particularly that of Davey Crockett. Dolson's account was confirmed by General Santa Ana's personal secretary, Ramón Martinez Caro. George M. Dolson's letter was published in the *Detroit Democratic Free Press* in September of 1846 but apparently went unnoticed by historians until the 1960's. A third descendent, Martha Dolsen (1804-1856) married William Chrysler, the great grandfather of the founder of Chrysler Motors, Walter Chrysler. According to one of Chrysler's biographers, Boyden Sparkes, the Chief Executive Officer (CEO) of the Chrysler Corporation was not especially interested in his ancestors but did share with others that his immigrant forebear was a sea-going Dutchman named Captain Jan Gerritsen Van Dalsen (Chrysler and Sparkes, 2011). Finally, there is Charles H. Dolson (1906-1992), the second CEO of Delta Airlines (*New York Times*, 6 September 1992).

While the author has not been able to confirm a direct lineage to Jacob [*Thuenis, Jan*], there is a likely possibility that another descendent of this branch was John L. Dolson (ca. 1840-1925), who with the assistance of his sons, developed and operated the Dolson Automobile Company beginning in 1904. Although the company only functioned for a period of four years, more than 700 "Durable Dolsons" were produced (Feltner, 2012).

Downey (2013) has reconstructed the family theorizing that children e-i existed based on Dutch family naming traditions prevalent at the time. Ample supporting evidence confirms the existence of Matthew, and there seems to be at least one confident sighting for Jacob. No records have been found for Sarah and Maritje. Additional details on several of the sons in this family (Thunis, Isaac, Matthew, and Jacob) will be provided later in this volume and in the Appendix.

The elder Jacob Dolsen [*Theunis, Jan*] served as a Justice of the Peace for the Town of Beekman for the period of 1739 to 1740. Doherty (1990), reports that a Jacob Dolsen took the oath as Justice on 16 January 1739.

In 1744, the Fishkill and Poughkeepsie congregations of the Dutch Reformed Church sent a joint request to Holland for the assignment of a *dominie* (pastor). Monies were collected for this purpose and in 1745 these efforts were memorialized in the following manner:

> **Augt den 7 dagh Anno 1745 dan hebben wey de name van de Lest van die Beloft habben an et beroep dat na hollandt is voor een domini:**[7]

> **...Jacob Dolsen 6 stivers, Abraham Dolsen 8 stivers...** (Van Glieson, 1893, pp. 116-118).

Two Dolson brothers, Jacob and Abraham, are listed as donors. Recognizable surnames among the other contributors include Hegeman, *Buis* [Buys], *Oostrom*, and *Delong*.

---

[7] Translation: *Aug. 7 of the year 1745, then have we the names of the list of those who have promised for the call to Holland for a minister… Jacob Dolsen 6 stivers, Abraham Dolsen 8 stivers…*

A Jacob *Dolfon*, defendant of *Swego* [Oswego], Beekmans Precinct is noted in a 14 March 1746 court complaint regarding a £50 debt to Johannes Tappen. In 1750, Jacob Dolsen of *Swego* filed a declaration with the Dutchess County court.

According to Cochrane (1887), Jacob Dolsen died at Marlborough, Ulster County and was buried there on 23 May 1775. He died of small pox. His wife Maritje Buys Dolsen is reported to have died at Marlborough on 22 September 1783 (Cochrane, 1887).

4. <u>Abraham Dolsen</u> was born ca. 1710, probably in the vicinity of Eastchester Town or as claimed by Hamlin (1905), in nearby Throggs Neck. Along with the rest of his family, Abraham moved to Dutchess County in 1726. He would have been sixteen years old upon his arrival in the Fishkills. An Abraham *Dolsing* is included on Rombout tax lists for the period 1734 to 1735. From 1738 to June 1753, Abraham is spotted in the Beekman Patent, in Oswego near his brothers, Johannis and Jacob.

On 10 November 1734, banns were announced at the Fishkill Dutch Reformed Church for Abraham *Dalsen* and Marytjen (*Marya, Maritje*) Slot. Marytjen was the daughter of Jonas Slot and Jannetje Oosterum. The marriage record indicates that Abraham was born in Westchester and Marytjen in Poughkeepsie. The writer has located Marytjen's baptismal record archived at the Kingston Dutch Reformed Church, even though there is a notation that her baptism took place at *Pakeepsy* [Poughkeepsie]:

> ***1714 Feb 02; Jonis Slot, Jannetjen Oosterum; <u>Marytjen</u>; Jan Oosterum, Magtelt Roelofs***

Sponsors for the baptism were the child's maternal grandparents.

The Slot and Oosterum Families
A Jan Pietersen Slot (Slott, Sloot, Sloat) was born ca. 1620 in Holstein, Denmark and immigrated first to Holland and then subsequently with his wife, Aeltje Jans, to Nieuw Amsterdam in 1650. The immigration record lists his profession as a *zimmerman* or builder (Boyer, 1978). For a period of time, Jan Pietersen Slot and Aeltje lived "along the Wall" in the lower end of Manhattan (Sloat, 1996).

Jan Pietersen Slot held public office as the president of the Board of Commissioners which became the first Court of Nieuw Harlem. In 1662 he purchased lots seven, eight, and nine at Van Keulen's Hook, Nieuw Harlem. In 1663 he was commander of the militia at Nieuw Harlem during the Esopus War.

Jan Pietersen Slot & Aeltje Jans Slot had at least one child, Pieter Jansen Slot. Pieter was born in Amsterdam, Holland, and immigrated with his parents to Nieuw Netherlandts in 1650. In 1665 he was a builder in Nieuw Harlem. He owned property near the present

City Hall in lower Manhattan, but made his residence from 1658 to 1664 in Nieuw Haarlem. Pieter was a cadet in the Third Company of the Nieuw Haarlem Militia in 1663. Aeltje Jans Slot, died before 1664 (Sloat, 1996). About the time of his mother's death, Peter Jansen Slot removed to the village of Bergen (Jersey City) along the west side of the Hudson River. In 1668 he purchased a patent in the Pembrepook Tract along the bay leading to the Hudson River. He remained at Bergen until 1671. In 1680 he was residing at Esopus (later renamed Kingston), New York. Jan Pietersen Slot died in New Amsterdam in 1688. For a period of time he served as the mayor of New Amsterdam. Pieter Jansen Slot married Marretje Jacobse Van Winkle, a daughter of Jacob Wallings Van Winkle and Tryntje Jacobs. Their marriage took place on 2 January 1663 at Nieuw Amsterdam. Marretje's father and uncle would later become two of the fourteen partners in the Acquackanonk Patent in present day New Jersey. Pieter Jansen Slot and Marretje Jacobse Van Winkle Slot had at least seven children, including Styntje, Jan Pietersen Jr., Arientje, Jacobus, Tryntie, Abeltie, and Jonas. After Marretje's death, Pieter married second, Claartje Domincus, with whom he had at least one additional daughter, Claartje Domincus Slot.

In the next generation several members of the Slot family resided in Ulster County. The Dutch colonized the area around present-day Kingston, New York ca. 1657 establishing a village that they first named Esopus and later Wiltwyck (Dutch for "Wild Woods"). Jonas Slot is recorded as having been born in Esopus. His baptism was recorded at the Kingston Dutch Reformed Church on 4 September 1681. Some thirty-two years later, on 4 October 1713, banns were registered for the marriage of Jonas Slot of Esopus and a Jannetjen Oosterum of Poughkeepsie at the Dutch Reformed Church in Kingston.

Eventually Jonas Slot's family relocates to the Rombout Patent in Dutchess County. On 21 November 1715, a Jonas Slodt is listed as a member of the Dutchess County militia under Captain Barend Z. Van Kleeck. A Jonas *Slott* is recorded on Dutchess County tax roles as a resident of the Middle Ward from August 1722 until 1735. The Fishkill and Poughkeepsie Dutch Reformed Churches, as well as county tax and military archives, indicate the presence of several Slot and Oosterum families in the Beekman Precinct. A Hendrick Slot is shown on the Beekman Precinct tax rolls between February 1757 and June 1766. Around the 1770s, a separate branch of this family under Steven Sloat founded Sloatsburg, a village in the Town of Ramapo in what is now Rockland County, New York. Jonas Slot was last sighted in Poughkeepsie in 1745, the same year as the baptism of his last known child, Marytjen.

Marytjen's mother, Jannetje Oosterum, was baptized 3 June 1694 at Poughkeepsie. Her baptism is recorded at the Dutch Reformed Church in Kingston. She was the daughter of Jan Hendrickse van Oosterum , baptized 24 June 1657 in Nieuw Amsterdam, and Mageltje Roelofse de Duyster, born before 1663 in Albany. At the time of Jannetje's marriage, she was living in Breuckelen [Brooklyn] on Long Island. In turn, Jan's parents were Hendrick Janzen Oosterum van Schalkwijk from Schalkwijk, Utrecht, Netherlands and Tryntje Lubbertsen of Fort Orange (Albany). This couple was married on 4 December 1652 at the Dutch Reformed Church in Nieuw Amsterdam. Tryntje's father, Lubbert Gysbertsen, a wheelwright by trade, was from Blaricum, near Naarden, in the Netherlands. The villages of Blaricum and Schalkwijk are very near each other and thus it is possible that the families of Oosterum and Gysbertsen were acquainted before immigrating to America.

The children of Abraham Dolsen and Marytjen Slot Dolsen, along with their corresponding baptismal dates and sponsors, are as follows:

a. <u>Jonas</u>: 15 May 1737, Johannes Dolsen and Elisabeth Buys at Fishkill
b. <u>Jannetjen</u>: 26 May 1739, Hedrick *Flip* and Marrtije *Oostrom* at Poughkeepsie
c. <u>Marregrieta</u>: 9 September 1740, Jacob Dolsen and Marytje Buys at Fishkill
d. <u>Aeltje</u>: 1 April 1743, Dirck Hegeman and Aeltje Dolsen at Poughkeepsie
e. <u>Marytje</u>: 28 April 1745, Hendrick *Phillip* and Marritje *Oostrum* at Fishkill

These children were baptized at the Fishkill and Poughkeepsie Dutch Reformed Churches. The first two children were named after maternal grandparents. The remaining daughters appear to be named alternatively after aunts on both sides of the family. Fishkill Dutch Reformed Church transcribers report that Marregrieta's name was reversed in the baptismal records with that of Cathrina, a daughter of neighbors, Abraham Fonteyn and Anneke Rouser. Marregrieta Dolsen and Cathrina Fonteyn coincidently were baptized on the same date. No substantiation available for possible children Sarah or Teunis. In addition to the five children listed above, Abraham Dolsen and his spouse Marytjen Slot Dolsen almost certainly had an additional son named Abraham Jr. Inexplicably, no baptismal record is on file for this child. Abraham Jr. may have been born ca. 1747 or as suggested by Downey (2013), around 1749. This Abraham most likely is the man known as Abraham Dolsen Jr. sighted in Warwick before the Revolution and who married Phoebe Benedict in that town ca. 1773. Additional information on Abraham Jr. is provided in the Appendix to this volume.

A Dutchess County deed (Liber 3, p. 67) of 22 September 1747 mentions Abraham Dolsen, his wife Marytjen, and solely their daughter, Marregrieta. Customarily, the names of all of the children living at the time would be included in a document such as the deed of 1747. One explanation, as incredible as it may seem, is that all five of the children born before 1947 may have died previous to the issuance of this deed. Except for the baptismal records, this writer has not located any definitive sightings in Dutchess or Orange County referring explicitly to a Jonas, Jannetje, Aeltje, and Marytje from this generation of this family.

Beekman Precinct road records of 1742 include a reference to Abraham's farm:

...following publick and common roads or high ways... to the southwest corner of the land of Joseph Crego Esqr., then along marked trees to a white oak tree marked at the north end of a hill where the people of the Vette Bergeh or fat him comes to this road... then along marked trees to the land of Abraham Dolson then from the last mentioned white oak tree along marked trees to the corner of Geessie De Langs and David Storms land then slanting through Abraham Vontyns land to the wagon path... (p. 175, Old Miscellaneous Records of Dutchess County, 1909**).**

This same farm is mentioned in the deed (Liber 3, p. 67) dated 22 September 1747. This document reaffirms that a property of 200 acres had been "demised" to an Abraham *Dolson*, his wife *Marritie*, and daughter, *Margaret,* by Gilbert Livingston. The farm was located on Lot Seventeen near properties belonging to Colonel Beekman, Abraham Fonteyn, and Johannes Buys.

After the mid-1750's, there are no further sightings of Abraham Dolsen in Dutchess County. It is possible that sometime after 1753, Abraham relocated to the Florida neighborhood of Warwick, Orange County. There are documented sightings of an Abraham Sr. in this area as early as 1775. If these sightings are not related to this Abraham Sr., then the author has no further documentation on this man after 1753. It is not known when or where he died[8]. Apparently, this Abraham did not leave a will. See the Appendix to this volume for additional clarifications regarding the several Dolson men named Abraham. Likewise, there is no documentation regarding the later years of Abraham Sr.'s wife, Marytjen Slot Dolsen, nor any definitive information regarding her death and place of burial.

5. Annetje Dolsen may have been born ca. 1710, probably in the vicinity of Eastchester Town. A wedding was recorded at the Fishkill Dutch Reformed Church on 6 June 1734 as follows:

Arie Delang, YM and Annatje Dolsen, YD

Arie Delong, born in New York City ca. 1705, was the son of *Frans De Lang* and Marytjen Van Schaack (Burt and Burt, 1997). This family was from Holland and in Dutchess by the 1714 census. *Frans Delang,* Arie's father, was a deacon at the Fishkill Dutch Reformed Church in 1732. However, the Fishkill marriage record for Arie De Long and Annatje Dolsen is almost certainly in error. There is a baptismal record of a child named Ruth at the Fishkill Dutch Reformed Church on 28 September 1737, whose parents are listed as

---

[8] Both Hamlin (1905) and Dolson (1932) mention a "tradition", a story about an Abraham being captured by Native Americans and taken to Detroit. This writer has not found any evidence to corroborate this tale.

Arie *de Lange* and Anna Wilson or *Dolson*. Burt and Burt (1997) report that Arie Delong married Anna Wiltsie in 1734 and that Anna Wiltsie bore all of Arie Delong's children. Faced with the available evidence, it appears that a marriage did not take place between Annetje Dolsen and Arie Delong. Since there are no other sightings of an Annetje Dolsen in Dutchess, it is quite possible that she died young or never married.

6. <u>Johanna Dolsen</u> was born ca. 1713, probably in the vicinity of Eastchester Town. While no marriage record has been found, Johanna Dolsen almost certainly was married to Nicholas Delong ca. 1733. Nicholas was the brother of Arie Delong mentioned previously. The following information has been garnered regarding the children of this couple:

   a. *Marya* baptized at the Fishkill Dutch Reformed Church on 21 March 1734. Parents are listed as Johanna *Dalson* and *Neclaes Delangh*.
   b. A child named <u>Frans</u> was baptized at the Poughkeepsie Dutch Reformed Church on 8 May 1740.
   c. <u>Nicholas DeLong</u> was born ca. 1750 (Dewald Jr., 2015).
   d. <u>Henry Delong</u> was born ca. 1754 (Dewald Jr., 2015; Baldwin, 1993).
   e. <u>Abraham DeLong</u> was born before 1755 (Dewald Jr., 2015; Baldwin, 1993).
   f. <u>Jacob DeLong</u> was born before 1755 in Dutchess County, New York and died ca. 1816 in Geauga County, Ohio (Dewald Jr., 2015; Baldwin, 1993).
   g. <u>John DeLong</u> was born ca. 1760 (Baldwin, 1993).

   Johanna's presumptive husband, *Niclaes De Lang,* was baptized at the Kingston Dutch Reformed Church on 10 August 1711. His parents were listed as *Frans De Lang* and Marytjen *Van Schaak*. The immigrant ancestor of the DeLong family was probably *Frans De Lang*'s father, Aire Fransen (AKA Adrianus Fanciscuszoon DeLanget), born ca. 1655 in Etten en Leur, Noord Brabent, Holland and who arrived in Nieuw Amsterdam on 2 December 1659 on the ship *De Trouw* (Burt, 1997). Nicholas Delong and Johanna Dolsen Delong are shown on a 1741 lease for a farm near what is now La Grange, Dutchess County. Nicholas DeLong is recorded as living in 1750 in Cumberland County, Pennsylvania (Downey, 2013). No records of the deaths of either Nicholas or Johanna have been located.

7. A <u>Sarah Dolsen</u> may have been born ca. 1715, probably in the vicinity of Eastchester Town but also conceivably in Mamaroneck. She is reported to have married Israel Rotsiker before 1736 (Plimley, 2011), which may have been her second marriage. On 25 May 1736 this couple baptized a child named Daniel Rotsiker at the Montgomery Dutch Reformed Church in Orange County (Downey, 2013). This writer has seen the baptismal transcript and concludes that the document in question is most likely not connected to the Sarah Dolsen from this family. No further records have been located.

Isaac's Transition to Orange County

The preponderance of evidence suggests that Isaac resided in Dutchess County until the mid-1750s. There are however, at least two reports that, on face value, make it appear as though he relocated to Orange County as early as the year 1735. The first is by Ruttenber and Clark (1881):

> *The Dolsen name was originally Van Dolsen and it is a tradition in the family that the first child born on Manhattan Island was a Van Dolsen. The original Dolsen tract comprised 700 acres. It was purchased in 1735 at one dollar per acre. Betty, one of the slaves of the early period lived down to with a few years, and could tell many stories of the Dolsen family and neighborhood* (p. 682).

The New York State Division of Military and Naval Affairs lists Isaac's home in its index of historic forts in the state (*http://dmna.state.ny.us*):

> *Dolson Blockhouse, 1735, Orange County, Middletown. Originally a fortified log house. 1750s erected a blockhouse and fortified stone house for protection during French and Indian raids. A fortified log home, originally built in 1735. Rebuilt as a stone house in the 1750's. A blockhouse was also built here in 1757 under orders of Capt. James Clinton.*

The wording of this entry suggests that when Isaac Dolsen obtained the property in the 1750s, a log fortification already existed and that he replaced the wooden construction with a stone structure.

Stickney (1863) elaborates on Eager's (1850) work to describe Isaac's coming to Orange County:

> *DOLSEN.—This family is said to be of Dutch origin. Eager says (p. 412) that there is a family tradition to the effect that the first male child born in New Amsterdam (now New York) was a Dolsen. The first of the name in this town was Isaac Dolsen, who came from Fishkill, in Duchess County, in 1756 before the French and Indian war, and purchased seven hundred acres in what is now known as Dolsentown. He was a millwright by trade, and married Polly Huzzy of New Jersey. He died in 1795, leaving two children, James and Isaac. Isaac was never married. James married Phebe Meeker, and their children were James, Asa, Samuel, Polly and Abby. The Indians committed some depredations near Dolsentown in the French and Indian war.*

While the evidence suggests the time of Isaac's relocation to Orange County was around 1756, it is difficult to pinpoint the exact date. This is primarily because no record of a land purchase has been located. Also, in several land records of Dutchess County, Isaac

Dolsen's name continued to be associated with his farm in Rombout Precinct as late as 1776 (Liber III, p. 432). This writer has noticed however, a tendency in the Dutchess records to refer to original owners when describing nearby land boundaries in deeds and mortgages.

Isaac's motivations to move to Orange County after spending nearly thirty years in Dutchess are unknown. Hamlin (1905) offers a logical explanation related to economics. While in Dutchess County, the Dolsons were merely tenants, that is, the land holding conditions imposed by the large landlords of the Rombout and Beekman Patents didn't allow most farmers the opportunity to purchase their own properties. Instead the farmers were forced to merely lease the land upon which they lived (Hamlin, 1905). As Isaac accumulated wealth, one of the few investments available to him would be the purchase of real estate. He probably had in mind the future financial wellbeing of his children. Additionally, the writer speculates that around this time, his first wife, Mary Hussey Dolsen, may have died. Accordingly, Isaac may have felt the need for a fresh start in a new location.

The author has not come across the deed for Isaac's original purchase of lands in Orange County. The writer surmises from various accounts and subsequent deeds, that Isaac's 700-acre tract was located near the place where current state routes 17M and 6 intersect. This is in an area just south of Middletown. The names of adjacent roads here, Dolson Avenue and Dolsentown Road, impart confidence to the hypothesis that the Dolson property lay in and around Pine Hill Cemetery, just a quarter of a mile west of the intersection mentioned, which is also known as Bradley Corners. An environmenta and cultural resourcesl study was conducted in 2005 and although no prehistoric archaeological resources were identified, the foundation walls of the Dolsen-Bradley house were identified as well as deposits of nineteenth-century cultural material: Eager (1846), notes that Isaac Dolsen:

> *...constructed a block house erected as protection against the Indians. The first home was log house, loop-holed for musquetry, and afterwards a stone house into which the inhabitants used to flee for safety as well as into the block house* (p. 412).

A stone in the wall of the dwelling-house was marked 1760 and is said to have been taken from the fort of 1756 (Ruttenber and Clark, 1881). This defensive structure eventually became known as the Dolson Blockhouse and is noted as an historical landmark of the French and Indian War (Stoetzel, 2008). Eager (1846) goes on to report that there was an Indian settlement in the meadow of the Dolson property near the residence and a burying ground on dry land in the vicinity. The Indian graves were so shallow that a plough passing over them would bring up bones. The Native Americans also had planted an apple orchard on this property.

The very first deed associated with Isaac's property is an indenture dated 22 October 1765 in which Isaac, and his wife Sarah, grant unto Isaac's son, James (Sr.), a parcel of land consisting of twenty-five acres. The price of the transaction was the token amount of £25. Mentioned in the indenture are various geographic points concerning the property in question including that (1) it was situated in the Westside of the Wallkills; (2) it adjoined the lands of Daniel Cooley; and (3), it was near the outlet of the Drowned Lands West Inhabitants. Both Isaac *Dalson* and Sarah Dolsen signed the document in their own hands. Witnesses were Margret Gardner (Dolsen), Isaac's daughter, and her husband, James Gardner.

The area where Isaac settled became known as Dolsentown, sometimes spelled *Dolsantown* or *Dolsontown*. Eager (1846) provides the following account regarding the origin of the community:

> *Dolsantown---This is some two miles west of Denton. Before the French and Indian war in 1756, an individual by the name of Isaac Dolsan came from Fishkill, Dutchess County and settled there. He purchased 700 acres which is now owned by Theophilus Dolsan, James Post, James Aldridge and Mr. Swezey.*
>
> *His children were James and Isaac; James married Phoebe Meeker. Their children were James, Asa, Samuel, Polly and Abby----of whom all are dead but Samuel, who is eighty-two years of age. Isaac never married. This family is Dutch and very old in America.* (p. 412).

Pages 677-678 of the volume by Ruttenber and Clark (1881) contain virtually the same text regarding the Dolson family. In the course of history, Dolsentown changed jurisdictions several times from Goshen to Minisink and finally to Wawayanda. In 1999, as part of the celebration of the sesquicentennial of the town of Wawayanda, Benjamin A. Gilman, Representative of New York, introduced a Congressional Resolution to acknowledge the earliest settlers of the area. The name of the Dolson family was included in this resolution (Congressional Record, 1 July 1999, p. 15407).

A Single Place with Many Names

Once settled in Orange County, Isaac Dolsen never relocated, but the name given to the area where his farm was situated changed several times. The history books, tax records, and other archives alternatively refer to the area as Dolsentown, Goshen, Minisink, Wallkill, and Wawayanda.

In 1738, the population of the Goshen Precinct was 1,017 and that of Minisink was 340 (Ruttenber and Clark, 1881). About the time of the French and Indian War, the only major settlement in the area was Goshen. The precinct remained rural for many years. As late as 1773, there was only one log house between Dolsentown and the Shawangunk Mountains. During these years and even until the Revolution, any happenings in the regions of Minisink, Wallkill, and even Warwick tended to be attributed earliest to Goshen Precinct and then subsequently to the Town of Goshen (e.g., Theunis Dalsen's obituary notice of 1766). The first deeds to village lots were recorded in Goshen in 1714 and the town had a major newspaper early. Around the 1730s, efforts were introduced to organize the Town of Minisink, but codification did not take place until 1788. The Precinct of Minisink (1772) and Town of Wallkill (1788) were adjacent and in the early days the boundaries of these precincts, towns, and hamlets shifted from time to time. Finally, in the mid-1800s, the Town of Wawayanda was incorporated. Previously, the surrounding area was referred to as the Wawayanda Patent and Middletown was considered to be part of Wallkill until 1888 (Orange County Genealogical Society, 1974, p. 20).

In New York State, towns usually contain several hamlets and villages and often encompass surrounding rural areas. Dolsentown was originally one of the hamlets of Minisink. Other nearby settlements included Graham, Brookfield, Ridgebury, Slate Hill, Jogee Hill, Westtown, and Gardnerville (Disturnell, 1843). By the time the Town of Wawayanda was formed in 1849, Dolsentown tended to be referred to as a neighborhood. Presently (2018), Dolsentown is solely an historical designation.

Notes archived in the collective vertical files of the Orange County Genealogical Society, developed primarily by Elizabeth Horton (but also including work by Helen Predmore, Myrtle Edwards, and Dab Burrows), suggest that Isaac Dolsen Sr. paid $1.00 an acre for his farm in 1756. Ruttenber and Clark (1881) is cited as the source for this information.

Almost all of the historians of early Orange County, New York make note of confrontations between Native Americans and the European settlers. Eager (1846) summarizes what he considered to be some of the noteworthy events:

During the French war the Indians came and killed a man in Dolsan's meadow, by the name of Owens, and he then removed to Goshen where he staid till the war was over. The Indians did not come in great numbers to this settlement, but only a few at a time, who secreted themselves in the woods of the neighborhood, and as opportunity served sallied out to rob and to murder. On one occasion three of them chased a man who ran and crept under the weeds and brush at the root of a tree which had been blown down; the Indians came, stood upon the tree, looked all around, yelling most savagely, but fortunately did not find him, and they left.

In old times it was customary to build ovens to bake in, in the vicinity of the house, and at the time we speak of a woman in the family of Mr. Cooley was engaged in baking, when some Indians passing at the time shot her while going from the oven to the house [Town of Minisink, p. 4].

There are several newspaper reports of the time that confirm some of the events that took place on or around Isaac's farm:

> *11 March 1756, Philadelphia. We hear from the Wallkill, in Orange County, that on Friday, the 25th of last month, one Morgan Owens was shot and scalped there by three Indians, who the day before were seen and known in that neighbourhood to be River Indians. It seems OWENS had just gone out of a house a few minutes before, in which he left one Silas Hulse, who hearing three guns go off, took up his gun and went out; he had not gone far before he saw the Indians making towards him, but none of their guns being loaded, he had room to run, the Indians being afraid to follow till they had loaded again, accordingly he pushed into a swamp where he hid himself, and saw his pursuers pass close by in search of him, but happily missed seeing him. Soon after the Indians leaving the swamp, he came out, and made the best of his way to some settlements, and a number of the inhabitants soon went out in pursuit of them (Pennsylvania Gazette).*

In Stickney's retelling of this story in *A History of the Minisink Region* (1867), the author claims that Dolsen immediately removed his family to Goshen for safety. This may be an error. Stickney writes that an Asa Dolsen [*James Sr., Isaac, Theunis, Jan*] was running the farm at the time of this incident (1756) but Asa was not born until 1761. In terms of this reference to Asa however, Stickney does correct the error. In the *errata* section of his book. Stickney indicates that the name "Asa" is to be replaced with the name "Isaac." Alas, many readers may not notice this correction.

In another entry in the same volume, this writer notes an additional misunderstanding on the part of Stickney (1863):

> *Isaac Dolson came to Minisink in the early 1700s and purchased seven hundred acres. His grandson, Asa built a stone house and block house as protection for his family and neighbors. The Indians killed a man named Morgan Owens in Dolsen's meadow and the family then moved to Goshen until peace was restored.*

The majority of the data are quite consistent in pinpointing Isaac's arrival in Orange County to a period between 1735 and 1756------not the early 1700s.

Additional incidents with local Native Americans were reported in 1758 in the *New Hampshire Gazette*:

> *15 September 1758, Portsmouth, New Hampshire. By express from Goshen we have advice, that on Sunday the 14th instant, one Samuel WEB, was inhumanly*

butchered and scalped by a party of Indians, as he was fetching home his cows, at the distance of about half a mile from his own house, and not above two miles from the Court House, which is situated in the thickest settled part of the town. We have also advice, that on Thursday following the wife of Isaac COOLEY was killed and scalped in her own house (which is half a mile within the blockhouse No. 1) and her three children carried away captives. And as Mr. COOLEY was coming up to the house, he was fired upon by 5 or 6 Indians, but being missed, fled to the town. He imagines there was a dozen or 15 in the party; and had it not been for the extraordinary alertness and activity of the Militia in pursuing the party, and scouring the woods, many more of the neighbours doubtless must have fallen, a sacrifice to the inhabitants of the wilderness, whose tender mercies are cruelty.

Stickney (1867) contributes another story about the Cooley family. He states that the wife of David Cooley, whose farm was adjacent to Dolsen's, was shot and killed by the Native Americans while walking between the outdoor oven and the house (p. 69). In this version of this incident, Cooley's farm is said to be located near Pine Hill Cemetery about a mile south of where Dolsen was located.

Michael VanDervoort, a docent with the Minisink Museum, has given a number of talks regarding the Dolsen family of Orange County at various civic, historical, and genealogical events in recent years. He theorizes that the local Native Americans were troubled by the fact that the Dolsens cultivated the land near and within the "Indian" burial grounds. This lack of respect for the Native Americans seems to have provoked the local indigenous peoples and most likely was one of the factors for their more assertive resistance to the early attempts of Europeans to settle in the Minisink region.

The mention that Isaac was not only a farmer, but also a millwright rings true. First, the original properties held in Dutchess County by Thuenis and Isaac were located along Sprout Creek. Secondly both Eager (1846) and Ruttenber and Clark (1881) report that several of the early settlers of Dolsentown, such as Christian Schultz and Isaac Finch, had mills on Mohegan Creek, a waterway which flowed along and through the Dolson property. The types of mills operating in Minisink in Isaac's time included fulling, grist, and saw mills as well as still houses (Ritterman, 1996). In a future generation, another Isaac Dolsen, this one from Warwick, would own an infamous grist mill situated on Wawayanda Creek.

Pioneering in Orange County

In 1775, the County of Orange conducted a comprehensive tax assessment. For the purposes of this assessment, the county was divided into ten districts. Contained in this tax record are the names of five Dolson men and several heads of associated families along with descriptions of the corresponding districts where these individuals lived.

Last Name	First Name	Assessment District
Baird	Frances	2
Benedict	James Sr.	2
Carpenter	John (Blacksmith)	10
Dolkin	Abraham	9
Dolsen	Isaac	10
Dolsen	James	10
Dolson	Isaac	8
Dolson	Isaac	9
Gardner	James	10
Harding	Abraham	10
Hathorn	John	2
Meeker	Benjamin Jr.	4

District No. 2 included a section of the present town of Warwick extending north and south from below Florida at some point to Amity, taking in also the Bellvale neighborhood and the settlements in the vicinity of what is now New Milford and the village of Warwick.

District No. 4 in the old precinct of Goshen includes other territory than the town of Chester. The district may be described somewhat in general terms as comprising East Chester, extending to Satterly Town, and including the Gray Court neighborhood; also West Chester, the families along the Somerville road, including the Conklingtown neighborhood in Goshen, and extending to Fort Hill.

District No. 8 was evidently the southwestern, or more correctly, perhaps, the western portion of the present town of Warwick, the neighborhood of Mount Eve, Amity to Pine Island, and to the New Jersey line, consisting in all of quite a portion of the fertile 17,000 acre tract.

District No. 9 comprised evidently the southern portion of the present town of Goshen, the Florida neighborhood of Warwick, and southward to the vicinity of Mount Eve, where, another district commenced. This district included an extensive portion of the valuable Drowned Lands, rich, fertile, and attractive to the early settlers.

District No. 10 was the rich Dolsentown neighborhood, comprising most of the town of Wawayanda, perhaps extending eastward across the Wallkill and including a portion of the present territory of Goshen, also extending westward to include any settlers in the north and northeast portions of Greenville.

(Original Source: Ruttenber and Clark, 1881; Copy entitled *1775 Assessment Roll of Orange County, NY* compiled by Thomas Cornell and posted at rootsweb.com. (Retrieved on 1 March 2011)

As expected, an Isaac Dolsen [*Thuenis, Jan*] and his son, James Dolsen [*Isaac, Theunis, Jan*], are found in District 10, which is referred to as the "rich" Dolsentown neighborhood.

We also see an Abraham *Dolkin,* possibly Abraham Dolsen Jr. [*Abraham, Theunis, Jan*], and an Isaac Dolsen in District 9, the Florida neighborhood, and surprisingly, another Isaac in District 8, Warwick. Other families associated with the Dolsons noted on the assessment rolls include John Hathorn, Nathaniel Minthorn, and James Benedict Sr. in District 2 and David Moore, Isaiah Vail, and Samuel Wickham in District 1. Henry Wisner was in District 5 and Daniel Carpenter in District 7.

The description of this tax assessment specifies that landowners are chronicled only once in the register. This raises questions not only regarding those Dolsons who may have owned properties in more than one district in the county as well as different Dolson men with the same given name. Additionally, the author assumes with some confidence, that to be listed as a landowner, a man had to be at least twenty-one years of age. Certainly, the identities of the various men named Isaac, who are listed in this tax assessment, beg for further clarification. Analyses are provided in the Appendix.

On 24 May 1775, the men of the Goshen Precinct were asked to sign the Articles of Association requested by the Continental Congress. Among men listed from the Minisink area who were signers are Isaac Dolsen [*Theunis, Jan*], James Dolsen [*Isaac, Theunis, Jan*], and an Isaac Dolsen Jr. [perhaps *Jacob, Theunis, Jan*] (*Calendar of historical manuscripts, relating to the war of the revolution,* 1868, p. 10). Other names of interest on this list are Peter Mills, Benjamin Meeker, and Abraham Harding. On Thursday, 6 July 1775, a *Tunis* Dolson [*Jacob, Theunis, Jan*] and a John Dolson [*Jacob, Theunis, Jan*] signed the Articles at Newburgh.

Isaac Sr. lived long enough to be included in the first U.S. Census taken in 1790. He is recorded as residing in the Minisink Township between the properties of James Owens and Abraham Harding, his son-in-law. In his household there were two free white males sixteen years and older and one free male under sixteen years of age, as well as three free white females.

Isaac's grandsons, James Jr. and Asa, are shown in the 1790 Census as having their individual farms in Minisink. James Jr. was located between Christian Hulse and Elijah Van Auken. He was reported to have several female slaves. Asa's farm was situated between the properties of James Hulse Sr. and Peter R. Ludlow. In Warwick, Abraham Dolsen, Abraham Dolsen Jr. and an Isaac Dolsen Jr. are listed. Other recognizable names of Orange

County residents enumerated in this first national census were: Abraham Harding, Theophilus Howell, James Little, Eusebius Austin, John Bradner, Peter Mills, Daniel Carpenter, and John Carpenter. The census for Chemung County includes *Tunis Dolson* [*Jacob, Theunis, Jan*] and *John Dolson* [probably *Thuenis, Jacob, Thuenis, Jan*].

Early Military and Political Matters

Plimley (2011) reports that Isaac Dalsen fought in the French and Indian War at the battles of Lake George and Ticonderoga in 1756 with the Company of Sir William Johnson. Johnson was Superintendent of Indian Affairs in North America for the British Empire. Plimley (2011) also states that Abraham served in Captain James Smith's Company in the French and Indian War with an agreement to be paid at three shillings. The writer of this sketch has been able to observe, in person, the original document related to these findings. The men identified by Plimley were undoubtedly Dolson men from the next generation of the family: Isaac [*Johannes, Theunis, Jan*] or Isaac [*Jacob, Thuenis, Jan*]; Abraham [*Johannes, Thuenis, Jan*] or Abraham Jr. [*Abraham, Theunis, Jan*]. Also identified on Captain Smith's roster is a James Dolsen, almost certainly Isaac Sr.'s son. Captain Smith's Company served under Sir William Johnson. The roster is dated 9 January 1756 and indicates that nineteen men, including the three Dolsons, were hired at the pay rate of three shillings a day for a period of twenty days to scout over the lands referred to as the Wallkills. Any man, aged sixteen to sixty in fit condition was eligible to volunteer and serve. The original, handwritten roster and cover letter are on file at the Goshen Public Library and Historical Society (Observed by author on 5 May 2017). Some writers speculate that, if any of the Dolsons mentioned above were the sons of Johannes [*Theunis, Jan*], this may explain, at least in part, why that family remained devoted to Sr. William Johnson and became Loyalists during the Revolution.

The famous Robert Rogers commanded the scouts and rangers under Sir. William Johnson (Ross, 2009). On 29 January 1756, only two weeks after the Dolson men enlisted as scouts along the shores of Lake George and Lake Champlain, Captain Rogers received orders to march to the French fortress at Crown Point which was located in the narrows of Lake Champlain. Following this expedition, on 7 February 1756, Rogers wrote the following report:

Fort Wm. Henry January ye 29th 1756
Set out with a partey of fifty men with orders to look into Crown Point &
advance batterys that is bult round it the first day we marched down the Lake
George aboute eighteen miles and camped so we preceed by, the westerd of the
Greate Mountains and continued our march until the 2nd of February than
climbed up a greate mounton to the west of Crown Point about one mile and
gave it the name of Ogdens Mount there we took a particular view of the said
fort and the rideouts that is built round it and a plan of the same we laide there
untell the evening then went down the mounten marched through a small
village about half a mile from the fort to the suthord there we laide in ambush

upon each side of the roade that leads from the fort through said village there
we laide until about nine of the clock or more and there came along one French
man which we took prisoner and 2 more were upon the roade accoming
towards us but discovered our ambush and made a speedy escape to the fort
and some of my men pursued them within gun shot of the fort but could not
overtake them so we being discovered thought it needles to waite any longer
for prisoners but imedently set fire to the barns and houses where was
abudance of wheat and other graiens and we kill there cattle, horses and hoogs
in number aboute fifty left none living in the said village to our knowledge about
11 o'colock we march home ward leving the village on fire the 5th instant In the
morning one of our men was taken sick so I stooped with seven men and sent
the rest home with Captain Cushinn and Lievant Ogden they arr at our fort
about 6 in the evening and I got home the next day about 4 o"clock in ye
afternoon with the remainder of my partey a true account by your Humble
Servant, Robert Rodgers Witness Seth Cushing (Hall, 1999).

The author has not encountered any documentation that any of the Dolson scouts participated in this march, or any other specific event of the French and Indian War. Still, Rogers' report provides an example of the types of activities in which the Dolson men were involved.

On 8 June 1775, male persons living in Orange County were asked to sign the Pledge to the Continental Congress at Goshen. Signers included an *Isaac Dollen* and a *James Dollen*. These men are undoubtedly Isaac Sr. and his son, James. Also signing at Goshen were Abraham *Dalsen* Jr. [perhaps *Abraham, Theunis, Jan*], Abraham Dolsen Sr. [perhaps *Theunis, Jan*], and Isaac Dolsen [perhaps *Jacob, Theunis, Jan*]. From collateral families we find David Carpenter, James Gardiner, and David Moore. A Theunis [*Jacob, Thuenis, Jan*] and probably his brother, John *Dolsan* [*Jacob, Thuenis, Jan*], are recorded as signing the Revolutionary Pledge in the Precinct of Newburgh.

In 1775, at the beginning of the Revolutionary War, the third generation of Dolson men, the sons of Theunis [*Jan*], would have been the following ages: Johannes Sr. 73, Jacob Sr. 71, Isaac Sr. 68, and Abraham Sr. 65. It is implausible that any of these men, in their advanced age, saw any active military duty in Revolutionary War units. As noted previously, there is documentation that Isaac Sr. was involved in the construction of military fortifications in Dolsentown in the late 1750s. These constructions were undertaken as defenses against Native Americans at the time of the French and Indian War (1754-1763). Johannes Dolsen participated in the Dutchess County colonial militia as early as 1739.

In the next chapter of this volume, additional information will be provided regarding the participation of Dolson men in the Revolutionary War.

Isaac Sr.'s Will

An impressive monument in Pine Hill Cemetery marks the grave of Isaac Sr. and that of his second wife, Sarah. Isaac's marker records the date of his death as 20 May 1794 and his age as eighty-seven years and fifty-seven days. Sarah's marker, inscribed on the adjacent side of the monument, shows her date of death as 14 March 1802, age seventy-nine years.

Isaac Dolsen wrote his will on 2 May 1794 (Liber A, p. 238). The will was proved on 26 May 1794. Following is a transcript of that document prepared by this writer:

In the name of God amen. I Isaac Dolsen of the Town of Minisink in the County of Orange in the State of New York being weak of body but of a sound and disposing mind and memory blessed be God do on this second day of May in the year of our Lord Christ one thousand seven hundred and ninety four make and publish this my last will and testament in manner and form that followith:

First it is my wish that all my just debts and funeral charges be first paid then I give and devise to my son Isaac my lands and buildings as by the deed may appear and whereas my sun Isaac is not fully compus mentus and fearing the same should grow upon him so as to render him incapable of managing for himself it is my will that my Executor hereafter mentioned should have the care and charge of his parte to order and direct it as he be provided a comfortable living and as to my personal estate it is my will that it be disposed of in the following manner. I give and bequeath to my grandson James Dolson my large pare of ____=ards. I give and bequeath to my beloved wife Sarah Dolson my brown mare and her side saddle allso shee taking her choice of one the uwes. Allso her bed and bedding and furnishere. I give and bequeath to my said wife the privilege of living in the house with my said sun Isaac and allso the keeping of the said mare and cow with pasture and hay both summer and winter and water and to have fire wood provided for her as long as she continues my widow and the remainder of my personal estate it is my will that it be equally divided between my said wife and my two daughters Margret Gardner and Alcha Harding share and share alike and at the death of my sun Isaac Dolson it is my will that the land_____ be the property of my daughter Alcha's two children Isaac and Sarah and lastly I do constitute and appoint my well beloved Sarah and James Dolson and my son in law Abraham Harding sole executors of this my last will and testament signed and sealed published and declared in the presence of us _____ of one of the ____ being first underlined the words as ____ _____ _____ Lideal Mapes, Abraham Osborn, David Sherwood-----

Isaac X Dolson

Blank spaces in the above transcript represent undecipherable passages. Isaac made his mark on the will indicating that he was not literate. Isaac mentions his daughters Margaret Gardener and *Alcha* Harding and two grandchildren, Isaac Harding and Sarah Harding[9], in the will. In fact, the Harding grandchildren were to inherit Isaac's farm.

Of important note is the fact the Isaac Sr. did not mention his first wife, Mary Hussey Dolsen, his eldest son, James Dolsen Sr. (previously deceased), his daughter Mary, nor an alleged son named Abraham in his will. By the time Isaac wrote his will, his first wife, Mary Hussey Dolsen, certainly had died since he refers to his current wife as Sarah. Except for her baptism, there are no other sightings of daughter Mary; she may have died at a young age. Despite differing claims, the author believes that a son named Abraham never belonged to this family.

In his will, Isaac Sr. states that his son, Isaac Jr., is *non-compos mentis* and directs his executor to not only care for Isaac Jr. but fundamentally gives the executor power of attorney over Isaac's Jr.'s affairs. The primary executor in this case was almost certainly James Jr. [*James Sr., Isaac, Theunis, Jan*]. Several Orange County historians concur with Eager's (1846) account that Isaac Jr. never married.

Who was Sarah?
Sarah Dolson wrote her will (Liber B, p. 306) on 25 October 1797. According to her tombstone, she died on 16 March 1802 at the age of seventy-nine years. Her will was proved on 20 March 1802. Sarah is buried in Pine Hill Cemetery in the same plot as her husband, Isaac. From the death date on her gravestone, the writer calculates that she was born in 1723. This means that she was only ten years old when James Sr. was born, Isaac's eldest child, and twenty-three years old when Altje, the youngest, was born. Sarah was too young to have been the mother of most of Isaac's children. In addition, the manner in which Sarah bequeathed her estate re-enforces the theory that she was not the biological mother of any of Isaac's children[10].

---

[9] Previous to Isaac's death, a third Harding child, name Ana, died. The name and date of birth of Ana Harding was noted in Mary Hussey Dolsen's bible. The transfer of Isaac's property to grandchildren, Sarah and Isaac Harding, probably did not take place. There are reports that the Harding family left Orange County before Isaac's grandchildren reached the age of maturity. According to land and tax records in Orange County, it appears that Isaac Dolsen's grandsons, James, Asa, and Samuel, all sons of James Sr., came into possession of the Dolsentown property----either by default or through some arrangement with the Harding family. James Jr. and Abraham Harding were executors of Isaac's will along with Sarah, Isaac Sr.'s second wife.

[10] Mary Hussey Dolsen's bible contains the names and corresponding birthdates of all of the children mentioned in Isaac's will; compelling evidence that she is the biological mother of these individuals.

I Sarah Dolson of the Town of Minisink, County of Orange and State of New York being well in health and of sound memory and understanding do make this my last will and testament in a manner and form following viz… First I will that all my just debts and funeral charges be paid by my Executor herein after named. Then I give to my niece Sarah Mills wife of Peter Mills one cow six sheep one bed and bedding one cupboard one table one _____ and bake pan also one note of hand against Richard Graham dated the twenty eighth day of February 1797. Also two notes against James Dolson the first for ten pounds eight shillings and three pence dated the 21 day of May 1794 and the last note for eight pounds dated the 21 day of February 1797. Also two notes against Abraham Harding the first for ten pounds dated the 20 Day of May 1794 the last for three pounds dated the 4 day of February 1796. And I will and positively order that the aforesaid sums of money and interest due and to become due thereon be paid to the said Sarah Mills according to the true intent and meaning hereof. And I also give to the said Sarah Mills all the rest and residue of my estate and property of my husband _____ to her and to her heirs and assigns forever. Lastly I appoint my friends Peter Mills and David Cooley Jr. both of the place aforesaid Executors of this my last will and testament to oversee and perform all things herein contained according to the true intent and meaning hereof in witness thereof I have hereunto set my hand and seal this twenty fifth day of October in the year of our Lord one thousand seven hundred and ninety seven----Signed Sealed and Delivered in the presents of David Cooley Jr., William Hallet.

Penelope X Bennet
Sarah XDolson

This will was transcribed by this writer in December of 2012. Blank spaces represent undecipherable passages. The author notices that the debts mentioned in the will owed by James Jr. and Abraham Harding are dated alternatively on the day of and the day after Isaac's death. This coincidence raises the possibility that the money may have been needed to cover medical or funeral costs.

As in the case of her husband, Sarah makes her mark on the document indicating her inability to sign. Of particular note, Sarah does not mention any step children nor step grandchildren except for James Jr., who is mentioned only in the context of the debt owed.

Sarah leaves her possessions, including notes against James *Dolson* Jr., Richard Graham, and Abraham Harding, to her niece, Sarah Mills (maiden name Foster). The writer has not been able to obtain additional information regarding the paternity of Sarah Foster Mills. Peter Mills, Sarah Foster Mills' husband, is named as one of two executors in Sarah Dolsen's will. Peter Mills was a captain in the Revolution. The immigrant ancestor of this family, George

Mills, was born in Yorkshire, England in 1581 and eventually settled in Jamaica, New York where he died around 1682 (Doherty, 1990). The Mills family, as the Dolsons, had previously been in Dutchess County but relocated to Minisink, now Wawayanda, Orange County (Heidgerd, 1977). A Peter Mills is included in the 1790 census in Minisink. A grave site for Peter Mills is located in Slate Hill Cemetery. The death date on his stone is given as 7 March 1831.

Of particular interest is the fact that a Peter Mills and a Sarah *Dolson* are listed as members of the Old School Baptist Church in Warwick as early as 1766 and also in 1767 (Hollbert, 1953). Foley (1934, p. 733) claims that an Isaac *Dolson* was a member in 1776 and Peter Mills in 1768 (p. 734). F.B. Sampson (2011) provides additional information on Peter Mills and indicates that his association with the Old School Baptist Church continued until at least 1790. This implies additional links between the Dolson branch of Minisink and the Dolsons of Warwick, where the father of Phoebe Benedict Dolson, James Benedict, was the founding pastor of the Old School Baptist Church. Phoebe Benedict married Abraham Dolsen Jr. [probably *Abraham, Theunis, Jan*]. Many years later, James Jr. [*James Sr., Isaac, Theunis, Jan*] would purchase a plot of land from Peter Mills and subsequently, Peter Mills served as a witness to James Jr.'s will. A Peter Mills is noted on Minisink jury lists between 1813 and 1825. No profession is noted. A Peter Mills Jr. is shown on Minisink jury lists in 1798 and 1806 and is identified as a carpenter. There are numerous documented interactions between the Dolson and Mills families as early as 1760 and as late as 1825.

The reader is cautioned however, that, the sightings of a Sarah and an Isaac *Dolson* at the Old School Baptist Church in Warwick might be other Dolson family members by the same first names. For example, Isaac is thought to have a daughter named Sarah, who was born 20 August 1735. There are several sightings of an adult male that appear to substantiate the presence of other Dolson men named Isaac in Orange County beginning in the mid-1770s. These younger Isaacs, possibly were sons of Isaac Sr.'s brothers, Jacob [*Theunis, Jan*] and Abraham [*Theunis, Jan*].

Doherty (1997) may err in speculating that Isaac's second wife was named Sarah Lossing, who was born 17 August 1723, the daughter of Peter Lossing and Cecilia Cook Lossing. The Lossing (*Lassing, Lassen*) family may have been the first European family to settle in Dutchess County, arriving in 1659 (McDermott, 1982). The Lossing farm was located in Oswego near the homes of Johannes, Jacob, and Abraham. As evidence of a relationship between Isaac Sr. and Sarah Lossing, Doherty points to a baptism registered at the Zion Evangelical Lutheran Church in Athens, New York, also referred to as Loonenburg in those times. An *Isaak Dolson* and a Sarah *Lassing* were sponsors for Sara, daughter of John Sanders and Gerdruyt, in January of 1763. The writer speculates that the baptismal sponsor in this record is likely another Isaac, probably the son of Johannes [*Theunis, Jan*] or perhaps the son of Jacob [*Theunis, Jan*]. These men were younger, unmarried, and lived in the vicinity of Poughkeepsie, where the baptism took place. There is no particular reason to believe that the *Isaak* who accompanied Sarah Lossing at Sara Sanders' baptism was Isaac Sr.

A manuscript on the Mills family archived at the Orange County Genealogical Society in Goshen contains a family chart developed by John Bartram Brouard (dated 29 January 1977), which identifies the father of Peter Mills as Samuel Mills of Jamaica, Long Island and Peter's wife as Sally Foster. Sally's mother in turn, was identified as Sara Losee. No supporting documentation is provided.

The evidence to refute Doherty's claim is circumstantial and not definitive. Isaac's second wife could perchance have been a Lossing or a Losee. But there are other possible explanations regarding this Sarah's identity (Horton, No Date):

- Perhaps Sarah was a Foster or a Mills or from another collateral family since the only heir mentioned in Sarah Dolsen's will was her niece, Sara Mills (née Foster). Interestingly, Mary Hussey Dolsen kept a record of the names and birthdates of eleven children from the Mills family born between 1766 and 1790 in her bible. The fact that Mary Hussey Dolsen, along with someone who had access to the bible after Mary's death, recorded there the names and birthdates of all the children of Peter Mills and Sarah Foster Mills suggests extraordinary familial ties between the Dolsen, Hussey, Foster, and Mills families. The list of eleven Mills children in Mary Hussey's bible matches perfectly the list of births contained in the Mills Family manuscript archived at the Orange County Genealogical Society in Goshen.

- Isaac Sr. wed Sarah after Mary Hussey Dolsen's death, probably after leaving Dutchess County, but certainly before 1765 when the names of Isaac and Sarah appear on a deed of sale to James Dolsen Sr. The Sarah in question may well be his second wife from another, yet-to-be-identified, Orange County family.

Sorting Out the Isaacs – Preliminary Findings
One of the more challenging aspects of conducting Dolson family history is the confusion surrounding individuals that carried the same first names and who lived during the same periods of time. Beginning in 1760 there were, at a minimum, three adult Dolsons named Isaac and over the lifetimes of these men, up to half a dozen Isaacs lived in and around Orange, Dutchess, and Ulster counties in New York. Often it is difficult and, in certain instances, absolutely impossible to conclusively identify which of the men named Isaac is associated with any particular event.

The first Isaac to carry the surname of Dolson is the subject of this chapter, the son of Theunis [*Jan*]. As mentioned, this Isaac was born ca. 1707 in Yonkers, Westchester County and died in Dolsentown, Orange County in 1794. This Isaac undoubtedly signed the Pledge and the Articles of Confederation in the Precinct of Goshen in 1775. This Isaac is also shown at Minisink on the Orange County Tax Assessment of 1775 and was enumerated in the first U.S. Census of 1790. Because this Isaac had a son and at least two nephews named Isaac, he is commonly referred to as Isaac Sr. in this volume.

In the fourth generation of the family there were three additional Dolson men named Isaac (Isaak). The second man to carry this name was Isaac, son of Johannes [*Theunis, Jan*], who was baptized at the Fishkill Dutch Reformed Church on 27 May 1739. This Isaac is the man who was a Loyalist and went to the Wyoming Valley in Pennsylvania as early as 1769. He subsequently relocated to Canada with his family at the culmination of the Revolutionary War. Therefore, with the exception of the Loyalist activities described in this volume, the writer concludes that any sightings of an Isaac during and after the Revolutionary War, in and around Minisink and Warwick, Orange County, should not be attributed to Johannes' son.

The third Isaac Dolsen was baptized on 27 May 1739. This Isaac was the son of Jacob [*Theunis, Jan*]. Because this man is reported to have the same baptismal date as Isaac [*Johannes, Theunis, Jan*] and because Jacob and his wife, *Mallie Buys,* are recorded on Fishkill Dutch Reformed Church transcripts as baptizing a child named Johannes on 15 May 1739, this writer considers that perhaps there is an error in the Dutch Reformed Church baptismal records. Another possibility is that this Isaac and/or his brother, Johannes, were not baptized immediately following their births. It is reasonable to believe that some of the sightings of an Isaac in Orange County after 1757, the year in which this Isaac would reach the age of maturity, could be attributed to this man.

The fourth Dolson to be named Isaac [*Isaac Sr., Theunis, Jan*] was born in 1743 and died date unknown. This Isaac Jr. is referred to in his father's will as "*non compos mentis*". The will was written in 1794 when Isaac Jr. would have been fifty-one years of age. This Isaac Jr. is reported to never have married (Ruttenber and Clark, 1881). Given these facts, it is unlikely that during his lifetime, this Isaac would have been considered sufficiently competent to own land, pay taxes, serve in the military, hold public office, or transact any public or legal matters. Therefore, this writer discounts any of sightings of an Isaac or Isaac Jr. in Orange County in the late 1700s and early 1800s as belonging to this individual.

And finally, a fifth Isaac was the son of Abraham Jr. [*Undetermined, Thuenis, Jan*]. Born on 24 May 1777 in Warwick. This Isaac died on 20 July 1838 in the same town (Plimley, 2011). The son of Abraham Jr. and Phoebe Benedict Dolson did not reach the age of maturity until 1798. Without any doubt, this is the man who married Catherine Sly and who was the owner of a problematic grist mill on Wawayanda Creek in Warwick around 1820.

There are several additional sightings of an Isaac Dolsen which this author has been unable to attribute confidently to a specific individual. For example, an Isaac Dolson was given Land Bounty Rights as a result of his participation in the Third Regiment of the Orange County

Militia during the Revolution. Candidates include Isaac [*Johannes, Theunis, Jan*] and Isaac [*Jacob, Theunis, Jan*]. An Isaac Jr. is listed as a member of John Hathorn's Warwick Fourth Regiment. Since the Isaac, son of Johannes, became a Loyalist, this Revolutionary War solder may have been Isaac, son of Jacob.

There is a 30 June 1797 Orange County deed in which an Isaac *Dolson* and wife, Elizabeth Weymer, both of Warwick, transfer ownership of land to Garret Vandervoort of the Town of New Hempstead for the amount of £525. The deed indicates that the land in question was adjacent to the farm of David Miller. The 1790 census shows a David Miller in Warwick between Josiah Holly and Peter Demerest. Of all of the men of maturity named Isaac, who were alive at that time, none are known to have been married to a woman named Elizabeth Weymer. An Orange County tax record of 1798 shows an assessment for an Isaac *Dolson* in the amount of $337.50 for a property in Minisink consisting of 100 acres. Since Isaac Sr. died in 1794, this tax record must pertain to the farm of some other Isaac. Also listed in the same assessment roll are Isaac Sr.'s grandsons, James Jr., Asa, and Samuel, each of whom are taxed on their own farms. In 1799, the owner of the famous Baird Tavern in Warwick obtained a Letter of Administration (C-32) associated with the estate of Isaac Dolsen. The letter is dated 12 August 1799, *"in the 24th year of our independence",* and grants fiscal authorization to Francis Baird regarding debts owed. If this matter is not linked to Isaac Dolsen Sr. [*Theunis, Jan*] who died in Minisink in 1794, then the existence of this document is perplexing. This writer has no corroborating information regarding the death of an Isaac Dolsen, in and around Warwick, just previous to or during the year of 1799. At the present time, the collective knowledge about the men named Isaac is not sufficient enough to be able to fully account for these and several other sightings of an Isaac Dolsen in Orange County in the latter half of the 1700s.

There were several additional Dolson men of later generations who carried the name Isaac. For example, in the fifth generation, an Isaac [*Johannes Jr., Johannes, Theunis, Jan*] was born 7 May 1767 and died on 23 September 1843 at the age of 76 (Plimley, 2011). This man apparently immigrated first to Cayuga and subsequently to Onondaga County, New York. He is buried in Plainville Cemetery, Lysander, Onondaga County. His brother, Peter, was known to be living in the same area (Doherty, 1997). The fact that this Isaac may have lived out his life in New York indicates that perhaps not all of the children and grandchildren of Johannes [*Theunis, Jan*] were active Loyalists and not all relocated to Canada during the Revolution. In fact, Beauchamp (1913) speculates that this Isaac was a member of the 4th L.B. Regiment. Based on this Isaac's age, he may have been a drummer during the Revolution. This man would have been eighteen years old in 1785 and therefore was not yet born or too young to account for most of the sightings of an Isaac in Minisink, Warwick, and other parts of Orange County before that year.

Another Isaac [*Matthew, Johannes, Theunis, Jan*] from the fifth generation was born in 1776 in Detroit (then part of Canada). Sometimes this Isaac is identified as "Junior" with the middle name of Matthew. Eventually this man went to Ontario, Canada with his family when Detroit was ceded to the United States. He married Peragie Dequindre and died in Dover Township, Kent, Ontario, Canada (Plimley, 2011). This Isaac never lived in Dutchess or Orange counties and therefore can be eliminated as one of the Isaacs sighted in these places. There was yet another Isaac Jr. [*Isaac, Johannes, Theunis, Jan*], who was also from the fifth generation and who also was Canadian. He was born in 1777 at Welland, Niagara Falls and died in 1855 (Plimley, 2011). This Isaac Jr. never resided in the United States.

Isaac Dolsen Sr.'s Heritage

In 1795, a deposition was appended to a Dutchess County deed originally recorded on 30 May 1738 (Liber XIII, p. 367) to document an exchange of property from Madame Brett to Jacobus Depeyster to which John Flewwelling and an Isaac *Dolson* were witnesses. The amendment reads:

> **April 7, 1795, by Peter Du Bois, surveyor, 71 years of age, that... he knew Isaac Dolson; that Isaac Dolson was an aged person many years past; that deponent has not heard of Isaac Dolson for a long time and he believes him dead.**

The surveyor's assumption was correct. Isaac Sr. had died eleven months earlier.

Some of Isaac Dolsen's notable accomplishments include:

- Successful farming and milling in Dutchess County to the extent that Isaac Sr. was able to accumulate sufficient wealth to purchase a large tract of land in Orange County. Also, while in Dutchess, Isaac gained valuable civic experience which would serve him well in later life.

- As noted in local histories, Isaac is considered to be one of the earliest and most prominent pioneers of Dutchess and Orange Counties. He was a founder of the community of Dolsentown in the Town of Minisink, now part of Wawayanda.

- With the purchase of 700 acres in the district that would become known as Dolsentown, Isaac Sr. established an estate for his descendants that would endure for several generations. Isaac's farm would serve as the Dolson family homestead for more than a century and his prudent investment would be an important financial asset for many of his descendents. In the case of our branch of the Dolsons, James Sr., James Jr., Frederick, and John C. all benefited directly from the Orange County property.

- Isaac Sr. witnessed the French and Indian War and the American Revolution. During the former conflict, he participated in the construction and management of a blockhouse which served as a refuge during conflicts with local Native American and British Tory troops.

- The evidence indicates that Isaac Sr. signed the Pledge to the Continental Congress and the Articles of Confederation. His son James Sr., as well as his grandson, James Jr., both served in Revolutionary War units. It is abundantly clear that Isaac and his immediate descendants were involved directly in the major sociopolitical events of their time.

- Isaac Sr. experienced several hardships in his life, most notably the death of at least one of his sons, James Sr.; the incapacity of another son, Isaac Jr.; and the loss of his first wife, Mary Hussey Dolsen.

- During Isaac Sr.'s lifetime, he almost certainly heard firsthand from his father, Theunis, of the accounts of the family's immigration from Holland and of the transition of New York from a Dutch to British colony. Undoubtedly, Isaac shared the interesting tales regarding these matters with his son, James Sr., and his other children, as well as with his many grandchildren, including James Jr.

Chapter IV - Fourth Generation

James Dolsen Sr.

[Isaac, Theunis, Jan]

According to his mother's bible and his grave marker in Pine Hill Cemetery, James Dolsen was born on 2 February 1734. His birth took place near Fishkill, Dutchess County, New York. He was named after his maternal grandfather, James Hussey. This James would be the first of many Dolson men to carry James as a first name. As far as can be discerned, James grew up on his parents' farm along Sprout Creek in the South Ward of the Rombout Patent, Dutchess County. When his father purchased a 700-acre farm in Orange County around 1756, the then twenty-two-year-old James moved with his family to the area that later became known as Dolsentown, located in present-day Wawayanda. Two years later, in 1758, James married a young woman named Phebe Meeker.

Phebe Meeker and Her Family
Phebe Meeker is reported to have been born in New Jersey on 1 December 1740. Yet her grave stone in Pine Hill Cemetery notes her year of birth as 1739. The latter date probably is in error. She was the daughter of Benjamin Meeker Jr. (1699-1761). While researchers have not identified the name of Phebe's mother, Phebe herself was named after her paternal grandmother, Phoebe Clark (1681-1755). Genealogists such as Meeker (1973) have traced the Meeker family line back to Albert Meeker born ca. 1594 in England. The immigrant ancestor was William Meeker (1620-1690). William was born at Lemington, Warwickshire, England and died at Elizabethtown, New Jersey.

William Meeker came to the Massachusetts Bay Colony ca 1635 and subsequently in 1646, married Sara Preston, daughter of William Preston and Elizabeth Sales Preston at New Haven, Connecticut. The Preston and Sales families were originally from England. William and his wife, Sarah, eventually resettled in New Jersey. William and Sarah had a son named Benjamin Meeker [Sr.].

Benjamin Meeker Sr. (1649-1707) was a planter and a carpenter and is credited with building the Meeker Homestead at Lyons Farms. His wife was Elizabeth Thompson (1654-ca. 1745) from Long Island. Her father, Thomas Thompson, was an immigrant from the British Isles. The couple married in 1673 and is reported to have had seven male children. One of their sons was named Benjamin Meeker [Jr.].

Benjamin Meeker Jr. (1680-ca. 1750) married Phoebe Clark who was born on 17 August 1681 at South Hampton, Long Island. Benjamin Jr., a blacksmith, died in 1750. Phoebe

Clark Meeker died in 1755 at Elizabethtown, New Jersey. The couple resided in Essex County. In his will dated 11 March 1750, Benjamin Meeker Jr. names the following children: Benjamin, Samuel, Phebe (wife of Nehemiah Ludlum), Ester (wife of Stephen Hindes), and Sara (wife of Isaac Woodruff). Executors were his wife, Phoebe, son-in-law, Stephen Hindes, and son, Samuel. Witnesses listed were John Clarke and David Meeker (Essex County, New Jersey, Liber E, p. 536).

The son named Benjamin born in Elizabethtown was, chronologically, Benjamin Meeker III (1700-1761). The author has not determined the name of his spouse. It is not known when Benjamin III married nor the date that this man relocated to Orange County. Benjamin Meeker III's oldest child was Benjamin Meeker IV, who was born ca. 1730. This means that Benjamin Meeker III's marriage presumptively occurred around 1728 or 1729. One of Benjamin III's daughters, Abigail, married Isaiah Vail and the couple bore a child named Mary on 4 September 1754. The birth is reported to have occurred in Orange County. This means that Benjamin Meeker III and his unidentified spouse were in Orange County, at the very least, some years before the birth of that grandchild.

According to several genealogists, Phebe Meeker Dolson had the following siblings: (1) Benjamin Meeker IV (ca. 1730-1790), (2) Stephen Meeker (ca. 1732-1790), (3) Abigail Meeker Vail (1734-1814), (4) Nathaniel Meeker (1741-1804), (5) Samuel Meeker (1747-1801), and (6) Elizabeth Meeker (1761-1824). This Elizabeth married Annanias Valentine Sr. at the Goshen Presbyterian Church on 15 October 1786.

This writer notes that a gentleman named James Little must have been a neighbor and friend of both the Meekers and the Dolsens. He was a witness to the deed (Liber C) of a sale of a piece of land located in Elizabethtown, New Jersey that was filed in Goshen, Orange County in 1761. A 146-acre farm was sold by Samuel Meeker to John Thompson for the sum of £130. The farm had originally belonged to Samuel's father, Benjamin Meeker III. James Little was also a witness to the will of James Dolsen Sr. in 1778. Benjamin Meeker IV, along with Thomas Gale and Annanias Valentine, was a witness to the will of James Little (Liber B, p. 38) of Brookfield on 3 April 1790. A few months later, Benjamin Meeker IV died during the month of July 1790 (Liber A, p. 111).

A number of contemporary Meekers, such as Phebe's brothers, Nathaniel and Samuel, were living in Wantage Township, Sussex County, New Jersey:

Meeker, Nathaniel of Wantage. 1023S-W. 15 Feb 1804: Filed 5 Sept 1804; Pro. 11 Jun 1806. Son: Jepth. Daughter: Mary Clark. Executors: Son, Jepth Meeker and cousin, Asa Dolsen. Witnesses: John Wisner Jr., Thaddeus Dickson, and John Beall.

In the will, Asa Dolsen [James Sr., Isaac, Theunis, Jan] and Jeptha Meeker, son of Nathaniel, are identified as cousins. Nathaniel and Jeptha are buried in the cemetery of the First Presbyterian Church of Westtown, Orange County.

Samuel Meeker purchased farms in Sussex County as early as 1763. His primary farm in Wantage was maintained until 1792, when Samuel sold off part of the farm. The remainder of the property was bequeathed to his son, Samuel Jr., on 24 August, 1801. The First Presbyterian Church (built in 1803), located at 807 Route 284 in Westtown, is situated on Samuel Meeker's former homestead (New Jersey Herald, 15 July 2018).

Wantage Township is situated along the New Jersey/New York state boundary---not distant from the towns of Sussex, Westown, and New Milford. The author notes that the line between these two states was in dispute over many years and properties once denoted as belonging to Sussex County, New Jersey are now in the jurisdiction of Orange County, New York.

Another of Phebe's brothers, Major Samuel Meeker, a somewhat controversial Revolutionary War figure, is reported to have led a group of militias on the impulsive chase to capture a band of marauding Native American warriors and a squad of Tory militia. In July of 1779, Loyalist and Indian guerillas raided settlements in the Minisink region. Most of the fatalities and abductions took place near the area now known as Port Jervis. There was a call to Minute Men to provide protection. It is said that Major Samuel Meeker, from Sussex County, N.J., created an unstoppable momentum when he mounted his horse, flourished his sword, and said, *"Let the brave men follow me! The cowards may stay behind"* (Privitar, 2012). The pursuit ended in the Battle of Minisink in which the pro-British forces led by Chief Joseph Brant defeated revolutionary troops under the command of Colonel John Hathorn of Warwick, New York (Gardner, 2014). Hathorn's troops suffered a great number of casualties and Major Meeker, himself, was seriously wounded in the battle (Haines, 1889).

Some of the information on the Meeker family mentioned in this section was retrieved from Ancestral Lines of Our Family (*mccurdyfamilylineage.com*) on 22 September 2016. This Website contains information on a number of families and was compiled by Kathy and Larry McCurdy of Okemos, Minnesota. Besides Meeker, another collateral family included in this compilation is Vail. An additional valuable source on the Meeker family is the sketch entitled *The Ancestors of Helen Pegg* developed by Karen M. Simmons and posted at *genealogy.com* (Retrieved on 23 September 2016). There is also a well-written and documented publication entitled *The Meeker Family of Early New Jersey* by Leroy J. Meeker (1973).

Phebe Meeker Dolsen died at the age of 68 in the year 1808. Her death was memorialized by the Goshen Presbyterian Church (Coleman, 1989) as:

March 5, 1808, Phebe Dolson, widow, 68 years old, old age.

Phebe is buried next to her husband, James Sr., in Pine Hill Cemetery, Wawayanda, New York.

The Children of James Sr. and Phebe
James Dolsen Sr. and Phebe Meeker Dolsen are known to have had five children:

1. James Dolsen Jr. was born in 1760. He is the ancestor of this line of the Dolson family. He was named after his father who in turn was named after James Hussey. James Jr. married Eleanor (Elinor) Carpenter and the couple had two children. Their home was located in Minisink.

2. Asa L. Dolsen was born on 3 January 1761. The origin of his first name is not known. Asa Dolsen married Mary Vail and lived on a farm in Minisink.

3. Mary Dolsen was born ca. 1764. Unfortunately, information regarding this Mary is limited. A Mary Dolsen Bloomer died on 10 September 1848 and is buried at Fallsburg Neversink Cemetery in Neversink, New York (*www.findagrave.com*). Additional details on this Mary Dolsen are contained in the next chapter.

4. Abigail Dolson was born ca. 1765. She was named after her maternal aunt, Abigail Meeker Vail. Nothing more is known about Abigail's life. She was living in February of 1778 as she is mentioned in her father's will.

5. Samuel Dolsen was born on 14 February 1766 and lived up to the age of ninety-four (Ruttenber and Clark, 1881). He was almost certainly named after his famous maternal uncle, Samuel Meeker. Samuel Dolsen married Fanny Vail and maintained a farm on the Dolsen tract in Dolsentown.

All of the children listed above, as well as his wife Phebe, are mentioned in James Sr.'s will written in 1778. James Jr., Asa, and Samuel were all successful farmers in and around Dolsentown. James Jr. is the ancestor in this branch of the family and therefore is the primary subject of the next chapter. That chapter also contains additional details regarding James Jr.'s brothers: Asa and Samuel.

James Sr. James Jr. and Others
According to his grave marker at Pine Hill Cemetery, James Sr. died on 23 February 1778 at the age of forty-four. Reamy and Reamy (2003) report that James Sr. was serving in a Revolutionary War regiment at the time of his death. His military obligation at West Point was assumed by his eighteen-year-old son, James Jr. (Ruttenber and Clark, 1881).

In this volume, the writer assumes that observations of a James Dolsen between 1733 and 1778 are attributable to James Sr. [*Isaac, Theunis, Jan*] and references after 1778, up to and including 1825, the year of his death, pertain to James Jr. [*James Sr., Isaac, Theunis, Jan*] and, perhaps in some cases, to one or the other of two contemporary Dolsen men, described as follows, also named James.

1. James Benedict Dolsen (1770-1852) was the son of Abraham Jr. [*Undetermined, Theunis, Jan*] and Phoebe Benedict Dolsen. This James was born and lived out his life in Warwick, New York. James Benedict Dolsen reached the age of majority (eighteen) in 1788. Additional information on this man and the Dolson line of Warwick is contained in the Appendix to this volume.

2. James Dolsen, was a son of Asa [*James Sr., Isaac, Theunis, Jan*]. This James was born on 11 November 1785 and would have reached the age of majority in 1803. It appears that this James resided in the Minisink area most of his life. He married Mary Van Scoy. He was still living in 1860 as he was enumerated as living with three granddaughters, Fanny, Celia, and Clara, in the census taken in that year.

The reader is alerted to the fact that some of the Orange County sightings of a James Dolsen between 1788 and 1825 could possibly be confusions between the James Jr. of this branch and his two cousins noted above.

Siblings of James Sr.

According to Plimley (2011) and Mary Hussey Dolsen's bible, James Sr. was the eldest child of Isaac Dolsen and Mary Hussey Dolsen. James Sr. had six siblings:

1. Sarah Dolsen, born on 20 August 1735. Nothing is known about Sarah. She may have died young. She was not mentioned in her father's will written in 1778. Sarah most likely was named after her paternal grandmother, Sarah Vermilyea Dolsen.

2. Mary Dolsen was baptized on 12 December 1738. As in the case of Sarah, nothing more is known about Mary. It is possible that she died young. The writer has found no further record regarding this person. Mary of course was named after her mother, Mary Hussey Dolsen.

3. Isaac Dolsen Jr. was baptized on 27 November 1743. Isaac was named after his father. This Isaac is reported to be mentally challenged and in his father's will, Isaac Sr. directs his executors, to be the caretakers of Isaac Jr. There are a number of reports that this Isaac Jr. did not marry. In alignment with this evidence, this writer has adopted the theory that Isaac Jr. suffered from a severe mental disability and hence was not sufficiently

competent to marry, own land, serve in the military, or sign social and legal documents. Therefore, the writer does not believe that any of the sightings of an Isaac Jr. in the latter half of the 1700s and the early decades of the 1800s pertain to this Isaac Jr. Such sightings are more likely attributable to one of Isaac Jr.'s cousins. The writer has not been able to determine when Isaac Jr. died but it may have been before the death of his stepmother, Sarah, in 1802 and undoubtedly before the death of his nephew, James Jr., in 1825. James Jr. had been appointed as one of Isaac Jr.'s caretakers. The wills of his stepmother and his nephew contain no mention of this Isaac Jr.

4. Margaret Dolsen was born on 23 February 1744 or 1745. Margaret married James Gardner. James Gardner was born in 1736 at Newburgh, Orange County, New York (Elizabeth Horton Notes, No Date, Orange County Genealogical Society). His parents were John Gardner and Christina Finch Gardner. James is listed on tax assessments as a farmer in Minisink, Orange County. James Gardner and Margaret Dolsen Gardner had several children: Abraham, Jemel Nafus, James, Asa, and Fanny. Margaret Dolsen Gardner died on 1 January 1810 at the age of sixty at Danby. Subsequently James Gardner remarried. He died on 1 February 1829 at the age of ninety-one years (Horton, No Date).

5. Altje Dolsen was born on 14 May 1750 and died in 1802 in Deer Park, Orange County. According to Plimley (2011), Altje (also referred to as *Alche, Aliha,* and *Alcha*) married Abraham Harding. Abraham Harding is noted as a son-in-law and as an executor in James Sr.'s will. According to Ruttenber and Clark (1881), Abraham Harding was one of the early settlers of Greenville, Orange County. Also noted as an early settler of Greenville was Eusebius Austin.

Early Orange County Historians

An extensive amount of information that is available on the Dolsen family between 1750 and 1825 derives from accounts of Orange County history written in the second half of the nineteenth century. In general, it appears that the regional historians often relied heavily on information gathered from conversations with pioneers or through interviews with individuals who were acquainted with the pioneers.

The nature of historical research during this period was commonly less standardized and, at times, less rigorous than might be normal for more modern works. True, the historians would consult primary documents and records. Additionally, they would interview individuals who shared first-hand accounts. Nonetheless, often hearsay, legends, and tales would creep into the narratives. On occasion, this writer senses that a few of the researchers employed literary license to fill in gaps that might be encountered in the historical record or to sensationalize events as a way of generating reader interest.

The earliest, exhaustive history of Orange County was written by Samuel Eager in 1846. A number of similar volumes followed including Stickney (1867), Ruttenber and Clark (1881), Headley (1908), and later Reamy and Reamy (2003, Revised).

Many of these historians addressed the same topics and events and when they did, it is quite clear that instead of relying on primary sources, they sometimes resorted to borrowing heavily from each other's works. The phrasing and word choices are just too coincidental to be original. This of course means that if an earlier historian made a mistake, the mistake was then picked up and repeated in the works of later historians. In the Dolson family genealogy, there are several instances where one historian identifies an error or omission in the work of another researcher and corrects or clarifies the record; however, just as often, inaccuracies have gone undetected, unaddressed, and unfortunately, reiterated.

Sightings of James Sr.
Even though James Sr. lived a mere forty-four years, markedly fewer years than any other Dolsen in this branch of the family, there are numerous mentions of this individual in Orange County records.

In January of 1756, James Dolsen is noted as a volunteer scout in the Wallkills under the command of British General, Sir William Johnson, during the French and Indian War.

Various records indicate that James Sr. was an owner of slaves and in at least one instance, in 1763, an overseer of an indentured servant. Referencing an original document on file at the archives of the New York Historical Society, Figliomeni (1997) states the following:

> ***Ester Spragg probably was not startled when her parents negotiated a five-year contract for her to be an apprentice "to learn the art of housekeeper." The indenture was made with James and Phebe Dolson (ca. 1763), fellow residents in the Wallkill region. Families frequently arranged for their daughters to earn their keep at household duties in a neighbor's home, so John and Hana Spragg felt that this arrangement was suitable and proper. The terms stipulated that the Dolsons were to give the Spraggs a cow in exchange for their daughter's services at the onset of the five-year period. Ester was bound to gladly obey their commands, to do them no damage, nor waste their goods, nor contract matrimony. In all, she agreed "to behave herself as a garl (sic) ought to do." The Dolsons promised to provide Ester with sufficient meat, drink, apparel, washing, and lodging. At the close of her five-year's service she***

was to receive a new freedom suit, a colored gown, a home-spun suit, and a young cow, too". (p. 146).

In October of 1765, James Sr. obtained a small farm of twenty-five acres from his father Isaac. The farm adjoined his father's property and was purchased at the bargain price of just £25. From this time forward, James Sr. would be an independent farmer in Minisink. Also, in 1765, on May to be precise, James Sr. was witness to a bond administered by attorney, William Wickham. Also noted in the matter was Eliphalet Lyon.

On 4 April 1770, James Dolsen of Wallkill signed a note to borrow the amount of £120 from Henry David, also of Wallkill in Orange County. Payment on the loan was to be made in the year 1772.

On 24 May 1775 James Dolsen Sr. signed the Articles of Association at Goshen along with his father, Isaac Sr. Other persons signing include an Isaac Jr., perhaps Isaac Sr.'s son but more likely Isaac [*Jacob, Theunis, Jan*], as well as other men associated with the Dolsens such as Benjamin Meeker [III], Gilbert Bradner, Peter Mills, James Gardner, Abraham Harding, and John Carpenter (*Calendar of historical manuscripts…*, 1868). Less than a month later, on 8 June 1775, Ruttenber and Clark (1881) note that a James *Dollen* and an Isaac *Dollen* were signers of the Pledge at Goshen.

A 1775 tax assessment record of Orange County residents contains the following recognizable names: James *Dolson* [Sr.], his father, Isaac Dolsen, and his brothers-in law, Abraham Harding and James Gardner. All of these individuals were assessed as landowners in District 10, the Dolsentown Neighborhood.

On 14 September 1775, James *Dolson*, with the rank of Lieutenant, is listed in Colonel Allison's Goshen Regiment, Westside of Wallkill Company of the New York Militia under Captain Gilbert Bradner. As early as 1775, James Sr. is reported to have been a Captain in the same company. Horton (No Date) notes that James Sr. was serving in the Revolutionary War at the time of his death on 23 February 1778.

In 1775, James Sr.'s cousins, Abraham *Dolson* Jr., Lieutenant, and *Matthew Dolson*, Ensign, were serving in Colonel Hathorn's Regiment in the Pond Company under Captain Henry Wisner Jr. (Ruttenber and Clark, 1881). The Pond Company consisted primarily of men from the Florida and Warwick areas of Orange County. According to Hull (2002), through the winter months, the Warwick militia drilled four hours each week in the warm attic of Francis Baird's Tavern. The heel marks of the militiamen's boots may still be seen in the wooden floorboards.

In the same year, James *Dolson* was serving as a Commissioner for the Wawayanda Patent. On 21 August 1775, the following notice appeared in the *New York Gazette* and the *New York Weekly Mercury*:

Whereas William Wickham and William Beekman did make, and with their hands subscribe, a certain writing, bearing date the ninth day of February, in the year of our Lord one thousand seven hundred and seventy five, and published the same twelve weeks successively in Hugh Gain's paper entitled, The New York Gazetteer, or the Connecticut, Hudson's River, New Jersey and Quebec Weekly Advertiser; two of the public newspapers of this colony. Which said writing was and is directed by the tenor thereof, to all persons interested in the land therein mentioned; containing 3000 acres; and recites that whereas Abraham Hasbrook, Jacobus Bruyn, and Richard Edsall, pursuant to law of the colony of New York, did divide a certain tract of land, commonly called the Wawayanda Patent, in the count of Orange. And whereas the said Commissioners did set apart to the persons holding the undivided right of the town of Goshen (commonly called the Goshen town rights) a certain tract of land of about 3000 acres, situate in the said patent, on the west side of the drowned lands and bounded as follows: Beginning at a heap of stones in the line of the Jersey claim, six miles from the Minisinck mountains; thence fourth 54 degrees west, 64 chains, to a white oak tree marked; thence north 45 degrees and 15 minutes west, 454 chains, to a traverse line run along the foot of said mountains; thence along the said line north-easterly, as it runs to the aforesaid Jersey claim; thence fourth 45 degrees and 15 minutes, 480 chains, to the place of the beginning; containing 3000 acres of land, as by the proceedings of the said Commissioners, filed in the Secretary's Office of the said colony and in the Clerk's Office of the said county of Orange, will fully appear. And did thereby give notice that Joshua Davis, Elnathan Corey, and James Dolson all of the precinct of Goshen, persons not interested in the said lands were appointed Commissioners to make partition thereof; and that the said Commissioners would meet on Monday the 15th day of May last at the home of Samuel Gale, in the town of Goshen, in the said county of Orange, inn-keeper, to proceed to the partition of the said land, and did then and there require all persons interested therein to attend then and there for that purpose by themselves or by their attorneys; Now therefore we the said Joshua Davis, Elnathan Corey, and James Dolson, Commissioners so appointed as aforesaid, do hereby dignify said appointment and do give notice that we will meet on Tuesday, the tenth day of October next, at the house of the said Samuel Gale, in Goshen aforesaid, to proceed on the said partition; and we desire all persons concerned to attend accordingly. In the mean time, in order to prevent as much as possible any doubts or difficulties that may arise from a chain of conveyances, it is requested of the claimants to the premises that they will be pleased to produce their title deeds to William Beekman in New York or to David Everitt, Henry Wisner, and Peter Closes in Goshen to the end, that by examining and comparing them, the true proportions may be known and their just proportions adjusted accordingly.

Given under our Hands at Goshen, the ninth day of August, Anno Domini, 1775

> *JOSHUA DAVIS,*
> *ELNATHAN COREY,*
> *JAMES DOLSON*

Finally, James Dolsen is included, along with brothers, Asa and Samuel, in an 1800 Assessment Roll of Real and Personal Estates for Minisink. His real property is valued at $4,375 and his personal property at $340. This was one of the largest real property evaluations in the county.

James Sr.'s Will

James Dolsen Sr. left a will dated 8 February 1778 (Liber 33, p. 110). Dying at the young age of forty-four, while serving as a Minute Man, suggests that James Sr. may have succumbed to a military-related illness or injury. His last testament reads as follows:

In the name of God, Amen. I, James Dolsen, of Goshen, in the County of Orange and in the State of New York being weak of body, but of a sound and disposing mind and memory (blessed by god for it), do this eighth day February in the year of our lord one thousand and seven hundred and seventy eight make and publish this my last will and testament in manner and form as followeth, Vizt., First, it is my will that all my just debts and funeral charges be paid. Then it is my will also that my family should keep together and carry on business agreeable to the direction of my executors hereafter mentioned, Until my son James arrives to the age of twenty one years, then I give and devise to my son James and his heirs and assigns for ever my dwelling house with all the buildings and the farm I now dwell on, he paying their share to my other two sons, Vizt., Asa and Samuel each the sum of two hundred pounds lawful money of the state of New York as soon as they shall severally arrive to the age of twenty one years. But if any of my said sons should die without leaving lawful issue of his or their bodies, then the share of him or them so happening to die to be equally divided among the surviving sons. Item, also I give and bequeath to my said son James the horse he calls his own. Item, also I give and bequeath to my son Asa a pair of steers that he calls his own. Item, I give and bequeath to my son Samuel the privilege of raising a pair of steers on the farm, and the remainder of my personal estate I would dispose of in the following manner. Vizt., I give and bequeath to my well beloved wife Phebe for ever my grey mare her saddle and one cow and also one third part of all the remainder of my cattle, goods furniture and effects whatsoever. Item, also I give and bequeath to my said loving wife the use of my dwelling and farm for the benefit of the family until my said son James comes to the age of twenty one years and after my said son arrives to agent give and bequeath to my said wife the privilege of living in the house or taking a room to herself is she desires it and likewise the privilege of keeping her mare and two cows while she continues my widow and no longer. Item, it is my will also that the remaining two thirds of my personal estate be equally divided between my two daughters Mary and Abigail share and share alike and if either of my said daughters should die without leaving lawful issue then the share of her so dying to fall to the surviving daughter. Item, it is my will also that a prudent care be taken that the shares of the younger children be put out to use as soon as the circumstances of the family will admit that it may be gaining until they come to age and lastly I do constitute and appoint my loving brothers-in-law Isaiah Veal [Vail] and Abraham Harding sole executors of this my will to see the same performed according to my intent and meaning in witness where I the said James Dolson have to this my last will and testament set my hand and seal the day and year within written.

James Dolsen
[In his own signature]

Noted in the will are his wife, Phebe; sons James, Asa, and Samuel; and daughters Mary and Abigail. The document contains the signatures of the following witnesses: Henry White, Benjamin Whitaker, and James Little. Taxation records indicate that these men were neighbors. There is an annotation to the will showing that it was proved by Benjamin Sutten Jr., Surrogate for the County of Orange. James Little, a witness, and Isaiah Vail and Abraham Harding, executors, appeared before the surrogate.

Subsequent to James Sr.'s death, the 1779-1787 Tax Assessment Rolls for Orange County list Phebe Dolsen on two separate occasions: initially assessed at £28 for real property and £12 for personal property and secondly, £141 for real property and £202 for personal property.

Vail Family Connections
Isaiah Vail was married to Abigail Meeker, Phebe Meeker Dolsen's sister. According to one account (Vail, 1902), the Vail family came early to America from England and the immigrant ancestor, Jeremiah Vail, settled in Southold, Long Island by 1639. Just after 1651, Jeremiah Vail took a position on the farm of Lyon Gardiner in South Hampton, Long Island. Thus, the Vail, Gardner, and Meeker families appear to have been acquainted many years before reconnecting in Orange County.

Isaiah Vail was born on Thursday, 27 September 1731 in either Long Island or possibly in Orange County, depending on the date when his parents relocated to Orange County. Isaiah was the son of Josiah Vail and Patience Corwin Vail (Vail, 1902). Isaiah Vail married Abigail Meeker, daughter of Benjamin Meeker III, in Goshen. Vail served on the side of the Colonies in the Revolutionary War as a Capitan in the Second Regiment of Ulster County under the command by Colonel James McClaghery. He was present at the capture of Fort Montgomery (Stickney, 1867). The 1800 U.S. Census includes the enumeration of Isaiah Vail as a resident of Wallkill, Orange County. Isaiah made his will on 31 May 1806 at the Town of Wallkill. He mentions his wife Abigail, his daughters: Phebe Smith, Irena Mapes, Abigail Mills, Mary Dolsen [wife of Asa Dolsen], and one granddaughter, Abigail Carpenter. He also mentions his sons: George Washington, Obadiah, Josiah, Isaiah, John, and Samuel Vail, as well as two grandsons.

Two Vail family members would marry Dolsons in future generations. Asa Dolsen, James Sr.'s son, married Mary Vail, daughter of Isaiah and Abigail. Isaiah's and Abigail's son, Obadiah (1752-1836), married Mary Cory and they had a daughter, Fanny Vail, who in turn married another of James Sr.'s sons, Samuel Dolsen, on 6 October 1793.

Major Events in James Sr.'s Life
Some of the key happenings in the life of James Dolsen Sr. include:

- James Sr. was twenty-three years of age at the time the Dolsens relocated from Dutchess to Orange County around 1756.
- He married in 1758, at twenty-five years of age. His first child, James Jr., was born when James Sr. was twenty-seven. James Jr. is the ancestor in this line of the Dolson family and the subject of the next chapter.
- James Sr. was approximately thirty-three years old when his grandfather, Theunis, died in 1766. If during his later years, Theunis was in good health and of clear mind, he must have shared with James Sr. many family stories regarding Jan Gerritzen de Vries van Dalsen's immigration to New Amsterdam from Holland, as well as Theunis' own adventures in New Harlem, Westchester County and Dutchess County.
- All of the evidence supports the characterization that James Sr. was a successful farmer and that he and his sons, James Jr., Asa, and Samuel, maintained and perhaps even expanded upon the tract purchased by his father, Isaac Dolsen.
- James Sr. seems to have had a particularly close relationship with his brother-in-law, Abraham Harding (husband of his sister, Altje), as well as with Isaiah Vail, father of Mary Vail, the wife of James Sr.'s son, Asa.
- James Sr., along with his wife Phebe, is buried at Pine Hill Cemetery in Wawayanda. His grave stone appears to be one of the oldest original markers in this burying ground. After her husband's death, Phebe would live on as his widow for another nineteen years.

- To date, James Sr. holds the unenviable record in this branch of the Dolsons of dying at the youngest age, forty-four years. His death occurred approximately fifteen years before that of his father, Isaac. He is the only Dolson man in this line of the family to die before his father. Although there are unconfirmed reports that James Sr. died of an illness, no documentation has been discovered which divulges the exact cause of his demise. Horton (No Date), as well as other genealogists, has noted that James Sr. died during his Revolutionary War service.
- Had he not died young, it appears that James Sr. was destined for civic prominence. He served as a Revolutionary War officer and as a county commissioner. In addition, he held several posts in the Minisink Township.

Chapter V - Fifth Generation

James Dolsen Jr.

[James Sr., Isaac, Theunis, Jan]

While neither birth nor baptismal documentation for James Dolsen Jr. has been located, his burial stone chronicles his year of birth as 1760. He was the first Dolson in this line of the family to be born on the property at Dolsentown. James Jr. appears to have spent his entire life tending to his farm and nearby properties in the Minisink area of Orange County, New York. His death occurred in 1825.

James Jr.'s Early Years
According to Ruttenber and Clark (1889) and other Orange County historians (e.g., Reamy and Reamy, 2003), James Jr. assumed his father's place in the Revolutionary War at West Point when James Sr. died in 1778. James Jr. would have been only eighteen years old at the time. His father had been a member of the West Side of Wallkill Company of the Goshen Regiment as early as 14 September 1775. Records indicate that James Jr. continued to serve in the same unit.

The West Side of Wallkill Company was part of the regiment that participated in the famous Battle of Minisink on 22 July of 1779. British Tories and their Indian warrior allies had made several raids into the Neversink Valley. After an incursion on 19 July resulted in a massacre of settlers, Minutemen from throughout Orange County responded to the alarm. The rebel troops were under the command of Colonel John Hathorn of Warwick. As colonel of the 4th Orange County Militia Regiment, Hathorn decided to send several companies to pursue the Tories. At Goshen, three companies consisting of 120 men from the local militia gathered and were ordered to shadow the enemy. Eventually the colonial troops caught up to the Loyalists and Native Americans along the Delaware River at Minisink Ford in Sullivan County. The Minutemen suffered a bloody defeat with at least forty-five killed and many more wounded. A few days after the battle, on 27 July 1779, Colonel Hathorn submitted his report to General Washington (Twichell, 1912).

While no documentation conclusively confirms their participation, it is possible that James Jr., a Lieutenant, was involved in this battle as well as perhaps two of his cousins, Abraham Dolsen Jr., Captain, and Matthew Dolsen, Ensign, both of whom were serving in the Pond Company under Captain Henry Wisner at the time. The West Side of Wallkill and Pond companies were under the command of Colonel Hathorn. It is reported that some men from these two companies fought at Minisink (Hendrickson, Inners, and Osborne, 2010). Also documented is the fact that contingents under Hathorn took the direct route from Goshen through Greenville and troops under Lieutenant Colonel Tusten came by way of the Old Minisink Road which ran from Goshen through Dolsentown (*Goshen Independent Republican,* 26 February 1904). With both locations near the properties of Isaac Dolsen and James Dolsen Jr., there is little doubt that the Dolsons were aware of circumstances. It is also known that approximately one hundred men from Hathorn's regiment had concurrently been assigned to guard British prisoners at Stony Point and additional militia took up support positions (e.g. guarding the horses and supplies) for the Minisink Battle but did not participate in the actual fighting (Clark, 1972). A John Carpenter, possibly a distant relative of Eleanor Carpenter Dolson, is reported to have died in this battle (*The Port Jervis Evening Gazette,* 10 May 1879).

Also participating in the Battle of Minisink were Pawling's Levies and other troops from Ulster County such as the Second Regiment of Ulster Militia (Hendrickson, Inners, and Osborne, 2010). Theunis Dolsen II, Jacob Dolsen II, and two John Dolsens were enlisted in these units. All of these Ulster Dolsons were descendants of Jacob Dolsen [*Theunis, Jan*].

Several years later, James Jr. is noted as hosting a mid-day meal for the officers of an expeditionary force led by Major General John Sullivan and Brigadier General James Clinton. Initiated in 1779, the purpose of the expedition was to mitigate the belligerent activities of British Tories and their Iroquois (Cayugas, Onondagas, and Senecas) allies in New York. The excerpt below comes from a diary kept by an ensign named John Barr. Dates refer to the period of 26-27 July 1782:

Friday 26th Set off from Pien Pack in Company with my waiter Timothy Howe and James Williams for to Join Capt Prentice Bowen's Company at Orange Town. Refreshed at William Roosa's on Shangum Mountain distance 4 miles coming over a very Rocky Mountain and Barren Land.

Friday 26th Thence proceeding through a very rough and Stonny Country to Mr. James Dolson's in Wallkill distance 9 Miles where we dined, thence throug[h] a pretty good Part of the Country to Mr. John Kenedy's in Florida distance 10 Miles total march 23 Miles and Expenses 3/6.

Saturday 27th from Mr. Kenedy's to Capt Minthorn's [Captain John Minthorn, 4th Regiment of Orange county militia, New York] *in Warwick through a fine Country distance 7 Miles, where we Eat Breakfast, thence over a very Steep Mountain to Mr. Macey's in the Bound of Sterling distance 5 miles where we refreshed—thence to Mr. Staggs at Sterling distance 5 miles where we Eat Dinner, thence to Mrs. Sidman's in the Clove where we Refreshed Passing Sterling Iron Works in 3 Places—from Staggs to Sidman's 7 Miles thence to*

Squire John Suffrans distance 3 Miles in New Antrim where we Lodged distance to Day 27 Miles Expences 10/6 (Talmadge, 1932).

The places mentioned as visited on 27 July 1782 are all locations in and around Warwick.

Other Dolsons in the Revolutionary War

Revolutionary War records confirm the participation of a number of Dolson men as members of colonial units fighting against the British. The service record of James Jr. has been depicted in the previous section of this chapter. A description of the participation of Dolson men from Warwick (Abraham Sr., Abraham Jr., and Isaac Jr.) is contained in the Appendix to this volume. In Chapter III, substantial details were provided regarding the colorful exploits of members of the Loyalist branch of the Dolson family, Johannes Dolsen [*Theunis, Jan*], including a narrative of the intrepid acts of Johannes' sons, Peter, Isaac, and Matthew. This section provides a summary of the participation of Dolson men belonging to the lineage of Jacob Dolsen [*Theunis, Jan*] and an unidentified individual or individuals referred to alternatively as Peter Dolsen and Peter *Dolson*.

In reviewing Revolutionary War rosters, it appears that it was common for individuals to enlist for multiple short term stretches and overtime, often to provide service in a variety of units. Much of the military data were taken from Fernow (1887) but also consulted was *New York in the Revolution as Colony and State* (1904). Another valuable resource has been the *Public Papers of George Clinton, First Governor of New York, 1777-1795* (1973).

Listed on the Land Bounty Rights roster for the Third Orange County Regiment is an Isaac *Dolson*. Many of the names of the men on this list are recognizable as being from Minisink (Fernow, 1887). This Isaac may have been a son of Jacob [*Jacob, Theunis, Jan*]. Isaac's son, Isaac Jr. is noted as having a severe mental disability. If he did serve in the militia it probably would have been in the capacity of a drummer or fifer. The following additional Dolson men are noted as eligible for Land Bounty Rights as a result of service in the Revolutionary War:

- A Jacob [Mier] *Dolson* [*Jacob, Theunis, Jan*] and a John Dolson [*Jacob Mier, Jacob, Theunis, Jan*] are documented as Levies, members of Pawling's Regiment of Ulster County.
- A John Dolson [*Theunis II, Jacob, Theunis I, Jan*], a Theunis *Dolson* [*Jacob, Theunis I, Jan*] and a Jacob Dolson [*Jacob, Theunis I, Jan*] are all enumerated with the Ulster County Third Regiment under Captains Uriah Drake and William Sammel (*New York in the Revolution as Colony and State* (1904). Fernow (1887) also shows these men serving under officers Johnson/Ostrander, Hays/Sickles, and Hays/Hogencamp.
- In addition, a John *Dolson* is found on the roster of the Fourth Ulster Regiment and a *Jacobus Van Dolson* in units under Hays/Sickles and also under Hays/Hogencamp.

- In terms of Land Bounty Rights for members of the Fourth Regiment of Ulster County, known as the Newburg companies, these same men are listed as John *Dolson*, Jacob Mier *Dolson*, *Tunes Dolson,* and *Tunis Dalson*. Interestingly, in some of the sightings of a *Jacobus* Dolsen, the individual in question is identified as a drummer. *Tunis Dalson* is shown as a private in Captain Arthur Smith's Newburgh Company on 24 April 1779. A John Dolson is identified as a private in Captain Jacob Conklin's Newburgh Company on 4 May 1778 (Barratt, 1928).

The military service records of two men named John Dolsen may be entangled. The elder of the two Johns was the son of Jacob [*Theunis, Jan*] who was baptized as Johannes on 15 May 1737. This man would have been thirty-nine years of age in 1776. He is probably the John *Dolson* who served in the Ulster Regiments. After the Revolution, he and his family resided in the Marlboro and Newburgh areas and later in Hackensack. In 1785, this John is noted as paying a tax assessment for highway labor in Newburgh (Ruttenbur, 1885). This John was married to Sarah Causbin and died in 1784 (Plimley, 2011). Ron Plimley is attached to this branch of the Dolson family (Plimely, 2011). The other John [*Theunis II, Jacob, Theunis I, Jan*] was born ca. 1754 and served in both the Revolutionary War and the War of 1812. According to his pension application (submitted 4 September 1832); he was assigned to a considerable number of units in Pennsylvania and New York and was involved in some of the most well-known events of the Revolution, including the Battle of Trenton where Washington's troops crossed the Delaware River on Christmas night of 1776. This John H. *Dolson*, the name used by several family researchers (e.g., Smith, Ian. Descendants of John H. Dolson posted at *FamilyTreeMaker.com*, retrieved on 7 October 2016), is also credited with participation in the Siege of Fort Meigs in May of 1813. In that battle, although Minutemen defenders persevered against an enemy onslaught, they concurrently suffered nearly a thousand casualties; approximately ten times that of the British and Indian forces. After the Revolution, this John relocated to Big Flats, near present-day Elmira, in Chemung County, New York with his father Theunis II. John was a soldier, farmer, inn keeper and tavern owner at Mud Creek, Bath, New York. Eventually, he and his family resettled near Battle Creek, Michigan Territory, where he died in April of 1836.

An interesting entry found in the *Public Papers of George Clinton, First Governor of New York, 1777-1795* (Volume VI, p. 588, 1973) is the case of a John *Dolson* who, on 22 January 1781, during a court martial proceeding at Poughkeepsie, pleaded guilty of dissertation. He was fined the sum of one pound and sixteen shillings. If unable pay, he was to serve an additional twenty days of military service. At the time of this incident, this John was in Captain Abraham Fort's Company, Colonel John Frear's Regiment, and General Jacobus Swartout's Ulster Militia (Public Papers of George Clinton, First Governor of New York. No. 3499). Noted from the court martial transcripts, many men were charged with the same offense, indicating that it was a common occurrence. Apparently, John's offense was his first or short lived since many of the other men charged with desertion were fined larger sums of money. Since the detailed pension application of John [*Theunis II, Jacob, Theunis, Jan*], does not mention any of these commanding officers, this writer concludes that the man cited in the court martial is most likely John [*Jacob, Theunis, Jan*] or possibly another unidentified John Dolson.

A noteworthy number of Revolutionary War records between 1776 and 1806 identify a Peter Dolsen as serving in various units, in particular the First and Third New York City Regiments. On 21 November 1776, a Peter *Dolson* was listed as an Ensign in Abraham Riker's First Company under the command of the Second Battalion's Colonel Phillip Van Courtlandt. These units were part of George Clinton's Brigade. There is also a Peter *Dolson* who was assigned to the Third New York Regiment under Colonel Rudolphus Ritzema (absent) in September of 1776. This Peter was a sergeant and was an author of an Orderly Book covering the period of 20 July to 12 September 1776. Entries in the book consist primarily of orders from headquarters and orders transmitted within Colonel Ritzema's Regiment. This was an interesting period as Ritzema, a Dutch immigrant, was court martialed on petty charges. He eventually became frustrated with superiors and deserted to the British. In 1777, an Ensign Peter Dolson was attached to the First Battalion in Captain Benjamin Pelton's Company (*Calendar of Historical Manuscripts, Relating to the War of the Revolution, In the Office of the Secretary of State, Albany, N.Y. Vol. I-II*, 1868). This writer has not identified any of the Dolson soldiers named Peter. There is a likelihood that the Peter serving in the First and Third New York Regiments was from New York City and therefore not a member of our Dolson family. There is also a possibility that one or more of the Peter Dolsen sightings may be linked to a Peter, who may be a yet-to-be-placed son or grandson of Jacob [*Theunis, Jan*]. This belief stems from the fact that both Johannes [*Theunis, Jan*] and his brother, Jacob, married sisters Elizabeth and Mary Buys respectively. These sisters had both a brother and an uncle named Peter. Out of respect for his in-laws, Johannes Dolsen named a son Peter, who was a Loyalist and after being imprisoned at Goshen, was killed in an attempt to escape from the local jail. If Jacob also had a son named Peter, he could be perchance one of the men named Peter discussed in this paragraph.

Copies of various Revolutionary War returns from the National Archives provide additional details on several of the Dolson soldiers mentioned previously in this section:

- John *Dolson*: 14 years old in August of 1776 (calculated birth of 1762 or 1763). Fifer in Levi Pawling's Regiment of the New York Militia, Ulster County, serving under Captain Jacob Conklin. A yeoman (a freeman, farmer, or laborer) of fair complexion with red hair. Based on his birth year, this young fifer may have been John Dolson [born 15 June 1764 according to Plimley (2011)], the son of Jacob Mier *Dolson* [*Jacob, Theunis, Jan*]. Fernow (1887) notes that both a *Jacobus Van Dolson* and a drummer named John *Dolson*, served together for periods of time during the Revolution under the command of Pawling and later under Hays/Hogencamp.

- Theunis *Dolson* [II]: age 41 in 1776 (born in 1735), cordwainer (a cobbler or shoemaker). Born in Dutchess County. 5 foot 10 inches, fair complexion, with brown hair and grey eyes. This man was undoubtedly Theunis II [*Jacob, Theunis I, Jan*].

- An interesting item related to a collateral family is that of Henry Bush, who, on the 14 November of 1780, married Catharine Dolson, daughter of Theunis Dolson II [*Jacob, Theunis I, Jan*]. Catharine was baptized at the Zion Evangelical Lutheran Church in Loonenburg on 22 November 1757. Henry was a descendent of Hendrick Abrachtson Busch who arrived to New Amsterdam on the ship *Faith* in 1658 from Leyden in the Netherlands. The younger Henry was a Revolutionary War soldier from Easton, PA. He enlisted on 9 July 1776 at the extremely early age of fifteen and a half (Winslow, 1978). During the winter of 1777, his company lost a battle at Fort Washington to Hessian troops and he was taken prisoner by the British. After a few months, he escaped and made his way home to Easton. In April of 1778, Henry enlisted in the Legion of General Casimir Pulaski as a cavalry trooper. He experienced various skirmishes and toward the end of his service, his legion was assigned to the Minisink area to defend against the incursions of Native Americans and Tories assigned to Colonel Joseph Brant. In 1779 Henry was discharged and he returned to Easton where he married Catharine Dolson. By the early 1790s, the couple had joined Catherine's father and brother, Theunis and John respectively, in Chemung, Montgomery County along Mud Creek. It was in this location that Catharine bore several children and raised them. Catharine Dolson Bush died at the age of seventy-eight on 3 May 1836. She is buried in the Peruville Cemetery next to Henry, who died in April of 1839 (Winslow, 1978).

- Jacob *Dolson*: Private in William Faulkner's New York Levies. Served eight months beginning in the summer of 1779 in Albert Pawling's Regiment at the pay rate of $6.66. Performed duty at Stony Point. This Jacob was most likely the son of Jacob [*Theunis, Jan*], also referred to as Jacob Mier *Dolson* and *Jacobus Dolson*.

James Jr.'s Siblings
According to Plimley (2011), James Jr.'s parents, Phebe Meeker Dolsen and James Dolsen Sr., had five children in the following order:

1. James Dolsen Jr. was born in 1760. James is the ancestor in this line of the Dolsons and his life events are described in this chapter.

2. Asa L. Dolsen was born on 3 January 1761. Asa was a successful farmer in Orange County. He lived near his brothers, James Jr. and Samuel. In 1803, Asa appears on a list of purchasers of pews at the Old School Baptist Church in Slate Hill. He obtained the seventh pew in the gallery for twenty-one dollars (Orange County Genealogical Society, 1977). Asa is noted as raising award-winning cattle. In 1820 an Asa *Dolsan* received an agricultural premium of fifteen dollars for "Best Bull" and in 1823, a three-dollar prize for

"Second Best Heifer" (Stickney, 1867). He married Mary Vail, daughter of Isaiah Vail and Abigail Meeker Vail. The marriage was reported in the *Goshen Independent Republican* (29 July 1842) as having taken place "*on the 21st instant between Asa Dolsen of Dolsentown and Miss Ana Maria Vail of Wallkill.*" This couple had two children: (1) son James (sometimes referred to as James Jr.), who married Mary Van Scoy, and (2) a daughter named Claracy, who married John T. Jansen. Mary Van Scoy was named as a beneficiary in the will of her mother, Rachel Van Scoy of Minisink, in 1822. James Jr. was a prominent farmer in Dolsentown. He is probably the *J. L. Dolson* who won prizes at the Orange County State Fair in 1842 for second best acre of oats and best acre of Mercer potatoes (*The Cultivator*, Vol. IX, 1842, Luther Tucker Publisher, New York). The immigrant ancestor of the Jansen family was Mathijs Jansen Van Ceulen (ca. 1600-1648), a fur trader and farmer who settled in Albany after reaching America from Cologne (Horton, No Date; D.G. Van Curen, No Date).

Asa Dolsen's will (Liber H, p. 362) was probated in Orange County on 14 January 1828 and mentions his wife, Mary, and his two children along with the following grandchildren: Asa, Charles M., Gabriel D., William Wallace, and John, all children of son James Dolsen; and Asa D., James, Charles, Claracy and Maria Jane, all children of his daughter Claracy Dolsen Jansen. Also mentioned is a great grandchild, a yet unnamed son of Gabriel Dolsen. Asa apparently was a wealthy man since he left significant sums of money and several tracts of land to his descendants. Executors of his will were James Dolsen (probably his son), Dr. John T. Jansen, a son-in-law, and John B. Booth. Witnesses to the will were William Arnout, Azubah Davis, Juliann Corwin, James Dolsen, Peter Holbert, and Daniel Dunning. Asa is buried in Pine Hill Cemetery. The date of death, as recorded on his tombstone, is 9 January 1828 (67 years and 6 days). Notice of his death at Minisink was published in the *New York Spectator* on 22 January 1828. The notice reports Asa's age as seventy-two. Asa's wife, Mary Vail, is reported to have died on 21 July 1831 (Plimley, 2011).

3. Mary Dolsen was born ca. 1765. This Mary appears to have married George Bloomer (ca. 1764-1854), son of Joseph Bloomer and Sarah Mygent. The date of marriage was likely before 1792 when a son named Seenotes Bloomer was born (Plimley, 2011). According to U.S. Census records, this couple lived in the Newburgh area until sometime between 1810 and 1820. Afterwards they are sighted in Neversink, Sullivan County, New York. According to an entry for Mary Polly Dolson Bloomer at *findagrave.com* (Retrieved on 5 October 2016), in addition to the son noted above, this couple had other children including at least two daughters: Elizabeth Bloomer Leroy (1793-1879) and Rachel Bloomer Kortright (1800-1870).

4. Abigail Dolsen was born around 1765. Nothing is known about Abigail except that she lived until her father's will was written in 1778.

5. Samuel Dolsen was born on 14 February 1766. Samuel was a successful farmer in Orange County and as his brothers, James Jr. and Asa; he lived on a property that was part of the original Dolsen tract purchased by his great grandfather, Isaac Sr. Samuel is recorded as having a sizeable farm in the 1790 U.S. Census including possession of one slave. Samuel, according to Plimley (2011), married Fanny Vail, daughter of Obadiah Vail and Mary Corwin Vail, on 6 October 1793 in Dolsentown. According to a manuscript entitled Descendants of Thomas Moore and Martha Youngs of Southold, LI. [Horton (No Date); Orange County Genealogical Society (No Date)], Samuel Dolsen and Fanny Vail Dolsen had the following seven children:

   a. Phebe Dolson was born ca. 1794. Nothing more is known about Phebe.
   b. Julia Jackson Dolson was born ca. 1797. The Jackson family had long standing ties with the Dolson family.
   c. Ira Vail Dolson was born ca. 1799. Ira lived for a time in Newburgh. Jury lists between 1828 and 1834 identify Ira as a farmer and an innkeeper. Ira eventually moved to Huntsville, Illinois where he died on 25 November 1842 (*Newburgh Journal*, 31 December 1842).
   d. Maria was born ca. 1802. She may have married David Irwin.
   e. William Meeker Dolson was born ca. 1810 and died in 1869. This man married first, Phoebe Ann Smith (1816-1866) and second, Mary H. Tuthill (1832-1898). A diary written by Mary Tuthill Dolson is on file at the Historical Association of Middletown and Wallkill. This diary covers family events over a multiyear period during the 1850s (Personal observation of the author. May 2017).
   f. Harriet Dolson was born ca. 1812. She married Emmet Moore, an ancestor of David Moore, father of Harriet Moore and Sarah Elizabeth Moore, on 24 March 1835 in Middletown (*Daily Albany Argus*, 28 March 1835). Harriet and Sarah Moore married James F. Dolson and Dewitt Clinton Dolson respectively; both sons of Frederick Dolson [*James Jr., James Sr., Isaac, Theunis, Jan*].
   g. Fanny Jane was born ca. 1808. Nothing more is known about Fanny.

Samuel Dolsen died on Sunday, 24 March 1850, "in the 84th year of his age…one of the oldest and most worthy citizens of his town" (*Goshen Independent Republican*, 5 April 1850). Ruttenber and Clark (1881) report that Samuel was still alive in 1850 and was able to recall the history of the region, including accounts regarding the local Indian inhabitants. His wife, Fanny, died on 27 November 1855. Her grave marker indicates that Fanny was eighty years old. According to the 1855 New York census, the widow, Fanny, was living with her son, William M. Dolson and his wife Phebe A. Dolson at the time of her death. Also, in the home at the time were five grandchildren and two Irish servants, Mary Kellarney and John Kipp, both aged twenty. Samuel Dolsen and Fanny Vail Dolsen are buried in Pine Hill Cemetery.

James Jr.'s Marriage to Eleanor

James Jr. married Eleanor Carpenter at the Goshen Presbyterian Church on 12 March 1780 (Coleman, 1989). Born on 17 April 1761 (Carpenter, 1996), Eleanor was nineteen at the time of the marriage and James Jr. was just twenty. Eleanor was the eldest child of Daniel Carpenter and Susannah Thompson Carpenter (Carpenter, 1996).

The Carpenter Family

Daniel Carpenter was born ca. 1720 and died at Goshen in 1791. Daniel was the son of John Carpenter of Jamaica, Long Island. Daniel's mother may have been Ruth Coe Carpenter who married second, a man named Benjamin Tustin or Thurston. The genealogy of Ruth Coe is ambiguous, but the lineage of the Carpenter family has been traced as far back as 1303 to a John Carpenter of England. The immigrant ancestor, William Carpenter, born in London in 1576, came to America on the ship *Bevis* in 1630, landing at Weymouth, Massachusetts (Carpenter, 1996).

Daniel Carpenter owned several farms in Orange County and was a hatter by trade. His will, proved in Goshen on 9 May 1791, includes mention of his wife Susannah, his brother John Carpenter, and his seven children: Susannah, Ruth, Eleanor, Sarah, Daniel, John, and Robert. There is no mention of daughter, Charity, reported to have been born in 1781 (Carpenter, 1898). In the will, Ruth, born on 5 March 1771, is identified as the youngest daughter and Robert as the youngest son. Of interest, Eleanor's sister, Susannah, married Theophilus Howell (perhaps the source of the name Theophilus in the Dolson family) and her younger sister, Ruth, was married to Henry B. Wisner, an associate of James Dolsen Jr. during and after the Revolutionary War.

Daniel's wife, Susannah Thompson Carpenter is reported to have been born on 7 February, 1733. This writer has not been able to connect this Susannah to any particular Thompson family in Orange County. A contemporary Thompson in Goshen was Judge William Thompson, who may have been a brother or cousin, but this is just guesswork. Susannah's death was announced by the First Presbyterian Church of Goshen on Wednesday, 3 March 1809. She is reported to have died at the age of seventy-six. Susannah Thompson Carpenter and Daniel Carpenter are interred in the Carpenter Burying Ground in Goshen on Route 17A opposite Houston Road.

There were several men named John Carpenter in Eleanor's family line. Besides her oldest known ancestor in England, her brother, and an uncle, she also had a paternal grandfather named John who was a well-respected citizen as well as a short-term sheriff of Orange County. Ruttenber and Clark (1881) indicate that on 10 July 1721, John Everett, John Carpenter II, and John Carpenter III, and others gave a deed of trust to establish the First Presbyterian Church, cemetery, parsonage and adjoining streets on approximately 140 acres in Goshen. This church is the oldest religious institution in Orange County.

As noted previously, a John Carpenter was documented as a Minuteman, who died at the Battle of Minisink in 1779. This man is buried at the Battle of Minisink Monument. In 1822, some 43 years after the Battle of Minisink, the bones of the slain patriots were recovered from the battle field. The remains were interred in two walnut coffins and buried in a mass grave in the church yard of the First Presbyterian Church of Goshen. A memorial was unveiled at the site and an elaborate ceremony, attended by over 15,000 people, was held to honor the fallen. The original memorial was replaced in 1862 with the current, more refined monument. The author speculates that this John Carpenter may be a distant relative of Eleanor Carpenter Dolsen. What the author is sure of is that James Jr.'s and Eleanor's grandson by way of their son, Frederick Dolsen, was named John Carpenter Dolson in honor of one of Eleanor Carpenter's male ancestors by the same name.

Eleanor along with several of her children and grandchildren were members of the First Presbyterian Church of Goshen (Coleman, 1989). Eleanor Carpenter Dolsen died 13 November 1821 (Coleman, 1989) and is buried in Pine Hill Cemetery alongside her husband, James Dolsen Jr. Her death was reported in a local newspaper as follows:

Died on the 13th instant at Minisink Mrs. Eleanor Dolsen in the 61st year of her age (*Orange County Patriot,* 19 November 1821).

Children of James Jr. and Eleanor
This couple had only two sons:

1. Theophilus Dolsen was born in 1782 at Minisink and died at the age of thirty-nine in 1820 at the same place (*New York Weekly Commercial Advertiser,* 23 September 1820).

2. Frederick Dolsen was born in 1784. He was a farmer and a harness race horse breeder. Frederick lived on the Dolsentown property in Minisink. He is the ancestor of this line of the Dolson family.

This is an unusually small family for the times. Perhaps the couple was unable to have additional children, but this is only a supposition.

James Dolsen Jr.'s Later Years
James Jr. was among the founders of the Town of Minisink. The first meeting of the town council was held in 1789 at the house of John Van Tyle in the Greenville section. The roll call of that meeting shows the presence of James *Dolson* and indicates that he held the posts of both assessor and constable concurrently (Bicentennial Commission of the Town of Minisink, 1988, p. 52). The second town meeting was held at Minisink at the home of James Dolsen, Esquire, on the first Tuesday in April 1790. In this instance, James Dolsen is listed as a commissioner of the highways. He is likewise noted as the highway master for Section 22,

while an Isaac Dolsen is shown as holding the same post for Section 21 (Ruttenber and Clark, 1881). These same historians note that James Dolsen also served as a justice and a tax assessor in 1790.

James Jr. was enumerated in the first U.S. Census administered in 1790. He was identified as James *Dalsen* on a property in Minisink located between Christian Hulse and Elijah Van Auken. This report indicates that three white males beyond the age of sixteen and two younger than sixteen were living in the household along with two white females. There were no slaves. Others reported in the 1790 Census are James Jr.'s brother, Asa (2/2/3/0), and his grandfather, Isaac (2/1/3/0), both in Minisink. Also, in Minisink were Eusebius Austin (1/1/2/1), Abraham Harding (2/2/2/0), Daniel Carpenter (1/2/2/0) and Peter Mills (2/6/2/0). Enumerated in Warwick were Abraham Dolsen, Isaac Dolsen, and Abraham Dolsen Jr. In New Marlborough, Ulster County there was a *Samuel Dollson* [*Jacob, Theunis, Jan*]. *Tuenis Dolson* [*Jacob, Theunis I, Jan*] and John Dolson [*Theunis II, Jacob, Theunis I, Jan*] were tallied in Chemung County, New York.

In the 1790s and early 1800s, James Dolsen Jr. was involved in several land transactions in Orange County. Examples include:

- A 14 April 1791 purchase (Liber E, p. 60) of one fifth ownership of a lot in Minisink from James McEvers of New York City for the sum of £80. The lot, part of the Wawayanda Patent, was originally owned by John Bridges. The land in question was adjacent to the properties of James Jr.'s grandfather, Isaac, and a neighbor, Derick Van den Berg.
- The deed number E-203 of 7 February 1793 documents the division of a large tract by County Commissioners. The tract was subdivided into five lots with Lot II granted to James *Dolson* and Asa *Dolson*. This land also was owned previously by John Bridges. Another deed of the same year shows a transaction between a James *Dolson* and a James Rivington.
- According to deed F-368, on 27 June 1796, John Carpenter, late of Goshen, sold to James *Dolson* a property consisting of 276 acres formally belonging to Nathaniel Cooley. Theophilus Howell was a witness to the transaction. The property lay along the Minisink Road.
- On 17 September 1805 James Dolsen purchased of David Cooley Jr. and his wife, Hannah, a sixty-eight-acre parcel in Minisink for the sum of $2,625 (Liber J, p. 138). This parcel bordered properties of Thomas Payne and Joseph Belnap. The land lay adjacent to James Dolsen's old farm.

In 1792, Thomas Greenleaf, a New York City publisher, printed a list of approximately three hundred subscribers and included it within a volume entitled the *New York Law Book*. Among the patrons from Orange County was James *Dolson* (Penross, 1987). The subscribers to this publication tended to be prominent lawyers, jurists, and politicians as well as elected officials including the current Mayor of New York City, the Governor of New York, and that state's Senator to the U.S. Congress. Also, in receipt of the book were several signers of the Declaration of Independence (Penross, 1987).

On Saturday, 27 April 1793, the *Farmers' Register*, a newspaper out of Ulster County, ran the following political announcement:

> **To The Electors of the Middle District**
> **Gentlemen, as two Senators are to be chosen at the ensuing Election for the Districts: We, Electors of the County of Orange, take the Liberty of recommending WILLIAM WICKHAM and JOHN ADDISON, Esquires, Persons in our Opinion adequate to perform the Duties of so important an Office. We therefore solicit your Aid in supporting the said WILLIAM WICKHAM and JOHN ADDISON.**

Appended to the ad was a list of prominent Orange County citizen supporters including Henry Wisner, John Bradner, Francis Baird, John Carpenter, and James *Dalson*.

A comprehensive tax assessment was conducted in Orange County in 1798. These records are quite detailed and contain the following information regarding residents of the town of Minisink:

- James Dolsen was on Goshen Road with a property of 380 acres. The house was on a one-acre lot and in good condition, two floors, 50x34 ft. with twenty-three windows. There was a barn (44x40 ft.), a cow barn (80x12 ft.), and one hay house (16x34 ft.). Improvements were valued at $4,375. James was reported to have one slave.
- Asa Dolsen had a house in good condition (27x27 ft.) with seven windows and another house measuring 20x24 ft. with two windows. He also had a barn, hay house, and cow house on a farm of 167 acres.
- Samuel Dolsen was next to Christian Schultz on 130 acres. His house was 25x25 ft. with four windows. He had two barns, 28x26 ft. and 38x28 ft. respectively.
- David Cooley Jr. leased a property from James Dolsen which contained two houses, one measuring 22x22 ft. and the other 33x33 ft.
- Nathanial Cooley also leased a ninety-eight-acre property from James *Dolson* which contained a home measuring 26x16 ft.
- Elihu Cary leased a property of sixty-four acres from Asa *Dolson* valued at $875.
- Isaac *Dolson* is listed on a property of 100 acres valued at $337.50. Since Isaac Sr. died in 1794, this assessment must refer to one of the junior family members who carried the same name such as Isaac [*Jacob, Theunis, Jan*].

Doherty (1990) also reports on the 1798 Farm Assessment, but his version diverges somewhat from that reported above which was taken from a copy on file at the Orange

County Genealogical Society in September 2010. It appears that Doherty may have erred in attributing ownership of the property of Isaac Dolsen to Daniel Drake and the farms of James Dolsen and Asa Dolsen to John Bradner. The Dolsons owned their respective properties. Drake and Bradner were their neighbors.

Minisink census data for the period of 1800 to 1820 are presented below. The results of the U.S. Census in 1810 and 1820 are somewhat thorny to interpret. In those years we see two men named James Dolsen. Based on the ownership of slaves, the author concludes that the man identified in the records simply as "James Dolsen" is the subject of this chapter, James Dolsen Jr. [*James Sr., Isaac, Theunis, Jan*]. The entry for the man enumerated as *"James Dolsen Jr."*, in point of fact, is the son of Asa Dolsen [*James Sr., Isaac, Theunis, Jan*]. This younger James would have been twenty-five years of age in 1810. Perplexingly, there does not seem to be a record for Samuel Dolsen (*James Sr., Isaac, Theunis, Jan*] in the 1810 census. This must be an error as Samuel reappears in 1820.

U.S. Census - Minisink, New York, 1800-1820				
Name	Number of White Males	Number of White Females	Others	Slaves
1800				
James *Dalsen* [Jr.]	3	3	0	1
Asa Dalsen	4	4	0	0
Samuel Dalsen	5	3	1	0
1810				
James Dolsen [Jr.]	8	5	0	2
Frederick Dolsen	2	3	0	0
Asa Dolsen	1	3	0	0
James Dolsen Jr.	4	1	0	0
1820				
James Dolsen [Jr.]	4	3	0	2
Frederick Dolsen	6	5	0	2
Asa Dolsen	3	2	0	0
Samuel Dolsen	4	4	0	1
James Dolsen Jr.	6	3	0	0
Liana Dolsen	4	3	0	0

The Liana listed in the 1820 census was the widow of Theophilus Dolson [Frederick, *James Jr., James Sr., Isaac, Theunis, Jan*]. We note that in these census years, none of the

Dolson households reported any foreigners or naturalized citizens as residing in their homes with the exception of Samuel, who in 1800 reported one other white person. The only profession noted for the heads of household was that of "engaged in agriculture." None of the Dolsons were reported to be involved in commerce or manufacturing.

The State of New York conducted a census in 1825. Among the persons enumerated in Minisink were Frederick, Asa, and Asa's son, James. Frederick is shown as owning a farm of 400 acres and having 100 cattle, five horses, twelve sheep, twenty pigs, and two "colored" persons. By the date of the 1825 census, James Jr. [*James Sr., Isaac, Theunis, Jan*] was deceased.

Slaves, Servants, and the Dolson Family
The U.S. Census has been administered every decade since 1790 and each enumeration contained a count of slaves in each household until the Emancipation Proclamation. In the case of the Dolsons, the first slave reported was that of Samuel Dolsen who reported ownership of one slave in 1800. The State of New York passed a statute in 1799 granting freedom to slaves effective on or before 1827. Children born of slaves in the interim were considered to be indentured persons but scheduled for manumission by their twenty-first birthday. The owners of the slave mothers were legal custodians of such children until their eighteenth birthday. After 1830, it appears that the Dolsons ceased to hold any slaves.

Around 1795, a free black farmer named McClaughry purchased a 490-acre property on which he established a village for African-Americans called Guinea, named after his homeland. The settlement was located between Scotchtown and Wallkill, not far from the Dolson farms in Minisink (Bilali, 1992). In 1800, there were 147 slaves and sixty free persons of African descent living in Wallkill.

In 1811 Orange County commenced registration of newborn slaves. The first recording, dated in April of that year, notes the birth of a "*female mulatto child named Charlotte*" by owner, George Phillips. Other Orange County residents filing similar notices included James *Dolson*, Elizabeth Wisner, Silas Hulse, and Susan Carpenter. In addition to the notice above, James Dolsen is listed among Orange County residents as transacting one or more manumissions. In New York, a Certificate of Manumission represented the legal document conceding freedom to a slave.

Additional particulars regarding slave ownership are contained in *The Slave Record Book of the Town of Minisink* (1811). On 14 February 1810, a female child was born to a slave referred to as "Sarah, wench from James Dolsen". The titleholder of the infant was identified as Noah Terry. On 9 August 1811, James Dolsen registered the birth of a male Negro child named Morris who was born on August 8th. The slave mother is listed as *Bets* (also known as Bett and Betty). Several years later, on 24 April 1817, James Dolsen registered another birth. Again, the mother was Bett and the child was listed without a name but described as "a male Mulato." In New York during this period, mulattos were defined as persons of mixed race.

The Slave Record Book of the Town of Minisink (1811) contains the following entries submitted by James Dolsen:

16 August 1811: Born of Bets a Slave to James Dolsen. Child named Morris on the 13 Day of July 11.

20 June 1817: Born in the house of the subscriber the 24 days of April 1817 a Mulatto boy of the body of a black woman by the name Bett. Recorded James Dolsen.

5 July 1823: Minisink. This is to certify that I James Dolsen together with the consent and approbation of David H. Saulson and Alexander Boyd overseers of the poor of said town have manumitted and freed my black woman named Bett of the age of thirty-two years agreeable to the act in that case made and provided. Signed James Dolsen.

Given the variation in dates of these entries, the 1811 date given to the Slave Record Book of the Town of Minisink is assumed to refer to the initial year in which births and manumissions were recorded. Perhaps just a coincidence, but on the U.S. Census report of 1860 for Theophilus Dolson II (spelled incorrectly as Dobson) lists a Black farm laborer, aged 50, named Morris Jarvis. The author wonders if the Morris enumerated in the 1860 census was the same person whose birth was noted in 1811 as a slave.

Ruttenber and Clark (1881) refer to an "old slave" owned by the Dolsons:

Betty, one of the slaves of the early period lived down to within a few years, and could tell many stories of the Dolsen family and neighborhood (p. 682).

The author notes that Betty was born in 1791 and therefore would have been ninety years old in 1881.

Of course, all of this background on slave matters raises a provocative question. As a result of slave ownership, are there any African-American ancestors in this branch of the Dolsen family? It was not uncommon for slaves, either kindred or not, to assume the surnames of former masters. The Orange County Genealogical Society has produced a six-volume series entitled *Genealogical History of Blacks in Orange County* (Brennan, 2001-2005). While there are a several African-American families identified in these volumes as carrying the surname Dolsen or Dolson, this writer, after a perfunctory investigation, has not encountered any evidence which would link any African-Americans of this surname to our Dolson family----neither by blood, adoption, nor by documents noting servitude or slave ownership. A more thorough study should be conducted to determine any possible relationships between European Dolsons and African-Americans Dolsons. This is particularly compelling because of the presence of a Black male of the same first name, Morris, living first with James Dolsen Jr. in 1811 and then again with Theophilus Dolson in 1860. An inquiry into the surname Jarvis may reveal additional information.

Besides slaves, some Dolsons also transacted contracts for indentured servants at their households. In Chapter IV, it was noted that during the 1760s-1770s James Dolsen Sr. and his wife, Phebe Meeker Dolsen, received a female minor named Ester Spragg for a five-year period of service (Figliomeni, 1997). According to Joslyn (2006), in December of 1831, Charles M. Dolsen [*James, Asa, James Sr., Isaac, Theunis, Jan*] of Minisink contracted to manage Delhi Heard, age seven years, until her eighteenth birthday to learn housewifery. For her service, Delhi was to receive the amount of twenty-five dollars.

Before 1850, the U.S. Census did not collect and publish the names of family members other than the heads of household. However, based on the relatively large number of individuals reported in Dolson family households, it can be safely assumed that persons other than biological relatives were present. In such instances these individuals may have been boarders or employees. In some cases, the persons counted were probably indentured servants, former slaves, or free-born persons of color. Commencing in 1850, Dolson census enumerations include the surnames of a number of Irish immigrants, undoubtedly domestic workers, whose employment conditions would likely have been similarly exacting as those of U.S.-born, indentured servants.

Two of the darkest events of American history have been the genocide and other mistreatments of indigenous peoples and slavery and the subsequent discrimination against African-Americans. Cleary the Dolsons were involved in both of these activities and the author considers that the behavior of some of our ancestors is adverse even in light of the time periods involved.

Based on the preliminary research conducted by this author, the breadth and depth of slavery as it existed in New Amsterdam and later in New York as colony and state was extensive. From 1749 to 1790, the number of slaves in Orange County grew from 360 to 966; in Dutchess from 421 to 1,856 and in Ulster, 1,006 to 2,906 (Stessin-Cohn and Hurlburt-Biagini, 2016). Apparently nearly as many immigrants from the Netherlands held slaves as those from English colonies. In a review between 1735 and 1811 of the languages spoken by runaway slaves, Dutch was reported by 145 and English by 189. Dutch was still being reported by monolingual and bilingual runaways as late as the 1820s (Stessin-Cohn and Hurlburt-Biagini, 2016).

In focusing on Orange, Dutchess, and Ulster counties, we find that the majority of slave holders came from the more prominent and wealthy families of the time. Surnames on slave rosters and runaway notices include Hasbrouck, Livingston, Beekman, Brett, Emigh, Wisner, Hathorn, Tusten, Wickham, Van Wyck and many others.

When slaves attempted to escape, owners would commonly place runaway notices in local newspapers. The author has found only one runaway notice placed by a Dolson but a number of notices from several collateral families and neighbors have been noticed.

Jacob Dolson [*probably Johannes, Jacob, Theunis, Jan*] of Fishkill, on 3 December 1823, placed a runaway notice for an indentured servant named John Ladue, a nineteen-year-old apprentice blacksmith. Although a two-dollar reward was offered, readers were warned not to harbor or employ the boy under penality of law. This Jacob was probably the grandson of Jacob [*Theunis, Jan*]; born on 11 May 1791; who submmtted a patent for a cast iron plough in Dutchess County in 1822; and who married Jane Coe at the Dutch Reformed Church at Hakensack. His parents were Johannes Dolsen and Sarah Cosman

On 6 June 1748, Samuel Wickham, the elder, published the following notice in the *New York Gazette*:

> **Run away the 5th of June last, from Samuel Wickham of Goshen in the County of _____ Orange, a negro Man named Jac, about 33 years of age, 5 feet high, very black, this country born, and speaks good English ... Whoever takes up or secures said fellow so that his Master may have him again shall have forty shillings rewarded all reasonable charges paid by me. Samuel Wickham. N. B. It is thought he took with him a bay mare.**

Much later, George Wickham, a prominent banker, and grandson of Samuel Wickham, sought the return of two of his mulatto slaves, James and Tomas, ages forty and thirty respectively. Wickham also mentions that his slaves were accompanied by Ceasar, a slave of neighbor, Anthony Dobbins. The notice contains mention that Tomas has *"a black mark from his left eye down his check, and has now a scrofulous complaint commonly called the King's evil on his neck."* A twenty-dollar reward was offered for each man (*Orange County Patriot*, 19 September 1812). George Wickham was the grandfather of Samuel S. Wickham, the husband of Ellen Adelia Dolson Wickham, daughter of Frederick Dolsen [*James Jr., James Sr., Isaac, Theunis, Jan*].

Charles Broadhead of Wallkill sought the return of Tom or Thomas Car on 11 August 1772. He offered a ten-dollar reward. It was noted that Tom *"spoke Low Dutch and English; was handy at all sorts of farmer work' and was a middling good shoemaker"* (*New York Gazette*, 24 August 1772). Broadhead was a collateral family associated with Josephine McMunn, daughter of Ellen McMunn Dolsen, whose father was Theophilus Dolsen [*James Jr., James*

Sr., Isaac, Thuenis, Jan]. The Broadhead family would publish another notice on 17 June 1806 regarding a runaway Negro man named Mink (*The Political Barometer*). Another collateral family, that of Abraham Vail of Goshen, offered a twenty-dollar reward for the return of Tone, five feet, ten or eleven inches with large feet and an excellent set of teeth (*Poughkeepsie Journal*, 10 June 1798).

At times, runaways fled from neighbors in and around Warwick, Minisink and even Dolsentown. Garret Post of Warwick, whose lands lay adjacent to those of Abraham Dolsen Jr. and his descendants, published the following announcement on 1 February 1816:

> ***Ten Dolars Reward***
> ***Ranaway from the subscriber on Christmas day---25*** *th* ***Dec. last, a NEGRO MAN named Jack, about 33 years old, thick set, something over 5 feet high, can speak good Dutch but speak indifferent English---had on a mixt grey coat and trowsers. The about reward and all reasonable charges will be paid to any person who will return said negro to the subscriber, or secure him and give information so that he may get him. GARRET POST, Warwick, Feb. 1, 1817.***

A decade earlier, another Orange County neighbor, Zephaniah Halsey of Blooming Grove, asked for the return of Sarah, who formerly was enslaved at Dolsentown:

> ***Five Dollars Reward.***
> ***Ran away from the subscriber on Sunday, the 9*** *th* ***inst; a negro woman named Sarah, 30 years of age, had on when she went away a blue and white calico shortgown, a homespun brown petticoat and old straw hat, a pair of old shoes that have been mended; she is supposed to be lurking about Goshen or Dolsentown, as she has lived at both those places: --Whoever will return her to the subscriber, or lodge her in Goshen jail, shall be entitled to the above reward and reasonable charges, ZEPHANIAH HALSEY, Blooming Grove, August 16, 1807*** (*Albany Gazette*, 10 January 1807).

In conducting the research for this volume, the author has read and heard comments from historians, librarians and fellow amateur genealogists that slavery as practiced by the Dutch was less cruel than that of the English or that slavery in New York was much more placid than plantation life in the South. The writer is not in a position to compare these claims; however, the wording in the runaway notices speaks for itself and the fact that between 1735 and 1831, at least 585 runaway notices were published to recover more than 750 slaves, is clear evidence of the inhumanity of the institution.

Orange County records for the year 1801 show the following tax assessment for James Dolsen Jr.: $4,075 Land and $293 Personal Property

In an 1803 Minisink tax levy, the three brothers were assessed as follows:

- James Jr.: $4,075 Land - $267 Personal Property
- Asa: $1,881 Land - $1,232 Personal Property
- Samuel: $1,407 Land - $151 Personal Property

Note that in both assessments James Jr.'s farm was more than twice the value of those of his brothers while in 1803, Asa's personal property was valued significantly greater than that of either James Jr. or Samuel. When compared to other residents of Orange County, the Dolsens tended to be somewhat wealthier than many of their neighbors.

On 16 September 1805, James Jr. was involved in a legal case administered by the imminent Orange County attorney, William Wickham. The matter concerned a receipt associated with the estate of Asa Smith. Also mentioned in the case was Sarah Smith, perhaps the widow.

The Will of James Dolsen Jr.
On 8 April 1825, the *New York Weekly Commercial Advertiser*, a newspaper operated by the renowned Noah Webster, ran a column entitled "Died". Among the obituary notices contained in the article was a brief announcement of just four words: "*At Goshen James Dolsen*".

James Dolsen Jr.'s will was written on 5 May 1824 and was probated nearly a year later on 2 April 1825. Wheeler Case was the presiding County Surrogate for all of the matters pertaining to the will. James Jr. was buried in Pine Hill Cemetery alongside his wife, Eleanor Carpenter Dolsen, who had passed away several years previous (13 November 1821). Following are the major provisions excerpted from James Jr.'s will:

- James Jr. bequeathed the farm on which he lived to his son, Frederick Dolsen. The farm is noted as containing 140 acres.
- He gave to his grandson, Henry W[isner] Dolsen [*Theophilus, James Jr., James Sr., Isaac, Theunis, Jan*], the sum of one thousand dollars and to another grandson, Theophilus Jr. [*Frederick, James Jr., James Sr., Isaac, Theunis, Jan*], three thousand dollars. The monies were to be paid to each grandson upon reaching the age of twenty-one years. James Jr. directed that the interest on these funds was to be paid beginning one year after his death. The four thousand dollars were to be paid from a lean on the farm which he had granted to Frederick.
- James Jr. conferred to his grandson, Henry W. Dolsen, seventy-five acres of land lying on the Minisink Road, a property which James Jr. purchased from Isaac Carpenter, as well as a lot of land which he obtained from Peter Mills

containing three acres. In addition, Henry W. received a lot containing roughly ten acres of cedar swamp which James Jr. had purchased from Dr. John Gale.

- James Jr. willed to the female children of his son, Frederick, all of his household furniture and one half of his remaining personal estate.
- He gave to his two grandsons, Henry W. and Frederick Dolsen, sons of his deceased son, Theophilus Dolsen, additional funds except for the sum of one thousand dollars which was to be given to his grandson, Dewitt Clinton Dolsen, son of Frederick [*James Jr., James Sr., Isaac, Theunis, Jan*], before any division of the personal estate was to be made.
- The remaining personal estate was to be divided equally among the children of his son Frederick, share and share alike.
- He appointed his son, Frederick Dolsen, along with Henry B. Wisner, and Henry G. Wisner, as executors.
- Witnesses to the will were Whitehead Halsted, Peter Mills, and David Lathrop.

James Dolsen Jr. signed his will simply as "James Dolsen". He did not make his mark which is taken as an indication that he was literate. When the will was proved, Peter Mills was a witness, providing further confirmation of a close association between the Dolson and the Mills families across three generations (Isaac Sr., James Sr., and James Jr.).

The Henry Wisner's
The first Henry Wisner (ca. 1720-March 4, 1790) was an American miller from Goshen, New York. He was a military and political leader during the American Revolution and represented New York in the Continental Congress.

Henry Wisner was born around 1720 in Florida, New York and spent his entire life as a resident of Orange County. He built and operated a grist mill in Goshen and became one of the town's leading citizens.

Orange County first elected him as a representative of the Province of New York Assembly in 1759 and returned him for eleven consecutive years. In 1768 he became a judge in the county's Court of Common Pleas. When New York created a revolutionary government in 1775, Wisner was sent to the New York Provincial Congress. That body, in turn, named him as a delegate to the Continental Congress where he served through 1776. Henry Wisner was a member of Congress when the Declaration of Independence was adopted.

While serving as a member of Congress, Henry Wisner became aware that one of the Continental Army's difficulties was obtaining adequate stores of powder and shot. When he returned home, he built three gunpowder mills in Orange County. For a period, Henry was shipping 1,000 pounds of gunpowder each week to Washington's army. He later financed the placement of cannon and other defensive works overlooking the Hudson that impeded the ability of the British to use the river in the Highlands Region.

In 1777, serving again in the provincial congress, Henry Wisner was a member of the committee that drafted the first constitution for the state of New York. Under that constitution, Wisner was a member of the state senate from 1777 until 1782. After the Revolutionary War he continued to remain active in civic affairs.

In 1784 Henry Wisner founded an academy in Goshen, and was one of the regents of the University of the State of New York from 1784 to 1787. In 1788, Wisner was a delegate to the state convention called to ratify the U.S. Constitution. He was one of those who opposed ratification, fearing that the strong central government would eventually infringe on state and individual rights. Henry Wisner died at his home in Goshen in 1790 and is buried in the Old Wallkill Cemetery in Wallkill, New York (Source: Wikipedia, retrieved 15 October 2011).

Henry B. Wisner and Henry W. Wisner were respectively, the son and grandson of the Henry Wisner described above. These men were contemporaries of James Sr. and James Jr. and were involved with them in military and civic matters. As noted previously, Theophilus Dolsen [*James Jr., James Sr., Isaac, Theunis, Jan*], in 1812, named one of his sons Henry Wisner Dolsen.

Highlights of James Dolsen Jr.'s Life

- James Jr. was born in 1760. He therefore possibly had some fleeting recollections of his great grandfather, Theunis, who died in 1766. He was probably very close to his grandfather, Isaac, who lived until 1794. This may well have been a particularly strong relationship owing to the fact that James Jr.'s father, James Sr., died at the relatively young age of forty-four in 1778.
- In 1794 James Jr. was named as the primary executor in his grandfather's will and was made custodian over his uncle, Isaac Jr., who was reported to be mentally challenged.
- James Jr. appears to have had a life as a farmer on the Dolson property in Minisink, save for his time away to perform military service during the Revolution.
- Since James Jr. was a subscriber to a law periodical and signed his own will in 1824, it is clear that he was literate and well educated. It is interesting to note that he consistently signed his name as "James Dolsen." Even though references to James Jr. alternate between "Dolson" and "Dolsen", in instances where he was in a position to influence the spelling, such as his will, he penned his surname as "Dolsen".
- As his previous ancestors, James Jr. appears to have been involved in business enterprises (e.g., land transactions) in addition to farming and civic matters (e.g., local town council and county politics). Records show that he rubbed elbows with some very prominent individuals.
- James Dolsen Jr., as well as several other members of the Dolson family, anteriorly and posteriorly, was a slave owner.

- Land, tax, and census records as well as his will, suggest that James Dolsen Jr. was well off financially and he was undoubtedly considered wealthy for the times.
- James Jr.'s son, Theophilus, died in 1820 of marasmus, a term used at the time to refer to a type of malnutrition that usually affected infants. Unfortunately, Theophilus was just thirty-six years of age and had a large family. This situation must have been a cause of much sadness and concern for James Jr.

Chapter VI - Sixth Generation

Frederick Dolsen

[James Jr., James Sr., Theunis, Isaac, Jan]

According to his grave stone at Pine Hill Cemetery, Frederick Dolsen was born in 1784. Court documents note his date of death as 11 April 1841. Nothing is documented regarding his childhood and his early adulthood previous to his marriage. The author surmises that Frederick grew up on his father's Dolsentown farm in Minisink, Orange County, New York. He would later inherit this farm and live on the property until his death at age fifty-seven.

Frederick Marriage to Margaret Moore

On 20 December 1806, Frederick's marriage to Margaret Moore was recorded at the First Presbyterian Church in Goshen (Coleman, 1989). According to Plimley (2011), Margaret Moore was born on 5 May 1788 at Goshen. Her obituary notice indicated that she died on 15 August 1863 at the age of seventy-three years, three months, and ten days. From these data, the author calculates her birth date to be 5 May 1790.

She was the daughter of William Moore and Elizabeth Howell. A William Moore appeared on local jury lists between 1798 and 1837 and was identified repeatedly as a farmer in Minisink and Mt. Hope but on one occasion as a blacksmith. The author has established few credible links between Margaret Moore and any specific Moore or Howell families. No connection to David Moore, the father-in-law of Frederick's and Margaret's sons, Dewitt Clinton and James F. has been discovered. One potential trace may reside with the fact that the Dolsens were related by marriage to Theophilus Howell (1760-1829), a well-known Orange County resident. Theophilus Howell's ancestors were of English origin and had been residents in Southampton, Suffolk County, New York before relocating to the Dolsentown area of Orange County in the late 1700s. Theophilus' father, Matthew Howell mentioned in his will, proved on 25 April 1786, his son, Theophilus, four daughters: Mary, Margaret, Elizabeth, and Jane, and two additional sons, Philetus and William, who appear to have been minors at the time of their father's decease. While these are common names, it may be more than a coincidence that Frederick Dolsen had a brother named Theophilus and that Frederick and Margaret named their second daughter, Elizabeth, and their eldest son, Theophilus. Another link between the Howells and the Dolsens is the fact that on 27 October 1792, Theophilus Howell married Susannah Carpenter, daughter of Daniel Carpenter and Susannah Thompson Carpenter and sister of Eleanor Carpenter Dolsen, wife of James Dolsen Jr. *[James Sr., Isaac, Theunis,*

Jan]. After Susannah Carpenter Howell's death, Theophilus Howell married second, Hanna Denton, a neighbor.

On 5 February 1839, a letter was submitted to the Surrogate's Office of Orange County which contained a written statement clarifying the status of a Revolutionary War pension application on behalf of William Moore. The following information was provided:

- William Moore of the County of Orange served about eighteen months as a private in the War of the Revolution and therefore is entitled to a pension under the law of 1832.
- The claimant's period of eligibility is from the time the law took effect (1832) to the time of his death on 29 January 1837.
- Mr. Moore was unable to apply as a result of mental infirmity and no application was ever made on his behalf.
- Subsequently a pension benefit was granted to his widow, Elizabeth, on 7 July 1838 for the amount of $52.22, effective from the date of her husband's death.

The letter goes on to request information regarding the continued eligibility for a benefit under current law to William Moore's widow and children. The Surrogate from Orange County, Charles Borland, responded on 13 July 1844, in the following manner:

> *... that, William Moore late of the County of Orange died on the 28th day of January 1837 and that he left surviving Elizabeth Moore his widow. And that she the aforesaid Elizabeth Moore died on the 26th day of February 1842 in the County of Orange aforesaid. And that she, the aforesaid Elizabeth Moore left her surviving the following named children viz. Maria Oliver, wife of David Oliver, Hannah Smith, wife of Thomas Smith, resident of the county and city of New York, Margaret Dolson, wife of Frederick Dolson, Elizabeth Montgomery, wife of Henry Montgomery, Jane Bailey, wife of William Bailey. ... And that the above named were all surviving children ... And that they are all of lawful age ... And that the said Elizabeth Moore applied for and received a pension under the act of July 1838 at the rate of fifty-two dollars and twenty two cents per annum. And was __[illegible]__ at the agency for paying pensions in the City of New York. And that she was a widow at the time of her death. The testimony whereof I have hereunto set my hand and affixed my official seal this thirteenth day of July in the year one thousand eight hundred and forty four. Charles Borland, Surrogate.*

While not totally clear, it appears that Surrogate Borland's response can be interpreted as an approval of the request and that the children of Elizabeth Moore were eligible to receive the benefit payments requested by the family.

Margaret Moore Dolsen was baptized as an adult at the First Presbyterian Church in Goshen on 14 December 1810 (Coleman, 1989). She is noted on the membership rolls of this congregation as Margaret Dolsen, wife of Frederick Dolsen. Apparently, Frederick did not join the church.

Plimley (2011) records the birth dates of Margaret Moore Dolsen's and Frederick Dolsen's nine children:

1. Emeline Dolson   20 October 1809
2. Elizabeth Dolson   11 April 1812
3. Theophilus Dolson (Sr.)   14 February 1813
4. Susan Dolson   9 May 1816
5. James F. Dolson   28 August 1818
6. Dewitt Clinton Dolson   23 April 1821
7. John Carpenter Dolson   4 April 1823
8. Ellen Adelia Dolson   18 March 1827
9. Oscar H. Dolson   1 December 1829

The first three children, Emeline, Elizabeth, and Theophilus, were baptized at the First Presbyterian Church of Goshen on 10 November 1814 (Coleman, 1989). Additional information on these nine individuals will be provided in the next chapter, which features, the seventh-born child, John Carpenter Dolson, the ancestor belonging to this line of the Dolson family.

Land transaction records in Orange County indicate that Margaret Moore Dolsen participated with Frederick Dolsen in the purchase, sale, and transfer of various properties during their marriage. Margaret continued to administer the remaining family properties during her widowhood, making sure that deeds were transferred into the names of her children, particularly sons James F. Dolson and Theophilus Dolson.

Margaret Moore Dolsen died on 15 August 1863 in Middletown. Her death was recorded in the *Goshen Independent Republican* newspaper:

Dolsen, Frederick, wife Margaret Wilson [Dolsen] **died at 73 years, 3 months, and 10 days on August 15, 1863 in Middletown at the home of son-in-law Samuel S. Wickham** (27 August 1863).

The Goshen newspaper mistakenly refers to Margaret, wife of Frederick Dolsen, as Margaret *Wilson*. The writer has researched this matter extensively and has found no corroborating evidence to suggest that either Margaret's maiden or middle name was Wilson. The First Presbyterian Church listed her surname as Moore at the time of her wedding to Frederick.

Her tombstone bears the same surname. Both are compelling confirmations of her family of origin.

According to the New York Census of 1855 and the U.S. Census of 1860, in the final years of her life, Margaret lived in Wallkill with the family of her daughter, Ellen Adelia Dolsen Wickham, and her son-in-law, Samuel S. Wickham, who was a dealer in lumber and coal. In 1860, also reported in the household was the presence of a young, female, Irish domestic worker.

Frederick's Brother, Theophilus
Frederick had a single sibling, a brother named Theophilus. Theophilus died at the young age of thirty-eight in 1820. This incident would have important consequences for the sixth and seventh generations of this line of the Dolson family.

Theophilus married Liana Austin ca. 1808 in Orange County (Plimley, 2011) and the couple had the following four children:

1. Ellen (Eleanor) Dolson (1808-1879). Ellen Dolson McMunn's obituary published in the Port Jervis Evening Gazette on Saturday, 24 May 1879, provides a summary of her life:

   Mrs. Ellen McMunn, aged 71 years, died at the residence of her son-in-law, Mr. George Brodhead, corner of Broome and Elizabeth Streets, Port Jervis, at nine o'clock Friday evening from the effects of pneumonia ... she will be interred at Hillside Cemetery, Middletown.

   Mrs. McMunn was born at Dolsentown, near Middletown, in April of 1808. She was the daughter of the late Frederick Dolson. Her parents owned nearly all the property in the vicinity of Dolsentown. Over 60 years ago she was married to the late Dr. McMunn, an eminent physician, well known not only in Orange county but throughout the country.

   In the spring of 1866 the family removed to Port Jervis. Two daughters survive: Mrs. Josephine, wife of Mr. George Brodhead of this village and Mrs. Louise Vanderbeek of Jersey City.

   Mrs. McMunn was a member of the [Dutch] Reformed Church of this village which she joined many years ago while the Rev. Dr. Mills was pastor ... Mrs. McMunn was a lady of rare intellectual powers ... She had been an invalid for many years but the immediate illness which resulted in death was of but short duration. She had made her home in the family of Mr. Brodhead ever since her coming to Port Jervis.

2. Henry Wisner Dolsen (23 August 1812-1868). Henry W. married Anna Thayer (1814-1893), daughter of William and Elizabeth C. Thayer. A jury record dated 1833 identifies Henry as a merchant residing in Newburgh. Anna Dolsen, a daughter of Henry Wisner Dolsen and Anna Thayer Dolsen, applied in 1895 to the National Society of the Daughters of the American Revolution to secure lineage recognition based on the record of Isaac Dolsen [*Theunis, Jan*] (DAR Record No. 10175). Although Henry's birth date is recorded as 1812, his grave stone in Pine Hill Cemetery notes his birth as 28 August 1810.

3. Frederick Dolsen II (1812-1859). Nothing is known about the profession of this man and it appears that he never married. In the New York Census of 1855, he is reported to be living with his brother, Aaron, and his mother, Liana, in Wallkill. On 2 November 1859, the local Middletown newspaper ran the following, short, obituary notice: *"Dolson, Liana, son Frederick d 26 Oct, 47yrs., Middletown"*. The *Goshen Independent Republication* also reported the death and noted that it took place at the Middletown residence of his mother, Mrs. Liana Dolson.

4. Aaron Austin Dolsen (1814-1871). This man appears to never have married. He is noted in census records of 1855 and 1860 as living with his mother in Wallkill. According to a Middletown directory, his house was located on North Street. His death was reported in the *Goshen Independent Republican* (7 December 1871) as having occurred on 4 December 1871 in Middletown during his fifty-seventh year. A photo of this man has been posted online by the Thrall Library (*www.thrall.org*) in a collection called Images of Local History. Aaron is standing in from of the Sweet's Hotel ca. 1860 wearing a "high" hat.

The exact birthdates of Ellen Dolsen and Aaron Dolsen are not known but all four of Frederick's and Liana's children were baptized collectively at the First Presbyterian Church in Goshen on 10 November 1814, the same date on which Margaret Moore Dolsen and three of her children, Emeline, Elizabeth and Theophilus, were baptized at the same congregation (Coleman, 1989).

The fact that Theophilus and Liana had a son named Henry Wisner Dolsen provides another link between the Dolsons of Minisink and those of Warwick since the line of famous men named Henry Wisner lived in the Warwick area. The Wisners were not only military, business, and civic leaders, but also served as executors and witnesses to at least two Dolson wills and to at least one Dolson family real estate transaction.

Theophilus I, II, and III
It is curious that Theophilus Dolsen and Liana Austin Dolsen did not name any of their male progeny Theophilus, but instead had a son named Frederick. On the other hand Frederick Dolsen and his wife, Margaret Moore Dolsen, had a son named Theophilus as well as one named Frederick. To confuse genealogists even further, Frederick's and Margaret's son,

Theophilus, was known later in his life as Theophilus Sr. since in 1843, his wife, Cecilia Hathaway Dolsen, gave birth to a son who was referred for a period during his lifetime as Theophilus Jr. At this point in time, there had been three generations of Dolsen men named Theophilus:

- Theophilus I, born in 1782, was the son of James Jr. [*James Sr., Isaac, Theunis, Jan*]. Theophilus I died in 1820 at the age of thirty-eight. He married Liana Austin and was a farmer in Dolsentown.
- Theophilus II, born in 1813, was the son of Frederick [*James Jr., James Sr., Isaac, Theunis, Jan*]. Theophilus II died in 1882 at the age of sixty-nine. He married Cecilia Hathaway. It seems that this man may have been referred to on occasion as Theophilus Jr. until the death of his uncle in 1820. Subsequent to the birth of his son in 1843, he sometimes was denoted as Theophilus Sr. Theophilus II is the man who sold off the remaining Dolson properties in Wawayanda in 1856.
- Theophilus III, born in 1843, was the son of Theophilus II [*Frederick, James Jr., James Sr., Isaac, Theunis, Jan*]. Theophilus III died in 1922 at the age of 79. He married (1) Sarah Elizabeth Masterson and (2) Annie Adelaid Ray (Plimley, 2011). Theophilus III was a Civil War veteran and an engineer for the Erie Railroad.

Additional information will be provided in the next chapter regarding Theophilus II and Theophilus III. There would be even more men named Theophilus in future generations of the family beyond the men by that name noted in this section.

Family of Liana Austin Dolson

Liana Austin Dolson was born 14 January 1787, the daughter of Eusebius Austin and Abigail Wood Austin. The Austin and Woods were both old and venerable Orange County families. The Austins were Minisink neighbors of the Dolsons and a prominent family in the region (*Fredericksburg Free Lance-Star*, 13 September 2009). Liana's father was noted as one of the Commissioners of the Poor at the first meeting of the town council of Minisink in 1790 (Ruttenber and Clark, 1881). He was also named as a Road Master for district number two on this occasion. Eusebius was a physician, a profession that he pursued as a result of his experience as a surgeon's mate in the Connecticut line during the Revolutionary War. For his service, he received an annual pension of ninety-six dollars between 1818 and 1835. In the 1798 tax assessment for Wallkill, Minisink, and Deerpark, Eusebius Austin is listed as owning a house, barn, stable and 206 acres. The real property was valued at $1,260 while the personal property was valued at $1,500. Eusebius Austin was a honorary member of the Tri-State Medical Society (Ruttenber and Clark, 1881). In 1803 he was taxed in Wallkill in the amount of $1,000 for real estate. During the period of 1805 to 1806, he was a contributor to the Ridgebury Presbyterian Church. Others noted as contributors include Asa *Dolson*, Annanias Valentine, James Little, Daniel Dunning, and William Fullerton. On 31 July 1809, Eusebius Austin recorded the following legally-required birth information in the Town of Wallkill Slave Record Book:

Rosanna, a female child born of Mary, the property of Eusebus Austin, born March 24th 1809. Signed Eusebus Austin.

Liana is noted as the founder of the Sabbath School in the village of Middletown (Seward, 1866). In a discourse delivered on 25 March 1866, the Reverend Augustus Seward stated:

A year later [1816] a Sabbath School was organized on the borders of the congregations of Middletown, Goshen, and Ridgebury, the children being collected from the families of these three societies and others living in the vicinity of the "Outlet." From this movement came the organization of a Sabbath School in the village of Middletown prior to 1824. From the commencement until the infirmities of years deprived her of the opportunity of laboring in the cause, these schools had no more zealous friend or efficient promoter of their interests than the Mother-in-Israel who was instrumental of their origin---Mrs. Lina [Liana] *Dolsen, now gone to her reward.*

The Reverend Seward further noted that he gleaned these facts from a narrative written by Liana Dolsen herself, and put into his hands at the time of her death.

Liana Dolsen was not only pious, but also patriotic. Based on numerous reports, she made an American Flag to honor the military sacrifices of her family members. According to Schemmer (2009), her flag is still in safekeeping at the Neversink Valley Museum of History and Innovation in Cuddebackville, New York. The flag is occasionally exhibited at museums and history centers around the country. The following article describes one such exhibition in Virginia:

Graffiti House Displays Unique 1861 Flag
"Unique" is a much overused word, cheapened by publicists and Madison Avenue hucksters. But it could hardly be more appropriate than when applied to the rare artifact now displayed at Culpeper County's Graffiti House.

"This is just glorious," visitor Floyd Houston said of the banner as it was unveiled Saturday inside the historic home at Brandy Station. "It is in glorious shape." Houston, a Marine from Burke, stood with two dozen others and admired the one of-a-kind U.S. flag, hand-sewn at the conflict's start by a 75-year-old widow whose kinfolk went off to war--and wound up at Brandy Station.

The banner has come to Culpeper through a partnership between Brandy Station Foundation, a nonprofit group preserving acreage where the Civil War's largest cavalry battle was fought, and the Neversink Valley Area Museum in Cuddebackville, N.Y. It was discovered in spring 2005 by Juanita Leisch

Jensen, a Neversink board member. Jensen "was poking around in the hot attic of the Museum, up in the eaves, and saw a small box," recounted Bob Luddy, former president of the Brandy Station Foundation. Written on top of it was 'American flag'. She opened it up and took it out, and realized this was far more than just an American flag. The only clue to the flag's history was in a handwritten note sewn into one of its white stripes:

"This flag was made by Liana Austin Dolson in 1861 when she was over seventy years of age. She was a daughter of Doctor Eusebius Austin who was in the Revolutionary War." Within a year of her making it, three of Dolson's family members would enlist in the Union Army.

Genealogical research continues, Luddy said, but it appears that at least three Dolsons served in the 124th New York Volunteer Infantry, known as the Orange Blossom Regiment. Theophilus Dolson, 18, probably Liana's grandson, was in Company D of the 124th.

The Orange Blossoms were on the field for the Battle of Brandy Station on June 9, 1863, and camped there with the Army of the Potomac from November 1863 through May 1864. It's thought that Liana Dolson's creation was a "home front" flag, hung in a window or on a wall of her Wallkill, N.Y., house as a reminder of the young men from Orange County, N.Y., serving in the Union Army, Luddy said. A flag expert examined it and found no evidence of soot or smoke, indicating it probably wasn't hung in a regimental camp or taken into battle, Luddy said. Sometimes, home front flags were carried to the front by individual soldiers.

The 124th took part in many of the war's key battles, suffering heavy casualties. Theophilus Dolson, who rose from corporal to first sergeant, participated in all of the regiment's major engagements: Chancellorsville, Brandy Station, Gettysburg, Wilderness and Spotsylvania Court House. In another link to the Fredericksburg area, he was involved in Confederate Brig. Gen. Fitzhugh Lee's cavalry raid at Hartwood Church in Stafford in February 1863, precipitating the Battle of Kelly's Ford in Culpeper on March 17, 1863, in which famed Confederate artillerist John Pelham was killed.

The Dolson flag is highly unusual for reasons other than its mere survival, immaculate condition and ties to Culpeper. Made of cotton, it has a double-sided canton, or blue field. Seen from the front, 21 stars are arranged as an exploding galaxy. Viewed from the reverse, one sees 13 stars arranged in a St. Andrew's cross. One theory is that Dolson designed the flag to acknowledge the secession of states loyal to the Confederacy as opposed to *those states remaining loyal to the Union, Luddy said. Another idea is that the stars' arrangement represents the 13 original states and the Union's later growth into the 21 states that formed the nation in 1861.*

A Brandy Station Foundation board member chanced upon the flag this June while at the Gettysburg Civil War Show, and realized its significance to Brandy Station and Culpeper County history. Talks with its stewards, the Neversink Valley Area Museum, led to its coming here for a temporary exhibition.

Next month, on the weekend of Oct. 17-18, re-enactors from the 124th New York Infantry will set up camp at the Graffiti House--so named for the amazing graffiti left inside it by soldiers during the war. The house will be open from 11 a.m. until 4 p.m. both days. The Dolson Flag will be on display at the Graffiti House until midNovember (Clint Schemmer, 13 September 2009, *Fredericksburg Free Lance-Star*).

Liana Austin Dolsen lived as a widow until her death at the age of seventy-seven. The 1855 New York Census records indicate that she was a widow, head of household, living with two single sons, Aaron and Frederick, ages forty-nine and forty-one respectively. Their frame house was located in Wallkill and valued at $800. A fourteen-year-old, black, female servant named Fanny Derby was also living in the home. In the 1860 U.S. Census Liana was shown as residing with her bachelor son, Aaron *Dolson*, in Wallkill. The 1860 census enumerates Aaron Dolson, age fifty, as head of household living in the home with mother, Liana, then age seventy-three. Also, noted was a young woman named Ruth A. McMann, age seventeen, who was living at the residence and attending school. Liana Dolsen's death was reported in the *Goshen Independent Republican* on 18 February 1864 as follows:

Feb. 4---In Middletown. Liana, widow of Theophilus Dolson, deceased, aged 77 years and 3 months.

Theophilus Dolsen died on 20 August 1820 at the age of thirty-three. He died intestate, meaning he did not leave a will. As a consequence, Frederick Dolson, Theophilus' brother, and James Gale, Theophilus' friend, petitioned the court on 15 September 1820 to be appointed as administrators of his estate.

Dolson Men in the Civil War

The names of several Dolsons are included in the *Annual Report of the Adjutant General of the State of New York for the Year 1903* (New York State Legislature, 1904). The three Dolson men listed below served in the 124th Infantry Regiment of New York from Orange

County. The regiment was known as the Orange Blossoms. In the late spring of 1865 the regiment returned to Orange County for the last time. Two hundred and fifty of their number were no longer present. They lay in graves, marked and unmarked, in battlefields with names such as Chancellorsville, Gettysburg, Wilderness, Spotsylvania, and Petersburg (Albanese, 2007).

- *Dolson, Jesseniah, age 20 years from Warwick. Enlisted August 9, 1862 at Goshen to serve three years, mustered in as private in Company D on September 5, 1862, wounded in action May 3, 1863 at Chancellorsville, wounded again on May 6, 1864 at the Battle of the Wilderness, Virginia and wounded a third time at Fredericksburg. Also served at Gettysburg. Jesseniah died of his cumulative injuries on May 25, 1864. This man was borne as Dolsen and Dolsin. His parents were Asa Dolson and Margaret LaCoste. Both father and son were reported to be laborers. Jesseniah had grey eyes, dark hair, and a dark complexion. He was 5'11" tall.*

- *Dolson, Theophilus* [Theophilus III], *age 19 years. Enlisted August 9, 1862 at Mount Hope to serve three years, mustered in as corporal in Company E on September 5, 1862, promoted to first sergeant prior to October 1864, mustered out with company on June 3, 1865 near Washington, D.C. Theophilus was referred to by the surnames of Dalson, Dolsen, and Dolson. On 16 August 1894, The Middletown Argus reported that Theophilus Dolson, a resident of Middletown and former member of Company E, attended on the previous day a reunion of the Orange Blossoms (the 124th Regiment).*

- *Dolson, William, age 22 years from Warwick. Enlisted August 7, 1862 at Goshen to serve three years, mustered in as private in Company D on September 5, 1862. He was discharged after the Battle of Fredericksburg on April 11, 1863 with a battle field disability. William was the son of Isaac Dolson and Eliza Sazer of Warwick. He and his father were harness makers. William had dark eyes, dark hair, and a dark complexion. He was 5'9" tall. This William also attended the reunion of the Orange Blossoms held in Warwick in 1894 (Middletown Argus, 16 August 1894). He is listed as a member of Company D.*

According to the *Town and City Clerks' Registers of Men Who Served in the Civil War*, Jesseniah was the son of an Asa Dolsen [*Peter, Abraham Jr., Undetermined, Theunis, Jan*] and Margaret Ann Lecoste. This family lived in Warwick. Of all the Dolsen men who served in the Civil War, the heroic exploits of Jesseniah, born in 1843, appear to be the best documented. He participated in several major battles including Chancellorsville, Gettysburg, Wilderness, and Fredericksburg. Jesseniah was wounded at least three times suffering a severe injury to the head and a fatal gunshot wound to the abdomen. He eventually died of his injuries on 25 May 1864. *The Town and City Clerks' Register* indicates that Jesseniah was twenty years old when he enlisted in August of 1862. He is noted as having grey eyes, dark hair, and a dark complexion. He measured five feet and eleven inches in height. The record indicates that he was buried in Fairfax County House 8 (notation difficult to decipher). A Memorial Urn in the Warwick Cemetery honoring the "Warwick Boys" includes an inscription with Jesseniah Dolson's name. His name is also included on the Civil War Monument in Minisink Square, Goshen. That monument commemorates the names of the war dead of the 124th Regiment of New York State Volunteers (Albanese, 2007; *Goshen Democrat* clipping in the Horton Scrapbook, Albert Wisner Library at Warwick, New York).

The Theophilus mentioned in the Adjutant General's report is undoubtedly Theophilus Dolsen III [*Theophilus II, Frederick, James Jr., James Sr., Isaac, Theunis, Jan*], born on 31 August 1843. On 26 May 1864, a dispatch published in the *Goshen Democrat* stated that a T. Dolsen of Company E was wounded in the side. Theophilus was mustered in as a Corporal but was promoted to First Sergeant by October 1864. He was discharged on 3 June 1865 near Washington D.C. A notation of "Distinguished Service" was attached to his military file. His obituary notes that Theophilus III participated in the battles of Fredericksburg, Chancellorsville, the siege of Petersburg, Gettysburg, the Wilderness, and the capture of Petersburg (*Port Jervis Gazette,* 28 November 1922). As mentioned previously, additional information on Theophilus III is provided in the succeeding chapter.

The *Warwick Valley Dispatch* (5 May 1886) reported that William Dolson of the 124th Regiment held the title of Junior Vice Commander. During one of his enlistments, he contracted small pox but survived. He was in involved in the Walden Raid and the Battle of Fredericksburg. In another report, William is said to have provided a total of three years of military service and after the war died of consumption.

Also noted on Civil War military documents are Oscar Dolson (born 11 June 1835) and Henry Dolson (born ca. 1841), Jesseniah's brothers. Oscar enlisted in 1863 and Henry in 1861, although Henry reenlisted in 1864. Both men were privates in Company D of the 56th New York Regiment and were listed as laborers from Warwick. Henry was discharged at Charleston in 1865 after serving four years. He is noted as twenty years old with dark eyes, dark hair, and a dark complexion. Henry stood five foot and seven inches tall. Oscar is reported as a member of the 7th New York Heavy Artillery and to have been involved in the Battle of Reams Station (Petersburg), Virginia, which took place on 25 August 1864. In that conflict, Union forces were deterred by Confederate troops when the former attempted to destroy the railroad facilities near Petersburg, Virginia. Oscar is noted as dying on 1 August 1865 after being discharged from the service. He died as a result of injuries sustained from an accident while working at a well.

There were a number of other Dolson men from various branches of the family that participated in the Civil War. For instance, a Henry Dolson from Mt. Hope enlisted in the 124th in 1861. James Mortimer Dolson enlisted as a Sergeant on 25 August 1863 and was promoted to Commissary Sergeant on 9 April 1864. James Mortimer Dolson died at the Chattahoochee River near Atlanta Georgia on 18 July 1863. He was a Commissary Sargeant in Company K of the 8th Iowa Cavalry, aged twenty-one years and five months (*Goshen Independent Republican*, 11 August 1864). He was the second son of John J. Dolson and John's wife, Emily W. Horton Dolson, of Muscatine, Iowa. Emily's father was William Horton, a medical doctor of Blooming Grove, Orange County. The author has discovered a photograph of James Mortimer Dolson online.

The John J. Dolson mentioned in this section is thought to be John Jansen Dolson, son of James Dolson Jr. [*Asa, James Sr., Isaac, Theunis, Jan*] and Mary Van Scoy.

Frederick Dolsen's Undertakings

Frederick farmed at his Orange County homestead for his entire life. As mentioned in the previous chapter, in the 1810 U.S. Census, he is reported as living next to his father, James Dolsen Jr. Frederick's family was enumerated as five persons in the household. The two Dolsen families were recorded in the town of Minisink between Ebenezer Auger and David Cooley. Also recorded nearby were Frederick's uncle, Asa Dolsen, and one of Asa's sons, James Dolsen Jr.

In 1819, Frederick Dolsen was mentioned at least twice in the *Orange Country Patriot* newspaper for outstanding agricultural production. Below are excerpts from these articles:

> **Extraordinary Yield—Mr. Frederick Dolson of Minisink, a few miles from this village, lately cut 88 shocks of rye from one acre, one half and two rods of land, strictly measured—good judges admit that every shock will produce a bushel** (29 July 1819).

> **We some time ago stated that Mr. Frederick Dolson, of Dolsentown, had cut 88 shocks of rye, on one acre, one half, and two rods of land---it was then conjectured that each shock would produce a bushel of rye---but since Mr. Dolson commenced threshing the crop, of which this was a part, we have understood, that the shocks average rather more than a bushel each---- namely, 14 bushels to 12 shocks, which will make about 60 bushels to the acre---this, at the present low price, will amount to near 40 dollars----for which an acre of tolerable good land might be bought---Here we have an instance of the advantage of good cultivation** (21 October 1819).

By the 1820 U.S. Census for Minisink, Frederick's family had grown dramatically. There were six white males and five white females. Additionally, one adult male slave and one adult female slave were registered. In the same census, Liana Dolsen, widow of Theophilus Sr., is reported to be located between Frederick and his father, James Jr. Frederick's uncles, Asa and Samuel Dolsen, as well as Asa's son, James Jr., are shown as living nearby. Between 1826 and 1833, Frederick Dolsen is shown on Minisink Township and Orange County records as reporting for jury duty on eleven occasions.

There are indications that Frederick Dolsen was involved in breeding harness race horses. A Poughkeepsie news article informed that "*On 3 October 1832, a Mr. Dolson's gg. Montgomery by Potomac, dam by Sarab, 5 years old, 96 lbs. completed the course of the Dutchess County Races in one minute and fifty-seven seconds*" (*Poughkeepsie Journal*, 10 October 1831, p. 3). The Orange County Government Website (*orangecountygov.com;* retrieved on 4 August 2008) posted an article from the *Goshen Independent Republican* entitled *Golden Hill Race Course for Horse Lovers* (21 January 1878). The article informed that a *Fred Dolsen* of Dolsentown raced horses over a multiyear period in Goshen. At the very last major race at the track, in June of 1832, Dolsen's horse called Hickory Colt, won the purse. Apparently, there was a line of renowned race horses that carried versions of the name Old Hickory and Hickory Colt. Frederick Dolsen's association with horses is mentioned by Wallace (1877) when he documents that a Theophilus *Dolson,* probably Theophilus II [*Theophilus, Frederick, James Jr., James Sr., Isaac, Theunis, Jan*] of Howells Depot, "*knows the history of the pedigree of the particular grey horse named Old Hickory*". This Theophilus also served as a judge of mares and geldings at a horse show in 1869 (*Port Jervis Evening Gazette*, 14 August 1869).

Between 1812 and his death in 1841, it appears that Frederick Dolsen served one or more terms as a commissioner for the Minisink, New York schools (Source: Minisink NY Early Schools. Posted at *old yearbooks.com;* retrieved on 25 April 2010).

On 20 May 1839, Samuel H. Seward wrote a letter of recommendation to his son, William H. Seward, regarding a vacant position as Property Appraiser for the Middletown Banking Company:

> **My Dear Child:**
> **David Moore of Minisink has called on me this morning to designate a proper person on the part of the Middletown Banking Co. to act as an appraiser of the various lands to be mortgaged by the said co. the comptroller. In casting my mind ... the Town of Minisink and Wallkill I do not think of a more suitable man than Frederick Dolson of Minisink. He is a man of propriety of clear discrimination and of stern integrity and in my impression will perform those duties to satisfaction.**

Samuel's son, William H. Seward responded to his father's communication with a brief message written at the bottom of the original letter:

> **I cheerfully recommend Frederick Dolson of Minisink and John E. Phillips to be appraisers of bonds and mortgages in the office of the comptroller by the Middletown Bank. They are very ... [illegible] ... May 22, 1830.**

[Signed] *William H. Seward.*

William H. Seward, born in Florida, New York was one of Orange County's most prominent citizens. He held several terms as a state legislator before being elected Senator from the state of New York from 1847 to 1861. Later he served as Secretary of State under Presidents Abraham Lincoln and Andrew Johnson. In his second term as Secretary of State, William H. Seward oversaw the acquisition of Alaska from Russia.

Seward was a staunch abolitionist. He participated in the Underground Railroad; provided funding to Frederick Douglas' North Star newspaper; and assisted Harriet Tubman to purchase property in his hometown of Auburn, New York.

Land: Purchases, Sales, and Mortgages
In the Orange County tax assessment of 1840, Frederick was taxed on two farms----one of 110 acres and the other of eighty with a total valuation of $3,300. Samuel Dolson appears in the same assessment on a farm of 140 acres valued at $2,800.

Frederick, along with his spouse, Margaret Moore Dolsen, was involved in a significant number of real estate transactions. Deeds on file at the Orange County Surrogate's Office indicate that he purchased and sold numerous properties, primarily in Minisink, but also at other locations in Orange County, most notably Warwick but also in Goshen and Slate Hill.

The Orange County deeds involving Frederick and his wife, Margaret, are listed in the two tables that follow, the first displaying purchases and the other sales. Information contained in the tables includes the year of the transaction, the name of the second party, the value of the property, the amount of acreage, location, and the archival number of the deed in Orange County records.

Purchases of Property by Frederick and Margaret Moore Dolson					
Year	Other Party	Value	Acreage	Location	Deed Number
1823	George Wickham	$1,375	55	Goshen	W-310
1826	Murray Hoffman	$ 661	50	Warwick	DD-491
1828	Master of Chancery	$ 950	16	Warwick	35-412
1831	George Canfield	$ 160	12	Minisink	43-364
1837	Estate J. Van Duzer	$1,245	? Farm	Minisink	62-352
1838	Trustees/J. Dolsen	$ 775	109	Minisink	63-170
1839	Charles Monell	$1,011	1	(Illegible)	64-241

Sales of Property by Frederick and/or Margaret Moore Dolson					
Year	Other Party	Value	Acreage	Location	Deed Number
1825	Eliphalet Stephens	$ 1,400	46.75	Minisink	Z-487
1826	Peter Mills	$ 756	47	Minisink	DD-375
1828	W. Halstead	$ 1,800	25	Minisink	36-285
1829	Peter Weed	$ 4,350	174	Minisink	37-11
1829	Henry Pelton et al.	$ 4,000	66	Warwick	37-192
1832	Increase Wood	$ 230	12	Minisink	46-8
1832	Samuel Davis	$ 150	½	Minisink	46-249
1838	James Post	$ 3,300	58	Minisink	62-4
1838	Ruth Carpenter	$ 1,350	Farm?	Minisink	62-353
1840	Charles Mills	$ 1,750	1	Slate Hill	67-3
1841	James F. Dolsen	$ 8,000	100	Minisink	70-35
1841	John J. Dolsen	$ 806	39	Minisink	70-44

There was an additional sale on 30 December 1838 to John J. Dolsen of two lots; the first containing seventy-five acres and the second, thirty-four acres. The sale price was $850 (Libers 61 and 62, misfiled).

According to these deeds, between 1823 and 1841, Frederick acquired approximately 243 acres of land, most of which was located adjacent to his properties in Minisink. He also purchased sixty-six acres of property in Warwick which contained a mill house and pond previously owned by Isaac Dolsen [*Abraham Jr., Undetermined, Theunis, Jan*]. The mill pond tended to overflow in the rainy season resulting in a scourge of malaria which plagued the citizens of Warwick. As a result, Isaac Dolsen and afterwards Frederick Dolsen, were caught up in legal, moral, and political quandaries during the period of 1826-1828. Details regarding these matters are contained in the Appendix to this volume.

The Orange County deeds indicate that during his life time, Frederick sold a total of 920 acres of land, all of which except 248 acres were sold to third parties outside of the Dolson family. An examination of the land transactions listed here suggests that Frederick sold off several sections of the original Dolson tract; lands originally acquired by his great grandfather, Isaac Dolsen, and passed down through his grandfather, James Dolsen Sr., and his father, James Dolson Jr. Near the end of his life, in 1841, Frederick transferred ownership of two plots of land to his son, James F. Dolsen. After Frederick's death, his widow, Margaret, transferred additional properties to her children, notably James F. Dolsen and Theophilus Dolsen.

In addition to the land transactions described in the two tables previously displayed, Frederick Dolsen also made formal real estate loans to a number of individuals. In all but two cases, the mortgages were associated with other Dolsen family members. As far as can be discerned from the records, with one exception as noted below, the monies were always repaid as stipulated. His son Theophilus acted as administrator for Frederick Dolsen's estate. Following are descriptions of the mortgages transacted by Frederick Dolsen on file in Orange County:

- 1823: Frederick sells three small lots in Minisink totaling seven acres to William Peppard Sr., William Peppard Jr., and his wife Sarah. As part of the sale, Frederick loans the purchasers $150, which is paid off in 1828 (Liber T, p. 312).
- 1825: In March of this year, Frederick Dolsen of Minisink loans Isaac Dolsen of Warwick the sum of $940 regarding two parcels of land containing fifty and sixteen acres respectively. The description of the property contained in this mortgage clearly shows that the property was located along Warwick [Wawayanda] Creek and contained a mill (Liber V, p. 87).
- 1828: Aaron A[ustin] Dolsen, son of Theophilus [*James Jr., James Sr., Isaac, Thuenis, Jan*] and Frederick Dolsen's nephew, borrowed from the latter the sum of $400 in March of 1828. As collateral Aaron deposited his one fourth interest in a farm consisting of eighty-seven acres. This farm was originally the property of James Dolsen Sr. and his spouse, Eleanor Carpenter Dolsen. Also included as collateral was a farm purchased of Benjamin Wood. This mortgage was paid off on the 16 April 1829 (Liber Y, p. 234).
- 1828: Ira V[ail] Dolsen borrowed $1,200 from Frederick Dolsen. Collateral was Ira's and his wife's (Ann Janes') property in Minisink. The land was described as acreage adjacent to the road from Frederick Dolsen's house to the Delaware River. The loan was repaid on 8 February 1832 (Liber Y, p. 415).
- 1829: Frederick in consortium with Aaron Dolsen, Ellen [Dolsen] Lewis, and Liana [Austin] Dolsen granted a mortgage of $950 to Peter Werd of Minisink. Payment of interest was to be made periodically to Liana for the remainder of her life. This document indicates that the mortgage was paid in full on 2 May 1862 (Liber Z, p. 482).
- 1838: In August of this year, Charles M[ortimer] Dolson and his wife Elizabeth took out a loan from Frederick in the amount of $800 for one acre of land in Minisink located along

the Turnpike Road (Liber 39, p. 429). After Frederick Dolsen's death the ownership of the mortgage was transferred to his son, Theophilus. It seems that Charles Mortimer Dolsen was indebted to Henry Elsworth for the amount of $295 stemming from a loan made in 1845 for the purchase of one acre of land. Theophilus repurchased the acre of land along with another of Charles Dolsen's parcels for $180 at an auction (Liber 374, p. 375).

- 1838: Frederick Dolsen loans to James Post and his wife, the amount of $3,000 for a fifty-eight-acre property in Minisink lying on both the Ridgebury Road and the Turnpike. The loan was paid in full on 21 November 1843 to Theophilus Dolsen, administrator for the estate of Frederick Dolsen (Liber 41, p. 88).

Frederick Dolsen's Passing

Frederick appears to have lived his entire life in Dolsentown. He seems to have been a skilled farmer and participated secondarily in breeding harness race horses. Unlike his father and grandfather, Frederick was not a military veteran nor does it look as if he participated in civic affairs to the same extent as his paternal ancestors.

Frederick Dolsen was listed in the 1840 U.S. Census. In this enumeration, seven white persons were residing in his household. Also counted were two free colored persons, a male thirty-five years or older and a female aged twenty-three or younger. All persons were employed in agriculture except for one who was categorized as working in manufacture and trade.

In the 1840 Minisink Tax Assessment, Frederick is listed as the owner of two separate properties. The first was a parcel of 110 acres valued at $2,500. The second was an 80-acre lot valued at $800.

According to a petition filed with the Surrogate Court of Orange County on 23 April 1841, Frederick Dolsen died on 11 April 1841. The petition contained the following additional information:

- The cause of death was identified as apoplexy, the characterization used at the time to denote a stroke or cerebral hemorrhage. Frederick died at his home in Minisink.
- Frederick Dolsen did not have a will.
- The deceased left the following relatives: Margaret Dolson, his widow and eight children; Elizabeth Dolson, wife of Charles M. Dolson; Susan Dolson, wife of William Wallace Dolson; John C. Dolson; Ellen A. Dolson; Oscar H. Dolson; Dewitt C. Dolson; and the two sons noted as the petitioners: Theophilus Dolson and James F. Dolson. These persons were said to represent all of the next of kin of Frederick Dolsen. The absence of daughter, Emeline, suggests that she died before her father. Note that daughter Elizabeth married first cousin, Charles M.

Dolsen, and that daughter Susan married first cousin, William Wallace Dolsen, both of these men were sons of James Dolsen Jr. (*Asa, James Sr., Isaac, Theunis, Jan*) and his wife, Mary Van Scoy Dolsen.

- John C. Dolson, Ellen A. Dolson, Oscar H. Dolson, and Dewitt C. Dolson were referred to as "infants", the term used in New York at the time as the legal definition of minors, persons younger than twenty-one years of age.
- On the date of the petition, all of the next of kin resided in Minisink except for the following: Dewitt Clinton Dolsen lived in Wallkill while Charles Meeker Dolsen with Elizabeth, his wife, and William W. Dolsen and Susan, his wife, lived in Schuyler County, Illinois.
- Frederick left goods, chattels, and credits, which in whole, did not exceed in value the sum of nine thousand dollars, exclusive of what the law allows the widow.
- The widow, Margaret, released all rights in the matter to the other petitioners.
- The petition was signed by Theophilus Dolson and James F. Dolsen in the presence of the County Surrogate, George M. Grier, in Goshen.

Subsequent to Frederick Dolsen's death, his wife, Margaret took steps to transfer ownership of any property still held in her name to family members, specifically sons, James F. Dolson and Theophilus Dolson. Additionally, a number of exchanges of land titles, including actual sales and purchases took place among and between Dolson siblings and cousins. Theophilus Dolson was at the center of several of these transactions. On 29 March 1856, Margaret Moore Dolsen sold three lots of land totaling 227 acres to Theophilus for the token amount of ten dollars (Liber 140, p. 629). A few days later, Theophilus is recorded as selling the last major family holdings in Dolsentown on 9 April 1856 to Simon Bradley of Wawayanda for the amount of $15,085 (Liber 140, p. 630).

Frederick Dolsen and Margaret Moore Dolsen are buried in Pine Hill Cemetery, Wawayanda. Frederick's gravestone is inscribed with the dates 1784--April 11, 1841 and that of Margaret, May 5, 1788--August 15, 1863. In this branch of the family, Frederick was the last of the line to commonly spell his surname as Dolsen. Subsequently, his sons, John Carpenter Dolson and Dewitt Clinton Dolson, both of whom eventually settled in California, and most of the other children and grandchildren of Frederick and Margaret Dolsen, penned their surname as Dolson on a consistent basis.

Chapter VII – Seventh Generation

John C. Dolson

[Frederick, James Jr., James Sr., Theunis, Isaac, Jan]

His grave marker records John Carpenter Dolson's birthdate as 7 April 1823. This date is consistent with census records and other accounts regarding the life of this man. John Carpenter was named after an ancestor from his grandmother's, Eleanor Carpenter Dolson's, side of the family.

John Dolson undoubtedly grew up on his father's farm in Dolsentown, where he lived until he ventured to California in 1850. His biographical file, archived at the Native Daughters of the Golden West (Davis, 1890), contains a statement that he was educated in New York which would mean that he had at least some basic schooling in Orange County. He was still a minor at the time of the deaths of his grandfather, James Sr., and his father, Frederick. Letters of administration were issued to his father and older brother, Theophilus, respectively, to manage John Dolson's share of these two inherences.

First Voyage to California
It appears that John Dolson participated in the California Gold Rush (Davis, 1890). He arrived in the state before the census of 1850, apparently traveling by ships via the Isthmus of Panama, a perilous overland journey through tropical rainforest (Native Daughters of the Golden West, Vol. 38, p. 72). One of the first independent sightings of John Dolson is in the U.S. Census of 1850. He is shown as living in the Georgetown area of El Dorado County, California. At that time, John's age was reported to be twenty-six and he is noted as a native of New York. He is shown as John *Dalson* living with a Gilbert *Dalson*, age twenty-nine, and an unidentified man named Jackson; age twenty-eight, also from New York. The three men were identified as involved in mining. The writer has not been able to place a contemporary Gilbert Dolson in the family. The Jackson man reported in the census was probably a member of the Jackson family, not only neighbors of the Dolsons in Orange County, but also associated perhaps, with Sara Jackson, mother of Cecilia Hathaway Dolson, wife of Theophilus II, John Carpenter Dolson's brother. The relationship between the Dolson and Jackson families must have been long standing. Earlier, Samuel Dolsen [*James Sr., Isaac, Theunis, Jan*] named one of his daughters Julia Jackson Dolsen.

Return to New York

It is clear that John Dolson did not strike it rich in the Gold Rush. In 1854 he returned to New York. While in Orange County, records show that he took the necessary steps to secure his inheritances from his father and grandfather. Several land transactions were recorded in the period of 1854-1855 between John and his mother, Margaret, and between John and his brother, Theophilus. The funds secured from these dealings were undoubtedly used to purchase a farm in San Joaquin Township (now Elk Grove), California in 1857.

The nature of John Dolson's inheritances affords an interesting story. First, John is mentioned in his grandfather's, James Sr.'s will as receiving an equal portion of the residual part of the estate. The value of this bequest may have been modest in nature since the residual was to be divided between several grandchildren. Frederick Dolsen was made administrator of this inheritance since John was a minor at the time of his grandfather's death. Upon Frederick's death in 1841, guardianships were issued for John and his minor siblings, Ellen and Oscar. Theophilus was named as administrator for John and Ellen while Margaret Moore Dolsen became administrator for her young son, Oscar H. Dolson. Orange County deeds indicate that John's share of the inheritance from his father consisted of at least three lots, one of which contained his father's homestead farm.

In 1854, during his return trip to New York, John deeded these parcels of land to his brother, Theophilus, for the amount of $1,950 (Liber 134, p. 354). Apparently, the funds were conveyed via a mortgage. In 1857, John filed a document granting power-of attorney to his brother-in-law, Samuel S. Wickham (husband of John's sister, Ellen Adelia Dolson Wickham), to authorize the collection of the debt from Theophilus (Liber 175, p. 148). According to the Orange County deed, this matter was resolved on 5 December 1863. The cause for the delay of payment is not known, but this matter may have strained relations between John and his brother, Theophilus.

Itemized in the Orange County deed (Liber 134, p. 354) associated with John Dolson's inheritances, were three separate properties. The first and largest tract consisted of 133 acres, thirty of which were identified as Frederick Dolsen's homestead farm. In 1854, this property was said to border the lands of the late James Aldrich and lands of late William Little, the highway leading from Middletown to Brookfield, the lands of the late James Post and Gabriel Swezy, with lands of the late Oliver A. Carpenter, and finally with the lands of James *Dolson*.

The second lot containing approximately forty acres was described in the following manner: adjacent to lands of Hannah Cooley, along the road leading from Benjamin Wood's store to Nathaniel Cooley's house, along Isaac Carpenter's land to the old Minisink Road, to the line of lands belonging to Christian Shultz, thereafter back to Hannah Cooley's property.

The third parcel consisted of ninety-two acres and was positioned from Abraham Bennet's farm to the Minisink Road, to the lands of Absalom Cary, and then back to the property of Abraham Bennet.

The deed in question makes clear that the exchange included any structures and improvements (tenements and appurtenances) existing on the properties. John C. Dolson signed the deed of sale on 29 May 1854 at Wawayanda, in person, in his own name, and in the presence of G. Houston, Justice of the Peace. John Dolson personally appeared before this Justice a second time, on 28 March 1855, to acknowledge the conveyance.

The writer does not know for certain if John Dolson ever became aware of the particulars concerning his brother Theophilus' subsequent sale of these lands in 1856 for a sum of $15,085 (Liber 140, p. 629). This was an amount ten times greater than the price of the 1854 exchange between the two brothers. If John did find out, he must have been chagrinned not only regarding the enormous profit realized by his brother, but also by the fact that it took Theophilus until December of 1863 to complete the payment of the $1,950. It should be highlighted however, that as part of Theophilus' sale of land to Simon Bradley, the deed clearly indicates that there were several outstanding mortgages on the property associated with Theophilus' siblings. Additionally, the handwriting as well as some of the archaic language used in old deed documents are sometimes difficult to decipher. Perhaps only a share of the sale belonged to John C. Dolson, the remainder to be distributed among several other siblings.

The precise locations of James Dolsen's properties in Orange County are difficult to pinpoint, but based on historic descriptions from Isaac Dolsen's times to later portrayals defined in various deeds, it is estimated that the Dolsen tract was located south of Middletown, New York in an area along present day U.S. Highway 6, bounded in the east by State Route 17M and in the south by Interstate 84. This area is crossed by Monhagan Creek. In fact, in describing the Bradley House, the home originally built by Isaac Dolsen, Parker Seese (1941) mentions that the house was probably located at the switchback where Mohagan Creek met Carpenter's Creek. Highway 6 links Middletown to Slate Hill (originally named Brookfield). Both the road to Brookfield and the Old Minisink Road are mentioned in the deeds. The Old Minisink Road, sometimes called the Minisink-Goshen Turnpike, is known as Highway 6 today. Pine Hill Cemetery, originally known as the Dolsen Burying Ground is found along U.S. Highway 6, approximately a quarter mile west of the intersection of Dolson Avenue and Dolsentown Road. The cemetery was reported to be located at the southern boundary of the Dolsen properties.

Hannah O'Connor and Children
During his 1854-1855 return trip to New York, John C. Dolson married Hannah O'Connor. A narrative of John C. Dolson's life provided to the Native Daughters of the Golden West by Alice Dolson Cutbirth, one of couple's daughters, stipulates that her parents married during

the month of December 1854 (Davis, 1890). According to the available evidence, John would have been thirty years of age and Hannah nineteen years. Even though there is an assumption that the marriage took place in Orange County, no marriage record has been located.

Very little is known about Hannah O'Connor. Based on census records and her tombstone, Hannah's date of birth is calculated to be 1835. Her place of birth is recorded as Ireland, a fact which coincides nicely with her maiden name. Her middle initial was "M", perhaps standing for Margaret or Mary since she had daughters by these names.

The writer has researched Orange County and New York State immigration records diligently for additional information regarding Hannah and her family without any success. At this time, a best guess is that Hannah O'Connor was a single, young lady, who immigrated to the United States from Ireland during or immediately following the infamous Potato Famine. She may have been employed in Orange County around 1854 as a domestic worker. An entry for Hannah O'Connor has not been located in the U.S. Census of 1850.

A review of census records in Orange County during the period of 1790 to 1830 show that some of the more affluent families often had one or two slaves working as farm hands and domestics. Gradually, in New York, manumissions were granted and slaves were given their freedom. By the 1830s, virtually all of the slaves in New York had been freed. Various documents indicate that Dolsen families in Minisink and Warwick were owners of slaves. As slaves were freed, they often were replaced by free Negroes and whites who worked as apprentices, ranch hands, and farm laborers. As early as the 1840s, but particularly by the 1850 census, there are numerous sightings at larger and wealthier Orange County households of young, female, domestic workers, commonly of Irish origin.

The pattern of holding slaves and white indentured servants, and subsequently employing free Negroes and Irish domestics occurred in several Dolsen households. In the first U.S. Census (1790), James Jr. reported as owning two slaves. Several years later, on 1 October 1798, as part of the tax assessment for Wallkill, Minisink, and Deerpark, James Jr. is recorded as the owner of one female slave. Even though the New York law of 1799 stipulated that all children born of a slave mother after July 4th of that year were considered to be free persons, it is clear that James Jr. and several other slave owners still regarded these children as slaves. James recorded one such birth as "a male slave child born of my black women Bet" (The Slave Record Book of the Town of Minisink, 1811). In 1820, Frederick Dolsen reported two slaves and then in 1840, two free Negroes living in his household. By 1850, Theophilus Dolsen, John C. Dolson's brother, reported in the U.S. Census of that year, the presence of several young people (ages 20-28) in his home, none of whom were relatives. Ten years later in 1860, John Dolson's mother, Margaret, was living with her daughter and son-in-law, Ellen and Samuel Wickham, and grandchildren Oscar D., age four, and Cecilia, age eight, in Wallkill. A young domestic woman of Irish origin, age twenty-five, by the name of Eliza Clark, was living in the home.

This writer suspects that Hannah O'Connor may have been a domestic worker in one of the Dolsen households or in that of an Orange County neighbor. It is not known if Hannah and John were acquainted before John ventured to California in 1850 or if they met upon his return to New York in 1854. In 1855 the couple, now married, returned to California, again via Panama, and two years later, settled on a farm in San Joaquin Township, now known as Elk Grove.

John Dolson and Hannah O'Connor Dolson had eight children who lived into adulthood. It is possible that one child died at birth. The surviving children's names and birthdates, listed here, are taken from Davis (1890) who apparently interviewed the family, or at least daughter, Alice, in 1890 while developing a compendium of biographies of local pioneers for the volume entitled *An Illustrated History of Sacramento County, California*:

1. Oscar J. Dolson   1 October 1855
2. John J. Dolson   17 November 1857
3. David P. Dolson   4 January 1861
4. Margaret M. Dolson   4 May 1863
5. William Dolson   22 May 1865
6. Mary E. Dolson   23 August 1869
7. Alice E. Dolson   31 December 1871
8. Joseph H. Dolson   23 October 1874

In the U.S. Census of 1900, Hannah O'Connor Dolson informed the census taker that, by that date, she had given birth to nine children. Clearly, since only eight children were listed in 1900, this signifies that one child was no longer living and had died young. The fact that the deceased child's name is not mentioned in any family or public records perchance indicates that the death took place late in pregnancy or at childbirth.

California voter registration records reveal the second names of several of the male children: John <u>James</u> Dolson, David <u>Pelton</u> Dolson, Oscar <u>Jackson</u> Dolson, and Joseph <u>Henry</u> Dolson. David Pelton Dolson is the ancestor belonging to this branch of the family and his life will be described in the next chapter.

It looks as if the first names of many of the children originated from Hannah O'Connor's family (about which this author has not discovered any information) or were selected arbitrarily by the couple. Few of the first names have direct historical links to the Dolson line. Oscar was the name of one of John C. Dolson's brothers in Orange County (Oscar H. Dolson, 1829-1900) and of course, John James was named after his father. The Dolson legacy also is represented through the selection of the second names for some of the children. For instance, David's middle name is Pelton, a surname of a prominent Orange County, New York family known to have had memorable ties to the Dolsons via the infamous 1820s Warwick mill pond incident described in the Appendix to this volume. Jackson was the surname found in a collateral family from Orange County and, as previously noted, a man from the Jackson family accompanied John C. and Gilbert Dolson to the Sierra Nevadas in 1850.

Hannah and John were married for a period of more than fifty years. The widow, Hannah O'Connor Dolson, died on 9 April 1911. The date of death is taken from her tombstone and is consistent with the date given in her obituary and will. Hannah was seventy-seven years old. She is buried alongside her husband at the Masonic Cemetery located on Elk Grove Boulevard adjacent to Highway 99 in Elk Grove, California. The following obituary was published in a local newspaper:

> *Hannah M. Dolson, wife of the late John C. Dolson, a well-known and highly regarded resident of this place, passed away suddenly last Saturday from an attack of apoplexy* [stroke]. *John Dolson came to California from New York, his native state, in 1850. In 1852 he returned to New York and was married in 1854. He came to California where the family has resided ever since. They moved to their ranch north of town in 1857, where all their children but one was born. Children: Oscar J., David Pelton, William, Joseph H., Maggie M. Bartlett, Mary E. Reeves, Alice E. Cutbirth, and John Dolson* (*Elk Grove Citizen*, April 1911).

An error noted in the article is the statement that John Dolson returned to New York in 1852 when in fact; most of the evidence indicates that he returned to Orange County in 1854, the same year in which he married Hannah O'Connor.

John's Siblings
John Carpenter Dolson had four sisters and three brothers. All of the siblings listed here are known to have lived into adulthood.

1. Emeline was born on 20 October 1809 in Goshen and died on 22 May 1837 at twenty-nine years of age (Plimley, 2011). She is buried at Pine Hill Cemetery in Wawayanda, New York. She apparently never married. Nothing more is known about Emeline.

2. Elizabeth was born on 11 April 1812 in Ridgebury, Orange County and she died before 1890 (Plimley, 2011). She was married to a distant cousin, Charles Mortimer Dolson, the son of James Dolson [*Asa, James Sr., Isaac, Theunis, Jan*] and Mary Van Scoy Dolson, on 25 November 1830 at Dolsentown. In October 1836, Elizabeth was a teacher at Brookfield School in Slate Hill. Around 1839, she and her family moved to Schuyler County, Illinois where she died on 10 November 1858 (Plimley, 2011).

3. Theophilus II was sometimes in his youth, denoted as Junior, and in his later years, sometimes as Senior. He was born on 14 February 1813 and died on 7 January 1882 in Orange County within a month of his sixty-ninth birthday. On 19 December 1837, a Tuesday evening, Theophilus married Cecilia Hathaway at the First Presbyterian Church in Goshen (*Goshen Independent Republican,* 23 December 1837). Cecilia was born on 28 January 1817 in Goshen. Her parents were Daniel Hathaway and Sarah Jackson Hathaway. She was admitted as a member of the Old School Baptist Church of Howells, New York before 1870 and continued as a member for many years (Foley, 1993). Cecelia died on a Tuesday morning, 23 August 1898, at her home in Howells, at more than eighty-one years of age, of general debility and old age (*Port Jervis Evening Gazette*, 24 August 1898). She was survived by eight children (*Goshen Independent Republican*, 26 August 1898).

In an 1850 tax assessment, Theophilus' farm is noted as consisting of 175 acres of which thirty-five acres were unimproved. The value of the land was assessed at $10,000. Theophilus had thirty-one milk cows, ten head of sheep, and produced 100 bushels of rye, 200 bushels of corn, and 400 bushels of oats.

As Frederick Dolsen's eldest son, the liquidation of the Dolsentown properties fell to Theophilus II [*Frederick, James Jr., James Sr., Isaac, Theunis, Jan*]. Orange County land records show that John C. Dolson deeded his share of the family inheritance to Theophilus Dolson II in 1855 for the sum of $1,950 (Liber 134, p. 354). On the same date, Margaret Dolsen transferred a portion of her interest in the same properties to Theophilus II for the token amount of five dollars. Later, on 1 March 1856, Margaret deeded the remaining interest in these three Dolsen lots to Theophilus II for ten dollars (Liber 140, p. 629). Afterward, on 1 April 1856, an Orange County deed (Liber 140, p. 630) indicates that Theophilus II sold most of the remaining Dolsen lands originally purchased by Isaac Dolsen, to a man named Simon Bradley for the amount of $15,085. The following newspaper article, reprinted in the *New York Times* on 6 May 1856, memorializes the event:

> **Value of Farm Property in Orange Co.**
> **---Theophilus Dolsen, of Dolsentown, (some three miles southeast of Middletown,) lately sold his farm, of over 100 acres, to a Mr. Benedict** [Bradley]**, for $115 per acre. This farm is a very valuable property, and is a portion of a tract of 700 acres purchased before the French and Indian war, (just one hundred years ago,) by his ancestor, ISAAC DOLSEN. In early times there was an Indian settlement in one of the meadows of the Dolsen property, and also an Indian burying ground on the high ground in the same vicinity. --Middletown Whig Press.**

On the same date, 1 April 1856, Theophilus' brother, James F. Dolson, sold a one-hundred acre parcel of the Dolsen tract to Benjamin Bradley for the sum of $10,000. As a result of these transactions, virtually all of the original 700 acres acquired by Isaac Dolsen ca. 1756 had been disposed. Of course, with monies garnered from farming profits and the land sales, many of the Dolson descendants were able to buy other properties, both near and far from Dolsentown.

Theophilus Dolsen II and Cecilia Hathaway Dolsen had the following children:

a. Frederick A. Dolson was born in 1840 and died in 1901. In October of 1863, a Frederick Dolson, living in Mount Hope, appeared on an Orange County Civil War Draft list. Following is Frederick's obituary notice:

> ***Frederick A. Dolson died last Saturday (December 22, 1901) at Denver, Colorado, age 62 years. He was a son of Theopolis Dolson, deceased of Howells. The following brothers and sister survive: R.H. Dolson of Middletown, J.W. Dolson of Wallkill, Theopolis, an Erie conductor of Port Jervis, Herbert of Norwich, and H.D. Dolson of Lincoln, Nebraska. The sisters are Mrs. Galen Otis and Mrs. James O. Davis, both of Howells.*** (*Obituaries for Various Newspapers,* Vol. I, pp. 187-188, Orange County Genealogical Society, 2000)

b. Martha S. Dolson was born 1841 and died after 1901. Mattie, as she was sometimes called, was admitted as a member to the Old School Baptist Church in Howells before 1861, where she married Galen Otis Jr. on 6 October 1863 (Foley, 1993). Notice of the marriage appeared in the *Goshen Whig Press* (21 October 1863). The couple continued to live at Howells until at least 1898 (*Port Jervis Evening Gazette,* 24 August 1898). In 1916 she was living in Bloomfield, N.J.

c. Annie Dolson was born around 1843 and died by 1898 (*Port Jervis Evening Gazette,* 24 August 1898). No further information is known regarding Annie.

d. Theophilus Dolson III was born on 31 August 1843 at the Dolson homestead in Dolsentown but subsequently lived in Mt. Hope and Port Jervis. He had a fifty-year career as a railroad conductor, retiring in 1922 (*Erie Railroad Employees Magazine,* 8 August 1922). In 1869, Theophilus Dolson of Mt. Hope appears on a list of judges for a horse show (*The Port Jervis Evening Gazette,* 14 August 1869). Theophilus III married first, Sarah Elizabeth Masterson, nicknamed Libbie, on 4 December 1867. The marriage ceremony took place in Wallkill and was officiated by the Elder Gilbert Beebe (*Orange County Genealogical Society Quarterly*, Vol. 44, No. 2). Libbie was born on 18 March 1845 and died on 13 February 1885. This couple had the following children: (a) Mattie Otis Dolson, (b) Herbert Grinnel

Dolson, (c) Oscar Crist Dolson, (d) Frank Masterson Dolson, and (e) Isabelle Dolson Hunt/Swinton. Sarah Elizabeth Masterson's parents were Louise Jane Hoyt and Zelotus Grinnel Masterson (Wheat, 1903).

Theophilus III married second, Anna Ray (1860-1930) of Goshen, on 23 February 1887 at New York City. His children, Herbert Dolson and Isabelle Dolson Swinton, were witnesses (Horton, No Date); *The Middletown Argus*, 24 February 1898). Beginning in 1849, Theophilus III participated on the committee formed to implement the division of the Town of Wawayanda from the Town of Minisink (Ruttenber and Clark, 1881). Theophilus Jr. died of cerebral apoplexy on 28 November 1922 (Coleman, 1989) at his home in Port Jervis (*Goshen Independent Republican*, 5 December 1922). He held insurance policy no. 151273 from the Mutual Life Insurance Company of New York in the amount of $5,000 (Annual Report of the Mutual Life Insurance Company of New York to Its Policy Holders). His funeral was held on 1 December 1922 and a portion of the ceremony took place at his home on 109 Ball Street in Port Jervis (*Port Jervis Evening Gazette*, 29 November 1922). He was buried in lot no. 71 of Howells Cemetery. Frank, Herbert, Oscar, and Rankin Dolson, as well as Frank Swinton (son-in-law), and Edward Ray (brother-in-law), were pall bearers.

Theophilus III was a veteran of the 124th Regiment, the Orange Blossoms, which saw action in several important battles of the Civil War. Details regarding Theophilus' military service and that of several other Dolson men who participated in the Civil War are summarized in another section of this volume. According to notes in the Dolson Family file at the Orange County Genealogical Society, Theophilus III purchased a farm in Howells and lived there after coming out of the Civil War (Horton, No Date).

e. Robert Hathaway Dolson lived from 1845 to 1915. He was a resident of Middletown. Robert Married Hattie L. Fullerton (Wedding card on file at Goshen Public Library) on 12 December 1872 (Horton, No Date). The couple had the following children: (a) Cecilia F. Dolson, (b) Beattie Dolson, (c) Clifford Dolson, (d) Irene Vollmer Dolson and, (e) James F. Dolson. Robert H. Dolson's death was memorialized by the Presbyterian Church of Middletown, noting the date 19 May 1915. Robert was the grandfather of Hildegard Dolson (1908-1981), a noted magazine journalist whose articles frequently appeared in periodicals such as *Harper's, Ladies Home Journal, McCall's*, and *Reader's Digest*. Hildegard was also a very prolific author. Some of her better-known titles include: *How About a Man*, 1938; *We Shook the Family Tree*, 1946; *My Brother Adlai*, 1956; *William Penn, Quaker Hero*, 1961; and *Please Omit Funeral*, 1977.

f. Henry D. Dolson, 1849-1922, moved to Vallisca, Iowa and then to Lincoln, Nebraska. He married Linda J. Merrell. The couple had four children (*Port Jervis Evening Gazette*, 24 August 1898). In 1881, the *Goshen Independent Republican* carried an announcement of a marriage in Des Moines, IA at the residence of J.H. Merrill. Henry is noted as being formerly of Middletown but currently residing in Villisca, IA. The bride is listed as Lida Jones (*Goshen Independent Republican,* 28 June 1881). Apparently, one or both of the newspapers printed incorrect information regarding the name of Henry's spouse. Another possibility is that in 1881, Henry married a Merril or Merrel woman, perhaps a widowed or divorced daughter, who had previously been married to a man named Jones.

g. James Wickham Dolson, 1851-1922, was living with his brother, Theophilus III, in 1880 at Port Jervis. By 1898 he was living in Middletown. James Wickham Dolson married second, Fannie Beyea in 1901.

h. Herbert Dolson's life span began on 14 December 1858 and ended on 28 December 1916. He married Anna E. Howell in Middletown on 16 November 1881. Anna was the daughter of Samuel Howell and Sally Jane Whitter. Herbert was a member of the Old School Baptist Church in Howells from before 1877 to 1888 (Foley, 1993) but later became a member of the First Congregational Church in Middletown. He lived in Middletown for thirty-four years, working in the grocery business. At the time of his mother's death, in 1898, he is noted as living in Norwich, NY. Henry's obituary notes his surviving widow, son, and siblings (*Middletown Times-Press*, 29 December 1916).

i. Alma E. Dolson was born in 1858 and died in 1927. Alma married Dr. James O. Davis. This couple erected a monument to Alma's father, Theophilus II, in Pine Hill Cemetery. The couple was living in Howells, NY in 1898 and 1901 and in Gilbertsville, NY in 1916.

Birth and death dates associated with Theophilus II's family members were taken from the notes of the Elizabeth Horton Collection at the Orange County Genealogical Society (No Date), cemetery headstones, as well as from U.S. and New York State Census records.

4. Susan Dolsen was born on 9 May 1816 and she died in October of 1842. Susan married William Wallace Dolson, a son of James Dolson [*Asa Dolsen, James Sr., Isaac, Theunis, Jan*] and Mary Van Scoy Dolson, on 22 January 1834 in Dolsentown. As in the case of her sister, Elizabeth, who married William Wallace Dolson's brother, Charles Mortimer Dolson, Susan's family moved to Schuyler County, Illinois. Later this family relocated to Muscatine, Iowa (Plimley, 2011).

5. James Frederick Dolsen was born on 28 August 1818 and died in 1889 at Middletown, New York (Plimley, 2011). James F. was a farmer in the Wallkill area for most of his life. Several properties were deeded to him by his parents before their deaths. He married Harriet Louisa Moore on 1 November 1837 at Middletown (*Goshen Independent Republican*, 4 November 1837). The couple did not have any children. The New York Census of 1855 shows James F. and Harriet L. both ages 38, living in a frame house in Wawayanda valued at $1,500. In 1880, Harriet Moore Dolson wrote a children's book entitled *Cloud Island* which was published by W.W. Smith of New York City (*Port Jervis Evening Gazette*, 30 December 1880). Harriet Moore Dolsen is known to have participated actively in the Women's Suffrage Society (*The New York Sun*, 6 August 1880). Harriet Moore Dolson died in September 1890 at the age of seventy-six.

Harriet's parents were David Moore II (1789-1872) and Elizabeth Fullerton Moore (1790-1864). The couple married on 23 February 1811. The Moore family members were descendants of John Moore of England, who immigrated to Lynn, Massachusetts in 1641 and eventually settled in Newtown, Long Island, where John died in 1657. David Moore II had brothers Wilmot, George W., and James E. Moore. Wilmot married Azubah Knapp 7 April 1791 at the Goshen Presbyterian Church. This couple had a son named Emmet Moore, who married Harriet L. Dolson, daughter of Samuel Dolson [*James Sr., Isaac, Thuenis, Jan*] on 24 March 1835 (Descendants of Thomas Moore and Martha Youngs of Southold, LI. Manuscript archived at the Orange County Genealogical Society, No Date). Elizabeth Fullerton Moore was the daughter of Captain Daniel Fullerton. When Captain Fullerton's will was probated in 1828, James *Dolson* served as executor. The Moore ancestor who resettled in Orange County, New York was David Moore I (1713-1789), husband of Hepzibah Wilmot. After arrival in Goshen, the couple settled on the Otterkill, at the location where this creek crossed Hamptonburgh Road. Later, David Moore I, in partnership with Samuel Wickham, purchased Lot 35 in the Minisink Angle along the edge of Middletown. This property consisted of 1,000 acres. This Moore family is not known to have any connection to the family of Margaret Moore Dolsen, wife of Frederick Dolsen.

Based on the description of his estate contained in his will (Orange County Liber 54, p. 254), James F. was a wealthy man. He left a share of the residual part of his estate to his brother, John C. Dolson. He also left a sum of money to the trustees of Pine Hill Cemetery with instructions to build a Dolsen Mausoleum and to care for the graves of the members of the Dolsen family located in this burying ground. Ruttenber and Clark (1881) document the Dolsen family's interest in Pine Hill Cemetery:

> ***Pine Hill Cemetery was incorporated by a certificate bearing date Oct. 8, 1861, and recorded in the office of the county clerk on the 9th. The chairman of the meeting for organization was Simon Bradley, and the secretary Samuel S. Wickham. The trustees named were James F. Dolsen, Benjamin***

Interestingly, James F., as well as his brother, Theophilus, and a cousin, William M. Dolsen, also were trustees for the Slate Hill Cemetery (Eager, 1881).

6. <u>Dewitt Clinton Dolson</u> was born on 23 April 1821 (Plimley, 2011). As his brother, James F., Dewitt also married a daughter of David Moore and Elizabeth Fullerton Moore. His marriage to Sarah Elizabeth Moore took place on 11 February 1846 in Minisink (*Goshen Independent Republican*, 27 February 1846). Sarah Elizabeth was born on the 28 June, 1821 and was twenty-three years old at the time of her marriage.

   Dewitt had a business in Middletown. In April 1848, as part of an annexation preceding, a landmark was identified by the court as "*Franklin Square near Dewitt C. Dolsen's storehouse*" (Williams, 1928, p. 45). Around 1850, Dewitt and his wife relocated to San Francisco, California. Apparently, the couple's infant daughter, Adelia, aged 2, was living with her Aunt, Sarah, in Wawayanda at the time (U.S. Census, 1850). In San Francisco, Dewitt opened a fish stall at the California Market in partnership with a man named Vail (*Daily Alta California*, 14 March 1853). The market, sometimes referred to as the Oriental Market, was located along Sacramento Street towards the Long Wharf. The writer wonders if his partner, identified only as Mr. Vail, might not be linked to the Vail family of Minisink, in-laws of Phebe Meeker, Asa Dolsen, and Samuel Dolsen. Later Dewitt partnered with a man named Trautman until the dissolution of that firm in 1869 (*Daily Alta California*, 23 June 1869). During the time his fish markets operated, Dewitt occasionally placed advertisements in the San Francisco newspapers such as the one printed in the *San Francisco Call Bulletin* dated 29 November 1856 containing the following details:

   > **D.C. Dolson, Dealer in Fresh and Salt Fish, located in stalls 29 and 30, Washington Market, San Francisco.**

   Around this time, according to information garnered from California Voter Registrations, Dewitt worked as a messenger for the Customs House in San Francisco. He lived at 10 Laskie Street between 8th and 9th Streets. He is shown on an 1864 tax assessment as an employee of the Customs House and he was required to pay five percent in taxes on a watch and two pianos.

   Dewitt Clinton Dolson and Sarah E. Moore Dolson had one daughter, Adelia (or Adeline) Elizabeth, born on 5 May 1848 in New York. She died in San Francisco. Her obituary notice was published in the *Daily Alta California* on 11 December 1872:

Died in this city December 10, Mrs. Adelia E. Caldwell, daughter of D.C. Dolson and S.E. Dolson. 24 years and 6 months. Funeral December 12, 11:00 A.M. First Congregational Church.

Based on this newspaper article depicting her surname as Caldwell, Adelia must have been married. It is striking that the death notice identifies her parents, but not her spouse. Given Adelia's young age at death (twenty-four), she may have died as a result of complications associated with pregnancy or childbirth.

In the last year of his life, 1892, Dewitt's voter registration indicates that he was seventy-two years of age; 5'8" tall; light complexioned with blue eyes. He was bald, but there was a notation that he "wears a wig". He was reported as not having an occupation at the time (probably retired) and living at 1169 Mission Street, San Francisco.

Dewitt Clinton Dolsen's death on 17 November 1892 was reported in the *San Francisco Call Bulletin (*20 November 1892). That notice specified that Dewitt Clinton Dolson was a native of New York; aged seventy-two years. His wife, Sarah, died four years earlier on 5 March 1888 (*San Francisco Call Bulletin*). Although Dewitt lived just ninety miles distant from the Sacramento area, there is no indication that his family had any contact with that of his brother, John C. Dolson, in Elk Grove.

Bits and pieces of information published in the *Daily Alta California* newspaper provide glimpses into the life of Dewitt during the time he lived in San Francisco:

- October 1851: **Two French gentlemen got into a fight on Commercial Street over a broken window. The workmen, acknowledged to be painters and glaziers, were fined a sum to replace the store window of Mr. Dolson.**
- 30 April 1869: **There was a severe accident on Market Street on Monday afternoon last. Mr. Dewitt C. Dolson was conducting the business wagon of Dolson and Trautmann near the junction of Eddy Street when he was run into by a two-horse brewery wagon which was moving at a reckless speed. The collision upset Mr. Dolson's wagon, breaking it into pieces, and throwing him to the street. He suffered a fractured right leg at the knee and other bruising which may confine him to bed for weeks if not months. The driver of the brewery wagon did not wait to learn the particulars but whipped up his horses and dashed out of sight. The police have an investigation in hand and it is hoped they will discover the perpetrator of the inexcusable deed that he may be brought to his deserved punishment.**

163

- 19 June 1869: ***DISSOLUTION—Dewitt Clinton Dolson and John Trautmann, 35 and 30 California Market, on this day dissolved by mutual consent. Dewitt C. Dolson will pay all liabilities and collect outstanding debts. The undersigned will continue the business at the old stand and hopes for a continuation of the very liberal patronage heretofore extended to the old concern. Signed Dewitt C. Dolson.***
- 30 June 1875: ***Polling places have been established for the upcoming primary election for the Third Election Precinct bounded by 8th Street, Market Street, Dolores Street, 16th Street, and Mission. One of the election judges is D.C. Dolson.***
- March 1893: ***Letters being held at the post office for gentlemen include one for Dewitt C. Dolson*** [Writer's Note: This was the last entry for Dewitt. He never received this letter since he and all of the members of his immediate family had died before this date].

7. Ellen Adelia Dolson was born on 18 March 1827 and died on 27 November 1868 at the age of forty-one. She married Samuel S. Wickham II (1821-1891), a well-regarded retail businessman from Middletown. At one-point Samuel established a coal, flour, and feed store in Middletown (*Port Jervis Union*, 12 September 1891). The wedding took place at Dolsentown on 16 September 1850 (*Goshen Independent Republican,* 27 September 1850). At the age of twenty-two, Samuel became a clerk at a dry goods store. In 1847 he purchased a majority interest in the Houston and Dill Tannery, a business that carried on until 1855. In that year, he purchased 1,500 acres of woodlands in Sullivan County, NY and engaged in large-scale lumbering. He is noted as erecting three sawmills (*Port Jervis Union*, 12 September 1891). Samuel was a trustee, along with several Dolsens, of Pine Hill Cemetery. According to census records, Ellen's mother, Margaret Moore Dolsen, lived with Ellen and Samuel in her old age. The couple is reported to have had up to five children, some of whom appear to have died young. After Ellen Adelia's death in 1868, Samuel Wickham remarried in 1870 to Marilee Raplee of Yates County, New York, with whom he had another child. Marilee died ca. 1873. Samuel died on Friday, 11 September 1891, suddenly and unexpectedly of nervous depression. He was seventy-nine years of age. Surviving children were Cecilia S. Wickham, Oscar D. Wickham, Almeda Wickham Demerest, and Laura Wickham, all of Middletown (*Port Jervis Union*, 12 September, 1891).

The Wickham family came early to Orange County and the first Samuel Wickham was considered an important pioneer of the area. He was wealthy and owned a number of slaves. His descendants were (1) William, a noted attorney, who had many dealings with the Dolsens in both Minisink and Warwick; (2) George, a well-known banker and business man in Goshen; and finally, (3) Samuel S. Wickham, who married Ellen Adelia Dolsen.

8. Oscar H. Dolson was born 1 December 1829 and died on 27 August 1900. He is buried in Pine Hill Cemetery. Oscar's obituary appeared in the *Goshen Independent Republican* on 28 August 1900:

> **Oscar H. Dolson died at Middletown yesterday, aged 71 years. Deceased was the son of Frederick and Margaret Dolson and he was born at Dolsentown, in the town of Wawayanda, on the site of** [what is now] **Supervisor John I. Bradley's residence. Mr. Dolson was married in 1854 to Esther Almeda North. She died March 9, 1880, at Goshen, and on November 14, 1888, Mr. Dolson was again wedded, this time to Angeline Butler, of Cold Spring, and she survives. Mr. Dolson was for a time a clerk in the County Clerk's office. For a long time he was in charge of the Erie freight depot in this village and afterwards conducted a cigar store in the store room now occupied by W.O. Sayer. He afterwards removed to Middletown where he held a position as clerk in the office of Dolson and Conklin.**

Oscar's second wife, Angeline P. Butler Dolson, is reported to have died on 20 March 1914.

Second Voyage and Settlement in Elk Grove

After his marriage to Hannah O'Connor, and with his inheritances in hand, John returned to California with his bride in 1855. As the case of the initial trip to California, the manner of travel selected was by ship to and from the Isthmus of Panama. He spent an additional year of prospecting in El Dorado and Placer counties before deciding to revert to his original vocation, farming. The family sojourned in Sacramento in 1856 and then settled in San Joaquin Township, now known as Elk Grove, in 1857. In a statement provided to the Native Daughters of the Golden West for the association's archives, Alice Dolson Cutbirth reported that the family arrived in Elk Grove on 5 July 1857(Davis 1890).

John, along with Hannah, lived on the farm in Elk Grove from 1857 until their deaths in 1909 and 1911 respectively. Various U.S. Census and government reports confirm the family's tenure on the 160-acre farm located approximately fifteen miles south of Sacramento.

- 1860: John C., famer, age thirty-five, a native of New York with wife Hannah, age twenty-five, a native of Ireland and two male children, O.J. five years and J.J. two years. A man named O. Barkman, age thirty-five, a native of Finland, was living on the farm.

- 1870: Besides John and Hannah, six children were listed: Oscar fourteen, John twelve, David nine, Maggie seven, William five, and Mary nine and one half months. None of the children attended school at this time. Property evaluations were reported as $2,000 for real estate and $1,000 in personal effects.

- In 1870, John paid $27.28 in property taxes to Sacramento County for his Elk Grove farm located in Road District 23 of NW ¼ Section 31. In this instance, the value of the real estate was $320 and the value of improvements and furnishings was $300 and $55 respectively. Other personal property was worth $475. John C. was reported to have one dog, two wagons, sixteen cattle and three horses. There was a notation on the tax form that a railroad track ran through the property.

- 1880: John C. continued to be listed as a farmer. Hannah's middle initial was recorded as "M" and she was noted as being a housekeeper. Children were: Oscar J., John J., David Pelton, Maggie M., William, Mary E., and newly added were Alice E., age eight, and Joseph H., age five. The adult children, Oscar and John, were listed as farm laborers. Interestingly, a school teacher named Ginnie Gage, age twenty-four, born in Michigan with parents from New York, resided with the Dolsons. The Gage family was well known in Elk Grove. Upon her death in 1909, Hannah O'Connor Dolson's estate inventory included a mortgage of $2,500 held against Norman Gage of the same family.

The agricultural production survey taken in 1880 contained the following details regarding John C. Dolson's farm:

- The value of the property was listed as $4,500 and machinery at $100
- Livestock, consisting of two horses was assessed at $100
- Labor costs for the year were reported to be $100 for five weeks of work
- Total income was reported at $800 with $155 coming from rents
- Land use consisted of twenty-five acres of mown hay, sixty acres of barley, ten acres in wheat, nine acres in peach orchards, one acre of apples, and two acres in vineyards

- 1890: No census data are available. Most records collected for the U.S. Census in 1890 were destroyed in a fire. John C. was listed in the Great Register of 1890 as being sixty-seven years old, living in the twentieth precinct of Elk Grove.

- 1900: By this year, William, age thirty-five, farmer, was registered as the head of the household. No occupation was noted for John. He probably was considered to be retired at the time. Along with Hannah, David, age forty, farm laborer, was still in the home. A thought-provoking detail contained in this census is that Hannah is recorded as the mother of nine children with eight surviving. Apparently one child died at birth or died very young. A grave of a Dolson infant has not been discovered at the Masonic Cemetery in Elk Grove nor at any other cemetery in the region.

Overtime, John C. Dolson was sighted frequently on voter registrations in Sacramento County. Several of these listings provide interesting details regarding John and other Dolson family members:

- *1874: John C. age 51 and Theophilus Dolson, age 37*
- *1888: John C. age 64 and sons, Willie 22, and David P. 27*
- *1890: John C. age 67 of the 20th precinct, from NY, mentioned sons David and William*
- *1898: John C. age 75, 5'8', light complexion, blue eyes, brown hair*
- *1900: John C., age 77 and sons living in Elk Grove*
- *1905: John C., age 82, farmer in Elk Grove*

The Theophilus Dolson, aged 37, mentioned in the 1874 voter registration was living in the Sutterville Precinct which, in contemporary times, is a neighborhood in the mid-southern section of the City of Sacramento along a road by the same name. This man may be Theophilus IV, who was born in 1837 in Muscatine, Iowa. He was the son of William Wallace Dolson and his wife Lutitia. The fact that Theophilus IV was in Sacramento at this time suggests that the Dolsons in California continued to have contacts with Dolson family members from other parts of the United States even as late as the mid-1770s.

James F. Dolsen, one of John's brothers residing New York died on 19 March 1888. In his will he left an inheritance to each of his siblings still living, including John. The amount of the bequest was to be calculated, share and share alike, from the residual of the estate. The amount could have been significant since, from all appearances, James F. Dolsen was well off financially.

During John C. Dolson's life in Elk Grove, a number of reports published by the *Sacramento Daily Union* provide interesting anecdotes about John and his family:

- 6 August 1860: *John C. Dolson, along with John Shannon, Thomas McAlpin, W. McCrosky, A.K. Bond, Thomas J. Thomson, J.H. Kerr, and Otis Barkway were jurors involved in a murder trial. A 57 year-old man named A. Blanchard, blacksmith, was killed on a Saturday night by two men. The incident took place in Thomas Mahan's field near adjacent to Buckner's house and pasture which is near Stockton Road. On his way home around 9:00 P.M. Blanchard was beat about the head with a spoke from a wagon wheel and a pick handle until he fell dead in a ditch. Before his body could be found it was partially mutilated by grazing pigs. Found guilty of the crime were William Williams, perpetrator, and Joseph Blake, accomplice. The motive: a lawsuit over disputed property.*

- 18 December 1869: *The following sum was paid into the County Treasury yesterday by John C. Dolson, $32, interest on state school land, location No. 285.*

- 6 December 1870: *John C. Dolson pays $312 taxes on the balance and principal due on state school land.*

- 23 April 1872: *John E. [C.] Dolson is listed as impaneled on the Grand Jury of the County Court.*

- 4 December 1872: *Persons chosen yesterday to serve as trial jurors during the October term of the County Court include John E. [C.] Dolson of San Joaquin Township.*

- 4 December 1873: *Elk Grove Schools. The County Superintendent reports that ... the following students are promoted to the fourth division: Fred Dickson, Willie Dolson, Nellie Davis, Alice Parker, and Minnie Siberwood.*

- 1 March 1881: *Wedding notice is given for Maggie M. Dolson and Christian Haavig, both residents of Elk Grove. The ceremony was held in the home of the bride's parents.*

- 26 May 1882: *Glass Balls---At Elk Grove next Sunday three teams will compete for a prize of $50 in shooting at glass balls. Each person will shoot at 50 balls. The names of the shooters are as follows: First Team Meiers, Gillespie, Coons and Dan Stevens; second team Dwight and Frank Coses; Third team Charles Graham and John Dolson. A special match between Lafeyette Derr and F. Coons is set for $100.*

- 7 February 1888: *The announcement has been made of several medals awarded to outstanding student scholars in the county for meritorious conduct. Victory School District: Miss A. Dolson.*

- 21 February 1888: *Self-proclaimed marksmen held a contest Sunday in Florin. Each was provided the opportunity to shoot 25 pigeons. The final score: John Dolson 10 and F. Coons 12.*

- 15 May 1888: *Graduation diplomas have been granted by the County Board of Education to students of the various schools. Victory District: Alice Dolson with a score of 76 percent.*

- 10 June 1892: *Capitol City Gun Club hosted a contest. The scores for the members of the Elk Grove Club include J. Dolson 21 and D.P. Dolson 17.*

- 10 June 1896: *Capital City Gun Club accepted the challenge and invitation of the Elk Grove Gun Club to shoot a twenty-five bird match for the "rocks" and a dinner at the hotel in Elk Grove last Sunday. Scores Elk Grove Club— J. Tavemer 23, J. Pickett 17, R. Maitland 20, J. Dolson 21, G. Tavemer 16, D.P. Dolson 17---Total 114.*

- December 30, 1899: *Transfer of land, J.C. Dolson to John Hurly, northeast quarter of sec. 81, township 7 north, range 6 east.*

In 1890, a collection of biographies of local pioneers was published in a volume entitled *The History of Sacramento County* (Davis, 1890), which included the following entry on John C. Dolson and his family:

John C. Dolson, a San Joaquin Township rancher, was born In Orange County, New York, April 7, 1823, a son of Frederick and Margaret (Moore) Dolson. His father was a native of Germany and a farmer by occupation, and in his family were five sons and four daughters. He died at the age of fifty-one years, and his wife at the age of sixty years, in Orange County, New York. Mr. Dolson, of this sketch, was brought up on the farm and came to California in 1850, by way of Panama, being three months on the route. He followed mining four years at Pilot Hill, near Georgetown, but he did not make much money, although the mines had been very rich. In 1854 he returned to Orange County, New York, again by way of the Isthmus; and during this year he was married to Hannah O'Connor, a native of Ireland. In 1855 he came again to this State and resumed mining for two years on the American River, with rather poor success. In 1857 he settled on his present ranch, a half mile from Elk Grove, and here he has prospered as a general farmer, as he has well deserved to do. He has eight children, in the following order: Oscar J., born October 1, 1855; John J., November 17, 1857; David P., January 4, 1861; Maggie M., May 4, 1863; Willie, May 22, 1865; Mary E., August 23, 1869; Alice E., December 31, 1871; and Joseph H., October 23, 1874.

This article by Davis (1890) contains a number of interesting details about the family. The obvious error in the piece however is the statement that Frederick Dolsen was a native of Germany. Reliable evidence indicates that Frederick was a fifth-generation American, born at Minisink, Orange County, New York of predominantly Dutch and secondarily, of British ancestry.

John C. Dolson's Legacy

According to probate case No. 5127 of Sacramento County, John C. Dolson died on 16 March, 1909 at the age of seventy-five years. His correct age however was eighty-six. He is buried in the Masonic Cemetery in Elk Grove. The following obituary was published:

> **Mr. John C. Dolson, one of the old settlers, died near Elk Grove March 16th. He was a native of New York and aged 86 years. He leaves a wife and 8 children. Mr. Dolson had been a semi-invalid for some time. He was a man of many good deeds and held in high esteem. The funeral service from his late residence was a large one. Internment in Masonic Cemetery** (*Elk Grove Citizen*, 20 March 1909).

Another version of the obituary was printed in the *Sacramento Bee*:

> **Dolson---Near Elk Grove, March 16, 1909. John C. Dolson, beloved husband of Hannah Dolson, father of Oscar, John, David, Maggie, Will, Mary, Alice, and Joseph Dolson, grandfather of Pearl Cuthbert, a native of New York, aged 86 years. Friends and acquaintances are respectfully invited to attend the funeral tomorrow afternoon at 2:30 o'clock from his late residence, near Elk Grove, where funeral services will be held. Internment in Masonic Cemetery, Elk Grove** (17 March 1909).

The only grandchild mentioned was Pearl Cutbirth, the daughter of Alice Dolson Cutbirth and her husband, Lincoln Cutbirth. No mention was made of any of the other grandchildren, deceased or living, including any of the children from the marriage of David Pelton Dolson and Caroline Van Ness. Granddaughters Katherine (deceased by this date), Elizabeth, and Vivian belonging to this couple were born before John C. Dolson's death.

Upon his father's passing, Joseph H. Dolson petitioned the Sacramento County Superior Court (Probate Case No. 5127) to become administrator of the estate. John C. Dolson did not leave a will. The petition was approved on 20 December 1909. The Court declared that John C. Dolson died intestate and that the deceased left real property and that said property is common property belonging to Hannah Dolson, his wife. The Final Account of Administration filed with the Court on 27 December 1909 describes the real estate holding as follows:

> **A tract of land consisting of 50.33 acres: Beginning at the Northwest corner of Section thirty one (31), Township Seven (7) North, Range six (6) East, Mount Diablo Base and Meridian: thence South along Section line forty and fifty one thousandths (40.051) chains to the quarter section corner of said Section thirty one (31); thence east eighteen and twenty nine hundredths (18.29) chains to the Sacramento Southern Railway Company's right of way; thence following said right of way north to the intersection of said right of way with the northern**

***boundary of said Section Thirty one (31); thence West eight and thirty five
thousandths (8.035) chains to the place of beginning.***

The writer estimates that John C. Dolson's farm was located roughly one mile north of the
center of the town of Elk Grove along Elk Grove-Florin Road immediately north of the
intersection of that road with Bond Road and along the course of the Southern Pacific
Railroad tracks up to the place where the tracks cross Elk Grove-Florin Road. As of 2018,
most of this parcel was undeveloped. There were no significant remnants on the property of
former buildings or indications of previous agricultural activity. The Dolson mansion that was
built on this property in 1880 was eventually moved to Elk Grove Boulevard by the Gage
family. The Gage family relocated the home for a second time in 2006 to 5623 Tegan Road,
Elk Grove, where it was still being used as a family residence in 2018. The location of the
original ranch was determined based on information contained in Hannah O'Connor's Letter
of Administration, *McKinney's Sacramento City and County Directory of 1884-85,* and
Husted's Sacramento Directory of 1889-90.

When Hannah M. O'Connor Dolson died on 9 April 1911, her son, Joseph H. Dolson, became
administrator of her estate (Probate Case No. 5520). The inventory of property consisted of
the following:

Moneys (cash) held by the deceased	$3,214.30
Note and Mortgage against Norman Gage	$2,500.00
Household goods	$ 20.00
Property[11]	$1,200.00
Cemetery Lot in North Elk Grove Masonic Cemetery	$ 20.00
Other cash received by the estate	$2,772.45

By the consent of the heirs, the administrator paid $185.00 for a granite monument over the
grave of the deceased. An attorney was employed to represent the administrator in the
matter of the estate. Hannah Dolson's funeral was conducted by the W.F. Gormley Mortuary.
Charges totaled $372.25.

Thus ends the saga of another generation of Dolsons of this branch of the family. In
summarizing the major events of John C. Dolson's life, the writer offers the following
observations:

- According to his voter registration profile, at age seventy-five, John C. was 5'8" tall,
  light complexioned, with blue eyes and brown hair.

---

[11] West fifty feet of Lot Number Eleven (11) in the H.S. Hill survey of the Town of Elk Grove Station
made June 12th 1876 by A.G. Winn.

- John was an authentic California pioneer. The first major event recorded in his adult life was leaving New York and traveling to California during the Gold Rush. John C. probably had a strong spirit of adventure. At the same time, it is possible that he did not see a viable future for himself in New York. The once large Dolson homestead in Orange County had been repeatedly subdivided among the male offspring for several generations. The dream of better opportunities in California must have influenced several of the Dolson men of this generation. Not only did John set out for the West in 1850, but his brother, Dewitt Clinton Dolson, relocated to San Francisco about the same time. Other siblings removed to the Midwest.

- Although John was not successful at mining during his early years in California, he eventually became a prosperous farmer in Elk Grove. The agricultural enterprise that John undertook and sustained was sufficient to adequately support a family of eight children during the period from 1857 to approximately 1910.

- The extent of schooling received by John's and Hannah's children is uncertain. Several census reports indicate that there were periods of time when some of the children did not attend school and several of the older boys were not considered to be literate at the time they reached maturity. On the other hand, Alice was a solid scholar and graduated from high school---a significant and uncommon achievement for a woman in the late 1800s. There is a record which shows that Willie (William) attended school through at least the third grade. Later census and voter registrations indicate that, eventually, all of the Dolson offspring were able to read and write.

- Comparable to his father, Frederick, John C. Dolson participated in relatively few civic affairs. John did serve as a juror and it is noteworthy that he and his sons consistently registered to vote. John did not serve in the military even though he would have been of age during the Civil War.

- John C. Dolson eventually settled far from his New York origins. This fact resulted in separation and relative isolation of his branch of the family from its ancestral core. At the same time, the cohesiveness of the family in Orange County, New York began to unravel. Some of John C. Dolson's siblings relocated to other parts of New York and several moved to other states. John's brothers, Theophilus II and James F., sold the remaining lots of the Dolson tract in Wawayanda. A third brother, Dewitt C. Dolson, resettled in San Francisco. By the early 1900s, the members of this branch of the Dolson family had scattered widely. Newspaper reports of the time show that John intermittently received letters at the Sacramento Post Office----quite possibly some of this correspondence represented communications from family members in New York, San Francisco, and perhaps even from John's siblings, who had resettled in other states such as Illinois, Iowa, and Nebraska.

Chapter VIII - Eighth Generation

David P. Dolson I

[John C., Frederick, James Sr., James Jr., Isaac, Theunis, Jan]

This volume contains an account on nine generations of a specific branch of the Dolson family over a time span of approximately 350 years. Of the Dolson men featured in this sketch, the writer has encountered less elucidating documentation on David Pelton Dolson I than on any of the other ancestors. This is somewhat surprising since David lived in a recent era which benefitted from better-kept government records and the availability of photographs. In fact the author is aware of only a single, existing photograph of this man. The reasons for this lack of relevant material may be connected to several factors. First and foremost, it seems that David lead a quiet and commonplace life. He appears to have participated in few extraordinary activities. Secondly, it is likely that the personality of his wife and a possible estrangement from his family over his marriage affected the course of David's life and what we know about it. Additionally, in his adult life, David experienced sporadic and low-paying employment, which suggests that he and his wife and children habitually lived in poverty. Each of these matters shall be discussed in further detail in later sections of this chapter.

Early Life in Elk Grove
David Pelton Dolson I was born on 4 January 1861 in San Joaquin Township now called Elk Grove, in Sacramento County, California. He was the third of six surviving children of John Carpenter Dolson and Hannah O'Connor Dolson.

No ancestors named David are observed previously in this branch of Dolson genealogy. Consequently, the writer assumes that the name David emanates from Hannah O'Connor's lineage. The second given name, Pelton, was taken from a prominent family in Orange County, New York. The Peltons were neighbors of the Dolsons at Warwick, NY during the early 1800s. An interesting story regarding the Pelton and Dolson family connection is recounted in the Appendix to this volume. As is the case with several other Dolsons, David had a nickname, in this instance, an abbreviated form of his middle name, "Pelt".

According to census records, David grew up on his parent's farm in Elk Grove. The U.S. Census of 1870 indicates that the then nine-year-old David was attending school along with his brothers, Oscar and John, fourteen and twelve years of age respectively. In 1880, at the age of nineteen, David continued to live at home, but was no longer enrolled in school. He is listed as a farm laborer, unemployed during two months of the previous year.

David stayed on at the Elk Grove property into adulthood. At the age of forty, he was shown as living with his aging parents and his younger brother, William, who was recorded as the head of the household (U.S. Census, 1900). The Dolsons were reported as owning the farm, free of mortgage. John Carpenter Dolson was categorized as retired, William as a farmer, and David Pelton as a laborer. The latter two men were employed full time. By this date, all of David's other siblings had left the family farm.

David's Marriage to Caroline Van Ness

According to a marriage certificate dated 2 October 1906, David married Caroline Van Ness in Sacramento. He was forty-five at the time and she twenty-one. The witness to the ceremony was Caroline's brother, Matthew Van Ness. Matthew signed his name to the certificate. Caroline stated at the time that her name was Carrie; that she was born in San Francisco; that she could not remember her father's name; and that her mother's name was Kate Sullivan. The couple was married by a Justice of the Peace. Both parties signed the marriage certificate indicating that they were able to write. This was the first marriage for both the bride and the groom.

The family of David P. Dolson and Caroline Van Ness Dolson consisted of seven children, six of whom lived into adulthood. All of the children are thought to have been born in Sacramento.

1. Katherine Van Ness was born on 5 March 1904[12] and died around 1906 or 1907. According to Caroline Van Ness, the death was related to the San Francisco earthquake of 1906, but there is no evidence to confirm this account. Katherine was named after her maternal grandmother, Katherine Sullivan. Since this child was born out of wedlock and the surname was recorded as Van Ness, it is plausible that David P. Dolson was not Katherine's biological father.

2. Elizabeth Hannah Dolson was born 12 October 1906. She was most commonly referred to as Bessie.

3. Vivian Hannah Dolson was born on 14 February 1909. She was given the nickname Dilly, which may have come from a popular song of the day. As in the case of her elder sister Bessie, Vivian's middle name was in honor of her paternal grandmother.

4. David Pelton Dolson II was born on 8 July 1911. He is the ancestor in this line of the family. His family nickname was Buddy. During his lifetime, there were extremely few instances when he was referred to as David Pelton Dolson Jr. More information will be provided on David II in the next chapter.

---

[12] The Sacramento County Recorder has on file birth records for the period 1872-1905. Page 44 of this registry contains the following entry: *Van Ness, Female, White, Born March 5, 1904.*

5. <u>Caroline Beverly Dolson</u> was born on 12 January 1914. Although named after her mother, and sometimes called Carrie, a nickname also used by her mother, she also had a second nickname, Tye.

6. <u>Josephine Johanna Dolson</u> was born on 12 October 1916. She was informally called Jo.

7. <u>James Ronald Dolson</u> was born on June 6, 1923. He was most commonly referred to by the diminutive of his middle name, Ronnie.

The writer speculates that the names Elizabeth, Vivian, Beverly, Josephine, and Ronald likely originated with maternal ancestors, specifically the Sullivan family. Only the names of David, Johanna (Hanna) and Pelton are found in recent Dolson family history. James and Elizabeth are longstanding Dolson names, but are common enough to possibly have existed in the Sullivan or Van Ness lines also.

Fact or Fiction

Caroline Van Ness' personality, along with her lack of knowledge, dearth of candidness, and questionable veracity, resulted in significant gaps in family history, particularly in regards to what we know about the collateral families of Van Ness, Sullivan, and Adams. Caroline commonly supplied "fuzzy" facts of every sort regarding details such as dates, ages, names, places, and nationalities.

For example, Caroline's father was William Henry Van Ness. Yet at the time of her marriage in 1906, she claimed that she did not know his name. Later, in 1941, when she applied for a Social Security Card, she gave the name of her father as Jack Van Ness. She alternately claimed that he was of Swedish, German, and Belgian origins. Actually, William Henry was born in Georgia, of a father from New York, probably of Dutch heritage.

Caroline had a difficult childhood and there is reason to believe that her mother and father were less than model parents. Even after her marriage to David P. Dolson I, her life remained vexatious.

Perhaps fibbing as a child and being untruthful as an adult were coping schemes that Caroline adopted to get through some very difficult circumstances. In hindsight, the writer realizes that much of the information that Caroline passed on to her children and grandchildren was inaccurate.

Caroline Van Ness

Caroline (Carrie) Van Ness was born on 3 June 1885 in San Francisco. Her middle name was probably Vivian. She was the daughter of William Henry Van Ness and Katherine (Kate) Sullivan.

By her own account, Caroline had a very problematic childhood. Her parents died while she was still a teenager and she claims to have been raised in a convent in San Francisco. The records of many institutions in San Francisco were destroyed in the 1906 earthquake and unfortunately, the writer has been unable to locate any documentation regarding Caroline's early childhood.

By the early 1850s, the San Francisco Diocese operated the San Francisco Roman Catholic Orphan Asylum and the Mount St. Joseph Baby House. Based on inquiries made by Patricia Loverde Hienrich of diocesan administrators between June 2000 and May 2003, the following information was obtained from the remaining ledgers of the Orphan Asylum:

- *On 10 February 1883, two abandoned children were admitted to the orphan asylum: Jennie Van Ness, age 4, and Matthew Van Ness, age 1. Both children were born in San Francisco.*
- *The children left the orphan asylum on 30 June 1883. There is no record of the subsequent living arrangement or conditions of the children.*
- *Both parents were living at the time of internment. The parents were reported to have come to California in 1854. The parents were married in St. Patrick's Church, San Francisco. The father was from Georgia and the mother from Boston, Massachusetts.*

St. Patrick's Church, established in 1851 by San Francisco's Irish community, was situated adjacent to the Orphan Asylum in the Mission District of San Francisco. Still at its original location, 756 Mission Street, the church was rebuilt after the devastating earthquake and fire of 1906. Scars from that event are still apparent on the original walls.

The reasons for the placement of the two Van Ness children in the asylum are unknown, but the notation that they were abandoned is disconcerting. Since both parents were reported to be living in 1883, perhaps the family experienced severe poverty, illness, alcoholism, separation, or a combination of these factors. It is surprising not to find the names of Caroline and her older brother, Henry, on the asylum registers.

Caroline Van Ness maintained that she was interned in a "convent" upon the death of her mother and remained there until she turned sixteen years of age in 1901. Katherine Sullivan is thought to have died ca. 1900, the year in which the second and last child from her relationship with John Adams was born. Consequently, Caroline may have resided at the San Francisco Orphan Asylum for a period as short as one or two years to slightly longer than a decade. In response to a question on the 1940 U.S. Census, Caroline reported that her schooling consisted of a sixth-grade education.

There is an alphabetized but clearly incomplete admissions list of the San Francisco Orphan Asylum for the same period (specific year not identified), which contains the name *Harriet*

Adams, No. 2684. The writer suspects that this Harriet may be Caroline's step sister. The name of her step brother, John J. Adams, is not found on this register.

The writer has yet to uncover any additional information about Caroline Van Ness' childhood nor her activities as a young adult previous to her marriage. The next sighting of Caroline is her marriage to David P. Dolson I in 1906. According to the U.S. Census of 1900, her brother Henry and her sister, Jennie Van Ness, were living together in Sacramento. Her brother, Mathew Van Ness, was living with the family of Adam Warner in Franklin, a small township just east of Elk Grove. A guardianship had been issued in 1900 to Adam Warner for Matthew. There is no directory or census listing in 1900 for Caroline. According to Caroline, she was still residing at the "convent". She would have been only fifteen years old in 1900 and according to her own recollection; she did not leave the convent until she reached the age of sixteen.

William Henry Van Ness and Family
William Henry Van Ness was born in Chatom County, Georgia in 1850. The first sighting of this man is in the U.S. Census of 1850. He is listed as two months old, living with his parents, two sisters, and an aunt in Chatom County.

According to a notation on records maintained by The San Francisco Orphan Asylum, William Henry Van Ness may have arrived in San Francisco as early as 1854; however, it is likely that this archive is inaccurate on this point as William would have been but four years old at the time. There are no corresponding records to indicate that the rest of his family relocated to San Francisco.

Henry eventually married Katherine Sullivan, a native of Boston, Massachusetts. According to records of the Catholic Diocese of San Francisco, the ceremony was held at St. Patrick's Church in San Francisco. In a 1949 interview with her granddaughter, Patricia Loverde Heinrich, Caroline claimed that her parents were married in 1877. Given the 1873 date of birth of the first born child, Henry, the writer considers that the marriage may have taken place several years earlier, perhaps 1871 or 1872. No marriage record has been located.

William Henry Van Ness and Katherine Sullivan Van Ness had at least the following children during their marriage:

1. Henry C. Van Ness   1873-After 1930
2. Isabel Van Ness   1874-1878
3. Mary Van Ness   1878-1879
4. Jennie F. Van Ness   1879-1961
5. Mathew Van Ness   1881-1960
6. Caroline Van Ness   1885-1970

Isabel died as a young child and Mary died as an infant. Their death notices were published in the *San Francisco Call Bulletin*:

Van Ness—In this city, January 31, Isabel, daughter of William H. and Kate Van Ness, aged 3 years, 9 months, and 5 days (1 February 1878)

Van Ness—In this city, February 1, Mary, daughter of William H. and Katie Van Ness, aged 1 year and 14 days (3 February 1879)

In the 1880 U.S. Census, William Henry Van Ness, age twenty-nine, and Kate Van Ness, age twenty-seven, are listed along with two children: Henry, age eight, and *Jane* [Jennie], age eight months. William H. and Kate were reported to be married. The father's occupation was reported as a waiter in a restaurant. Kate was keeping house.

There are a number of sightings of William Henry in San Francisco during the 1880s. Most of this information comes from Langley's San Francisco Directories[13] and voter registration forms:

- **1880: William Henry, age 29, Georgia, waiter, 515 8th Street, 2nd floor.**
- **1880-81: William H. employed at a restaurant, 813 Market Street. Terrance Healy, an Irish immigrant, was associated with this establishment.**
- **William H., waiter, residence West Hampshire between Solano and Butte Streets.**
- **1881-82: William H., cook, residence at 515 8th Street.**
- **1882: William Henry: age 31, Georgia, waiter, West York Between 18th and 19th Streets.**
- **1886: William Henry, age 37, Georgia, waiter, Bonanza Lodging House, 2nd floor, room 31.**
- **1887: William H., waiter, residence 869 Market Street.**
- **1887-88: William H., waiter, Main Restaurant at 719 Market Street, residence 445 Clementina Street.**
- **1890: William Henry, age 39, from Georgia, bartender, residing at 519 Sacramento Street** (Great Register of 1890).
- **1892: William Henry, age 41, Georgia, waiter, dark complexioned, brown eyes, dark hair, pock mark, Adams House, 1st floor, room 110.**
- **1893: William H., waiter, Adams House.**

---

[13] *Langley's San Francisco Directory* was published annually by the Directory Publishing Company from 1857 to 1895. In subsequent years, the same directory was published by the H.S. Crocker Company and even later by the R.L. Polk Company. All of these publishers were located in San Francisco.

- *1896: William Henry, age 51, 5'6", dark complexioned, hazel eyes, brown hair, Georgia, 217 Third St., 2nd floor, room 31, literate.*
- *1898: William Henry, age 50, 5'3 ¾", dark complexioned, dark hair, dark eyes, 217 Third St., 2nd floor, room 124.*

These records provide many interesting details regarding William Henry Van Ness and his circumstances during the 1880s. It is interesting to note that he appears to have changed residences and employment often and that several of the locations where William Henry resided after 1890 are evidently single rooms at boarding houses. This then raises the prospect that during these years, he may not have resided with his wife, Katherine Sullivan Van Ness, and the children.

There are no sightings of William Henry Van Ness after 1899. Caroline Van Ness Dolson, when interviewed in 1949, gave the date of her father's death as 1887. However, there are a number of credible sightings of William Henry through 1898.

The *San Francisco Call Bulletin* reported the death of a *William Van Ness,* age 50, in 1899. The San Francisco Coroner records contain the following entry: *"Night of 10 April 1899, William Van Nest, waiter at race track, natural causes."* There is a record of an internment of a *William Van Ness* at an Odd Fellows Cemeteries in San Francisco. The reported date of death is 1899. The deceased's ashes were placed in the dome section of the San Francisco Columbarium (Deubler, 2003). This plausibly refers to our William Henry Van Ness. Several of the Van Ness and Adams offspring and a number of Dolsons are buried in other cemeteries managed by Odd Fellows in Elk Grove and Sacramento[14].

Before William Henry died, he must have separated from or divorced Katherine Sullivan Van Ness. No divorce documentation has been located. Katherine subsequently had two more children with a man thought to be named *John Q. Adams:*

1. Harriet Ruth Adams born on 19 April 1888
2. John James Adams born on 15 April 1889

The births associated with the two children from her relationship with John Adams predate William Henry Vaness' death.

It appears that William Henry Van Ness and John Q. Adams shared the vocation of being waiters and may have worked at times at the same locations. In the Great Register of 1890,

---

[14] The Van Ness family's connection to the Order of the Odd Fellows raises questions about the state of health of William Henry Van Ness. The Odd Fellows were established in Britain in the mid-1700s to aid and comfort to the sick. Perhaps William Henry Van Ness suffered from a serious illness during the 1880s and received some sort of support from this organization. His ill health may have contributed to the placement of the children in the San Francisco Orphan Asylum.

John Quincy Adams is listed as a sixty-two-year-old barkeeper from New York and living at 1132 21st Street in San Francisco. Ironically, in 1892-93, it appears that William Henry was employed as a waiter or boarded at an enterprise owned by the Adams' family called the Adams House. Given these circumstances, Katherine, almost certainly was acquainted with John Q. Adams while still married to William Henry. She may have had an affair with John Q. Adams and eventually lived with this man for a time. No wedding, divorce, or death documentation has been found for Katherine Sullivan or John Adams. The available evidence is not sufficient to support any definitive theory regarding the exact nature of the legal and social relationship between and among these two individuals.

According to Caroline Van Ness Dolson, John Adams may have operated a shoe repair shop. Additionally, Caroline suggested that this John may have been a cousin of the well-known actress of stage and films, Maude Adams (1872-1953). There is no documentation to confirm either of these assertions.

Earlier Van Ness Ancestors
William Henry Van Ness' parents were Seneca Van Ness and Mary A. Richardson. Seneca was born in New York and Mary in Georgia. This couple is listed in the U.S. Census of 1850 as living in Chatom County, Georgia with the following persons in the household:

1. *S.H. Van Ness, male, age 27 years, head of household, merchant*
2. *Mary A. Van Ness, female, age 27*
3. *Mary Van Ness, female, age 20, born in New York* [probably Seneca's sister]
4. *Georgia Van Ness, female, age 8, born in Georgia*
5. *Dora Van Ness, female, age 4, born in Georgia*
6. *William Van Ness, male, age 2 months, born in Georgia*

A marriage certificate is on file showing that Seneca H. Van Ness and Mary S. Richardson, single, were married in Chatom County on 7 August 1839. Officiating at the ceremony was the Reverend *John Sewell* (Handwriting is difficult to decipher). An Eduard Wilson may have been a witness as his signature is affixed to the certificate.

In 1850 another Van Ness man was living in Chatom County. His name was Garrett Van Ness, age twenty-three. He is reported to have been born in New York and was working as a merchant. The writer ventures that Garrett and Seneca may have been brothers. Regrettably, the author has not been able to discover any credible link between the two Van Ness men living in 1850 in Georgia to any particular Van Ness family from the state of New York.

<u>Katherine Sullivan</u>

Katherine Sullivan was a native of Massachusetts. She married first, William Henry Van Ness ca. 1872 in San Francisco and, as mentioned previously, this couple had the following children. Henry Van Ness, Isabel Van Ness, Jennie Van Ness, Mary Van Ness, Caroline Van Ness, and Matthew Van Ness. She had a subsequent relationship and may have married second, John Q. Adams, around 1889. Katherine had two more children as a result of the second relationship: Harriet Ruth Adams and John James Adams.

According to the U.S. Census of 1880, Katherine was born in 1853 in Boston. The census also indicates that both of her parents were born in Ireland. With such a common Irish surname, the writer has been unable to discover any additional information on Katherine or this particular Sullivan family from Boston, MA on any immigration records.

The records of the San Francisco Orphan Asylum stipulate that Katherine Sullivan came to San Francisco in 1854. This probably is not the case. Katherine would have been an infant of one year of age in 1854. Additionally, there is no evidence that Katherine's parents or any other members of her family ever resided in San Francisco. Consequently, the writer believes that it more likely that Katherine Sullivan arrived in San Francisco as a young woman, sometime before she met William Henry Van Ness and had her first child with him in 1883.

Subsequent to a separation or divorce from William Henry Van Ness, Katherine may have remarried. The writer has not found records of any of these events. Her second relationship was with a fellow named Adams. His first and second names may be John Quincy. There were a number of men named John Adams listed in San Francisco and Sacramento directories at the time. In 1893, a John Q. Adams is listed at a restaurant with the address of 1442 Harrison Street (Langley's Directory). In the same year, William H. Van Ness is listed in the Langley Directory as a waiter residing in the Adams House. This circumstance is probably more than a mere coincidence. Since William Henry and John Q. may have lived or worked together at the same establishment, it is possible that Katherine and John Q. became acquainted around this time. Given the birthdates of the two Adams children (1888 and 1889), Katherine's relationship with John Q. Adams appears to have commenced before William Henry's death.

There is no record indicating that John Q. Adams adopted any of the Van Ness children: Henry, Jennie, Caroline, or Matthew. These individuals maintained their Van Ness surname into adulthood and throughout their lives.

It is not known for certain when or where Katherine Sullivan died. In 1900, a guardianship was issued for Matthew Van Ness to Adam Warner of the Franklin Township near Elk Grove. Matthew was seventeen years old at the time and signed the document himself. Also signing the guardianship were Matthew's brother and sister, Henry and Jennie Van Ness. According to the U.S. Census, Henry and Jennie were residing together in Sacramento in 1900. It is logical to assume that the guardianship was necessary as a result of Katherine Sullivan Van Ness' death. There is also a possibility that the guardianship was related to the death of William Henry Van Ness in 1899. Oddly, even though she was still a minor, no guardianship was issued for Caroline Van Ness, perhaps because she continued to be interned at the Catholic children's home in San Francisco. By 1900, it appears that the Van Ness and Adams offspring were orphans.

Siblings of David P. Dolson I

Between 1855 and 1874 Hannah O'Connor Dolson, David's mother, gave birth to four sons and three daughters who survived into adulthood:

1. Oscar Jackson Dolson was born 1 October 1855 and died 11 May 1935. Oscar probably was named after a paternal uncle from Orange County. Jackson is a collateral family name also from New York. Given the 1855 date of birth, Oscar was born somewhere along the American River in the Sierras. Although in California as early as 1855, John C. Dolson and his wife, Hannah, did not settle in Elk Grove until 1857.

    According to various records (voter registrations, city directories, and the U.S. Census), Oscar lived out his life in and around Sacramento working as a general laborer, farm hand, and as a sheep shearer. As early as 1880, he moved from Elk Grove to the City of Sacramento. The following extract was originally featured in the "State News in Brief" section of the *Gridley Herald* and was reprinted by a San Francisco newspaper:

    > ***Oscar Dolsen has brought in from Butte Creek a white swan measuring 8 feet and 1 and a half inches from tip to tip. The bird will be stuffed and placed in a saloon in Sacramento. It is the largest of its species ever killed in this neighborhood*** (*San Francisco Daily Evening Bulletin*, 05 December 1881).

    On 23 October 1897, Oscar married Martha (Mattie) E. Robinson (1851-1933). Their marriage affidavit is on file at the Sacramento County Recorder's Office (Marriage Book 3, p. 453). The couple married when they were forty-two and forty-six years of age respectively. The marriage took place on 10 November 1897 at the home of the bride's mother in Elk Grove (The *Sacramento Record-Union*, 19 November 1897). According to census data, Martha was born in February of 1851 and was a native of Louisiana. Her father was from France and her mother, Winnie Robinson, was born in Louisiana in 1831. In 1900, Winnie Robinson was living with Oscar and Martha. Oscar's mother-in-law was noted to be a widow whose mother was from Pennsylvania and whose father came from Scotland. Around 1896, Oscar relocated to Roseville where he and his wife lived for several years. At this point in his life, Oscar was described as six feet tall, light complexioned, with blue eyes and black/brown hair. From 1903 to 1910, the couple resided at 2416 V Street in Sacramento and Oscar registered to vote as a Republican. Martha registered as a Prohibitionist. In 1910, Oscar's voter registration card indicated that he was working as a gardener. According to the census records of 1920 and 1930, the couple was living in the San Joaquin Township on a property which they owned. Oscar was working as a sheep shearer in 1920. Martha died on 25 March 1933. Oscar died two years later on 15 May 1935, at the age of 80. Both are buried in Odd Fellows Cemetery in Sacramento. Oscar died intestate and left no real property. His personal property was valued at approximately $1,000. In an affidavit filed on 22 November 1939, Oscar's siblings were deposed regarding family associations at the time of his death. He was a widower whose sole heirs were his siblings and the siblings of his deceased wife. In the end, each of these individuals received $91.38. Surnames included were Dolson, and the collateral families of Cutbirth, Bartlett, and Reeves as well as Robinson in-laws: Jenkins, Simpson, Nelson, Comstock, and Harris.

2. <u>John James Dolson</u> was born on 17 November 1857 and died in Sacramento on 5 July 1945. As several of his brothers, John worked primarily as a farm laborer with a particular focus on sheep shearing. On 12 July 1897, at the age of thirty-nine, John married Bertie Jolley, age twenty-eight, who was born in 1869 in Pennsylvania (Sacramento County, Book S, Page 603)[15]. When John registered to vote at the age of forty, he was reported to be 5'8" tall, light complexioned, with brown hair and eyes. In 1908, John resided at 411 K Street in Sacramento and was registered as a Republican. Around 1912 he was living with his brother, Joseph, at a boarding house located at 812½ J Street and later in 1926, he resided at 800 O Street. John continued at this address until at least 1932. Later, there are sightings of a John J. Dolson in Sacramento directories, between 1937 and 1945, as residing at 1104 V Street. John James Dolson died in 1945 at the age of eighty-eight (Probate File 25537, Sacramento, County). He is buried in Odd Fellows Cemetery, Sacramento.

3. <u>Margaret (Maggie) May Dolson</u> was born 4 May 1863 at Elk Grove and died on 26 January 1949. On 27 February 1881, she married Christian Haavig (*Sacramento Record Union*, 2 January 1882). Haavig, according to census records, was born in Norway. In May 1888, Christian Haavig was reported to be thirty-seven years old, which would mean that he was born in 1851. In the 1900 U.S. Census, Maggie Haavig is reported to be a widow, head of household, living in San Joaquin Township. Subsequently, Maggie married an Elk Grove man named George Bartlett, who was a neighbor of the Dolson family. The following story originally appeared in a local newspaper on 14 May 1910 and was republished 100 years later:

---

[15] The following, perplexing notice appeared in a local newspaper on 29 November 1897:
NOTICES: CARD TO THE PUBLIC---The article published in the Sunday News of to-day, stating that I had married an inmate of an L Street den, is false. Neither was I married in the Salvation Army barracks as stated. My wife was living with her mother at the time of our marriage. JOHN J. DOLSON.

One of George Bartlett's horses fell dead from fright on the road to the park Saturday. An automobile suddenly passed by the horse which fell dead immediately. (Elk Grove Citizen, Wednesday, 10 May 2010)

Maggie and George Bartlett are enumerated on the 1920 U.S. Census as living on a farm in the San Joaquin Township. They were reported to own the property. At the time, Maggie was fifty-five and George fifty-six years old. He was working as a laborer on county roads. In the 1930 U.S. Census, the couple, each reported to be sixty-six years of age, continued to reside in San Joaquin Township. Their property was valued at $3,500. Maggie is reported to have been born in California and George in New York. Previous to his marriage to Maggie, George Bartlett was living with his uncle, Stewart Silas, on a San Joaquin Township farm (U.S. Census, 1900). On a voter registration in 1896, George Bartlett was said to be 5'9", with a dark complexion, brown eyes, and black hair. Sometime in the 1930s, the couple moved to San Bernardino. When George Bartlett died before 1939, he bequeathed a small share of his estate to each of Maggie Dolson Bartlett's siblings (Probate Case No. 16891, Sacramento County).

4. <u>William Dolson</u> was born on 22 May 1865. At age thirty-three, William was said to be 5'8", light complexioned, with brown hair and eyes. In 1903, William was living in Elk Grove with his father and brothers. He was listed as an orchardist while the rest of the Dolson men were listed as farmers. At ages forty-three and forty-nine, William was reported on both occasions to be a farmer in Elk Grove. Apparently, William never married. William Dolson was buried in Odd Fellows Cemetery following his death on 16 September 1932. He was sixty-seven years old. His funeral was conducted by George L. Klumpp, Funeral Director, located at 808 O Street. The total cost of the funeral was $380. Line item expenses were reported as follows:

Casket	$220	Tent & Chairs	$12
Box	$10	Minister	$5
Embalming	$20	Permit	$1
Digging Grave	$15	Notices in Papers	$6
Hearse	$10	Suit & Underwear	$20
Personal Service	$20	Flowers	$5
Grave (site)	$30	Telephone Calls	$1

William left a very small estate consisting of cash in a bank account totaling $2,200. His brother, John Joseph Dolson, petitioned the court (Probate Case No. 15506) to distribute the funds, in equal portions, share and share alike, among each of William Dolson's siblings. Accordingly, the court ordered that the residue of the estate be allocated to each of the following persons:

184

J.J. Dolson,	Petitioner
Oscar J. Dolson	Elk Grove, CA
Maggie Dolson Bartlett	Elk Grove, CA
D.P. Dolson	56th and V Streets, Sacramento
Alice Dolson Cutbirth	Elk Grove, CA
Mary E. Dolson Reeves	Hollister, CA
J.H. Dolson	San Bernardino, CA

5. <u>Mary Elizabeth Dolson</u> was born on 23 August 1869 and died in Hollister, San Benito County, California on 26 January 1947. She married George B. Reeves in 1898. In 1886, George was twenty-seven years old and living in Mayfield, Santa Clara County, California. His occupation was listed as a hostler (stableman or horse groomer). By 1890, he had relocated to the Elk Grove area and registered to vote in the Twentieth Precinct along with the Dolson family. In the 1910 U.S. Census, George, age fifty, and Mary, age forty-one, are shown as living in Fremont, California. George indicated that he was born in Ohio. His father was from England and his mother from Illinois. Mary reported her parents were from New York and Ireland. The Reeves had been married for twelve years and there were no children from this marriage. In 1920, the couple, now sixty and fifty-one years of age respectively, was living in Las Tablas, San Luis Obispo County, California.[16] Interestingly, Mary then claimed her parents were from Pennsylvania and Ireland. The last sighting of the couple is in the 1930 U.S. Census. They were living in San Benito County, aged seventy and sixty-two. They owned their home situated on a farm valued at $8,000. Again, George B. Reeves reported that he was born in Ohio with parents from England and Illinois. In this instance, Mary states that her parents were from Holland and Ireland.

6. <u>Alice E. Dolson</u> was born on 31 December 1871 and died on 15 October 1962. Several newspaper reports show that, as a child and young woman, Alice was an exemplary student. For example, she not only completed high school, but also was awarded a scholar's medal on 7 February 1885 (*Sacramento Bee*). Alice married Lincoln H. Cutbirth on 15 November 1890. The wedding took place at the Dolson residence in Elk Grove[17] (*Sacramento Union*). The Reverend W.C. Scott presided. This was the first marriage for

---

[16] The writer notes that some 1920 census transcriptions show the Reeves surname mistakenly displayed as Bower. A closer examination of the original document confirms however that the family consisted of two persons: George B. Reeves and Mary E. Reeves.

[17] In 1880, John C. Dolson, with the technical assistance of his future son-in-law, Lincoln Cutbirth, built a two-story, three bedroom mansion on the farm. Lincoln was a master carpenter. Around 1910, the Gage family purchased the Dolson property in Elk Grove and in 1953, moved the mansion to 9239 Elk Grove Boulevard. After 2006, the house, a historically-significant structure, was moved by Richard and Shirlyn Gage to its current three-acre site at 5623 Tegan Road between Franklin Blvd. and Laguna Park Drive, Elk Grove (Armstrong, 2006; Gage Park History, No date).

Alice but the second for Lincoln. He had married first, Harriet Buel on 1 February 1883. Lincoln H. Cutbirth, born on 3 June 1860, was a native of Iowa. He was a well-regarded Elk Grove pioneer. It is presumed that Harriet Buel died before 1890.

On 30 October 1909, the *Elk Grove Citizen* contained the following notice:

> ***Among the real estate transfers, we note Mr. Cutbirth has purchased the beautiful home of Mrs. LeBoyd, corner of Main and Florin roads. Mrs. Cutbirth is a daughter of Mr. John Dolson, early settler of Elk Grove.***

In 1913, both Alice and Lincoln were reported to be officers in the Elk Grove chapter of the Rebekahs (*Sacramento Union*, 28 July 1913). Lincoln died on 16 June 1934. Alice died on 15 October 1962. Both are buried in the Odd Fellows Cemetery on Riverside Boulevard in Sacramento.

Alice Dolson Cutbirth and Lincoln H. Cutbirth had a daughter named Pearl Mae Cutbirth born on 7 September 1891. Pearl married Thomas Valentine Wightman Sr. (1885-1952), born in Olney, Illinois. He had a 320-acre ranch on Sheldon Road until the 1950s. His wife Pearl Cutbirth Wightman died on 23 February 1991 in her one hundredth year. She was buried in Odd Fellow's Cemetery in Sacramento on 26 February 1991, alongside her husband.

Pearl Cutbirth Wightman and Thomas Valentine Wightman had two sons: (1) Mark Lincoln Wightman, born on 28 December 1918; and (2) Thomas Valentine Wightman II, born 7 October 1921. Mark Wightman's obituary appeared in the *Elk Grove Citizen* on 4 January 2011:

> ***Mark Lincoln Wightman, Elk Grove native whose family came to this area in 1885 died Dec. 14, 2010 in Hillsborough, just 14 days shy of his 92nd birthday.***
>
> ***He was born Dec. 28, 1918 to Thomas V. and Pearl Mae Wightman, the older of two boys. His younger brother was named Thomas. Mark was named after his uncle, Mark Newman Wightman, the only Elk Grove graduate killed in action Oct. 3, 1918 during World War I, and one of only two local area soldiers whose bodies were shipped home and buried locally. Mr. Wightman grew up here, graduating from Elk Grove High School in 1936 and then attending Sacramento Junior College. He graduated from the University of California, Berkeley in 1941 with an A.B. degree in Economics. World War II was on, and he went to work in the Supply Department, Sacramento Air Depot, and Headquarters IV Air Service Area Command coordinating aviation fuel shipments. In 1942 he married Grace Ruth Brown***

Johnson, also born and raised in Elk Grove. Mr. Wightman worked for various departments in the state of California before moving to the Bay Area and employment with Santa Clara County. He returned to the state with the Department of Alcohol and Drug Enforcement, retiring in 1982. In retirement he became a licensed real estate broker in the Bay Area and assisted his wife in the management of the family's real estate assets. The couple traveled extensively in Europe, South America, Southeast Asia, China, Australia, Tahiti and Easter Island. Mr. Wightman was also an avid reader of history and biography. Mrs. Wightman preceded him in death in 2000, and he became active with the Elk Grove Historical Society especially with the Hotel & Stage Stop Museum where a memorial fund was established in his wife's name. The Grace Ruth Brown Wightman [1917-2000] fund will continue to be administered by the Wightman Family Trust. Mr. Wightman was a member of the Masonic order for 69 years and belonged to lodges in both Elk Grove and Burlingame. He is survived by his daughters, Ruth Wightman of Elk Grove and Alice Sgourakis of Oakland. Services were held Dec. 22 with burial in East Lawn Memorial Park, 43rd and Folsom Boulevard [Sacramento].

Thomas Wightman married Patricia Thorson but left no children. *Who's Who in America* (1999) contained an entry for Wightman, Thomas Valentine:

Rancher, researcher, b. Sacramento, Oct. 7, 1921; S. Thomas Valentine [Sr.] and Pearl Mae (Cutbirth) ... Student, U. Calif., Berkeley, 1945-46; B of animal Husbandry. U. Calif., Davis, 1949; student, Cal. Poly 1949-50. Jr. aircraft mechanic SAD (War Dept.), Sacramento, Calif., 1940-42; rancher Wightman Ranch, Elk Grove, Calif., 1950-59; machinist Craig Ship-Bldg. Co., Long Beach, Calif., 1959-70; rancher Wightman Ranch, Austin, Nev., 1970-88; dir. Wightman Found, Sacramento, 1988---. Dir. Med. Research.; Staff Sergeant U.S. Army, 1942-43. Recipient of scholarship U.S. Fed. Govt., 1945-50; Fellow NRA, VFW, U. Calif. Alumni Assn., U. Calif. Davis Alumni Assn., Bowies Hall Assn., mem. Confederate Air Force, the Oxford Club, Republican. Avocations: antique automobiles and aircraft. Home and Office: Wightman Foundation, 2130 51ˢᵗ St. Apt. 129, Sacramento, CA 95817-1507.

Thomas died on 11 January 2003. His obituary indicated that he was a glider pilot in World War II and upon his return to civilian life, he became a cattle rancher (*Sacramento Bee*, 19 January 2003).

7. Joseph Henry Dolson was born on 23 October 1874 in Elk Grove and died on 23 May 1951 in Monterey, California. When Joseph was twenty-three, his voter registration card

records his height as 5'10", complexion light, eyes blue, and hair brown. Around 1912, Joseph and his brother, John, were shearing sheep and living at a boarding house at 812½ J Street in Sacramento. In later life, Joseph appears to have married a woman named Margaret J. O'Brian. In the 1920 U.S. Census, Joseph H. (age given as forty-five) and his wife Margaret J. (age given as forty) were living in San Joaquin Township. His occupation was listed as a harvester and Margaret was operating a hair salon. Her birthplace was indicated as New York. The couple is mentioned in the following resolution found in Sacramento City Council records:

RESOLUTION ACCEPTING QUITCLAIM

Whereas, J.H. Dolson and Margaret Dolson, his wife, have made, executed and delivered to the City of Sacramento the following real property in the City of Sacramento, County of Sacramento, State of California, bonded and particularly described as follows:

Lot 50 "Alta Vista" according to the official plat thereof filed in the office of the Recorder of Sacramento County, California, on July 12, 1905, in Book 6 of Maps, Map No. 17; EXCEPTING the east forty (40) feet of said lot [30 September 1937].

In 1940, there is a voter registration for a Joseph Henry Dolson, a filling station manager in San Bernardino, California. Margaret Dolson, housewife, is shown at the same address. They are both registered as Democrats. There is a California death record for a Margaret Dolson, born in New York on 18 August 1875, with a paternal maiden surname of O'Brian and a maternal maiden surname of Lavery. The date of death is 18 December 1954. The author trusts that this is Joseph Henry Dolson's widow.

Siblings of Caroline Van Ness

Caroline Van Ness Dolson had three full siblings resulting from the marriage of Katherine Sullivan Van Ness and William Henry Van Ness. She had two additional half siblings from her mother's relationship with John Q. Adams.

1. Henry C. Van Ness (1872-1910). According to the 1880 U.S. Census, Henry, then eight years old, was residing with his family and attending school in San Francisco. In 1900, he was living in Sacramento with his sister, Jennie. The address was noted as 918 Alley between Q and R Streets. In 1907 Henry is included in a Sacramento directory as living in Broderick (West Sacramento) and working for the Southern Pacific Railroad Company. Subsequently, Henry left California and relocated to Nevada. In 1910, Henry Van Ness was living in New River, Churchill County, Nevada. He was a lodger at a boarding house, age thirty-seven, divorced, and working as a janitor in a building (U.S. Census, 1910). In

the 1920 U.S. Census, Henry was now in Fallon, Churchill County, Nevada. He is reported to be age forty-three, owned his home, and was working. In 1930, he is reported in the U.S. Census as living in New River again, age fifty-seven, but now married to a Lyda J. (maiden surname unknown), age thirty-nine. Lyda was born in Iowa with a father from Missouri and a mother from Iowa. Henry and Lyda had been married one year. They owned their house valued at $2,300. Henry's middle initial is reported to be C. He was not a veteran. Henry was working as a caretaker at a high school. Lyda was not employed. This is the last sighting of Henry Van Ness and his wife.

2. <u>Jennie F. Van Ness</u> (1 October 1879 - 26 May 1961). Born in San Francisco, Jennie came to Sacramento as early as 1900, when according to census records she was residing in the Capital with her brother, Henry. In 1903 there is a sighting of a Jennie F. Van Ness living at 2111 9th Street. A marriage certificate is on file at the Sacramento County Recorder's Office showing that Jennie Van Ness of Sacramento wed George Metz of Sacramento on 5 July 1903. The couple was married by Phillip Brady, a Catholic Priest. Witness to the ceremony was Ernest Metz, probably the brother of the groom. Another man named Ernest Frederick Heinrich Metz was George's father. He was born in 1820 and was a native of Prussia.

    Jennie was twenty-three years old and George twenty-one years old at the time of their wedding. Over a great part of her life, Jennie Metz lived at a home located at 2301 P Street. She was at this address as early as 1913. Until the early 1940s, she and George Metz are listed as living together at this same address. George worked as a baker, beginning as early as 1911 until his death. In 1913, the address of the bakery was reported as 515 12th Street. In 1915, George was reported to be a baker for Noceti and Weltman. In the 1940 U.S. Census, George was described to be fifty-seven years old and retired. His highest level of schooling was the sixth grade. Jennie is reported to be fifty-six years old, not working, and schooled only to the third grade. After George Metz' death on 19 August 1944, Jennie eventually moved into a smaller first-floor apartment of the large Victorian home located at 2301 P Street. In the late 1950s, John Cabral and Matt Loverde customarily picked up Jennie and brought her to family Thanksgiving and Christmas dinners, alternatively held at one of the family homes located on Fruitridge Road (personal observation). Jennie would then be given a ride home after dinner. The writer recalls tagging along on one such occasion on Christmas night of 1960. Jennie Metz died on 31 May 1961. She is interred in the same plot (Section C, Lot 14, Grave 23) as her husband, George Metz, in Odd Fellows Cemetery, Sacramento. Before her death, Jennie gave permission for the shared-use of this plot for the burial of her brother, Matthew Van Ness, who died in 1960.

3. <u>Matthew Van Ness</u> (1881-1960). Matthew was admitted in 1883 to the San Francisco Orphan Asylum. In 1900, he was made the ward of Adam Warner as the result of an order of guardianship issued by the Sacramento County Court. The 1900 U.S. Census

shows a *Marten Van Ness*, age seventeen, living with Adam Warner and his wife, Katie, in Franklin Township, Sacramento County. On 12 September 1918, Matthew presented himself at the Sacramento Courthouse for his initial draft registration:

Address:	*Elk Grove*	*Age:*	*39*
Occupation:	*Laborer*	*DOB:*	*Nov. 1, 1878*
Employer:	*G.M. Colton*	*Contact:*	*Jennie Metz*

In this instance, Matthew's birthdate is given as 1878. If another report of his birthdate (1881) is correct, he was only 18 or 19 years old in 1900 and 36 or 37 in 1918. Matthew reported to the Draft Board that his address was 2301 P Street in Sacramento, the home of his sister, Jennie Van Ness Metz.

In 1920, Matthew Van Ness was listed on the U.S. Census as a forty-year-old, single man living with the family of George Colton in Elk Grove. This seems to be the same Colton family which was reported on Matthew's draft registration two years previous. He was working on a dairy farm. In 1941, Matthew, then sixty-two, registered for the draft a second time. He lists his address as 2100 K Street, which is the same address that he provided for his employer, the Western Café. He again gives the name of his sister, Jennie Metz, who was living at 2301 P Street, as a contact person. In the same year, a Sacramento directory has a listing for a Matthew Van Ness residing at 1630 20th Street. Matthew Van Ness died on 6 February 1960. Odd Fellows Cemetery has a record on file indicating that Matthew's burial plot is located at Section C, Lot 14, Grave Site 23, the same plot in which his sister, Jennie Van Ness Metz, and his brother-in-law, George Metz, are interred.

4. <u>John James Adams</u> (15 April 1889 - 28 February 1960). Little is known about John. There is a John J. Adams in a 1907 Sacramento directory listed as a baker, living at 414 Alley between L and M Streets. This John J. Adams would have been seventeen years old at the time. According to the 1930 U.S. Census, John J. Adams was living with his sister, Hattie Adams Kelly, and his brother-in-law, Frank Kelly. At that time, John was employed at a mortuary and cemetery. In 1940, a John Adams was working as a janitor at the Francesca Apartments. His address is listed as 2311 C Street. John J. Adams may have lived in Sacramento for all or a great part of his life. On one occasion in the late 1950s, the author recalls accompanying David Pelton Dolson II (the writer's father), on a visit to John's house. The writer remembers John J. as a very old, white-haired gentleman. He lived alone in an extremely humble abode, a wooden shack, along the Sacramento River.

There is no record that John ever married. John James Adams died in 1960. He was cremated and interred at Odd Fellows Cemetery in Sacramento. His ashes were placed at the same grave site as his brother-in-law, David P. Dolson I. David P. Dolson II may have made the arrangements for John's burial in this plot.

5. <u>Harriet (Hattie) Ruth Adams</u> (19 April 1888 - 28 December 1957). As noted previously, Harriet may have been interned in the San Francisco Orphan Asylum as a child. In the 1900 U.S. Census there is an entry for a Frank J. Kelly, age twenty-three, married to Hattie Adams, age nineteen. They are reported to have been married for two years and to have a daughter named Alice Kelly, then three months old. In a 1905 Sacramento directory, a Miss Hattie Adams is shown as living at 1815 12th Street. She was working as a clerk. Hattie and Frank Kelly may have been separated around this time. It appears that in 1905, Hattie Adams married a man named Fayette Harlow (Sacramento County Index to Marriage Certificates, Book 27, Page 97), which resulted in the birth of a male child named David Harlow in Sacramento on 10 March 1908 (California Birth Index, 1905-1910). Nothing more is known about these two Harlow individuals.

In the 1930 Census, Frank Kelly and Harriet were living together once again. Frank Kelly, now reported to be forty years old, was working as a butcher. He indicated that both of his parents were born in Ireland. Hattie reported that her parents were born in New York and Ireland. A John J. Adams, age forty-one, was living in the home. John was working at a mortuary and cemetery. Hattie and Frank were living at 1931 8th Street in 1933. In 1940, the census data indicate that Frank was fifty-one and born in 1888. Hattie was fifty-two and born in 1889. They lived at 701 N Street. At that time, Frank worked as a watchman for a public warehouse. He earned $1,200 during the previous tax year. Both Frank and Hattie reported that they had completed the eighth grade. In Sacramento directories between 1937 and 1949, the couple continued to reside at 701 N Street. Frank was variously reported to be working as a watchman for the Argonaut Liquor Company, a laborer for the Southern Pacific Railroad Company, and as an electrician. There is a listing for a Frank R. Kelly in the California Death Index as born on 20 November 1888 and who died on 30 January 1958. The writer remembers that Aunt Hattie would attend family Thanksgiving and Christmas celebrations in her later years. She was living alone during this time. She had white hair and was known for wearing flamboyant hats. Harriet Adams Kelly died in 1957.

<u>David Dolson I's Life in Sacramento</u>
Most of the details that the writer has garnered on David I's activities were obtained from voter registrations, city directories, and the U.S. Census.

After his marriage to Caroline Van Ness Dolson, some of the earliest sightings of David Dolson I include the following:

- 1909, Truck man for the Southern Pacific Company
- 1910, Residence at 311 N Street, laborer at Southern Pacific Company
- 1910, Age forty-nine, living at 208 M Street, Sacramento, registered Republican
- 1911, Laborer at SP Co., living at 208 M Street
- 1913, Laborer at 1422 2nd Street
- 1914, Laborer at 1022½ 5th Street, registered Republican along with wife Carrie, housewife
- 1915, Taylor House, 1022½ 5th Street
- 1916, Laborer, R.D.2, Box 645, City [Sacramento], registered Republican
- 1919, Laborer, 645 40th Street
- 1920, Laborer, wife Carrie V., housewife, 645 Fortieth Street, registered Republican
- 1930, Mill man, Sacramento Box and Lumber Company, Route 1, Box 1299
- 1930, Brighton (neighborhood in eastern section of Sacramento)

The above data indicate that the Dolson household moved frequently. Many of the addresses imply that the family lived on rental properties, in marginal neighborhoods, in humble abodes.

The 1910 U.S. Census shows a D.P. Dolson, age forty-four, as a head of household living in Sacramento with wife, Carrie, twenty-nine, in a rented home. The address was 312 Sutter Avenue. David I was reported to be a common laborer, but not working at the time of the census. The couple was described as having been married for four years and having had a total of three children, two of whom were living. The surviving children are identified as Bessie, four years of age, and Vivian, two years old. It is noteworthy that the birthplaces of both David's and Carrie's parents are listed as unknown.

In the 1920 U.S. Census, David was listed as age forty-five and he continued to live with Carrie, now age twenty-nine, in a rented home in Sacramento. David was working as a sheep shearer on a ranch. Surprisingly, David's father is listed as being from Ireland. Carrie's father is reported to have been born in the USA and her mother in Ireland. Children are Bessie nineteen, Vivian nine, David eight, and Carrie, four and a half. In this instance, young Carrie was a reference to daughter Caroline, also known as Tye. All of the children except Carrie were enrolled in school and were reported to be able to read and write. A possible explanation for the errors in ages and places of birth recorded on this census administration is that David and/or Caroline may have provided inaccurate information to the census takers.

According to daughter, Josephine Dolson Loverde, around 1927, the family lived in a big farmhouse on Fruitridge Road. This farmhouse was located near the intersection of 71st Street on the south side of Fruitridge Road. During this time, Josephine attended Elder

Creek Elementary School where she met her future husband, Matthew Loverde. Ronald Pile, Jr., son of Elizabeth H. Dolson Pile, recalls that the family had chickens. Ronald further recounts that Caroline Dolson used to scrub the clothes and the grandkids in a washtub with Fell's Naphtha soap.

In 1930, the census records show David I as age sixty-nine, living with his wife Caroline, age forty-nine, son David II eighteen, daughters Caroline thirteen, Josephine twelve, and son, Ronald, six years of age. The family was paying rent in the amount of ten dollars per month. David I and Caroline's ages at marriage are reported as forty-six and nineteen respectively. David II was not in school, but working. All of the other children were enrolled in school. Everyone in the family was reported to be literate. Birthplaces of David I's parents are listed as New York and Ireland and for Caroline's parents, California and Ireland. This information was incorrect since Caroline's father was born in Georgia and her mother in Boston. David I was categorized as not having a trade and was not employed at the time. David II is reported to be a laborer currently working at a box factory.

In 1932, David P. Dolson I is reported to be a laborer residing at 5601 V Street and registered as a Republican. A 1933 voter registration shows David Pelton Dolson, laborer, living at 1821 11th Street. Also living at the same address is David P. Dolson Jr., mill man, and Miss *Carolyn* Dolson, waitress. This *Carolyn* was daughter, Tye, as she was referred to as "Miss" in this instance. All family members were registered as Democrats.

The Sacramento Directory shows David I and Caroline living at 415 9th Street in 1939. At the time of David I's death in August, 1940, Ronald Pile Jr. recalls that the family was still living at 415 9th Street. The house was located on 9th Street near D Street. However, a 1940 voter registration shows David I living at 1223 P Street. His political affiliation was reported to be Democrat and he was classified as retired.

In 1941, Caroline Dolson, now shown as the widow of David Pelton Dolson, was listed in a Sacramento directory as living at 1321 P Street.

The Heritage of David Dolson I
David Pelton Dolson I died on 7 August 1940. The funeral was conducted by the Klumpp Mortuary and the burial took place at Odd Fellows Cemetery, Sacramento. He was seventy-nine years, seven months, and one day old. After her husband's death, Caroline lived with the family of her daughter, Josephine Dolson Loverde, at their home on Fruitridge Road, adjacent to the Loverde Shopping Center. A small cottage was built in the backyard of the main house. In the last years of her life, Caroline lived with her daughter, Elizabeth, and grandson, Ronald. Caroline Van Ness Dolson died on 30 May 1970 and is buried in St. Mary's Cemetery, Sacramento. She was eighty-four years and eleven months old at the time of her decease.

As indicated earlier, David I led a rather lackluster life. He lived on his parents' ranch until he was at least forty years of age. Once married, he appears to have continued to work at the family farm for a short time and later sought out odd jobs as a common laborer. From 1909 to 1911, he was employed by the Southern Pacific Railroad. Over the years, his primary source of employment appears to have been that of a sheep shearer, an endeavor which he pursued in partnership with his brothers. Around 1930, he worked briefly at the Sacramento Box Factory along with his son, David II. Records show that David I was retired in 1940, the same year as his death. Based on David I's sporadic employment history in lower-paying jobs and the fact that his wife, Caroline, was a housewife, the family's income must have been meager and unpredictable. Clearly, David I, Caroline, and their children lived in poverty for prolonged periods of time. As far as is known, only a single photograph exists of David P. Dolson I, a portrait taken ca. 1912 with his young daughters Bessie and Vivian, and his infant son, David II.

As a result of his marriage to Caroline in 1906, David I may have become estranged from his family in Elk Grove. His father, John C. Dolson, died in 1909 and his mother, Hannah, passed away three years later. The incensed feelings of this era may have persisted between David I and some of his siblings, even after the deaths of their parents.

The tension caused by the marriage resulted in a gap not only in family relations, but in family history. The knowledge of the family's Dutch legacy and particulars regarding the migrations to New Amsterdam, Westchester, Dutchess, and Orange counties in New York were not passed on from one generation to the next. Since David I was in his mid-forties by the time he married, he must have had some notions of his family's heritage. Whatever he did know, he ostensibly did not share with his children or grandchildren. The contemporary generations of the family knew essentially nothing regarding their ancestry previous to the time that John C. Dolson and Hannah O'Connor Dolson settled in Elk Grove. The earlier Dolson heritage only came to light after the year 2000 when Patricia Loverde Heinrich [*Josephine, David I, John C., Frederick, James Jr., James Sr., Isaac, Theunis, Jan*] initiated genealogical studies and contacted Ron Plimley in New York (Plimely, 2011). Subsequently, Patricia's cousin, David Dolson III, continued the investigative efforts and the resulting body of research is contained in this volume.

Chapter IX - Ninth Generation

David Pelton Dolson II

[David I, John C., Frederick, James Jr., James Sr., Isaac, Theunis, Jan]

David Pelton Dolson II was born on 7 July 1911. Around the time of his birth, his parents, David P. Dolson I and Caroline Van Ness Dolson resided at 1022½ 5th Street in Sacramento, California.

Writer's Note
The description of David P. Dolson II is unique among the chapters of this volume. David II was the father of the writer and the only Dolson ancestor featured in this sketch that was personally known to this author. Much of the information contained in this chapter is based on the author's experiences and observations and from face-to-face conversations between David II and David III as well as with other family members of this and subsequent generations. Whenever possible, particulars contained in this chapter are supported by primary or secondary sources but when references are not cited, unless otherwise noted, the reader should assume that the information was obtained through personal experiences of the author.

David II's Early Years
According to David II's own accounts, during his childhood, his family was very poor and moved often from one low-rent dwelling to another. In 1918, a severe influenza epidemic struck Sacramento and everyone in the Dolson household became ill. David II remembers that, for a time, the only food available in the house was a sack of oranges. His first job as a young boy was picking hops at the age of eleven in rural Sacramento County.

As a child, David II had limited contact with the Dolson family in Elk Grove. Both of his paternal grandparents were deceased by the time of his birth. He did however recall one or two instances when he visited the Dolson farm with his father, travelling from Sacramento to Elk Grove by horse-drawn wagon. According to David II, these were positive experiences and he remembered the family in Elk Grove as being "well off" and generous. During times of extreme hardship, David II's father would, on infrequent occasions, visit the family in Elk Grove to ask for assistance.

David II shared little information about his father but in general, seemed to have endearing memories of him. He remembered his mother however, as sometimes being harsh and aloof. In one instance as a young boy, when David II forgot to close the corral gate behind the family cow as requested, his mother struck him on the head with a large rock with enough force to cause him to go unconscious.

Previous to his marriage, David II, as early as 1930, was working as a mill man and residing at Route 2, Box 1299 in Sacramento. Earlier that same year, he was reported in the U.S. Census as residing with his parents in the Brighton District. In 1934 David II was living at 5610 V Street and registered as a Democrat. He was reported to be working as a mill man at the time. In 1937, he was listed in the Sacramento Directory as employed at the Sacramento Box and Lumber Company with a residential address of Route 1, Box 1605.

Marriage to Marion C. Cabral

Marion Cassandra Cabral was born on 20 March 1917 in Sacramento, California. She was the daughter of José de Freitas Cabral and María de Jesus Lourenço, both residents of Fajã Grande das Flores, Azores Islands, Portugal at the time of immigration to the USA.

David Pelton Dolson II and Marion Cassandra Cabral were married on 25 September 1937 in Reno, Nevada. A Justice of the Peace named Harry Dunseath officiated. Witnesses were Vivian Dolson Gaddi and Calvin Barrigan. The marriage license was reported in the *Nevada State Journal* of Reno on Sunday, 26 September 1937:

> **Marriage License: David Dolson 26 and Marion Cabral 20, both of Sacramento** (p. 8).

It is not known if the couple celebrated their honeymoon immediately or at a later date but there is evidence that this event took place in San Francisco. After David II's death in 1989, his son, David III, discovered a number of mementos that had been saved over the years. They included materials from Alioto's at Fisherman's Wharf, Lefty O'Doul's Cocktail Bar on Powell Street, Techau Cocktails at 247 Powell Street, and the Cameo Cocktail Lounge at the Drake Wiltshire Hotel on Stockton Street-----all locations in San Francisco.

Marion spent her childhood at her family's small ranch which at the time was located just outside the city limits of Sacramento. This property was located directly across Fruitridge Road from St. Mary's Cemetery. She attended Elder Creek Elementary School, perhaps completing the eighth grade. Before her marriage in 1934, Marion is listed on a voter registration as employed as a waitress, living at Route 4 - Box 2465, and voting Republican.

Cabral and Lourenço Families

Marion's father, José de Freitas Cabral, was born on 7 January 1878 in the village of Fajã Grande, District of Lajes, Island of Flores, Azores (*Certidão Narrativa de Assento de Nascimento*). His parents were Manuel Cabral and Mariana Luiza de Freitas Fagundes, both single at the time of José's birth. Manuel was a native of Vila do Porto, Island of Santa Maria.

Manuel's paternal grandparents were José Cabral and María Julia and his maternal grandparents were António José de Freitas and María Joaquina.

Sometime before his marriage on 2 March 1878 at Fajã Grande, Manuel Cabral, migrated from Santa María Island to Flores Island. At the latter location, he married Mariana Luiza de Freitas Fagundes. This couple's marriage certificate, translated by the author, provides the following information:

> ### Certidão de Matrimonio - No. 6, 2 March 1878
>
> **Manoel Cabral: age 23, native of Vila do Porto Santa Maria, single, laborer living in Fajã Grande. Baptized in Vila do Porto** [Santa Maria]. **Son of José Cabral, laborer, and Maria Julia, housekeeper, both natives of Santa Maria. Luiza de Freitas: single, housekeeper, age 28, living in Fajã Grande, and baptized in Fajazinha. The daughter of Antonio José de Freitas, laborer, and Maria de Jesus dos Santos. Witnesses: Lauriano de Freitas Henriques, married, and João Joaquin André, single. Priest: Antonio José de Freitas**

According to this certificate, Manuel was born in 1855 and Luiza de Freitas in 1850. The fact that Mariana Luiza was baptized in Fajazinha, a small village near Fajã Grande, may be an indication regarding Mariana Luiza's family origin. Noting that the name of the priest, AntonioJosé de Freitas is the same as Luiza's father allows the author to venture these men were brothers, cousins, or uncle and nephew.

According to available baptismal certificates, Manuel and Mariana Luiza had only two children, José and a daughter named María, born on 24 February 1879 at Fajã Grande. Nothing more is known about this María.

José's wife, María de Jesus de Freitas Lourenço, was born at Fajã Grande on 25 April 1874 (*Certidão Narrativa de Assento de Nascimento*). Her parents were João de Freitas Lourenço II and Luciana Margarida Fagundes. Her paternal grandparents were João de Freitas Lourenço Sr. and María de Jesus. Her maternal grandparents were José António Fagundes and Mariana Margarida. María de Jesus had the following siblings:

1. María da Fontina Lourenço Fragueiro Cardoso was born on 14 February 1867 and died on 10 February 1955. She was married and lived her entire life at Fajã Grande. María da Fontina was survived by one son, Raulino Fragueiro Cardoso.

2. Ana Lourenço Silva was born in Fajã Grande on 15 April 1868. She married and had several children. The writer is uncertain if she immigrated to the United States before or after her marriage but she eventually resided for many years in Sonora, California. Ana was a widow when she died sometime before 1963.

3. João de Freitas Lourenço III was born on 27 March 1872 at Fajã Grande. His *Certidão* lists his first name as José but the writer is certain that he was named João, after his father and grandfather. He traveled to the United States in the very late 1890s or early 1900s but returned to Fajã Grande before 1911. This João died in 1944.

4. Mariana Lourenço Fagundes Felizardo was born at Fajã Grande on 23 March 1870. She married Mateus Rodrigues Felizardo on 21 February 1895. Mateus died at Fajã Grande on 15 March 1955. Mariana died at the same village on 16 January 1964. The couple had several children including Mateus Rodrigues Felizardo, who corresponded with the writer during the 1960s. Mateus had one son and three daughters. One of his daughters was named Vitória Santo Cristo Felizardo. She married José Lourenço Fagundes Jr. This couple hosted the writer during his visit to Fajã Grande in 2000. One of Mariana's grandsons, and a cousin of the aforementioned Vitória, was Luis Felizardo Cardoso, who also corresponded with several Cabral family members in Sacramento. Luis immigrated to Canada around 1963 and eventually settled in San Jose, California. Luis died in 1995.

5. María de Ceu Lourenço was born ca. 1871 and died on 1 December 1949. She lived her entire life in Fajã Grande and never married.

Children of José and Maria

In 1897, José de Freitas Cabral was living on Rua Tronqueira in Fajã Grande and María de Jesus lived on Rua Assumada in the same village. On January 30, 1899, José de Freitas Cabral, age 21, and María de Jesus de Freitas Lourenço, age 24, were married at the parish church of São José in Fajã Grande. María and José had the following children:

1. José Freitas Cabral Jr. was born at Fajã Grande on 19 December 1897 and came to the United States on 11 June 1911. On 4 November 1917 he married Mary Julio Souza. Their marriage was reported in the *Sacramento Union* on 4 October 1917. Mary was born on 28 October 1903 at Ribeirinha, Pico, Azores. She was the daughter of Francisco and Mariana Souza. The family immigrated to America when Mary was just an infant. For many years, Mary participated in various Portuguese Community activities in Sacramento. She conducted a Portuguese language radio program called *Ecos do Capital*. In 1991 Mary received an award from the Portuguese Government for outstanding service to the Luso-American community.

As a young man, José Freitas Cabral Jr. worked as a farm hand but later became a carpenter and worked in construction in the Sacramento area. Around 1927, Joe Jr. and Mary purchased a forty-acre ranch off Kiefer Boulevard near the present-day Mirandy Drive. Here, José managed a small farm which included olive trees, grapes, and other crops as well as some livestock. Part of this land was sold and currently, the Albert

Einstein Middle School is located on this former ranch. In 2018, daughters, Jo Ann Cabral Wilson and Violet Marie Cabral Boehl, continued to reside on properties which were once a part of the original family tract purchased in 1927. José Freitas Cabral Jr. died on 11 June 1983. Mary Julio Souza Cabral died on 20 December 1999. Both are buried in St. Mary's Cemetery. Joe Cabral Jr. and Mary Souza Cabral had the following children:

a   William Joseph Cabral was born in August 1922 and died on 19 November 2004.
b   Violet Marie Cabral Boehl was born in January 1927 and was living in Sacramento in 2018.
c   Elizabeth (Betty) Jean Cabral Lopes was born on 14 May 1937 and died from cancer on 16 April 1976.
d   Jo Ann Cabral Wilson was born in January 1942 and was living in Sacramento in 2018.

2. Alberto Freitas Cabral (Cabeal)[18] was born at Fajã Grande on 19 October 1899. He came to California with his mother and brothers in 1911 and subsequently purchased a farm of approximately forty acres at 7804 Wachtel Way in Citrus Heights, California, where he lived until his death. He registered for the draft on 21 September 1918 as Albert F. Cabral and was noted as being tall, slender, with brown eyes and black hair. His U.S. nationality status was noted as stemming from his father's naturalization. He attended school only until the third grade. He married Muriel Elva King (1901-1990) in 1923 (Book 62, p. 425, Sacramento County). Census records indicate that Muriel had a father born in Portugal and a mother born in the USA. She had an eighth-grade education. Albert worked at various agricultural jobs until a two-year stint with the railroad between 1922 and 1924. He eventually obtained long-term employment with a gold dredging company. In 1940 he earned $1,600 doing this work (U.S. Census). After becoming a widow, Alberto's mother-in-law, Ricka A. King, lived with the family for many years. Alberto Freitas Cabeal died on 4 January 1980. Alberto and his wife, Muriel King Cabeal, had the following children:

a   Marjorie Viola Cabeal Barns was born on 23 November 1923 and died on 19 January 1995.
b   Jackie Albert Cabeal was born on 18 February 1934 and died on 31 August 2013. He attended San Juan High School. Jackie married Mary Katherine Smith on 10 December 1954.

---

[18] Sometime before 1930, Alberto changed the orthography of his surname from Cabral to Cabeal based on the notion that, perhaps on some immigration documents, the surname was spelled in this fashion. To date, the writer has never encountered any primary documents to corroborate this spelling. Cabral is a common Portuguese surname and all of the other documents regarding the family contain this version of the spelling without exception.

3. Manuel Freitas Cabral was also born in Fajã Grande and also made the journey to the United States in 1911 with his mother and brothers. His baptismal certificate notes his birthdate as 21 April 1901 but his grave marker specifies 1 April 1901. After working as a farm hand, a ship's carpenter, and as a meat curer for the Western Meat Company in 1930, Manuel had a career with the Southern Pacific Railroad Company in Sacramento. He married first, Angelina Nevis (21 April 1909 - 3 April 1940), daughter of Manuel C. Nevis and Mary C. Dutra Nevis. This marriage took place when Manuel was twenty-five and Angelina was seventeen years of age, ca. 1926. Manuel Cabral and Angelina Nevis Cabral had the following children:

    a. Lucille June Cabral Gamba (9 June 1927 – 6 March 2017).
    b. Wilma L. Cabral Graham (13 February 1930 - 2 August 2015).
    c. Dorothy Cabral Grijalva (June 1931 - living in 2018).
    d. Rosemary Cabral Walker (1 June 1936 - 29 October 1981).

    Angelina Nevis Cabral died in 1940 and Manuel married second, Nell (perhaps her formal name was Helen). Nell's maiden name is unknown. There were no children from the second marriage. Manuel died on 29 September 1955 from lung cancer. He is buried in St. Mary's Cemetery alongside his first wife, Angelina, and his daughter, Rosemary Cabral Walker.

4. Lucille C. Cabral was the first child in this family to be born in the United States. She was born on 1 May 1914. In 1930, Lucille married João Francisco Barreiros, an immigrant from São Jorge Island in the Azores[19]. João was born in 1896 and came to the United States in 1920. He was a construction worker. Lucille had a career working for the Campbell Soup Company. João died on 24 July 1975 from complications associated with diabetes. Lucille died on 14 May 1994 after surgery for a malignant brain tumor. Both João and Lucille are buried in St. Mary's Cemetery. Lucille Cabral Barreiros and João F. Barrieros had the following children:

    a. Lucille Barreiros Dolson Dawson (2 April 1930 - 28 March 1997). She died of cancer.
    b. Isabel Barreiros I (26 November 1931 - 24 May 1933). This child died from whooping cough.
    c. Isabel Barreiros II Thexton (6 April 1934 - 16 September 2002). Isabel died of heart disease and complications following cardiac surgery.
    d. John Barreiros Jr. (8 August 1936 - 30 August 2002). John served in the Navy where he acquired firefighting skills. He had a thirty-year career in the Fire Service starting as a firefighter with the Florin Fire Department and ending as the Chief of the Pacific Fire District. John Barreiros Jr. died in Redding, California of

---

[19] João Barreiros' grandson, Robert Barreiros, alleges that his grandfather was born on the Island of Terceira, Azores. No documentation is available to confirm this matter.

Asbestosis and Emphysema, undoubtedly contracted during his service as a firefighter.

5. <u>John Lawrence Cabral IV</u> was born on 17 September 1915 and died on 16 July 2006. Additional information on John Cabral is included in the section addressing Vivian H. Dolson, sister of David P. Dolson II.

6. <u>Marion Cassandra Cabral Dolson</u> was born on 20 March 1917. She married David Pelton Dolson II, who is the Dolson ancestor featured in this chapter. Additional information on Marion can be found in several other sections of this chapter.

Immigration to the United States

According to family tradition, Manuel Cabral, father of José Sr., journeyed to the United States in the late 1800s and subsequently obtained U.S. citizenship. The writer has been unable to verify either of these events.

Records archived at Ellis Island indicate that José de Freitas Cabral (1 July 1878-28 December 1940) disembarked at Flores on 28 June 1901. His destination was San Francisco, California and he traveled on the ship S.S. Peninsular. He arrived in New York on 7 July 1901. He claimed to be meeting an uncle named João F. (surname illegible) in San Francisco. This João F. could possibly be João de Freitas Lourenço, María de Jesus de Freitas Lourenço Cabral's brother. Perhaps he was identified as an uncle instead of as a brother-in-law because José Sr. was unable to say the latter in English at the time he was questioned. The ship's manifest indicates that José was twenty-three years of age and a laborer. He could read and write. José had twenty dollars in funds and he reported that it was his first trip to the United States. José Sr. is said to have resided both in the San Francisco Bay Area and in Fresno after arriving in California.

In 1911 María de Jesus de Freitas Lourenço Cabral came to the United States on the ship, S.S. Canopic, sailing from São Miguel, Azores on 30 October and arriving in Boston on 5 November 1911. She, at the age of thirty-seven, was accompanied on this trip by her three sons, José Jr. (age thirteen), Alberto (age eleven), and Manuel (age ten). Maria de Jesus stated that the purpose of her trip was to join her husband, José, and that he was living in Turlock, California at the time. His address was given as Route 3, Box 45. She reported that she was carrying eighty dollars in funds. Neither she nor any of her sons were able to read or write. Maria de Jesus and the boys are thought to have made the final leg of the trip from Boston to California by train.

At the time of Maria's arrival in the United States, José was in serious legal trouble and had been involved in an affair. The marriage must have been strained. On 29 November 1919, the *Sacramento Union* reported that a suit for divorce had been filed by *Mary* Cabral against *Joe* Cabral. Clearly, this matter did not proceed further as no divorce was ever granted.

There is an lesser chance that the *Sacramento Union* notice may refer to Joe Cabral Jr. and his wife, Mary, as they had been married in 1917 and in 1919 had yet to have any children.

After being reunited, the family settled in Sacramento and lived for a while in the Brighton District off Fruitridge Road near the Sacramento Signal Deport (U.S. Census, 1920). In 1920, the Cabrals relocated to a thirteen-acre property at 6528 Fruitridge Road, located between 65th and 66th Streets, across from St. Mary's Cemetery (U.S. Census, 1930). The purchase of this property from Frederick A. Miller was noticed in the *Sacramento Union* on 25 December 1920. José and María lived at this address until their deaths.

José was a farmer. In Fajã Grande, he and his parents owned several homes on Rua da Tronqueira. He also cultivated various fields and managed a number of pasture lots which were located on the outskirts of the village. Two of the Cabral homes were still in the family's possession as late as the year 2000. They were owned by a distant cousin, José Cardoso de Sousa. Another Cabral property had been taken over at the time of the death of Mariana Luiza Cabral by a family that had been serving as her caretakers. The name of the head of that family was José Puresa Greves Sr. Greves' son, José Jr., was still living in the former Cabral house on Rua Tronqueira in 2000. A fourth Cabral home on this same street had been purchased by a man named Pereira around 1998.

María de Jesus' father, João de Freitas Lourenço Sr., was also a farmer. The Lourenço family homestead was located on Rua Assumada on a hillside overlooking both the ocean and the village of Fajã Grande. In 2000, this home was occupied by María do Rosário Jorge Lourenço, the widow of João de Freitas Lourenço IV, María de Jesus' nephew. The couple's son, João de Freitas Lourenço V, was working in Santa Cruz das Flores as an airport traffic controller in 2000.

The stories relating to the history of the Cabral and Lourenço properties are interesting. The following accounts were written down in letters sent in 1968 from Mateus Rodrigues Felizardo Cardoso to the writer. Manuel Cabral was not a native of Fajã Grande. He was born in Vila do Porto, Santa María and nothing is known regarding the reasons for his migration to Flores. It appears that he was the first person from this Cabral family in Fajã Grande. Manuel and Mariana Luisa Cabral traveled to the United States in the late 1920s or early 1930s to visit their son, José. The couple returned to Fajã Grande after a few months. Manuel is said to have died from a fall while working on a neighbor's roof. His wife lived into old age. She was cared for by the Greves family to which a power of attorney was granted for one of the properties. When Mariana Luisa died, the Greves family took possession of one of the Cabral houses as compensation for debts owed. The remaining houses and farm lots passed to Cabral family members.

In the case of the Lourenço property in Fajã Grande, María de Jesus' parents lived in the home on Rua Assumada until their deaths. This house and adjacent properties were then bequeathed to their children, share and share alike. A son, João de Freitas Lourenço III, had been in the United States in the early 1900s working as a ranch hand in Northern California. While digging fence posts, he came across a box of money containing several thousand dollars. With these funds, he decided to return to the Azores shortly before 1911. Upon his homecoming to Fajã Grande, his sister, María de Jesus, asked him for a loan to purchase passage for herself and her three sons to America. The money was loaned and years later, in return, María gave her brother, João de Freitas Lourenço III, her share of the interest in the Lourenço estate. Subsequently, this João obtained the full ownership of the Lourenço properties which were still held by his descendants in 2000. This account of the Lourenço property was shared with the author in a letter dated 18 April 1963 from Mateus Rodrigues Felizardo, who stated that he obtained the information from the wife of João de Freitas Lourenço III.

In Sacramento on Fruitridge Road, the Cabrals cultivated some of their land and used the rest for pasture. Early, two acres were in grapes. There was also a large garden, a barn, and a number of sheds. In the period of the 1950s and 1960s, livestock consisted of a milk cow, plough horses, and a herd of sheep. There were also chickens, pigeons, and rabbits. The farm was too small to sustain a family. As the sons grew up, they sought outside jobs, first as ranch hands, and then more steady work such as construction, the Southern Pacific Company, dredging, and the Pepsi Cola plant. During and after Prohibition, José Sr. dabbled in wine making and distilling whiskey. His activities were, unfortunately, discovered on more than one occasion by authorities (*Sacramento Bee* article, date unknown). José and María attended various Portuguese community organization events in Sacramento, in particular the Holy Ghost Festivals and St. Elizabeth's Church.

José de Freitas Cabral died on 28 December 1941. His wife, María de Jesus Lourenço Cabral died on 7 October 1960 at the age of eighty-six. Both are buried in St. Mary's Cemetery.

Before traveling to America, María de Jesus prayed at the parish church in Fajã Grande for safe passage and for the reunification of her family. After her wishes were granted, María de Jesus, as is the custom of Azoreans, showed her thanks by sponsoring a *festa* (festival) for the entire village of Fajã Grande. There was a parade, an orchestra, a mass, and of course a banquet of *sopas* and *carne.* Based on the dates of correspondence between the USA and Fajã Grande, regarding the *festa* underwritten by María de Jesus, the event took place sometime between the late 1940s to early 1950s[20].

---

[20] After María de Jesús died in 1960, the author discovered a number of letters and photographs that had been saved in the very trunk which his grandmother had used when she immigrated to the United States in 1911. The trunk had been stored in the cellar of the house on Fruitridge Road. It contained a number of interesting items including correspondence from Flores which María de Jesús had received over many years. There were also a number of photographs including one of María de Jesús and her family on the day she departed from Flores and another, unfortunately torn in half, of the festa in Flores, which she sponsored many years after arriving in the United States.

<u>Azorean Legends</u>
There are several tales associated with the Cabrals that have been passed down from one generation to another. As far as the writer has been able to determine, there is no documentary evidence to support any of these stories.

Manuel Cabral was said to be light complexioned. This has caused speculation that his ethnicity might be other than Portuguese. One story has him surviving the sinking of an Irish ship and becoming stranded on Flores. Nevertheless, according to the marriage certificate, Manuel was born in Vila do Porto, Santa María. His parents and grandparents had Portuguese given names and surnames. Given these facts, there is little doubt that Manuel was a native of the Azores. His light complexion could be related to other factors. For example, a significant number of Flemish (Dutch) families were present early in the Azores and Manuel might have had such roots. Some Flemish names have been translated to Portuguese versions (e.g., Van der Haggen = Silveira). There is also a possibility that Manuel and his ancestors were Jews. Alcoves and underground storage spaces in at least two of Manuel's homes on Rua da Tronqueira in Fajã Grande have been noted by subsequent family residents of these houses. Portuguese Sephardim (also known as *Conversos, Novos Cristiãos*, and *Maranos*) commonly used such spaces to display and then hide religious artifacts.

Manuel was said to be from a "wealthy" family which was involved in the shipping industry. In fact, it is said that he traveled to the United States on a ship owned by the family. There is also conjecture that Manuel was a U.S. citizen and passed this entitlement down to his son, José. While the Cabral family had several houses and some other farm land in Fajã Grande, there is no evidence of a former business or significant affluence in the family. Some family members claim to have seen a naturalization document but the writer has been unable to authenticate Manuel's U.S. citizenship.

José de Freitas Cabral came to the United States unaccompanied and was in California for almost a decade before reuniting with his family. During this time it is said that he established another family with the surname Freitas in Fresno or at another location in the Central Valley or Bay Area.

These family legends have been shared by many relatives, including the Cabral offspring for many years. There are a number of versions to each story. As mentioned previously, although intriguing, no compelling evidence has been uncovered to validate any of these accounts.

One of stories that the author originally thought was a legend is actually supported by evidence. There was a story that in his early years in America, José had a mistress and that he was involved in an altercation with her boyfriend ca. 1910. During the altercation, the boyfriend was supposedly severely injured or killed. The girlfriend may have been the perpetrator but José is said to have taken responsibility for the incident and was incarcerated at San Quentin for a time. Upon becoming aware of José's troubles, María de Jesus decided to come to the United States to assist her husband. While the details relating to this incident are a bit different from the family's retellings, the facts were documented by a local newspaper.

A Girlfriend and a Gun: Folsom Prison

It is frequently repeated that the truth can often be stranger than fiction. Because that seems to be the case with the following account about Joseph Freitas Cabral Sr., the author has decided to relate the story faithfully according to articles which appeared in the *Sacramento Union* during the period 1911-1912:

> 20 June 1911: ***SHOOTS WOMAN IN FACE; SLASHES OWN THROAT - Jealousy Cause of Attempt at Murder and Suicide of Dredge Fireman-Holds Pursuers at Bay-Hiding in Empty Box Car, Enraged Man Cuts Throat at Sight of Police. Enraged by the attentions of other men were paying to the woman, Joseph Cabral, a dredger fireman, last night shot Mrs. May Osborne, also known as May Perry, with whom he had consorted for months past, then, fleeing from the scene of his crime at Fourth and N Streets to the water front, took refuge in an empty box car and there, holding at bay a crowd of men and boys that pursued him, drew a pocket knife and cut his throat from ear to ear.***
>
> ***The woman was shot through the left cheek and was not seriously wounded. When Cabral slashed his throat he severed his windpipe and the sternoclido mastoid muscles on either side, but failed to reach the jugular vein. He probably will live.***
>
> ***The incident occurred in front of the John H. Gallagher grocery store and saloon at 331 N Street. The Osborne woman was leaving the store at 6 o'clock when Cabral stepped up to her and asked her to stop and speak with him.***
>
> ***FIRES ON WOMAN. When she refused Cabral drew a revolver and fired directly into her face. The woman turned and ran screaming into the store. Cabral pursued, firing at her. Several persons in the store at the time sought places of safety without attempting to interfere. The woman ran from the store to the saloon adjoining and hid behind the bar. When Cabral emptied his pistol he fled down N Street to the water front with a number of men and boys following.***
>
> ***The man reached an empty box car between M and N on the waterfront a few second before Captain of Police Pennish and a squad of officers from the police station composed of Patrol Sergeant Byan, Detectives Biggs, Kramer, and Koening and Patrolmen Hallanan, Balsz, and Realth, arrived. While holding his***

pursuers off, Cabral saw the police and pulling out a knife, stabbed viciously at his throat, then staggered to the end of the car, threw the knife out of a window and fell unconscious. He was hurried to the receiving hospital, where Drs. Lindsay and Heurickson attended to him. It required a dozen interior stitches and seventeen surface stitches to close the long, ragged cut.

GUARDED BY DEPUTIES. Cabral was removed to the county hospital, and a deputy from the sheriff's office was detailed to keep a guard over him, the physicians stating that he had a good chance of recovering.

May Osborne had an exceedingly narrow escape. The bullet which passed through her cheek missed her left eye by an inch and just grazed the cheek bone. Had she not turned her head at the instant that Cabral fired she probably would have been killed instantly. She is being held at the police station pending the outcome of Cabral's wounds.

The woman has been boarding at 222 Q Street. She has no relatives in this country, her parents living in Ireland. Cabral has been employed on the dredger Yolo as a fireman for two years.

ANOTHER ADMIRER? A mysterious feature of the affair is that a half hour before the shooting Cabral spoke with police, the very police patrol with Patrolmen Hallanan and Balsz, who were seeking Joseph Stephani, wanted on a warrant charging battery which was sworn to by Cabral.

At Fourth and N Cabral pointed out a man who he said was Stephani, and saying that Stephani carried a gun and would shoot him on sight he got out of the patrol, while Hallanan and Balsz proceeded up N to Fifth and arrested the man who had been pointed out.

That was the last the patrolmen saw of Cabral until they found him in the box car on the waterfront. The man arrested was not Stephani. The police are investigating to determine if Stephani has any connection with the tragedy. It is said Stephani was one of those whose attentions to the Osborne woman aroused Cabral to attempt murder. Up to a late hour last night Stephani had not been arrested.

21 June 1911: *CABRAL MAY LIVE TO STAND TRIAL – Man Who attempted to Kill Woman Improving. Joe Cabral, the dredger fireman, who Monday night shot and slightly wounded Mrs. May Osborne, his former consort, and slashed his own throat in an attempt at suicide, will live to face trial for his crime,*

according to a report from the county hospital last night. The attending physician said that the man probably would recover.

Investigation yesterday developed the fact that the man Cabral was jealous of Joseph Stephani, who as stated in the Union yesterday, was believed by the police to be mixed up in the case. Stephani, who is a married man, deserted his wife and paid attentions to Mrs. Osborne, who was living with Cabral. Mrs. Osborne left Cabral, and the latter, to spite both Stephani and Mrs. Osborne, made love to Mrs. Stephani.

A many-sided row ensued. Stephani last week assaulted Cabral, who swore to a complaint charging his enemy with battery. It was while Cabral was accompanying Patrolman Hallanan and Balsz to Fourth and N Streets Monday night in search of Stephani that he saw Mrs. Osborne enter the Gallagher grocery store at 331 N, left the officers and attempted to murder the woman and kill himself.

4 July 1911: *CABRAL HEARING SET. Hearing of the case of Joe Cabral, dredger fireman, who shot Mrs. May Osborne, also known as May Perry, and attempted to kill himself on June 19, has been set for tomorrow in the court of City Justice Anderson. Cabral shot the woman in the cheek, inflicting a slight would, and then cut his throat failing to cause a mortal wound. Trial of the case is expected to straighten out a complicated row between Cabral and the Osborne woman and Joseph Stephani and wife, which has engaged the attention of the police at different times.*

7 July 1911: *DISAPPEARS TO SAVE LOVER FROM TRIAL. A bench warrant has been issued by City Justice Anderson for Mrs. May Osborne, also known as May Perry, who was shot by her lover, Jose Cabral, and who is wanted as prosecuting witness in the trial of Cabral on a charge of attempt to commit murder. When the case was called Wednesday, the Osborne woman failed to put in an appearance. It is believed she disappeared in the hope that the case against Cabral would be dropped.*

A rumor that Mrs. Osborne committed suicide by jumping into the river is not credited by the police. Cabral shot Mrs. Osborne in the cheek and then tried to kill himself by slashing his throat with a knife.

8 July 1911: *CABRAL TRIAL TO GO ON WITHOUT WOMAN WITNESS. Although May Osborne, alias Perry, the complaining witness is still missing, the trial of Manual [Joseph] Cabral, charged with attempting to murder the Osborne woman several weeks ago, will be taken up before Judge Anderson today.*

After the shooting affray in which May Osborne received a cheek wound, Cabral attempt to commit suicide by cutting his throat and both were taken in the county hospital for treatment.

June 23, when Cabral's trial was called, they were both brought in from the hospital. The trial was continued until July 5 and Cabral was kept in the city jail, while the Osborne woman was supposedly living at 224 Q Street. When the trail was called on July 5, May Osborne was missing. She left her belongings at 224 Q Street and whether she committed suicide or dropped out of sight in order to save Cabral, is a question.

9 July 1911: *HOLD CABRAL TO ANSWER. In spite of the disappearance of the complaining witness, Mrs. May Osborne, Joe Cabral yesterday was held to by City Justice Clarken, sitting for Justice Anderson. Cabral shot the Osborne woman and then tried to commit suicide. Mrs. Osborne has left town to escape testifying against her lover.*

28 September 1911: *CABRAL PLEADS. Joe Cabral, charged with attempted murder was arraigned before Superior Jude Shilds, acting for Judge Hughes, yesterday, and entered a plea of not guilty. His trial was set for October 9.Cabral shot May Osborne, also known as May Powell, several weeks ago. Cabral and the woman had been living together. Jealousy was the cause. Cabral was captured in a box car on the waterfront with his throat cut. He had tried to commit suicide.*

1 October 1911: *CABRAL TRIAL IS TO START ON OCTOBER 16 ... The trial of Joe Cabral, charged with the attempted murder of May Powell, also known as May Howard, with whom he was living, was set for trial for October 16. Cabral, after shooting the woman, went into a box car on the river front and cut his own throat with suicidal intent.*

17 October 1911: *CABRAL SENTENCED TO TWO YEARS IN PRISON. Joe Cabral, who several months ago shot and wounded May Osborne, also known as May Powell, with whom he had been living without the formality of a marriage license and who, after he had done the shooting went to a box car on the water front and there cut his throat, making a poor job of it, yesterday pleaded guilty to a charge of assault with a deadly weapon and was sentenced to serve two years in the State Prison at Folsom.*

Cabral had been charged with an assault to commit murder, but the woman who was shot had dropped out of sight and the charge was reduced with the understanding that Cabral would enter a plea of guilty. This arrangement was carried out.

11 September 1912: **ADVERTISEMFNT. Notice Is hereby given that I intend to apply to the State Board of Prison Directors to be paroled from the state prison at Folsom, according to law. JOE CABRAL.**

12 September 1912: *JOE CABRAL WANTS PAROLE FROM FOLSOM. Joe Cabral serving a sentence of two years in the Folsom prison for an assault with a deadly weapon on a woman in this city in June 1912 will apply to the state board of prison directors next month for parole.*

Cabral shot a woman with a revolver at Third and M Streets and then ran to Front Street, where he hid in a box car and tried to cut his own throat. He was captured by Captain Pennish and Detective Ryan.

The woman disappeared shortly after the shooting and has not been heard from since. The police swore to a complaint and he was found guilty. He was taken to Folsom October 17, 1911. He has filed notice that he intends to apply for parole.

The 12 September 1912 entry in the *Sacramento Union* is the last mention of this case that the author has encountered. It is not known if Joe Cabral was paroled or if he was required to serve out his full sentence. His wife and children had recently arrived in the United States and may have secured legal assistance.

The incident described above would not be José's only brush with the law. As noted in another section of this chapter, he was also arrested on one occasion for bootlegging homemade wine during Prohibition.

Family Connections
By the 1920s, the Cabral and Dolson families were acquainted, probably as a result of the families living in close proximity of the Sacramento Signal Depot. Three marriages would take place between these families. Eventually David Dolson II married Marion C. Cabral; Vivian H. Dolson married John L. Cabral; and Ronald J. Dolson married Lucille Barrieros, daughter of Lucille Cabral Barreiros and João Barreiros.

David and Marion's Children
David Pelton Dolson II and Marion Cassandra Cabral Dolson had two children:

1. <u>Sharon Lee Dolson</u> was born on 20 April 1941 in Sacramento. Sharon attended William Land and Earl Warren Elementary Schools in Sacramento. She graduated from Elk Grove High School in 1958 and in the next year married Jimmie Louis Rogers on 1 February 1959. The ceremony took place in St. Peter's Church and the reception at the Del Prado Restaurant on Stockton Boulevard. Jimmie was born in Modesto, California on 14 April 1939, the son of Weldon Rogers and his wife, Myrtle Adelaide Moore Rogers. Jimmie Rogers died in Sacramento, California on 4 April 2015. He worked at Foremost Foods for more than a decade and later established Wallcraft, a wall paper-hanging company. His last employment was with Button Transportation as a safety engineer. The couple divorced on 2 February 1974. Sharon worked for twenty-three years at the California Department of Transportation in Sacramento. Sharon Lee Dolson Rogers died on 9 December 2013 and her ashes were scattered at the Ice House Reservoir, El Dorado County, in the Sierra Nevada Mountains of California.

Sharon L. Dolson Rogers and Jimmie L. Rogers had three children:

a. Kimberly Ann Rogers was born in December 1959 and was living in 2018. She married first Samir Farid Doumit, a native of Lebanon on 12 July 1980 at St. George's Byzantine Catholic Church in Sacramento. This couple had two children: (1) Amanda Samir Doumit, born in March 1984 a living in Sacramento in 2018 and (2) Joseph Samir Doumit, who was born in October 1985. Joseph married Taylor Rawlings and the couple was living in Placerville, CA in 2018.

Kim married second Doug Fisher and subsequently divorced. There were no children from the second marriage.

b. Jimmie Louis Rogers [II] was born on 8 February 1961. He married Claire Juhasz on 7 June 1986 at Immaculate Conception Church in Sacramento. Jimmie and Claire had three children:

- Curtis James Julius Rogers born in February 1989.
- Cody James Julius Rogers born in April 1991.
- Christine Claire Rogers born in January 1995.

Jimmie Louis Rogers died on 11 January 2014.

c. Tammara Lynne Rogers was born in February 1963. She married Raymond Cheung on 12 August 1989 at Lake Tahoe, California. Tammara and Raymond had two children:

- Steven Raymond Cheung born in November 1990.
- Christopher Raymond Cheung born in February 1995.

All of the children of Sharon Dolson Rogers and Jimmie L. Rogers were born in Sacramento and Kimberly and Tammara were still living in that city in 2018. The grandchildren were all born in Sacramento but by 2018 were living in various locations such as San Francisco, New York, and Georgia.

2. <u>David Pelton Dolson III</u> was born in March 1946. He attended Earl Warren Elementary School, Peter Lassen Middle School, and graduated from Hiram W. Johnson Senior High School in Sacramento in 1964. He subsequently went on to college and graduated from the University of California, Santa Barbara with a bachelor's degree in 1968. David III earned a M.S. degree from the University of Southern California in 1973 and a doctorate in Education from the University of San Francisco in 1984. He had a thirty-year career with the California Department of Education.

After serving in the Peace Corps in Bolivia (1967-1970), David married Miriam Libertad Salazar Tapia of La Paz, Bolivia on 6 June 1970. The ceremony and reception took place at Cristo Rey Church in the Sopocachi neighborhood of La Paz. Miriam was born in February 1950 in La Paz and was the daughter of Luis Sixto Salazar Escobar, a native of Cuzco, Peru, and Mercedes Tapia De La Fuente de Salazar, born in Cochabamba, Bolivia. Miriam had a career in the Sacramento area as a dental assistant. David III and Miriam had two children:

a. David Pelton Dolson IV was born in Santa Paula, California in October 1974. He graduated from John F. Kennedy High School in Sacramento in 1992 and later obtained a B.S. degree from Chapman College. David IV was a Firefighter and Captain for the Sacramento Fire Department for more than twenty years. In 2015 he became the Chief of Emergency Medical Services and Training for the Roseville Fire Department. David P. Dolson IV was living in Sacramento in 2018.

b. Andres Luis Dolson was born in Sacramento in May 1977. He graduated from John F. Kennedy High School in 1996 and obtained a B.S. degree in Construction Management from California Polytechnic University at San Luis Obispo, California in 2002. In that year he moved to San Diego and began work with an engineering firm. In 2011, he married Nicole Sanchez of Tipton, California. Nicole's parents were Raymond Sanchez, whose family was from Texas and Gloria Urrutia, whose family was from California. Both of Nicole's parents were of Mexican heritage. Nicole graduated from California State University, Fresno in 2002 and subsequently worked for the San Diego County Probation Department as an administrator. The couple had a daughter, Penelope Riley Dolson, born in November 2013 in San Diego. Andres Luis Dolson and family were living in the San Carlos neighborhood of San Diego, California in 2018.

David Dolson II's Siblings
David II had six siblings, five sisters and one brother:

1. <u>Katherine Van Ness</u> was born on 5 March 1904 and died as a young child around 1906.

2. <u>Elizabeth Hannah Dolson</u> was born on 12 October 1906. Bessie, as she was known, lived in Sacramento and ran Maguel's Reducing Salon, a slenderizing service for women that provided facials, saunas, massages, exercise sessions, and steam rooms. This business operated from 1945 until 1962. She married first, Frank Leroy Pile on 30 October 1926. Frank was born on 11 September 1900 and died on 26 October 1962. She married second, George Menzel. George was born in September 1906 and died in March 1977. Elizabeth Hannah Dolson had three children with Frank Leroy Pile, two of whom died in infancy. These children were:

    a. Shirley May Pile (3 July 1932 - 29 April 1936). Shirley died as a young child.

    b. William Dolson Pile (10 September 1927 - 22 November 1927). William died as an infant.

    c. Ronald Leroy Pile (12 June 1929 – 6 February 2013). He was this couple's only child to survive into adulthood and resided in Sacramento for his entire life. Ronald, nicknamed Tootie, served in the U.S. Coast Guard and U.S. Navy during the Korean War. He was stationed at New London, Connecticut and deployed on The USS Escanaba which was assigned to the Bearing Sea. Ron had a career in Sacramento and Auburn in the brewery and beer distribution businesses. On 13 September 1953, Ronald Pile married Lavina Marie O'Neil (6 June 1935 and living in 2018) at St. Francis Catholic Church in Sacramento. The reception following the ceremony was held in the Tuesday Club House at 2227 L Street. Lavina was the daughter of John Hugh O'Neil. This couple had seven biological children and one adopted son. The names of these children including corresponding birth years are listed below. All of the biological children of Ronald Pile and Lavina O'Neil Pile were living in 2018.

        - David Arthur Pile (July 1954)
        - Frank Thomas Pile (March 1956)
        - Rhonda Marie Pile (August 1958)

- John Kelly Pile (December 1960)
- Andrea Pile (January 1963)
- Kally Ann Pile Phelps (March 1964)
- Shannon Kay Pile Clarke (October 1965)
- Maxwell Burton Pile (born 12 June 1987; adopted and was deceased before 2012)

In her later years, Bessie lived with her son Ron and her daughter-in-law, Lavina. Elizabeth Hannah Dolson passed away on 6 December 1996 and is interred at St. Mary's Cemetery in Sacramento.

3. Vivian (Dillie) Hannah Dolson was born on 14 February 1909 in Sacramento. Dillie married first, George Joseph Gaddi (18 May 1905 - 9 December 1988). The marriage took place in 1928. George's parents were natives of Italy named Narciso Joseph Gaddi and Alicia Maria Checcetini Gaddi. He had several siblings: Ester Mary Gaddi, Augustine Gaddi, Joseph Gaddi, and Josephine V. Gaddi. In 1920, the family was living in Brighton. Apparently, it was in this township on the eastern side of Sacramento that the Dolson, Cabral, and Gaddi families became acquainted. George Joseph Gaddi married Vivian Hannah Dolson in 1928. She was twenty-one years of age at the time. George Gaddi was employed most of his career at the Sacramento Box and Lumber Company as a sawyer.

In the 1940 U.S. Census, George Gaddi is reported to be thirty-four, with one year of high school education, working at the box factory, and earning $1,800. Vivian was thirty-one years old and reported to have finished three years of high school. Their residence was 4224 Solano Avenue in Brighton. Sometime after 1940, the family moved to 5630 Broadway, Sacramento. This home was located across the street from the old California State Fair Grounds. This couple divorced in October 1955. George Gaddi married second, a widow named Marie Voris Parish Balthorn on 6 December 1955. There were no children from this marriage. Marie's maiden name was Parish. She was born in San Francisco in 1908 to parents, Lewis B. Parish and Anna Parish. Her siblings were, in order of birth, Harry, Olive, Perry, and Pearl. Marie married first, Ed Balthorn ca. 1931. Marie died in Sacramento on 20 September 1999. She was interred at Sacramento Memorial Lawn at 6100 Stockton Boulevard. Marie's first husband, Ed Balthorn was a veteran of World War II. For many years Marie participated in the Women's Auxiliary of the American Legion.

Vivian Dolson Gaddi married second, John Cabral on 22 October 1955. The couple had a long relationship before they married. John Lawrence Cabral was a brother of Marion C. Cabral Dolson.

After her marriage to John Cabral, the couple lived on the Cabral property located on Fruitridge Road at 66th Street. Vivian H. Dolson Cabral died on 23 December 1964 of breast cancer that had metastasized to the brain. She was buried in St. Mary's Cemetery.

John Lawrence Cabral's nickname was Cabbie, which was short for Cabral. His middle name, Lawrence, is the translation of the Portuguese Lourenço, the surname of his maternal grandfather. He was born on 17 September 1915 and died on 16 July 2006. During World War II, John served in the U.S. Coast Guard and was a Second-Class Boatswain's Mate. After the war, he was employed by the Pepsi Cola Bottling Company where he had a thirty-year career. John inherited the remaining property at 6528 Fruitridge Road when his mother, María de Jesus Lourenço Cabral, died in 1960. In 1965, John Cabral married second, Viola (Winkie) Baldwin, and relocated for a time to a property in Rio Linda. He then returned to the Fruitridge Road location briefly but eventually moved to a small ranch in Galt where he lived until his death in 2006. At John's request, no funeral services were held. His ashes were scattered at an Oregon farm owned by his stepson, Alford "Chip" Morris. Viola Baldwin Cabral, at the age of 76, preceded John L. Cabral in death.

Vivian Dolson Gaddi Cabral had two children:

a. Patricia Nancy Gaddi (26 August 1932 - 22 June 1933). This child died as an infant.

b. Geraldine Bernice Gaddi [Cabral], born in May 1935 and was living in 2018. Geraldine's biological father is thought to be John Lawrence Cabral. Geraldine's DNA assessment result showed her ancestry to be twenty-six percent Iberian (Spain/Portugal) while only two percent Italian.

    Geraldine Bernice Gaddi Cabral graduated from St. Francis High School on 8 June of 1953. On the very night of her graduation, she eloped with Gerald Lee Fryer. The couple remained together for only a few years, but the marriage was not legally dissolved until the 1960s. Gerald L. Fryer died in Michigan Bluff, CA in June 1973. After her first marriage, Geraldine Gaddi Fryer had a number of relationships and several additional children. At age thirty she married, Don E. Mason, age thirty-four, on 18 January 1963 in Monterey, California. Don adopted the children from Geraldine's previous relationships. Geraldine Gaddi Mason and Don Mason eventually divorced. Don Mason died on 21 January 2005 in Oregon.

Geradine's children along with corresponding birth years are:

- Kevin James Mason   (December 1954)
- John Lawrence Mason   (4 January 1956)
- Candice Lee Mason   (October 1957)
- Vivian Leslie Mason   (October 1959)
- Gail Elaine Mason   (19 October 1962)
- Kelly Anne Mason   (February 1964)
- Paul Edward Mason   (June 1967)

Gail, Kelly, and Paul are biological children with Don Mason. All of Geraldine's children, except John and Gale, were living in 2018. John passed away from coronary heart disease in March 2010 and Gail died tragically on 10 April 2015 as part of a murder/suicide perpetrated by her second husband, Terry Martinez.

4. <u>Caroline Dolson</u> was born on 12 January 1914 in Sacramento. Caroline, also called Tye, also called Carrie, was born with a severe birth defect. She had curvature of the spine and never reached a normal height as an adult. In her youth Caroline was a talented singer and dancer. She entered singing contests at the State Fair. As a young woman, Tye worked for a time as a waitress. In 1937, Tye was listed in the Sacramento Directory as residing at 1425 8th Street. There is some indication that Caroline Dolson married first, a man named Bill Page, but no marriage certificate has been located and there were no children from this marriage.

Around 1952, Caroline Beverly Dolson married James Edward Overton. James was born on 21 November 1919 and died on 11 March 1969. He worked for the Pacific Telephone Company. James had served in the Navy in World War II and his position with the telephone company required him to work on ships in and around San Francisco Bay. The couple lived in San Francisco and subsequently in Pacifica at 368 San Pedro Avenue. The couple had a son in 1954, but the pregnancy was problematic for Tye and she died from complications of childbirth on 12 June 1954, eight days after the delivery. In 1955 James Overton Sr. married second, Mary B. (surname unknown). On 11 March 1969, James E. Overton Sr. committed suicide off a barge in San Francisco Bay.

Caroline B. Dolson Overton and James Overton had only one child, James Edward Overton Jr., born on 4 June 1954. During the first few months of his life, James Jr. was cared for by his Aunt, Geraldine Gaddi Fryer, at her home at 4920 Alcott Drive in Sacramento. After his father remarried in 1955, James Jr. went to live with his father and step mother in Pacifica, California. James Jr. was only fifteen years old when his father died.

As an adult, James Overton Jr. was referred to as Jimmy and Big Jim. He worked at a variety of part time jobs, but his passion was music. James Jr. was a member of the musician's union and often performed as a drummer for the Green Street Mortuary and Powell Street Blues bands in San Francisco. James Jr. married Robin Wiley on 7 September 1985. Jim died at the age of forty-seven from coronary heart disease on 4 September 2001. According to a story conveyed to his cousin, Kevin Mason, James Jr. was walking his dog near his home in Fremont when he collapsed in pain. A passerby attempted to assist him but he could not be revived. James Overton Jr.'s funeral took place on 10 September 2001 at the Green Street Mortuary in San Francisco. Afterwards a reception was held at The Saloon located at 1232 Grant Street. Donations were requested to be directed to the Music in the School Organization (*San Francisco Chronicle*, Sunday, 9 September 2001, p. A-28).

5. <u>Josephine Johanna Dolson</u> was born 12 October 1916. She attended Elder Creek Elementary School on Lemon Hill Avenue in Sacramento. On 21 September 1934 she married Mathew (Matt) Leonard Loverde, whom she met during elementary school days. Mathew was born on 10 September 1915 and died 8 October 1980. He was the son of Nicholas Loverde (1889-1983) and Ellen Silva (1895-1987). The Loverde family was originally from Sicily in Italy and Ellen Silva Loverde was born on Faial Island, Azores.

In World War II, Matt served as an airplane mechanic for the Navy at the Alameda, CA Naval Air Base. Upon his return to civilian life, Mathew Loverde worked as a mechanic for Miller Automobile Company for a time. Soon after, Matt and his wife, Josephine, along with Matt's brothers, William and Leonard, established Loverde Shopping Center on the south side of Fruitridge Road between 66th and 71st Streets. The shopping center consisted of a barber shop, grocery, variety, and hardware stores. There was also a lumber yard and afterwards a cocktail lounge called the Idle Hour. The couple worked at and oversaw the shopping center between 1950 and 1970. Matt and Jo lived in a house just west of the shopping center at 6700 Fruitridge Road. Later the couple built a larger, modern home on a hilltop on the Jackson Highway at the corner of Excelsior Road. Subsequently Mathew and Josephine moved to a house on Westholme Way in the Valley Hi neighborhood of South Sacramento. Jo volunteered from 1975 to 2001, initially at Methodist Hospital and later at the Bruceville Terrace Nursing Facility. She was also beloved among family and friends for her delicious chili bean recipe and her skill in making and gifting Raggedy Ann Dolls. Matt Loverde died in 1980 and Jo passed away on 24 June 2006. Both are buried at Sacramento Memorial Lawn Cemetery on Stockton Boulevard in Sacramento.

Josephine Dolson Loverde and Mathew Loverde had two children:

a. Patricia Ellen Loverde was born in June 1935. Pat had a career as an elementary school teacher. Her first assignment was Mark Twain Elementary School in the

216

Sacramento Unified School District. She worked at Mark Twain from 1958 to 1968 and then transferred to Peter Burnett Elementary from 1968 to 1975. After a ten-year absence from the education field, Pat returned to teaching as a kindergarten teacher for the Elk Grove Unified School District. She spent the decade of 1985 to 1995 at Prairie Elementary School. Patricia married first, Don Lee Singleterry on 29 June 1958. Don was born on 7 July 1928 and died on 12 November 2006. Patricia married second, Albert William Heinrich on 15 May 1988 at Fremont Presbyterian Church in Sacramento. Albert was born on 13 January 1920 in Germany and died on 26 June 2003 in Sacramento. He came to the USA as an infant. There were no children from either of Patricia's marriages. Pat was living in Elk Grove in 2018.

b. Carol Jo Loverde was born on 29 March 1937 and died on 10 November 2000. Her birth and death took place in Sacramento, CA. Carol worked for more than thirty years as a secretary for the State of California. She retired in May 2000. She married first, Wayne Anthony Silva on 6 February 1955. Wayne was born on 15 September 1934 and died on 16 September 2013 in Sloughhouse, CA. Wayne Anthony Silva married second, Susan Carter. This couple had two additional biological children and adopted a baby girl. Carol married second, Charles E. Kosobud on 18 May 1985. Charles was born in May 1943 and was still living in 2018. There were no children from the second marriage.

Carol Loverde Silva and Wayne Silva had two children:

- Mathew Wayne Silva was born in March 1956 and was living in El Dorado Hills in 2018. Mathew married Grace Colon on 1 September 1979. Mathew had a career as a firefighter and administrator with the California Department of Forestry. Mathew Silva and Grace Colon Silva had two sons: Jeffery Wayne Silva, who was born in March 1981 and Robert Mathew Silva, born in May 1983.

- Michael Anthony Silva was born on 25 December 1960 and was living in Citrus Heights in 2018. Michael had a career as an aviation mechanic. Michael married Janice Elaine Nellis on 13 September 1997. This couple had one daughter, Kaitlyn Jo Silva, born in April 1998.

6. James Ronald Dolson was born on 6 June 1923. In World War II, Ron served in the Marines and experienced combat in the South Pacific. He was awarded several medals. During the war, the Sacramento Bee published a photo (ca. 1944, date not verified) entitled "Sacramentan on South Sea Isle" which identified *PFC. James R. Dolsen of Route 4, Box 2465, Sacramento.* The photo showed Ronnie in front of a fox hole with several other marines from California. Another *Sacramento Bee* article (date unknown), with the simple header "Honor Roll", contains the photographs of four servicemen from

Sacramento. The Marine in the photo located in the lower left corner of the article is noted as James Dolson of 1726 N Street. Ronnie's World War II combat experience may have resulted in undiagnosed, Post-Traumatic Stress Disorder, as in later life, Ron suffered from alcoholism. By trade, James Ronald Dolson was a talented tile setter and he worked intermittently for many years as a tile contractor. Around 1949, James R. Dolson married Lucille Barrieros[21] (2 April 1930 - 28 March 1997), daughter of João Barreiros and Lucille Cabral Barreiros. Lucille Cabral Barreiros was Marion Cabral Dolson's sister.

For many years, Ronald and Lucille lived in their home at 5844 Cindy Lane, just two blocks distant from the Barreiros house on 66th Street in Sacramento.

James Ronald Dolson and Lucille Barreiros Dolson had three children:

a. James Ronald Dolson Jr. was born in March 1950 and was living in Sacramento in 2018. James married first, Betty Carol McWilliams and second, _____ Mugleston. He married third, Beatrice Araya Dolson.

b. Terrell Lynn Dolson was born in July 1951 and was living in Sacramento in 2018. She married first, Michael McErlain and second, Jeff Jeffries.

c. William Dolson was born in June 1955 and living in Sacramento in 2018. William married first, Kathy Despain.

Ronald Dolson and Lucille Barreiros Dolson eventually divorced. James Sr. never remarried. James Ronald Dolson Sr. died on 24 July 1987 of cardio-pulmonary arrest. He is interred at St. Mary's Cemetery. His grave is located adjacent to those of his former wife, parents, siblings, and in-laws.

David Dolson II's Career and Business

Even though David II found it necessary to enter the workforce at an early age, he was always proud of the fact that he returned to school and obtained his diploma from Sacramento High School. During the Depression, David II joined the California Conservation Corps and was assigned to forestry work in the area around Fort Smith near the California-Oregon border. This experience may have led to his involvement in the Christmas tree business. For at least two seasons, David II cut trees and transported them to various lots in Sacramento where the trees were sold during the holidays. For a short time, David II was involved in operating a restaurant. The establishment was called the Gilt Edge and was located near 11th and T Streets in downtown Sacramento.

---

[21] Lucille Barreiros Dolson married second, John W. Dawson. The couple did not have any children and were divorced on 19 February 1980. This marriage was the singular connection between the Dolson and Dawson families.

During the 1930s, David II worked as a mill man at the Sacramento Box and Lumber Company. While working at the "Box Factory", David II joined the labor union and became an activist. He recalled being present at confrontations between the employees and club-carrying thugs hired by the company. On several occasions when the union held demonstrations to organize the workers or to protest for better wages and benefits, the company would respond ruthlessly. From that time forward, David II consistently registered with and voted for the Democratic Party, with the exception of Dwight D. Eisenhower's first term as President.

Around 1940, David II went into business for himself and established Camellia Lunch and Distribution Service with a partner named Edmond A. Mount. To help finance the business, David II took out a loan of $264 with Bank of America in June of 1941. This he paid back in full by June 1942.

Camellia Lunch and Distribution Service was located at 3701 Freeport Boulevard, across the street from McClatchy High School. The building in 2018 was being used as a restaurant. The partnership with Edmond Mount continued until 13 September 1947 when a notice of dissolution was issued. For a short time, David II was sole proprietor, operating the business under the name of Camellia Lunch Service. Soon afterwards, David II entered into a second partnership with an individual named Russell Burns. The partnership continued with the same name.

Box lunches were prepared and delivered to bars, restaurants, markets, and cafeterias. Soon World War II came along. During the war, Camellia Lunch Service was given a tremendous boost through government contracts to serve military troop trains that passed through the Southern Pacific rail yards in Sacramento. During these years, lunches were also delivered to trains carrying *braceros*, Mexican farm workers. As Camellia Lunch Service grew, accounts were added that included various California state government offices, local college cafeterias, the State Fair, and several highway stands such as the Giant Orange chain.

A number of family members, including David II's wife, sisters, and mother-in-law all worked at different times for the business. Over the years, the most noted employee at Camellia Lunch Service was Edna Saint, who prepared sandwiches at the shop for more than thirty years.

The box lunches were simple affairs consisting of one or two sandwiches wrapped in wax paper. The cardboard boxes usually contained a piece of fruit (an apple, orange, or banana) and a dessert such as a pie or a package of cupcakes. A carton of milk or a bottle of soda water often accompanied the meal. For Mexican workers, chili peppers were added. Popular sandwiches included bologna, ham, salami and cheese, roast beef, egg salad, and David II's delicious tuna fish salad recipe. There were also several exotic varieties of sandwiches such as peanut butter and jelly, and deviled-ham. So many loaves of bread were used daily that each evening, David II would bring home a barrel full of heels which were eagerly consumed by the sheep and poultry on the premises of the Fruitridge Road farm.

Most of the work of preparing the sandwiches and box lunches had to be done during the overnight hours. The company had a small fleet of approximately four vans that were pressed into service to deliver the sandwiches to the various retail locations by 11:00 a.m. each morning. Camellia Lunch Service prospered until the 1960s when fast food restaurants such as McDonald's and Kentucky Fried Chicken proved to be stiff competition. David II worked at Camellia Lunch Service until his retirement in 1969. He sold his interest in the company to his partner, Russ Burns.

Early Residences and Fruitridge Road

In the first years of their marriage, David II and Marion lived in a number of rented apartments and houses. These residences are recorded in various Sacramento directories and voter registration lists:

> *1939: David P. Dolson and Cassie, factory worker, 415 9th Street, living with David P. Dolson I and Caroline.*
> *1940: David P. Dolson and Marion, attendant at Ott Bros., 1468½ 33rd Street.*
> *1940: Marion C. Dolson, waitress, 1830 8th Street.*
> *1940: David P. Dolson, 3285 62nd Street.*
> *1941: David P. and Marion C., Box lunches, 2433 32nd Street.*
> *1942: David P. and Marion, Merchant, 2433 32nd Street.*
> *1945: David P., Camellia Lunch Service, residence at 1104½ T Street.*
> *1947: David P., Camellia Lunch Service, residence at 1104½ T Street.*
> *1949: David P., Box Lunches, 3071 Freeport Blvd, residence at 1104½ T*
> *1953: David P., Camellia Lunch Service, Freeport Blvd.*
> *1955: David P., Residence at 6528 Fruitridge Road.*
> *1956: David P., Residence at 6528 Fruitridge Road.*

In the mid-1920s, José de Freitas Cabral and María Lourenço Cabral purchased approximately thirteen acres of land at the corner of 66th Street and Fruitridge Road. Originally the couple intended to give each of their children a two-acre lot. By 1950, Lucille Cabral Barreiros and Manuel Cabral had taken possession of their acreage, which consisted of two lots along 66th Street at the southern extreme of the property. Joe and Albert Cabral had purchased larger ranches by this time and they did not receive any shares. It was understood that the youngest son, John Cabral, would inherit any remaining acreage upon the death of his parents.

In 1950 Marion C. and David P. II decided that, rather than accept a two-acre parcel on 66th Street, they would renegotiate for a smaller lot on Fruitridge Road. The lot in question is described in the following Grant Deed of Joint Tenancy (Book 1793, p. 380) on file in the county of Sacramento:

All that portion of Section 27, Township 8 North, Range 5 East, M.D.B. & M.,
described as follows: Beginning at a point on the North line of said Section 27
and in the center line of Fruitridge Road, located East 270.8 feet from the
Northwest corner of said Section 17; thence from said point of beginning East 60
feet along the North line of said Section 17 and the center line of Fruitridge Road;
thence South 01 degree 28' West 150 feet; thence West 60 feet to a point in a
fence; thence North 01 degree 28' East 150 feet along said fence and its
extension North to the point of the beginning.

María Cabral was unable to sign this document but made her mark on 3 March 1950. In lay terms, this lot was located mid-way between 65th and 66th Streets on the south side of Fruitridge Road directly across from St. Mary's Cemetery.

In 1950, Marion and David II built a three-bedroom home on their lot at 6528 Fruitridge Road. Many years later the address of the house was administratively revised by the Post Office to 6532 Fruitridge Road. According to records of the Anglo California National Bank, on 30 October 1950, the couple took out a loan of $5,000 to finance the construction. Final payment on this loan was recorded on 3 June 1960. The family took possession of the home in the summer of 1950. Marion lived in this home until her death in 1967. David II remained in the home, as a widower, until he relocated to live with his son in 1976. Daughter, Sharon Dolson Rogers, received title of the property in 1976 and eventually sold the home in 2001.

Events in the Lives of David II and Marion
While a partner at Camellia Lunch Service, David II dabbled in other business interests. For example, over the years he dealt in real estate. He purchased and sold several lots in the city. He also purchased and then rented several homes, notably two small houses on Yale Street just one block from the corner of Broadway and 10th Street. On 11 April 1941, David P. Dolson II and Marion Cabral Dolson, his wife, transferred the following property to George J. Gaddi and Vivian Dolson Gaddi:

Lot 14 Block "E" Fairmond, (as the same is shown on the official map or plat
thereof filed in the office of the County Recorder of the County of Sacramento,
State of California).

This is the home located at 5630 Broadway, across from the former California State Fair Grounds. Vivian, David II's sister, lived at this address while she was married to George Gaddi. In 1955, she married second, John L. Cabral and moved to the Cabral property at 6528 Fruitridge Road. The above transfer of deed probably indicates that, as a way to assist his sister and brother-in-law, David II, along with his wife, was the initial holder of the mortgage.

Over the years, David P. Dolson II made a number of real estate investments. For example, on 18 February 1949, he, in conjunction with his wife, Marion, and a partner named Edwin Furano, obtained title insurance to a property described thusly: *The east ¼ of lot 2 in the block bounded by J and K and 6th and 7th Streets of the City of Sacramento* (Policy No. 77905, Title Insurance and Guaranty Company). In 1949, after a decade of ownership, David II sold one-fourth interest in a lot bounded by J and K streets and 6th and 7th streets in downtown Sacramento for the sum of $20,000. Not only was this a substantial amount of money for the times, but the location was considered, during this period, to be prime Sacramento real estate. Until the early 1960s, J and K streets made up the main shopping district of the city. This area contained several first-class movie theaters and major department stores such as Weinstock-Lubin, Wards, Kress, Breuners, and Woolworths. During this period, K Street was considered to be Sacramento's "Main Street".

David II also had a modest investment portfolio, primarily in large corporate bonds such as American Telephone and Telegraph (AT&T) and Pacific Gas and Electric (PG&E). In the mid-1950s, he purchased a minor interest ($5,000) in the Diablo Toy Company in partnership with his brother-in-law, Matt Loverde, and others. The Diablo was a plastic, Chinese-style, string yoyo. Unfortunately, the Diablo was somewhat difficult to manipulate and sales never took off. For many years after this investment, David II had a large supply of Diablos stashed out of sight in his garage. His family made light of the investment folly by retrieving and gifting him Diablos on special occasions such as his birthday and at Christmas time.

In the early years of their marriage, Marion worked outside the home. She applied for a Social Security Card on 2 June 1937. In August of that year, she went to work for the Del Monte Cannery at the corner of Stockton and Alhambra Boulevards. She was a member of the Cannery Workers Union No. 20324 of Sacramento County until at least 1943. Subsequently, Marion became a homemaker. On a 1960 California Driver's License, Marion is reported as: Marion Cassie Dolson, 6528 Fruitridge Road, brown hair, brown eyes, 5'7", 132 lbs., married, age 42. During the mid-1950s, Marion's health began to fail. She suffered from ulcers and in 1961, experienced a cerebral aneurysm, which left her completely paralyzed on the left side of her body. Miriam Cassandra Cabral Dolson died on 5 March 1967 at Sutter Memorial Hospital. Her death certificate indicates that she died at 11:10 a.m. of Uremia as a result of chronic active pyelonephritis and generalized but severe arteriosclerosis with complications of thrombosis of the abdominal aorta and iliac arteries. Her physician, Dr. Gail King, had been treating her for these and other conditions since 1958.

During his career at Camellia Lunch Service, David II typically worked Monday through Friday and half days on Saturday. His regular work day started at 4:00 a.m. and he would not return home until nearly twelve hours later. From time to time, he had to make deliveries in the evenings and on Sundays. When workers called in sick or when especially large orders were received, he was required to work a night shift. Being a co-owner of Camellia Lunch Service was a challenging endeavor. Over the years, David II suffered from stress, anxiety, and exhaustion. By age forty, he had developed severe hypertension. For many years, David looked forward to retirement which he entered into at the age of fifty-eight in 1969.

In 1975, David II's California Driver License data indicated that he had brown hair and blue eyes, was 5'10' tall, and weighed 180 lbs. He was a widower, aged 71 years.

Until 1976, David II lived at his home on Fruitridge Road with his daughter, Sharon Rogers and her family. In January 1976, when his son David III returned to Sacramento to take a job at the California Department of Education, David II moved in with his son's family with whom he lived until his death in December of 1989. David II lived at 9 Nautilus Court at the time of his decease.

Summary of David Dolson II
Around 1979, as a result of his hypertension, David II's heart began to fail and he underwent surgery for insertion of a pacemaker. He struggled with this condition for a decade. A few days after Thanksgiving in 1989, David II suffered a severe heart attack. After almost three weeks at Sutter Memorial Hospital, he was allowed to go home on Friday, 15 December 1989 but two days later, on Sunday, 17 December 1989, at approximately 10:00 a.m., he suffered a second heart attack which he did not survive. David Pelton Dolson II was buried at St. Mary's cemetery next to the grave of his wife, Marion. David II's death certificate indicates that he died of cardiac arrest at Sutter General Hospital as a result arteriosclerosis and chronic hypertension, conditions for which his attending physician, Dr. Donald Shaffer, had treated him since 31 August 1972.

David II left a will. In this document he notes that before his death, he transferred the deed of the property at 6528 Fruitridge Road to his daughter Sharon Rogers as her inheritance. He also provided gifts of $1,000 to his surviving sisters, Bessie Dolson Menzel and Josephine Dolson Loverde. The residual of his estate was bequeathed to his son, David P. Dolson III.

David II had a difficult childhood. He grew up in poverty and his parents were unable to provide much financial and social support. His childhood was cut short when he had to seek employment at the very young age of eleven. It was only through his extraordinary motivation and perseverance that he was able to finish high school.

Throughout his working life, David II dedicated the majority of his waking hours to Camellia Lunch Service. The poverty he experienced as a child and the imprint left by the Great Depression were major motivations for him to ensure that he was successful in business and able to provide a comfortable home life for his wife and children. As a result, David II did not engage in many civic activities. However, when his son David III joined the Boy Scouts in 1954, David II served as a regional representative for the Golden Empire Council for several years. In addition, when the Fruitridge Little League established baseball fields at St. Mary's

Cemetery in 1954, David II, with the assistance of John Cabral, oversaw the irrigation needed to assure that the newly seeded baseball diamonds would sprout and take hold.

Some of David II's favorite activities included attending opening day to watch the Sacramento Solons baseball team at Edmonds Field; reading the *Sacramento Union* newspaper in the morning and the *Sacramento Bee* in the afternoon; watching comedy shows on television as well as sports programs such as baseball and boxing. He particularly enjoyed spending time with his grandchildren.

David II's marriage with Marion had its challenges. Their courtship and the early years of their marriage must have been the most enjoyable. Marion could be hard headed and difficult at times. She was a heavy smoker which contributed to her ill health for most of her adult life. In her late thirties she suffered from anxiety and eventually developed duodenal ulcers for which several surgeries were required beginning in 1954. During these years, she became addicted to prescription pain medications, a circumstance that would eventually diminish her physical and mental health until she suffered a cerebral aneurysm in 1961. Marion barely survived the subsequent brain surgery performed at Sutter General Hospital. After the operation, the left side of her body was paralyzed and she was bed ridden for the remainder of her life. To add to these difficulties, Marion's health insurance had been cancelled soon after she was treated for ulcers. The costs for the brain surgery, hospital stays, home care, medical visits, and medications totaled tens of thousands of dollars. This was a tremendous sum of money in the 1960s and David II had to cope with this demanding financial burden. Marion Cassandra Dolson died on 3 March 1967 at the age of forty-nine.

Regrettably, David II was not aware of many aspects of his family heritage. He knew that he had relatives in Elk Grove and had visited his aunts and uncles infrequently during his early childhood. His father apparently shared very few details about Dolson family history. Much of what his mother told him about the Dolson, Van Ness, Adams, and Sullivan branches of the family tended to be incomplete and even at times, inaccurate. Although he knew little about his ancestry, he assumed that he was primarily of Irish heritage. He also had a vague, if errant notion, that the Dolsons may be linked in some way to the Pennsylvania Dutch[22]. Of all of the Dolsons, David II no doubt, would be the family member most interested in this genealogical sketch. It is sad to think that he died more than twenty-nine years before this volume was published.

David II, although known to be a worrier, also was viewed as a happy-go-lucky person with a unique laugh. Throughout his life, he made great efforts to be fair with everyone he encountered: family, friends and business associates. Most who knew him would comment that he was a good and honest person.

---

[22] Actually the so called Pennsylvania Dutch are Amish, Old Order Mennonites. They are descendants from eighteenth century, religiously-orthodox, German-speaking immigrants to the United States, Canada, and other parts of the Americas.

Epilogue

As stated in the Prologue, this volume encompasses comprehensive portrayals of nine generations of a specific branch of the Dolson family. The descriptions contained herein follow a line of ancestors beginning with Jan Gerritsen de Vries van Dalsen (ca. 1638-1692), born in the Netherlands, and ending with David P. Dolson II (1911-1989), born in Sacramento, California.

Jan's father, Gerrit, is mentioned in the volume but is not counted as the first generation depicted since the author has not been able to garner a single piece of documentation regarding this individual or any of the other ancestors in the Netherlands. First of all, the name Gerrit is only an assumption, even though a firm one. The Dutch at the time faithfully used a naming pattern called patronymics which resulted in sons carrying a name meaning "son of". In Jan's case, his patronymic "Gerritsen" clearly indicates "*son of Gerrit*". Secondly, since the author theorizes that Jan may have had at least two brothers, the patronymic of his father may have been alternatively Gerrit Jansen, Gerrit Lubbertsen, or possibly Gerrit Reynerson. The patronymic of Jan's father can't be determined conclusively since it is not known if Jan were the first-born son; nor how many siblings he may have had; nor if Lubbert Gerritsen or Reyner Gerritsen were definitively his brothers. We can approximate, albeit roughly, Gerrit's life span. Jan reasonably was born when his father was between approximately twenty and thirty years of age. If we estimate that Jan was born in 1630, then Gerrit might have been born ca. 1600 to 1610. If Gerrit lived to be sixty years old, he would have died between 1660 and 1680. These timeframes are all suppositions of course.

Full descriptions of the Dolsons from the most recent three generations of this branch of the family were omitted from this sketch. These are the contemporary descendants who were alive at the time this volume was written. The lives of these individuals continue to unfold, and for reasons of discretion and objectively, the writer has decided not to incorporate elaborations on these persons and their families in this volume. Instead, a capsulized profile of each of these individuals was included in Chapter IX. The personalities constituting this group are David Pelton Dolson III [*David II, David I, John C., Frederick, James Jr., James Sr., Isaac, Theunis, Jan*]; his sons David Pelton Dolson IV and Andres Luis Dolson; and his granddaughter, Penelope Riley Dolson [*Andres, David III, David II, David I, John C., Frederick, James II, James I, Isaac, Theunis, Jan*].

As an added note, the author, David P. Dolson III took two DNA tests before 2018. The first test around 2010 was conducted by 23AndMe and the second in 2017 by Family Tree DNA. The results of both assessments corresponded to the findings of this genealogical study. Ninety-five percent of the author's lineage is European with approximately a third contributed by people from Northern Europe (e.g., Netherlands and Germany); about a third from the British Isles, including Ireland, and the remaining third from Portugal and the Azores Islands.

The latter finding can be attributed to the author's maternal heritage while the Northern European findings correlate nicely with his paternal ancestry. Future DNA studies may result in even more detailed findings. As the pool of individuals tested increases, the number in particular subgroups may become sufficient to discern more specific distinctions such as British verses Irish verses Dutch.

This then completes the sketch of this particular branch of the Dolson family. Commencing with Gerrit and culminating with Penelope, a total of thirteen generations of the family have been noticed while nine have been depicted in detail. The writer is confident that some energetic Dolson cousin will take on the challenge to: (1) discover the stories of our ancient ancestors in the Netherlands and perhaps even earlier, (2) add, clarify, and correct information contained in this volume, and (3), document the lives of the contemporary and future generations of the family.

Appendix

The Dolson Line of Warwick

This segment of the sketch contains information on several Dolson families resident in Warwick, New York, between the mid-1700s to the late 1800s. This tract, placed purposefully in the appendix, stands apart from the principal nine chapters for a number of reasons. First, this subdivision addresses several generations of the family in Warwick and does not focus on a single ancestor, as is the case of the central body of the text. Secondly, the author has not been able to ascertain, with any level of certainty, the identity of the earliest Dolsons to settle in Warwick nor determine confidently these descendants' affiliations to any particular branch of the family. The amount and nature of guesswork contained in this appendix far surpasses the more grounded assumptions and theories characteristic of the main chapters. The ambiguities of the Dolson family in Warwick are many and complex; nevertheless, in the process of developing this volume, the author became aware of the remarkable deeds of the Dolsons in this region and felt that this information should be shared. In addition, there is a distinct possibility that some of the Warwick Dolsons are direct descendants of the writer's line of the family.

The Warwick families were involved in pioneering important homesteads and operating significant businesses. They constructed impressive homes, several of which still stand today. Several of the Warwick Dolsons had distinguished military records, but others were troubled by allegations of misconduct. The Dolsons of this locale entered into a number of marriages which forged relations with several prominent collateral families of the region. As was the case in Minisink, the Dolsons were involved in local civic matters, generally contributing affirmatively to the community but also, in at least one instance, prompting a great deal of misery for their neighbors. In all, the stories associated with this branch of the family make for intriguing reading.

Earliest Sightings
Unfortunately, there is considerable uncertainty regarding the precise date, the exact number, and the specific identities of the original Dolsons to settle in Warwick. There are several possible candidates. Whoever these individuals were, various local historians estimate that the first Dolsons came to Warwick before the Revolutionary War (Parker Seese, 1941). In her book entitled *Old Houses of Orange County* (1941), Parker Seese suggests that:

> **Richard Johnson and William Armstrong had come to the region about 1750. Abraham Dolson Jr., a few years later.** (p. 84)

The earliest known record of a Dolson in Warwick is that of the membership list of the Old School Baptist for the year 1766. Identified on this roster are an Isaac Dolsen and a Sarah Dolsen, possibly Isaac Sr. [*Theunis, Jan*] from Minisink and his second wife (maiden name unknown). The following year, Peter Mills, is noticed as a member of the congregation. The Mills family may have had a familial relationship to this Sarah Dolson and were concurrently, very good friends with several generations of Dolsons, such as Isaac Sr., Mary Hussey Dolsen, James Dolsen Sr., and James Dolsen, Jr. It is also possible that the Isaac and Sarah noticed at the Old School Baptist Church were Dolsons from later generations such as Isaac [*Jacob, Theunis, Jan*] and Sarah Dolsen [*Isaac Sr., Theunis, Jan*].

Warwick was the location of a famous Revolutionary War era inn called Baird's Tavern. Francis Baird, the innkeeper, maintained ledgers detailing his clients' transactions. For the time period between 5 December 1773 and 20 May 1774, the following accounts were noted by number and name:

Account No	Surname	First Name
45	*Dalson*	Abram / Abram Jr. / Abraham
74	*Dalson/Dolsen*	Isaac
127	*Dalson*	Matthew
135	*Dalson*	Jacob
145	*Dalsen/Dolsen*	Matthew

Unfortunately, Baird's Ledger does not contain the particular dates of individual transactions, but we know that the time period was late 1773 to early 1774. The largest number of entries was for account number 45, attributed alternatively to *Abram, Abraham,* and *Abraham Jr.* Based on the solitary account number, this could signify references to a single individual but of course, there is also the possibility that Abram and Abram Jr. were two different men who shared the same account. A later entry in the ledger for an *Abraham*, dated between 27 July 1785 and 31 October 1786, indicates that a charge was made to his "father". This means that a father and son pair named Abraham was alive and present in Warwick during the period 1785-1786.

Other ledger entries for Abraham Sr. indicate that his daughter frequented Baird's Tavern on behalf of her father. Abraham Sr. [*Theunis, Jan*] baptized a daughter named Marregrieta at the Dutch Reformed Church in Dutchess County on 9 September 1740. This woman would have been approximately thirty-five years of age in 1775. Abraham Jr.'s eldest daughter, Mary, was not born until 1787.

Also noted in the Baird's Ledger are a significant number of entries for an Isaac under account no. 74. Although the surname is sometimes spelled "Dalson" and at other times "Dolsen", this may be of no consequence given the circumstances of orthography in those days. However, other sightings of an Isaac and an Isaac Jr. during the period between 1773 and 1800 suggest the presence of at least two or three men by the name of Isaac in Warwick and still others in Dolsentown.

Varied spellings of the Dolson surname also occurred with a relatively small number of transactions credited to a Matthew. However, in these cases, the surname was not only spelled in a different manner but in addition, two account numbers were issued, signifying the possibility that these references may have been to two separate individuals with the same name.

Important notes contained in ledger entries provide additional clues. In one instance, a purchase by Isaac included the notation "*for his cousin Matthew.*" A "*Matthew Sen.*" is inscribed in another entry, a telltale sign that there was a need to differentiate between a Matthew Sr. and a Matthew Jr.

Typical purchases for the Dolsons included: rum, linens and sewing supplies such as buttons and thread, tea, molasses, allspice, shears, and grog.

In addition to the Baird Tavern Ledger, there are other early sightings of Dolson men in and around Warwick in civic, taxation and military records. Included on a 24 May 1775 list of Associators taken at Goshen are the names James Dolsen, Isaac Dolsen, and *Isaac Dolsen Jun.* On 7 June 1775, a roster of signers of the Pledge to the Continental Congress taken at Goshen, the names of an *Abm Dolsen Sen.,* and *Abram Dolsen Jun.* are included. Adjacent on the same list are the names of well-known men from Warwick such as Francis Baird, Henry Wisner, and Nathaniel Minthorn.

There is a 1775 Orange County tax assessment roll (Ruttenber and Clark, 1881) with the names of an *Abraham Dolkin* and Isaac Dolson in District 9, which is described as the Florida neighborhood between Goshen and Warwick. Abraham was assessed a sizeable sum of £5, 16s, and 1d meaning five pounds, sixteen shillings, and one pence. Isaac's taxes were much more modest at 16s and 1d. Importantly, another Isaac Dolson was assessed in District 8, the western section of Warwick. His assessment was somewhat more substantial at £4, 1s, and 11d. Finally as expected we see Isaac Dolsen Sr. [*Theunis, Jan*] and his son, James Dolsen Sr. [*Isaac Sr., Theunis, Jan*] taxed in District 10, the Dolsentown neighborhood.

Albeit no marriage record has been found, there is plentiful documentation to establish a marriage between a man referred to as Abraham Dolsen Jr. and Phoebe Benedict, daughter of James Benedict, the founding pastor of the Old School Baptist Church in Warwick. The couple's eldest child, Isaac, was baptized on 24 May 1777 (Van Duzer, 1923; Plimely, 2011), suggesting that the marriage between Abraham Jr. and Phoebe took place ca. 1775 or 1776 in Warwick.

The earliest military documentation for an Abraham is that of a February 1776 entry in the *New York Congressional Record*, cited later in this appendix under military matters. The record consists of a request by Colonel Hathorn for approval of nominations of two Dolsen men for posts in the Pond Company of Warwick. Here we see the name of an *Abraham Dolson* for Captain and a *Matthias Dolson* for Ensign. This writer accepts that Matthias is a reference to Matthew Dolsen.

Curiously in another letter from John Hathorn to the New York Congress (Vol. 5, p. 147), on 9 March 1776, the General states the following:

> **John Hooper, who was appointed Second Lieutenant in Captain Dolson's Company in Florida and Warwick Regiment, refuses to accept his commission. Returned in his place, Matthew Dolson, Jun. Second Lieutenant and John Tebons, Ensign, in the room of Matthew Dolson, being advanced.**
>
> **... I also inform your Honour, that a mistake appears in the commission for the First Lieutenant of Captain Dolson's Company. The commission is come for Henry Bartolf, which should have been for Peter Bartolf, he being the person elected in the Company.**

This last letter implies that two men named Matthew Dolson were involved in the regiments and the one referred to as Matthew Jr. was promoted to at least a Second Lieutenant. The phrase "*in the room of Matthew Dolson*" implies that the second man named Matthew was also an officer.

There are a number of lists that exist to denote those Revolutionary War veterans who qualified for land bounty rights. In one such roster of the First Regiment of the Orange County Militia under Major Zachariah Du Bois (*New York in the Revolution as Colony and State*, 1904) are found the names of *Abm. Dolson Sr., Abraham Dolson, Isaac Dolson, Jacob Mier Dolson, Tunes Dolson,* and a second sighting of an *Isaac Dolson*. The names are listed in groups, each group representing a particular neighborhood in Orange County. Abraham Sr., Abraham, and Isaac are listed in a paragraph of men from Warwick. *Jacob* and *Tunes* are listed with residents from Ulster County and Newburgh. A singular *Isaac Dolson* is shown with men from Minisink. Unfortunately, the roster does not contain information on dates of service. A similar roster of soldiers qualifying for land bounty rights as a result of service in the Fourth Regiment of Orange County lists an *Abraham Dolson* as a Lieutenant and Captain in Nicholl's Regiment of New York Levies. This Abraham is noted as fit for duty on 4 October 1776.

Much later, at a town meeting in April 1789, an Abraham Dolsen Jr. was elected as one of the Road Masters for the Town of Warwick (Ruttenber and Clark, 1881). And finally, an Abraham Dolsen, an Isaac Dolsen, and an Abraham Dolsen Jr were all enumerated in Warwick as part of the U.S. Census of 1790. Abraham was recorded as [10300] meaning one adult male, zero young males, three females, no other white persons, and no slaves. Isaac was recorded as [23400] and Abraham Jr. as [23401]. The configurations of these families suggest that Abraham may have been significantly older than either Isaac or Abraham Jr.

The various documents referenced in this section appear to identify a minimum of four and perhaps as many as seven Dolson men who resided in Warwick between 1766 and 1790.

Disentangling The Abrahams

The first Dolson in Warwick for whom unequivocal documentation is available is Abraham Jr. The Fishkill Dutch Reformed Church records clearly state that Isaac Sr. and his wife, Maritje, baptized a child named Abraham on 4 October 1741; however, all of the children belonging to this couple are assumed to be listed in Mary Hussey Dolson's personal bible. None on that list is named Abraham. Also, when Isaac Sr. wrote his will in 1794, he mentioned all of his known children. There is no mention of an Abraham. Abraham Jr.'s first son was named Isaac, which would be expected if Isaac Sr. were his paternal grandfather. From the early sightings of a Dolson in Warwick until the mid-1850s, there seems to be a fair number of documented interactions between members of the Dolson family in Minisink and members in Warwick. For example, in the 1820s, the names of Frederick Dolsen [*James Jr., James Sr., Isaac, Theunis, Jan*] and his wife, Margaret Moore Dolsen, are observed on several deeds with Isaac Dolsen and his wife, Catherine Sly Dolsen, regarding lands associated with the notorious mill pond incident. Still, the issue of Abraham Jr.'s paternity remains in question.

While no baptismal record has been found for a child named Abraham with the parentage of Abraham Sr. and Marya Slot, several genealogists and local historians understandably credit Abraham Jr.'s birth to this couple. The many sightings of an Abraham Sr., Abraham, and Abraham Jr. in Warwick insinuate a father-son relationship. Creating doubt on this supposition is the fact that all of the baptisms of Abraham Sr.'s and Marya Slot Dolson's other children are archived at the Dutch Reformed Church records of Fishkill and Poughkeepsie. Additionally, the baptismal date of 4 October 1741 does not fit chronologically within the documented baptismal dates of this couple's other children. Furthermore, Abraham Jr. and Phoebe Benedict Dolson did not name their eldest son Abraham, which would be expected if the grandfather were Abraham Sr. They did name their second son, James, after his maternal grandfather, James Benedict. Also, this author has observed that the use of the terms *senior* and *junior*, during the time period in question, was clearly not restricted to father and son combinations but could be applied also to an uncle and his nephew and even perhaps, as will be suggested later in this section, to distinguish older and younger cousins of the same name.

As previously mentioned, several historians note Abraham Jr.'s settlement in the Florida neighborhood of Warwick sometime before the Revolutionary War. Mildred Parker Seese

231

(1941) asserts that Abraham Jr. was the first Dolson to purchase land in Warwick. Sayer (1927) seems to agree:

> **Settled by Abraham Dolson in about 17??. His wife was Phoebe Benedict. Next James B. Dolson, son of Abraham Dolson in 1796. Next Joseph Miller whose wife was a Dolson? Her second husband was James Vail. Next Joshua Miller. Next J. E. V. Miller. Next Howard Miller est. sold to Abuja Utter. In 1794 Abram Dolson was granted a license and ran a hotel in part of the house that now stands on this farm. He died before 1805. The part of the house used as a hotel stood in the corner of the meadow across the road at the junction of the Long Ridge Road with the crossroad, going toward the Armstrong District. In 1796 James B. Dolson** (Sayer, 1927).

Regardless of his paternity, we know that Abraham Dolson Jr. married Phoebe Benedict ca. 1775-1776. She was the daughter of James Benedict and Mary Blackman Benedict (Plimley, 2011). Phoebe was born on 14 August 1753 at Ridgefield, Fairfield County, Connecticut. A Phoebe Dolson appears on the Warwick tax assessment for the year 1830. Phoebe Benedict Dolson died 31 October 1831 at Warwick, Orange County and was buried at the Old School Baptist Cemetery in the same town.

Phoebe's father, James Benedict (1717-1789), was the founding pastor of the Old School Baptist Church in Warwick. He was a very prominent resident of Warwick and his Old School Baptist Church played a central role in the early years of the community. The church edifice has been moved from its original location but is still standing and is considered to be an important Warwick landmark. It is now located on High Street, one block off of Main Street[23]. Phoebe Benedict's mother was Mary Blackman Benedict. She was born in 1741 at Green Farms, now the oldest neighborhood of Westport, Connecticut. Her parents were married in 1740 and relocated to Warwick in 1764 from Stratfield, Connecticut (Van Duzer, 1923). Additional genealogical information regarding the Benedict and Blackman families can be found at The Morris Clan (Retrieved on 19 June 2017 at *http://www.themorrisclan.com/*) and in *Elder James Benedict - The Pioneer Preacher of the Warwick and Wyoming Valleys* by Elizabeth C. Van Duzer (1923).

---

[23] Original Old School Baptist Meeting Site and adjacent cemetery location: Corner of Forester and Galloway streets. A marker stands in the small field across Forester Avenue from the Methodist Church. It commemorates the original site of the log meeting house of the Old School Baptist Church and the unmarked graves of some of Warwick's first settlers. The text of the marker reads: **Site of log meeting house of the Baptist Church of Warwick. James Benedict organized and installed as pastor Nov. 7, 1765 was the first minister and this first church in the valley. He died Sept. 9, 1792, aged 72 years. His wife, Mary Blackman, is buried beside him this churchyard, which is filled with the unmarked graves of his pioneer congregation, among them those of several Revolutionary War soldiers.**

Phoebe Benedict Dolson and Abraham Dolson Jr. had the following children, listed here according to their birthdates taken from Plimley (2011), tombstones, and obituaries:

1. Isaac Dolson was born on 24 May 1777.
2. James B. Dolson was born in May 1779.
3. John Dolson [Sr.] was born in 1785.
4. Jane Dolson was born on 20 April 1787.
5. Mary Dolson was born on 9 February 1790.
6. Jesse Dolson was born on 13 December 1791.
7. William Dolson was born in 1794.
8. Christian Dolson on 12 November 1795.
9. Nancy Dolson was born on 4 May 1799.

Additional details regarding the lives of these persons are provided later in this appendix.

Of the utmost genealogical importance is the fact that this couple did not have a son named Abraham, thereby negating the possibility that any sighting of any Abraham in Warwick could be an offspring of this family. Abraham and Phoebe did have a son named Isaac born in March of 1777 but based on this birthdate, he could not account for any sightings in Warwick (or Minisink for that matter) until at a least 1795 or more likely, 1798, the year in which this Isaac would reach the age of majority.

Who then were the Dolson men named Abraham spotted in Warwick as early as 1771? Even after extensive research and considerable analyses, the author remains perplexed. In fact, he is not steadily sure of the exact number of Abrahams. Surely there was more than one Abraham. There would be no need to use the suffixes *Sr.* and *Jr.* if only a single Abraham existed. However, it is much more challenging to determine if there were two Abrahams or three. There is even an outside prospect that four men carried this name.

One theory suggests that Abraham Sr. [*Theunis, Jan*] moved to Orange County around 1756, about the same year in which his brother, Isaac, relocated to Minisink, Orange County from Dutchess County. During his lifetime, this Abraham would definitely have been referred to as Abraham Sr. As in the case of Isaac, Abraham Sr.'s wife, Marya Slot, may have died ca. 1756 and Abraham Sr. may have decided to make a new start, perhaps in Warwick. However, unlike his brother, there is no indication that Abraham Sr. remarried. We do not find any evidence of his demise (a will or other legal documents) nor burial. Conflicting with this theory is the idea that an Abraham Dolson Sr. is noted as a military officer in 1776. Abraham Sr. [*Theunis, Jan*] would have been sixty-six years old at the time---significantly older than what would be typical for Revolutionary War service.

Another possibility is that local historians may be correct in supposing that the first Abraham to settle in Warwick was Abraham Jr., whether the son of Isaac Sr. [*Theunis, Jan*] or his brother, Abraham Sr. If we accept that Abraham Jr. [*Undetermined, Jan, Theunis*], was the first Dolson in Warwick, this then would allow us to theorize that a second Abraham Dolson relocated to Warwick during Abraham Jr.'s lifetime, thus explaining the need to modify the first names with Sr. and Jr. and rotating these suffixes overtime. This still leaves unanswered the question of the identity of the second Abraham. There are a couple of possibilities:

1. Either Isaac Sr. or Abraham Sr. or both may have had sons named Abraham. Perhaps the second Abraham to reach Warwick was one or the other of these men.

2. The second Abraham may have been the son of Johannes [*Theunis, Jan*] or somewhat less likely, the son of Jacob [*Theunis, Jan*]. The theory that one of these men could have resided in Warwick for a number of years and then relocated elsewhere is not unwarranted. Even if there is compelling evidence that two or three men named Abraham were present in Warwick between 1773 and 1790, there is virtually no evidence concerning the corresponding families of the other two men. There is not a single sighting in Warwick of a marriage, a baptism, a deed, a will, or a burial of any other Abraham or a related family with the singular exception of Abraham Jr.

To conclude, the author is reluctant to recommend one particular theory over the others regarding the identity of the men named Abraham. After all, it is even possible that one of the Abrahams sighted in Warwick is an unrecognized, contemporary Dolson from some other branch of the family or even an Abraham from a subsequent generation. Theunis' four sons, Johannes, Jacob, Abraham and Isaac, all married in the early 1730s and some of their children were born as early as one or two years after their marriages. This means that some of their grandchildren could have reached the age of twenty-one ca. 1775, approximately the same time as the earliest sightings of an Abraham in Warwick. The author does hold the unsubstantiated notion that the Abraham Sr. and Abraham Jr. first spotted in Warwick might have been cousins, one older than the other, and thus warranting the use of senior and junior to differentiate between the two men. These two Abrahams may have been grandsons of Theunis, and their fathers could have been in order of probability either Johannes, Abraham, Isaac, or Jacob.

Disentangling the Isaacs
The ambiguities regarding the identity of the Dolson men named Isaac are no less puzzling than those obscurities surrounding the Abrahams. Still, it may be possible to dispense with some of the usual suspects or at least narrow the scope of considerations.

According to Fishkill Dutch Reformed Church baptismal records, Isaac Sr. [*Theunis, Jan*] baptized a son named Isaac on 27 November 1743. This individual would reach twenty-one years of age in 1763. This son was mentioned in Isaac Sr.'s will as *non-compos mentis,* and Isaac Sr. included provisions for his son's care noting that he feared the condition would worsen in the future. Isaac Sr.'s will was written on 2 May 1794. At that time, Isaac Jr. would have been fifty-one years old. Based on this context, the author assumes that Isaac Jr.'s condition did not allow him to marry nor was he capable of owning land or serving in the military. Furthermore, it is assumed that this Isaac Jr. required specialized care for the remainder of his life. The author thinks that it is extremely unlikely that any of the sightings of an Isaac or Isaac Jr. in Warwick or Minisink pertain to Isaac Sr.'s mentally-challenged son.

Isaac's brother, Johannes, is also documented as having a son named Isaac or Isaak, who was born ca. 1739. This man however, along with his father and brother, Matthew, was a well-known Tory, a Loyalist to the British during the Revolutionary War. He was from Dutchess County and his family relocated ca. 1769 to the Wyoming Valley of Pennsylvania and subsequently to Niagara, Detroit, and eventually to Chatham, Ontario, Canada. His whereabouts and his activities as a Loyalist argue against this man being any one of the Isaacs sighted repeatedly over a number of years in Warwick in the late 1700s and early 1800s.

If not Isaac Jr. [*Isaac Sr., Theunis, Jan*], nor Isaac [*Johannes, Theunis, Jan*], who were the men by this name present in Warwick? An Isaac *Dolsen*, along with a Sarah Dolsen, was identified as a member of the Old School Baptist Church in Warwick as early as 1766. This very early sighting may have been Isaac Sr. [*Theunis, Jan*] and his second wife, Sarah (Doherty, 1990). Another resident of Minisink, Peter Mills, is noted as a member of the Old School Baptist Church in 1767. The dates of birth of Peter Mills' children are inscribed in Marytje Hussey Dolsen's bible and Peter's wife, Sarah Foster Mills, was the primary beneficiary of Sarah Dolsen's estate. Even though Isaac and Mary Hussey baptized their children at the Dutch Reformed Church in Fishkill, it appears that Isaac Sr.'s second wife was not of Dutch heritage and may have been associated with a different religious congregation. Perhaps Isaac and Sarah became members of the Old School Baptist Church for a time, but the distance between Minisink and Warwick probably deterred their regular participation.

Even allowing for the possibility that Isaac Sr. may have ventured to Warwick on infrequent occasions to attend church or even transact business at Baird's Tavern, the numerous other sightings of an Isaac and an Isaac Jr. in both Minisink and Warwick during the years in question assert the existence of at least one other, but more likely, two other men by this name in Orange County.

Even though there are no supporting baptismal record, it is theoretically possible that Theunis' sons, Jacob and Abraham, had sons named Isaac. After all, such offspring would have been old enough to be included on the 1775 tax assessments, on the rolls of the pledges in 1776, and on the rosters of the militia during the Revolution.

On 30 June 1797, an Isaac Dolson is noticed in a mortgage with Garret Vandevoort for the substantial amount of £525, using as collateral a lot in Warwick consisting of ninety-seven and one half acres (Liber H, p. 164). The property lay adjacent to the lands of David Miller.

In this indenture, Isaac's wife is identified as Elizabeth, no maiden name included, but this is probably Elizabeth Weymer. An obituary of William Dolson published in the *Warwick Advertiser* identifies William's father as Isaac Dolsen and his mother as Elizabeth Weymer:

> ***Another respected veteran of this town has departed in the death of William Dolson, which took place at the home of his daughter, Mrs. George E. Decker in Newburgh on Monday afternoon. He was born in this neighborhood on June 15, 1839, a son of Isaac Dolson and Elizabeth Weymer. He was married to Anne Cronk who died on Oct. 15, 1912. Mr. Dolson was an enthusiastic fireman and helped organize the Goodwill Hook and Ladder Company. He was a genial man with many friends. He was an earnest G.A.R. man and a faithful member of the Methodist Church and the Brotherhood. He went into the Union Army early in 1864 being in Co. A. 7th N.Y. Artillery. He is survived by the following children: William of Monroe; Jeanette La Pearl of Newburgh; Rebecca Buck of Providence, R.I.; Ada Clark of Goshen; Luella Decker of Newburgh; and Hollie Dolson of Providence. His funeral will be held from the Methodist Church this afternoon at two o'clock Rev. F. Withey officiating*** (*Warwick Advertiser*, 10 July 1919*).*

A Civil War enlistment record for Warwick notes a William Dolson, age 22 in 1862, as the son of Isaac Dolson and Eliza Sazer of Warwick. The spouse's name may be an error as this William appears to be the same man as noted in the *Warwick Advertiser* article.

Unfortunately, no wills for this Isaac or his wife, Elizabeth Weymer (Sazer) Dolson, have been located and no births of children, with the exception of the William mentioned above, have been discovered, which can be attributed conclusively to this couple. However, In the census of 1850, William is noted as eleven years old and living with the family of Henry Bertholf. Two other Dolson children in Warwick are observed in the 1850 census as living with other families: Abraham Dolson, age 14, was living with the Elizabeth *Wisener* family; Oscar Dolson, age 16 was living with the John A. Ackerman family. If the three children mentioned in this paragraph belonged to the family of Isaac Dolson and Elizabeth Weymer, then the author ventures that by 1850, both parents were deceased or otherwise unable to care for their children. Perplexing is the fact that if the couple were married as early as the recording of the 1797 deed, they would be expected to have had several children beginning in the late 1790's and continuing into the 1800s, 1810s and 1820s.

In summary, Isaac Jr. [*Isaac Sr., Theunis, Jan*] is reported to never have married. Isaac [*Johannes, Theunis, Jan*] married Mary Field, and moreover, was residing in Canada by this time period. Another Isaac Jr. [*Abraham Jr., Undetermined, Theunis, Jan*] from Warwick married Catherine Sly and was not born until 1777. If either Jacob or Abraham Sr. had a son named Isaac, this may be the man or men who account for the sightings mentioned. The author favors the idea that it was Jacob who had a son named Isaac for the reason that, although no baptismal record has been uncovered, it is almost certain that Jacob also had a son named Matthew. Jacob and Johannes Dolsen were married to sisters, Mary and Elizabeth Buys, respectively. Matthew was a prevalent name in the Buys family. There is military correspondence between Governor George Clinton and Sheriff Isaac Nicholls dated April 1779 specifying that a Matthew Dolsen of Orange, assisted his cousin, Matthew Dolsen [*Johannes, Theunis, Jan*] of Susquehanna, to break out of the Goshen jail along with several men including another cousin named Peter [*Johannes, Theunis, Jan*] (*Public Papers of Governor George Clinton,*1899). This Matthew and his brother, Peter, had been involved in Loyalist activities. Peter was killed by colonial militia during the escape attempt. Both Matthews managed to elude their pursuers. Subsequently Matthew of Orange County was captured and convicted of committing crimes as a member of the infamous Claudius Smith gang. It appears that the court confused the identities of the two Matthews. Matthew of Orange, along with Claudius Smith, and three other members of the gang were sentenced to hang in Goshen on 22 January 1779. Additional correspondence between Orange County Sheriff Isaac Nichols and Governor Clinton (*The Public Papers of Governor George Clinton*, 1899) indicates that Matthew was eventually pardoned. The pardon of two members of Claudius Smith's gang was also noticed by a militiaman who served as a guard at the Goshen jail. David Dean of Hopewell testified to this fact as part of his pension application (M-804, Roll 777) in 1832 (Hendrickson, Inners, and Osborne, 2010). Jacob's family was observed in Marlborough during these years, then part of Orange County. Based on this analysis, the author reasons that if genealogists missed placing a son named Matthew in Jacob's family, it is possible that they also overlooked a son named Isaac. Therefore, hypothetically, a son of Jacob named Isaac, could be the man noted as Isaac Jr. who participated in the following activities in Warwick:

- Taxed in 1775.
- Signing the articles and pledges in 1776.
- Enlisted in the militia in 1776.
- Owning land in Warwick before 1797.
- Married to Elizabeth Weymer. A woman by this name appears as Isaac Dolson's wife on a Warwick deed dated 7 May 1797.

Finally, the family of an Isaac Dolson was enumerated in the U.S. Census of 1800, the same year in which Isaac [*Abraham Jr., Undetermined, Theunis, Jan*] was married to Catherine Sly. The data from this census indicates that there were two men between the ages of sixteen and twenty-five living in the home as well as one girl under the age of ten, and two young women between the ages of sixteen and twenty-five. If this report pertains to Isaac [*Abraham Jr., Undetermined, Theunis, Jan*], there is no accounting for all of these individuals. This must be another sighting of Isaac [*Jacob, Theunis, Jan*].

From 1810 to 1840, a Peter *Dalson* or *Dolson* was enumerated in the U.S. Census reports taken at Warwick. It is significant to note that in the New York Census for Warwick in 1855, this Peter Dolson was noted as originally from Ulster County, perhaps Marlborough. Eventaully, Peter is listed as widowed and living in the home of his married daughter, Sarah J. Dolson Carpenter. This supports the idea that Peter and perhaps, Isaac were from Jacob's [*Theunis, Jan*] line. The spouse of one of Peter's later descendants, Blanche Decker Dolson, widow of Isaac Ten Eyck Dolson [possibly, *Jesseniah, Peter, Johannes Jr., Johannes Sr., Theunis, Jan*] is recorded as presiding over the transfer of the deed of the original Old School Baptist Church property in Warwick to the local historical society in 1952 (Hull, 2007; Morris, 2011). In the New York Census of 1925, Isaac Ten Eyck Dolson is enumerated as a railroad worker and his wife, Blanche, as a laundress. Their residence was located at 18 Forrester Avenue in Warwick. Also living in the home was James H. Decker, age 77, presumably Blanche's father. The author notes here a possible family connection. In the previously-presented obituary for William Dolson, son of Isaac Dolson and Elizabeth Weymer Dolson, a Luella Decker is listed as one of William's daughters. In the 1930 U.S. Census, Isaac T. (born ca. 1871) and Blanche (born ca. 1881) are shown as still living in Warwick. Also in the home was a stepson, George Wood, age twenty-one. This seems to indicate that Blanche was married previously to a man with the surname Wood. In the 1910 U.S. Census, Isaac T. Dolsen is shown as head of household and married to Sarah I Dolsen, age 40. Children are noted as Chauncy C, age five and Lillian Peal, age three. Residing at the same home are Harry C. Scudder, brother, and his wife, Emma Scudder, along with a nephew, Harry Crammer.

Again, the evidence is insufficient to advance a full-bodied theory regarding the early sightings of Isaac in Warwick. The author hazards a supposition that an Isaac in Warwick could have been the son of Abraham Sr., relocating to Warwick along with his father or brother Abraham Jr. There is also the prospect that one of the Isaacs in question may have been a son of Johannes Jr. [*Johannes Sr., Theunis, Jan*], who was born ca. 1775 at Marbletown (Marlborough), Ulster County. Less likely, an Isaac in Warwick could have been another genealogically-overlooked son of Jacob [*Theunis, Jan*] or another descendant in Jacob's line. And, as in case with the several men named Abraham, the individuals named Isaac may have been from another generation of the Dolson family or even from another branch. The substantial research conducted by this author has not resulted in any definitive answers.

Military Endeavors
A number of military documents indicate the participation of several Warwick Dolsons in Revolutionary War units during the 1770s. There is no doubt that Abraham Dolson Jr. and Matthew Dolsen participated in the Revolution. Their appointments as Captain and Ensign were recorded in the *New York Congressional Record* as follows:

Commissions for Sundry Officers Ordered Die Jovis, 10 ho. AM February 29, 1776.

The Congress met pursuant to adjournment. Present: Brigadier-General Woodhull, President. FOR NEW-YORK. — Colonel Lott, Mr. Prince, Mr. Rutgers, Captain Rutgers, Mr. Denning, Mr. J. Van Cortlandt. FOR ORANGE. — Colonel Allison.

Return of Officers to fill up several vacancies occasioned by promotions in the Florida and Warwick Regiments, subscribed by John Hathorn, Chairman, dated at Goshen, the 28th instant, was read and filed. They thereby return for Officers in the late Captain Henry Wisner's Company: Abraham Dolson for Captain; Henry Bartolf, First Lieutenant; John Hopper, Second Lieutenant; and Matthias Dolson, Ensign.

... Ordered, that commissions be issued for those gentlemen. (Source: [1776-02-29] New York Congress [S4-V5-p0319]).

During Abraham Dolson Jr.'s tenure as Captain, roll calls of his company were taken periodically. Following are data from one of these registers dated 2 November 1776:

Capt. Dolson Appears as shown below on a Return of the Regiment of Foot, in the Service of the United Colonies, commanded by Coll. Isaac Nicoll's return dated Nov 7, 1776 Capt. Abraham Dolson's Company:

- *Officers Present 1 Captain 1 First Lt. 3 sergeants 2 Drummer & Fiffers*
- *Rank and File Present fit for duty 18 Sick Present 10 Sick Absent 10 On Command 5*
- *Total 43 Alterations Since Last Return Deserted 4*

Within a few months of his Captain's commission, Col. John Hathorn recommended Abraham Dolson Jr. for a promotion as First Lieutenant:

Warwick, April 20, 1776
To the New-York Congress.
GENTLEMEN: I have herein made a return of the officers chosen in Captain John Wisner's Company of Minute-men, of the Regiment of Florida and Warwick, in the Precinct of Goshen, and County of Orange, agreeable to a return made to me by two of the members of the Committee of this Precinct, declaring their attending at the election of the said company, on the 26th day of March last; and were chosen (agreeable to a certain resolve of the Provincial Congress of this Province, made respecting the regulation of the Militia and

Minute Companies) Abraham Dolson, First Lieutenant; Nathan Sayre, Second Lieutenant, and Asa Wisner, Ensign; and hope your honourable body will issue commissions accordingly.

I am, on behalf of the Committee, your most obedient and humble servant,

JOHN HATHORN, Chairman

Several military reports describe Abraham's military experiences. On 2 November 1776, a Return of the Regiment of Foot in the Service of the United Colonies commanded by Col. Isaac Nicoll was submitted. For the Company of Abraham Dolson, the report shows the presence of one Captain, one First Lieutenant, three Sergeants, two drummers and fifers, and forty-six rank and file. Of the rank and file, twenty-three were reported as fit for duty, seven were present but sick, and sixteen were sick but absent. Seven privates had requested permission to complete service. A week later, on 7 November 1776, the number of rank and file had dwindled as a result of four desertions, and five privates were placed on command. Two additional returns during the same period of time show that Captain Dolson's company was fielding thirty-eight and forty rank and file troops respectively. One of the returns mentions that the regiment consisted of eight companies and was referred to as Isaac Nicholl's Charge of Minutemen. The return dated 2 November 1776 was taken at White Plains, New York.

Although the preceding documents seem to indicate that Abraham was performing satisfactory military service, there are also a number of reports that an Abraham *Dolson* was court martialed for stealing a subordinate's blanket (Doherty, 1997). Doherty cites the *Published Papers of Governor Clinton, First Governor of New York* as his source. The following tracts consist of several excerpts taken from Doherty (1997):

Capt. Abraham Dolson of Col. Nicoll's Regiment was accused of "feloniously taking and marking and selling a blanket belonging to a soldier". He was Court Martialed at Peekskill 6 Dec. 1776. [AA 1097]. The Court Martial was held at the house of Mr. John Mandivells, Colonel Ward, President: Captain Abraham Dolson, of Colonel Nicoll's regiment, arrested by the said Colonel Nicolls for feloniously taking and marking and selling a blanket belonging to a soldier. The prisoner being arraigned pleads Not guilty.

Lieutenant Gore, under oath, saith Captain Dolson told him that he had a blanket that he would sell him; and soon after a soldier in Captain Little's company came to the tent of the prisoner and said he had lost a blanket, and thought that blanket present was his blanket. Soon after the soldier was gone the Captain came to the tent, and I was at the fire, and told him that the blanket he offered for sale is like to have an owner, and the Captain said, Is the blanket gone? I told No. Then he said he would go into the tent and mark it, for it was

240

not marked; and took out his knife and went to the tent; and when he came out, as he was shutting his knife, and said he had marked the blanket. He asked the Captain how he came by the blanket; the Captain told him he took it up booauoo it could not give the countersign. At another time he told him he found it by the root of a tree. After Captain Little challenged the blanket, Captain Dolson told me that Captain Little had been to him about that blanket, and says if you will stand by me, I will do well enough, for, says he, I am told Captain Little I brought it from King's Bridge, and you may say that, and not tell a lie, for I brought it far enough from King's Bridge, you know; and further says he, I told him I bought it of a New-England man, and gave him twelve shillings for it.

Reuben Hall, Captain Dolson's waiter, under oath, saith that he heard the captain tell the Lieutenant, that he had found a blanket, and it could not give the countersign, and took it up. Some time after I heard of a New-England man at King's Bridge, and gave him twelve shillings for it; and Captain Dolson marked the blanket, and after some time sold the blanket that was in contest to Joel Frost. George Gore confirms the evidence of Rheuben Hall.

Joel Frost, under oath, saith, that he was passing by the tent of Captain Dolson, and Captain Dolson offered him a blanket for sale, and I agreed and gave him two dollars for the blanket and carried it home to my tent, and offered to sell it to my tent mates, and one of them agreed to have it; and the next morning he told me that he should not have the blanket for there was like to be an owner for it. And after Captain Little challenged the blanket he sold me, I told him I had sent it home; he said that blanket could not give the countersign; and further saith about the time said Dolson was arrested, he asked me what I had done with the blanket; I told him I had sent it home, and I told him if he came as honestly by the blanket as I did, he would not be ashamed to have the blanket seen; and told him if he would give me leave I would go home and bring it: and he told me he would go to the Colonel and try to get me a furlough, and said he wished that he could, for then I could go home and get the blanket and alter or mark it so that the blanket should not be known.

The within Court having examined the evidences against the prisoner, find him guilty of the charge alleged against him, and adjudge him to be cashiered and posted as described in section 14th, article 22d, in the Rules and Regulations of the Army, and he be mulcted eight dollars, four to be paid the soldier that lost the blanket, and the rest to be disposed of as directed by act of Congress.

Attest: J. Ward, President. I do approve of the above sentence. W. Heath, Major-General

There is little doubt that the Abraham involved in this event was a Dolson ancestor. An article printed in the *Newport Gazette,* dated 20 March 1777, clearly identifies the Abraham in question:

FISHKILL Jan, 30:
At a GENERAL COURT MARTIAL,
Held by order of Major Gen. Heath
At Peek's Kill Dec. 6, 1776.
Co. Ward, Lieutenant Colonel Harmon, Major Wood, Capt. Maxwell, Capt. Masa,
Capt. Newell, Capt. Sumaer, Capt. Paine, Capt. Ladew, Captain, Wright, Capt.
Bartlet, Capt. Barlow, and Capt. Brown, members.

CAPTAIN ABRAHAM DOLSON of Col. Nicolls's regiment arrested by Colonel
Nicolls for feloniously taking, marking, and selling a BLANKET, Belonging to a
SOLDIER, was brought before said court. The Court having examined the
evidence are of the opinion that the said DOLSON is guilty and adjudge that he
be cashiered, fined eight dollars, four of which to be paid to the soldier who lost
his blanket and the other four to be appropriated for the fine and publication in
public papers. December 18th: The Major General having approved of the
above sentence, it is published herein. Said Dolson belongs to Florida in
Orange County, in the State of New York.

Abraham Dolson's court martial took place in December of 1776. The following entry among the papers of Governor Clinton may refer to a different matter; may be dated incorrectly; or, for whatever reason, was posted at a later date:

In 1777 the Clinton papers note that Capt. Dolson was a suspect "has silver and
a ruffled shirt." He was of Orange County. [GCP 989] (Doherty, 1997, Pages 368-369).

A quote was taken regarding the same entry (No. 989) from the *Public Papers of George Clinton* by this author and it reads as follows:

Capt. John Wisener, Capt. Dolson, Jonathan Thompson; all have silver and
Ruffeld Shurts; Thomson has a Silver and White and plunder at Richard Wood
at Goshen. Jacob Vanskike privet at Warwick. *(p. 626)*

Gardiner (2008) explains that during the Revolutionary War men were assigned to particular units but records indicate that they often ended up serving in various units over their terms of service. This occurred because militiamen were called up for alarms such as the Battle of Minisink in July of 1779. In other instances, men were asked to re-enforce other units temporarily for a specific assignment. When on occasion soldiers became separated from their home units during battles or other deployments, they sometimes joined other units until they were able to return to their original troops. Finally, records also show that some militiamen enlisted for relatively short periods of time and then re-enlisted for a second and even a third term, often in different units on each occasion.

Colonel John Hathorn was perhaps the most well-known Revolutionary War figure from Warwick. He led his regiment on a number of important engagements including the Battle of Minisink in July 1779. His home, now an historical landmark, is located at the corner of Hathorn Road and Highway 94, just north of the Village of Warwick. To the extent that Colonel Hathorn operated out of his home, it is possible that Captain Abraham Dolson Jr. (Pond Company), Ensign Matthew Dolsen (Pond Company) as well as Lt. James Dolsen [Jr.] (West Side of Wallkill Company) may have reported for duty to his house.

While there is no documentation, it is also possible that any one of these Dolson men may have participated in some way in the Battle of Minisink. Some men from both the Pond and Wallkill companies responded to the alarm (Gardiner, 2008). In addition, the path from Goshen to the battle site taken by Hathorn's militia passed through Isaac's Dolsen's blockhouse in Minisink. Certainly, this would have attracted the attention of James Dolsen Jr. [*James Sr., Isaac, Theunis, Jan*]. What raises doubt about the inclusion of the Dolson men on the actual battle field at Minisink are the facts that (1) none of the Dolsons appear on any list of combatants, (2) it is known that some of Hathorn's troops were given support assignments such as quartering the horses, securing supplies, and guarding the rear and (3) a few days before the battle, Hathorn had been ordered by Washington to provide one hundred men to guard British prisoners being transported to Easton, PA (Hains, 1889).

As late as the mid-1780s, in a compilation of service records for Colonel Hathorn's Regiment (Gardiner, 2008), there were listings of the following individuals:

- *Dobson, Abraham (Dolson?) 1784/12/31: Receipt roll (pay) Certificates and sums.*
- *Dobson, Isaac (Dolson?) 1784/12/31: Receipt roll (pay) Certificates and sums.*
- *Dolson, John 1785/04/03: Order Capt. Ostrander please pay Wm. Birdsall for my service. Signed John Dolson, witness Henry Demler.*

Homes and Homesteading in Warwick
The coming of the Dolsons to Warwick is described by Mildred Parker Seese (1941) in a book published by the Albert Wisner Library in Warwick:

Dolson Homestead/Old Ridge Rd

The Dolsons came early to the Warwick Valley, sometime between the French and Indian and the Revolutionary Wars. They came from New Amsterdam by way of the Valley of the Ramapo, where they had been for possibly the space of a generation neighbors of the Van Duzers, Van Alens, and Van Blarcums[24]. They, too, had inherited a two-part name. It had been Van Dalsen when they came from Holland, and their Ramapo neighbors, whose descendants yet retain the Van, were quite disdainful of the family which had so far ignored its origins as to render its name, to their minds, meaningless. The feeling did not, however, interfere with a Dolson-Van Duzer marriage, when in another generation branches of the same two Dutch families found themselves neighbors at Warwick. John Dolson, son of Abraham, Jr., married Susan Van Duzer and built a house on his share of his father's estate, between the Van Duzer and the Dolson homesteads. This, the Dolson home place, is set high in the Y of the old road to Florida, originally an Indian trail northward from the Delaware, and the connecting road past the Johnsons to the Armstrong Neighborhood. It was not chance that placed the Dolson home so neatly in the fork. Not long after James Benedict Dolson had come into possession of the home farm at his father's death in 1803, he decided to establish a tavern, and the fact that the house was not well situated for such an enterprise did not deter him. The Indian trail from which the road had developed had in turn followed a natural course along the top of the ridge. James Dolson, probably at his own expense, rerouted the road by pulling it down from the ridge top to its present course, so that none could overlook the Dolson tavern. The Dolson tract, bought before the Revolution by Abraham, Jr., lay just east of the property already held or soon acquired by the Johnsons and Armstrongs. Beside a spring on a southerly slope the Dolson house was built. It must have been substantial, for years later, when they built again near the crest of the ridge, that old house was moved up the hill and across the little road to become part of this larger dwelling which, from its front porch, seems to have the world at its feet. There is no indication of when the move was made. Perhaps it was when Abraham, Jr. and Phoebe Benedict, daughter of the first settled pastor in the Warwick Valley, were married about 1775. Or it may have been when their growing family, nine children in all, required a much larger house. It was, in any case before Abraham made his will in 1803, for he designated boundaries of

---

[24] Two of Parker Seese's statements appear to be inaccurate. The Dolson family did not come to Warwick via Ramapo but rather from Dutchess County. Secondly, there is no evidence that the "van" segment of their surname was dropped because of any disdain for their Dutch heritage. A more consistent explanation is that the original moniker, Jan Gerritsen de Vries van Dalsen, was observed to be very long and unwieldy, leading to frequent complications in a primarily English-speaking society. In a move away from patronymics, the "Gerritsen and de Vries" parts of the name were dropped in the second generation. Also during Theunis' time, the "van" was left by the wayside, probably as part of a natural progression towards further simplification of a Dutch surname in a British colony.

James's farm by noting, "the place where the old house stood." It was and is a plain gabled rectangle built, one might almost say, between two fire places with broad backs dominating each end wall.

The above excerpt was accompanied by a photograph of Abraham Dolson Jr.'s initial homestead which Parker Seese (1941) entitled as "Dolson Set Home Neatly in the Fork". In 1976, the Division for Historic Preservation of the New York State Parks and Recreation Department produced a Building-Structure Inventory for this home which contained the following information:

- Location: N. side of Ridge Rd., Warwick, Orange County.
- Name and Use: Dolson original homestead.
- Exterior visible from public road: Yes.
- Materials: Clapboard with wood frame and interlocking joints.
- Condition: Good.
- Integrity: Moved (ca. 1775-1790), new roof and windows ca. 1950, addition to rear in early 1900s.
- Map and surroundings: situated on a small knoll on the northeast corner of West Ridge Road and Ridge Road; much of the area is former farm land withdrawn from active use because of increasing tax pressure.
- Historic and architectural importance: Abraham Dolson bought this land and built this house before the Revolution. Subsequently the house was moved to this site and enlarged, perhaps about 1775 when he married Phoebe Benedict, daughter of the first settled minister in the Warwick area. Upon Abraham's death in 1803 his son James Benedict Dolson, established a tavern in the house, and at his own expense re-routed the nearby road to have it pass closer to the house. In Parker Seese's 1941 photograph, the house has 2/2 windows, a tin roof, and a shed-roof porch. Subsequent owners have "restored" the house by installing 9/6 windows, removing the porch, and adding small scroll type brackets under the shallow eaves.

The author of the present volume includes the following interesting passage regarding the home which was retrieved from a genealogy manuscript posted online. The citation, although ambiguous and incomplete, appears to be copied from archival material.

The wall of one room in this house is said to have been decorated by an Indian. No trace of it now appears, though careful removal of paper and paint might reveal it. Such an undertaking by Mrs. Elizabeth Crissey Van Duzer in the Baird Tavern at Warwick a few years ago confirmed a tradition that roses decorated its ballroom wall. (Source: Dorothy Helen Martin Genealogy, Generation No. 5. Posted at *http://familytreemaker.genealogy.com;* retrieved on 27 March 2011).

Parker Seese (1941) also featured Isaac Dolson's [*Abraham Jr., Undetermined, Theunis, Jan*] home in her book about old houses in Orange County. The home is noted as meticulously restored and maintained by the current owners, Mr. and Mrs. Frank Gibson, of Johnson Road. Parker Seese (1941) further reports that the diary of an early mistress of the house informs that the state of the home was:

> *... topsy-turvy while we whiten [widen] the dining room. Consequently, the Gibsons have completed the work of enlarging the dining room and also installing dormers in the lower wing. Little else has been changed in the house.*

When Abraham Dolson wrote his will in 1803 he noted that he already had given his son, Isaac, the part of his estate which he felt he deserved. On this property Isaac built his house and was established in it by the time that Abraham Jr. died (Parker Seese, 1941). Isaac had married Catherine Sly, a neighbor's daughter who had come into a considerable dower of gold on her wedding day. That may explain the comparatively fine house Isaac built, the first of several Warwick structures of more than ordinary excellence attributed to him (Parker Seese, 1941).

As was the case with his father's homestead, the Division for Historic Preservation developed a Building-Structure Inventory for Isaac's home on 6 February 1976:

- Location: N. side of Ridge Rd.
- Original use: Residence of Isaac Dolson.
- Visible from public Road: Yes.
- Material: Clapboard.
- Structural System: wood frame with interlocking joints.
- Condition: Good.
- Integrity: Original site, dormers added, extensive interior renovation in 1935.
- Mapping: On north side of West Ridge Road approximately one half mile west of Ridge Road.
- Outbuildings: Barn.
- Surroundings: Open woodland dotted with scattered buildings.
- Notable features: Two and one half stories, gambrel roof, 6/6 windows, doorway with sidelights, small gable porch on two square columns, interior end chimney.
- Historic notes: Built by Isaac Dolsen before 1803 on land inherited from his father, Abraham Jr. Isaac was a skilled builder. Isaac Dolson is buried beside his father-in-law, Conrad Sly, in the Old School Baptist Churchyard.

Isaac Dolson lived at his home on Long Ridge Road until 1805. Remarkably, this house was featured in an article published in the *New York Times* in 1997:

It was love at front sight. One day five years ago, Mario Rodriguez, a woodworking teacher, was driving on a rural road in Orange County, N.Y., toward a house he had been told was for sale. What he saw was a wooden doorway unlike anything he had ever seen before.

There, on the modest frame building was a Federal-period front doorway whose dimensions alone distinguished it. It was 9 feet tall and 6 feet wide, punctuated by a glass transom at the top and glass sidelights. But the Greek chorus of statuesque carved wooden decorations on the old door was raising a call for help.

The call went through. Mr. Rodriguez and his wife, Judy, were looking for a house to buy. The 180-year-old doorway carried him across the threshold. The Booth family, which was selling the house, had helped spare the period work with 60 years of proud Yankee frugality. Nothing had been damaged or removed.

Mr. Rodriguez, who teaches in the woodwork restoration program at Fashion Institute of Technology in Manhattan and also offers classes in 18th-century hand woodworking techniques at his own studio in Warwick, made a wise decision. To preserve what he could of the original doorway, he carefully removed it and retired it from active service. To replace it, he created a replica to within a sixteenth of an inch. There were more than 100 parts, from the four pilasters supporting four fluted urns to the stacked frieze of shelf moldings on top. Though Mr. Rodriguez had been a woodworker for 20 years, taking the doorway apart taught him much about traditional technique. "In working, I found myself making the same decisions that yielded the same exact results of the original," he said. "What you experience is this immediate connection between you and an 18th-century woodworker."

Like a man trying to identify an ancestor, Mr. Rodriguez called on the Warwick Historical Society to find out more about his house. Built in the late 18th century by a family of prosperous Dutch farmers, the original cabin-like house was added to early in the 19th-century by Isaac Dolson. Mr. Dolson was a climber: he built a large drawing room in front of the cabin with bedrooms above, and on one side, an entry hall with a stairway. The imposing door capped Mr. Dolson's social ambitions. If a front door is a house's best foot forward, Mr. Dolson's doorway was designed to trip passers-by on the road. It looked more like a fine breakfront than architecture. Built in 1812, it is an early example of Greek revival style (Hamilton, 1997).

The 21 September 1957 issue of the *Minisink & Wallkill Precinct Historical Chronicle* contained a brief article concerning a previous week's visit by members to several old homes in Warwick. Isaac's house was mentioned in the following manner:

> **The Gibson home, the old home of Isaac Van Dolson, one of the old Dutch settlers. This was a lovely home, nice location out of town on the Ridge Road, the old fireplaces, the old furniture, the old hand-hewn beams in the kitchen, upstairs it had been modernized but not harmed historically ... Then you came out down a fireplace stairs----so you did not have to retrace your steps thru the house.**

A number of varied but interesting details regarding the genealogy and history of the Warwick Dolsons were highlighted by Sayer (1927) as follows:

- *According to Michael McCreery: Parents Abraham Dolson b 1710 and Marytje Sloat*
- *Grandparents Teunis Van Dalsen b 1664 in NYC and Sarah Vermilye b 1673*
- *Great Grandparents Jan Gerritson Van Dalsen b 1647 in Dalsen, near Zwolle in Overyssle, Netherlands and Gristie Cray/Kray*
- *Rt. 94 N. Abram Dolson*
- *Abram Dolson married Phebe Benedict, daughter of Elder James Benedict. The part of the farm across the Long Ridge Road west of the school house before 1800. Abram Dolson owned part of it.*
- *More Deeds April 25, 1816 John Dolson & Susan his wife and Phebe Benedict Dolson widow of Abram Dolson sold to Moses Mather 43 acres.*
- *Jan 23, 1835 James Benedict Dolson sold to Wm. Vail 18 acres.*

These records confirm that Abraham Dolson Jr. purchased land in the Florida neighborhood of Warwick, at the intersection of West Ridge and Old Ridge Roads (Sayer, 1927; Ruttenber and Clark, 1881). These homes were still standing in 2018 and are registered with the Warwick Historical Society.

In April of 1796, the records of the Warwick chapter of Masons, St. John's Lodge, include a member named *Abe Dolson* (Ruttenber and Clark, 1881). Most of the meetings were held in Florida but some meetings were also held in Warwick. Members in 1797 included: Abraham Genung, John Burns, James Wisner, William Wood, and an Abraham *Dolson* (*The Warwick Advertiser*, July 1965). Earlier, Abraham Dolson was on the roster of Little Britain Lodge No. 6 of the New York Free Masons. Abraham was noted in this roster as enlisted in the Orange County Militia.

At the first town meeting of Warwick in April of 1789, an *Abraham Dolsan* was named as one of several Road Masters. Each Road Master was to be a Pound Master for their respective district. Sayer (1927) states that in 1794, an *Abram Dolson* was granted a license to run a hotel in a wing of the house that now stands on what used to be Abraham's farm.

Abraham Dolson Jr. died in January of 1803. He and his wife, Phoebe, are buried in the Cemetery of the Old School Baptist Church. Apparently, the relationship with the Old School Baptist Church, incurred even before Abraham and Phoebe's marriage, would endure for several generations in this and other branches of the Dolson family. One hundred and fifty years later, at an open house celebration, Blanche Decker Dolson, the widow of Isaac Ten Eyck Dolson [possibly *Jesseniah, Peter, Johannes Jr., Johannes Sr., Theunis, Jan*], participated in the transfer of the deed of the church property to the Warwick Historical Society:

> ***On July 27, 1952, the deed was given by Mrs. Isaac Dolson, one of two surviving members of the congregation, to Lawrence Stage, Treasurer of the Historical Society and custodian of the Records. It was agreed that the building would not be de-consecrated and that religious services could be held there in the future on special request*** (Hull, 2007; Morris, 2011).

Following is a transcript prepared by this author of Abraham Dolson Jr.'s will, which was proved on 15 January 1803:

> ***In the name of God Amen. I Abraham Dolson of the Town of Warwick, County of Orange, and the State of New York being in a weak and low state of body but of a sound mind and disposing memory do this ordain and make my last will and testament. For the first place I recommend my soul to God who gave it and my body to be decently interred in a Christian like manner and as for my worldly estate that it has pleased God to endow me with I give and bequeath in manner following. I do give unto my beloved wife Phebe Dolson one bed and bedding and decent support out of my estate as long as she continues my widow and likewise a horse to ride whenever she chooses. Likewise I give to my son James one hundred acres of land together with my buildings and one ... and his south ... beginning in the line of Gerret Post and running on line near where the well is where the old house stood and from thence to an elm tree near the stone fence and along the same to the road that leads to Richard Johnson's and that he together with my son John Dolson pay all the just debts that is due from my estate and likewise I give my son John the remaining part of my lands supposed to be upwards of fifty acres be the same more or less and that he shall have the lower meadow adjoining William Johnson's land and plough ... adjoining the same north make up the compliment of land intended to be given and he to live with James and help support the family until he is twenty one and have equal shares of profits with him and I give to son William the sum of one hundred pounds at the time he arrives at the age of twenty one years which***

money is to be paid by my son Isaac and for the use of the money which Isaac owes me I allow my son William to live with and he to give him schooling and when able to go to a trade that suit his inclination best to be put thereto and I give to my son Jesse the sum of one hundred pounds when he arrives at the age of twenty one and that live with son James and receive schooling until he is fit to go to a trade and he my son James pay him the said sum and I give to my daughter Jane one cup board and one cow, one bed and bedding, half dozen chairs, three sheep, one chest of drawers, two wheels, one large and one small, one looking glass valued at five dollars, two tables of the value of nine dollars, 1 sett knives and forks, six pewter plates and three pewter table spoons, and tea spoons half dozen of each, half dozen earthen plates and three platters, one tea pott, milk pott, sugar dish, a sett of cups and saucers, shovel and tongs, and a pair of hand irons, two potts, one large one small, one tea kettle, two new pails, one wash tub and a churn, one candle stick, one common chest and I do give to my daughters Mary Christian and Nancy the same articles that I give to my daughter Jan except the cupboard they to have their legacies whenever they marry or arrive at the age of eighteen and to be delivered by my wife and son James and their complying, I give them all my personal property and my said daughters to live with James until they may marry or arrive to the age of eighteen and my will is that Jesse have the colt I gave him this last fall and the he be kept on the place until he goes to a trade unless he chooses to sell him before and as to my son Isaac, I have already given him that part of my estate that I thought proper and therefore have not considered him in this my last will and lastly I do appoint my wife Phebe Dolson executor and Isaac and James Dolson executors to this my last will and testament and I do dismiss all former wills and declare this to be my last will and testament. Dated this fourteenth day of March, one thousand eight hundred and two. Sealed, signed, and acknowledged in the presence of us John Houston, William Johnson, and Isaac Clark. Signed Abraham Dolson

All nine of Abraham Jr.'s children were named in the will as was his wife, *Phebe*.

The Subsequent Generations

As noted, Abraham Dolson Jr. and Phoebe Benedict Dolson are recorded as having at least nine children. Following are brief portrayals of each of these offspring except Isaac. Because of the number of remarkable stories and interesting family connections associated with the life of Isaac, the author concludes this Appendix with a detailed description of this man in a separate section.

1. Isaac Dolson was born on 24 May 1777.

2. <u>James B. Dolson</u> was born on 24 May 1779. He was baptized at the Old School Baptist Church in 1816 (Foley, 1938). Plimely (2011) and Van Duzer (1923) assert that James Benedict Dolson was married to Maria Ackerson, daughter of Garret Ackerson and his wife, Dorcass (surname unknown). When Gerret Ackerson wrote his will in 1811, he named James Dolson of Warwick and identified him as a son-in-law. Maria was born on 23 January 1786 (Van Duzer, 1923). Maria Ackerson Dolson and James Benedict Dolson had four children: (1) Phebe Maria born on 8 November 1804, (2) Julianer born 26 July 1806, (3) Sally Ann born 2 May 1808, and (4) Jane Eliza born 28 March 1810 (Plimely, 2011). Between 1810 and 1820, James was a member of the Old School Baptist Church and records show that he made donations to that organization as late as 1829. Nevertheless, in 1814, his wife, Maria, was a member of the Reformed Church of Warwick. On 20 May 1800, Abraham Dolson deeded to his son, James Benedict Dolson, a twenty-acre lot for the sum of $284. The lot is described as lying along the former highway from Warwick to Florida and bordering the lands of Abe Genung and Robert Armstrong (Liber D, p. 292). After his father's death in 1803, James Dolson is reported to have established a tavern on the Dolson property along the old road to Florida. Given that the original homestead's location was not well suited for the purpose, James rerouted the old road from Warwick to Florida so that all who passed by would not miss noticing the tavern. Ruttenber and Clark (1881) inform that religious services were held in the "Long Room" of Dolson's place in 1811-1812, while a proper house of worship was being constructed for the Presbyterian Congregation. In 1815 James was subscribed to a pew (No. 56) located on the lower level of the Old School Baptist meeting house. James B. was assessed as a musician in 1813 and 1814. James B. Dolson is noted as a Constable in Warwick for the period of 1818-1819. James Benedict Dolson, farmer, served as a juror between 1830 and 1836 on seven occasions.

Foley (1938) claims that James Dolson died on 13 May 1852 but there are subsequent sightings of this man. Maria Ackerson Dolson must have died before 1855 as the New York State Census in that year shows that James was living as a widower with his daughter, Phoebe, and her husband William Vail. In 1857 James provided testimony in an affidavit to support the Revolutionary War pension application of Catherine Johnson, widow of William Johnson, a former neighbor from Long Ridge. In the affidavit James indicated that he recalled the marriage of the couple in February 1793 and that the following spring, Johnson traded horses with James' father, Abraham Jr. Johnson needed better horses as he had been elected Constable. James further stated that Catherine and William Johnson lived within one half mile of his father's house. James Benedict Dolson is buried in Warwick Cemetery. His remains were transferred in 1889 from the Old School Baptist Church burying grounds along with those of his wife, Maria, and children, Jolaner and Sara Ann.

3. <u>John Dolson [Sr.]</u> was born in 1785. He married Susan Van Duzer (1792-after 1855), daughter of Christopher Van Duzer and Juliana (Julianer) Tusten ca. 1810. Upon his death in 1812, Christopher Van Duzer bequeathed $60.00 to Susan Dolson. Executors of the will were Christian Van Duzer, David Foster, William Foster, and Sarah Foster, the last three mentioned perhaps the parents or other relatives of Sarah Foster Mills, who married Peter Mills of Minisink before 1802. Susan Van Duzer was a niece of Benjamin Tusten, the medical officer who died heroically at the Battle of Minisink in 1779. Susan's mother, Juliana Tusten Van Duzer was Benjamin Tusten's sister.

On 25 of April 1816, John Dolsen and Susan, his wife, in consort with *Phebe* Dolsen, widow of Abraham Dolsen Jr., sold forty-three acres of land in Warwick to Moses Mather, of Connecticut, for the sum of $2,150 (Libers Q-R). John and Susan Dolson are credited with constructing a home on the Dolson tract between the Van Duzer estate and the homestead established by Abraham Dolsen Jr. Even though John was the grandson of a Baptist minister, Susan Van Duzer became a member of the Reformed Church of Warwick in 1813. In her widowed years, Susan Van Duzer Dolson resided in the Cornwall home of her daughter, Mary A. Dolson Reeve, wife of Ruben Reeve (New York State Census, 1855). Susan Van Duzer Dolson is thought to have died sometime between 1863 and 1867. She is buried in the Reeve family plot in Cornwall. According to Van Duzer (1923), John Dolson and Susan Van Duzer Dolson had six children: (1) James Dolson born ca. 1811, (2) Mary Ann Dolson Reeve born in 1812, (3) William Dolson born in 1814. He married Ann Elizabeth Galley of New York City, (4) Jane Dolson Ferdinand (1816-1838), (5) Nathan Westcott Dolson (1825-1911), who on 10 July 1850 married Rebecca Weed, and (6), John Dolson [Jr.] (1826-1866), who was married to Rachel Mott (ca. 1830-1909) in 1849.

John Dolson Sr. died in February 1866. Again, the death date given by Van Duzer (1923) for John Jr. is suspicious since it is the exact same date as given for the death of John Jr. A funeral announcement for a John Dolson appeared in a local newspaper as follows:

> ***In this place, Feb. 20th, 1866, Mr. John Dolson (Also Dolsen). Returning from auction sale of Cash Arnot on the 15th, near the corner at the widow Huston's, thrown from his sled.***

John Jr. was a farmer and also worked as a farm laborer. He was reported as being illiterate. John Dolson Jr. was noted on the ledger of the Bellvale Store from 1858 and 1860. John Dolson Jr. and Rachel Mott had two children, a daughter named Sarah Ann Dolson Brown (1850-1934) and a son named Edison Dolson. Rachel Mott Dolson worked as a dressmaker after her husband's death. When Rachel died in October of 1909, a local newspaper published the following obituary:

Mrs. Rachel Dolson died at her home in Sugar Loaf on Monday, aged 79 years. She was a daughter of William and Rachel [Sarah] Mott, long since deceased and was born at Glenwood, N.J. Forty-eight [fifty-eight] years ago, she married John Dolson, who has been dead a number of years. The deceased is survived by one daughter, Sarah, widow of Edward Brown, four grandchildren and six great grandchildren. Mrs. Dolson and her daughter had lived together in Sugar Loaf for a long time. The deceased had been a member of the Methodist Church for about forty years. Funeral services were held Wednesday and the remains interred in Locust Hill Cemetery (Van Duzer, 1923).

Van Duzer (1923) assumes that John Dolson Jr. is also buried in Locust Hill Cemetery. Although there are no stones, there is a Dolson section in this cemetery, including the burial sites of Oscar and Henry Dolson, Civil War veterans.

4. Jane Dolson was born on 20 April 1787. Jane was baptized at the Old School Baptist Church in 1821. Jane Dolson is recorded as a member of the Old School Baptist Church from 1820 to 1830. Her grave maker in the cemetery of the same church records the date of death as 20 April 1830 and notes that she was forty-three years of age. It appears that Jane never married.

5. Mary Dolson was born on 9 February 1790 and died on 20 May 1813, at the age of 23. She appears to never have married.

6. Jesse Dolson was born on 13 December 1791. Jesse Dolson married Elizabeth Burt, granddaughter of Colonel John Hathorn, on 17 December 1812 (Horton, No Date). Elizabeth, born in 1790, was the daughter of Belden Burt and Sally Hathorn Burt. Elizabeth was bequeathed the sum of $5.00 in the will of her uncle, Andrew Hathorn in 1814. Jesse Dolson and Elizabeth Burt Dolson had at least the following children: (1) Samuel B., Belden, (2) Jeremiah, (3) William, (4) Benjamin, and (5) Abraham. Jesse Dolson died on 22 April 1831. He was buried in the Old School Baptist cemetery but his remains, along with those of his wife, Elizabeth, were moved in 1867 to the Warwick Cemetery. Importantly, a notation regarding Jesse Dolson's burial identifies him as a veteran of the War of 1812. It appears that Elizabeth Burt Dolson died before 1850 as in that year, the U.S. Census seems to indicate that the children from this marriage were living among several Warwick families including the Bertholfs, Wisners, and Ackermans.

7. William Dolson was born in 1794. He married Elizabeth Ann McCamly (21 August 1802 - 28 August 1823) on 1 March 1824. Elizabeth was the daughter of Colonel David McCamly and Phoebe Sands McCamly. One of the couple's grandsons, William Dolson Mills, graduated from Yale University in 1871. Dan Burrows (1950) wrote a sketch of the

McCamly family which was published in the Warwick Historical Papers. That sketch contained the following story regarding William Dolson:

... coincident with that famous year without a summer, 1816. Wherein every month of the year saw frost and the farmers of the country were poor in consequence, a young boy came to live with the family [McCamly] and to earn his living at such pursuits as he was fitted for. The exact circumstances are unknown. The boy's name was William Dolson. Several years later he married Elizabeth Ann, but their happiness ended shorty when she died at the age of twenty-one. William Dolson never remarried. He remained all his life with the two [McCamly] brothers, David and Rodman, who lived on adjoining farms and was unswerving loyal to them as a brother and as a faithful family retainer. He died at the age of seventy-one years in 1865, and his monument is in the McCamly family cemetery.

Who was William Dolson? ---I myself have done a good deal of puzzling since the days when I was a small child ... I noted in a collection of pictures and accounts of old homesteads in Orange County, one of the old Dolson houses located on the Ridge beyond Warwick. This particular account tells about Abraham Dolson's house stipulating in the aforementioned will that his underaged son, William, was to live with his brother, Isaac, until he came of age, meanwhile to be allowed schooling and go to a trade if he chooses. The account says that it is probable that William chose a trade. Little is known of him. Now let us consider. If William Dolson, who married Elizabeth Ann McCamly was seventy-one years of age in 1865, he would have been in 94. In 1803 he would have been nine years of age and therefore far from major years ... If little was ever known about him, obviously, he disappeared from the memory of his family and their descendants, possibly from a break with them. The probability is that William found life with his brother, Isaac, none too pleasant; Isaac was probably glad to be rid of the boy whom the McCamlys obviously thought a great deal of. Certainly, his years of devotion to them prove he had reason to be grateful for some measure of kindness.

8. <u>Christian Dolson</u> was born on 12 November 1795 and died on 10 May 1844 at the age of forty-eight years, five months, and twenty-eight days. Christian is buried in the Old School Baptist Church Cemetery. Apparently, she never married.

9. <u>Nancy Dolson</u> was born on 4 May 1799. Nothing more is known about this individual.

It appears that virtually all of Abraham Jr.'s and Phoebe's children were born in and lived out most of their lives in Warwick.

The Adventures of Isaac Dolson of Warwick

Isaac Dolson, Abraham Jr.'s and Phoebe Benedict Dolson's eldest child was born on 24 May 1777 in Warwick and died on 20 July 1838 at the same place (Plimley, 2011). This Isaac lived at the Dolson tract of the Florida neighborhood just north of Warwick. Before his father's death in 1803, he had built a house on his share of the property. According to Sayer (1927), Isaac sold this property in 1805.

This Isaac married Catherine Sly, daughter of Conrad Sly and Anna Ward. The couple's first child was born in 1801 suggesting that the marriage took place ca. 1800. Conrad Sly's descendants claim he was of German birth and immigrated to America around 1770 (Sly, 2016). Conrad was a blacksmith by trade. Conrad's family was from the Town of Pfalzburg, located in Germany near the French border in the province of Alsace-Lorraine. Conrad Sly subsequently may have lived in Long Pond, New Jersey. Long Pond was a settlement involved in the iron mining and smelting industry. There, he married Anna Ward, the daughter of Thomas Ward, a shopkeeper from the Village of Long Pond. According to Sly (2010), there is a 1776 map which indicates that a Sly/Ward family lived on the Old Post Road somewhat south of White Plains in Westchester County, New York. Conrad resettled in Warwick, Orange County, New York ca. 1778.

Conrad Sly purchased several lots from Abraham Dolson Jr. after the Revolutionary War (Sayer, 1927). The first transfer consisted of fifty acres in 1784 and then there was another transaction of a single acre in 1793. Conrad Sly was a celebrated citizen of Warwick. His homestead was located at what is now the Landmark Inn on State Route 94, not far from the Dolson tract. An historical marker has been placed at the site and reads as follows:

> **Conrad Sly Homestead. Settled in Warwick 1778 A Blacksmith who forged Revolutionary War chain that crossed Hudson River at West Point. Pvt. in Col. Hathorn's Regiment.**

According to various historians such as Hull (1996), Conrad Sly was a principal participant in the manufacture of the colossal chain that was strung across the Hudson River to impede the passage of British war ships during the Revolutionary War. Portions of this chain are on exhibit at various locations including Washington's Headquarters in Newburgh. Conrad may have fought at the Battle of Newtown during the American Revolution. The battle was the culmination of the "Sullivan Campaign" ordered by General George Washington (Sly, 2010).

Apparently, Isaac Dolson and Conrad Sly enjoyed a close relationship. When the latter neared death in 1812, Conrad, now in his 60's, asked that his son-in-law be buried next to him in the Old Baptist School Cemetery (Parker Seese, 1941). Indeed, Isaac Dolsen's tombstone, dated 1838, is near the same tree as the markers for *Coonrad* Sly and his wife, Anna Ward Sly. Anna was born on 20 October 1751 in Ramapo, Bergan County, New

Jersey and died 14 August 1822 in Warwick. In his will, Conrad mentions his daughter, *Catherine Dolson*, and provides her with an inheritance of $250.

Sly (2010) provides the following passage about Isaac Dolson in a narrative posted at the Conrad Sly Homepage:

> *Isaac was from Warwick, New York. He built a hotel, a store, and grist mill below the Village of Warwick. The "Sly History" reports that he was a "heavy dealer" in fat stock but that he met with financial reverses which reduced him to day labor. He died from a fall from a load of grain near Warwick thereby breaking his neck. He was a member of the Dolson Family on Long Ridge in Warwick. Isaac owned the plot in the Old Baptist Cemetery where his father-in-law and mother-in-law, Conrad and Anna Sly, were buried. Isaac was also buried in the Old Baptist Cemetery. Unfortunately, his stone has not been located* (Retrieved on 4 October 2012 from.*familytreemaker.com).*

In 2010, this writer visited the Old School Baptist Cemetery and located the grave stones of both Isaac and Catherine Sly Dolson as well as those of *Coonrad* and Anna Ward Sly. Conrad's date of death is indicated as 7 April 1812. Isaac's stone is inscribed "*20 July 1838, 61 years, 1 month, 26 days.*"

Catherine Sly Dolson's stone shows that she was the wife of Isaac and died on 13 October 1823 at the age of forty-four years, eleven months, and eleven days. Her birthdate is noted as 12 November 1779 (Sly, 2010). A letter of administration dated 28 February 1824 regarding Catherine Sly *Dolson* is on file in the Surrogates Office of Orange County (Liber E, p. 276). Little more is known about Isaac's wife. Parker Seese (1941), claims that upon marrying Isaac, Catherine had a large dower of gold. Catherine Sly Dolson and Isaac Dolson had the following two children (Plimley 2011; Sly 2010):

1. Ann Dolson was born ca. 1801. She married a lawyer in Newburgh, a man named Crary.
2. John Dolson was born ca. 1805.

In 1808, Isaac Dolson is noted on town records as providing land for an animal pound and hence was elected Pound Master.

Isaac Dolson was involved in three legal cases with William Wickham, Orange County's first attorney and later a judge. William Wickham was also an owner of large tract of land (Parker Seese, 1960). Later, his son, Samuel, would marry Ellen Adelia Dolsen, daughter of Frederick and Margaret Moore Dolsen. In a case denoted as Phillips vs. Dolson, dated 8 June 1812, Isaac was a defendant. His attorney was Henry G. Wisner. A second case took place on 11 March 1818 and fellow litigants were Henry G. Wisner and John Sutton. In a third case, we again see Isaac as a defendant along with Henry G. Wisner, his advocate, in a case described as a levy on the assets of Dolson in favor of Ball. This last action took place on 9 January 1823. The dates of these cases seem to coincide with the period of Isaac's imprudent real estate purchases and the scandalous mill pond incident.

An Isaac *Dolson* is noted on multiple, Orange County deeds in Warwick from as early as 1792 and 1801 (Liber H, p. 164) to as late as 1836 (Liber 56, p. 570). The 1792 deed contains the names of Isaac Dolsen and his wife Elizabeth (probably Elizabeth Weymer). For many years, subsequent deeds clearly denote Isaac and his wife, Catherine (Sly), as parties of the first part. However, on 13 April 1824, in a transaction with James Hoyt for sixteen acres, only the name Isaac Dolson appears. The name of a wife is omitted. On 8 October 1832, a quarter acre lot is sold to Nicholas Demorest for $85 by a man who signs his name *Isaac Dolsen Junior* with his wife, Margaret. Finally, on 1 May 1834, another quarter acre lot is sold to James McWhorter for $50. In this case, the Dolson party makes his mark as Isaac Dolsen Jr. The author has not discovered conclusively the identities of the Isaac who married Elizabeth Weymer, the Isaac who married Margaret (surname unknown) nor the Isaac who identified himself in Warwick as Isaac Jr in 1834. These could all be different men or they could be one or two men who married more than once or used temporarily the moniker Junior.

An Isaac *Dolson* appears on the Warwick tax assessments for the years 1813 and 1815. In 1814, the citizens of Warwick founded an association to establish a public library. The first meeting of this committee was held at the home of Isaac Dolson on 12 December 1814 (Ruttenber and Clark, 1881, p. 597). An Isaac Dolson is noted as a Constable of Warwick from 1803 to 1805. An Isaac was subscribed to pew number 20 located on the lower floor of the Old School Baptist meeting house in 1815.

An Isaac Dolson was also involved in Orange County land transactions in 1815 with Jacob Jew (Liber Q, p. 395). Before 1820, for a relatively short time, Isaac owned the Masonic Brick Building located at Main and West streets in Warwick (Sayer, 1927).

Isaac was not only a farmer and hotelkeeper but also a miller. There are numerous accounts in Warwick historical documents of a grist and sawmill operated first by an Isaac Dolson and later owned by Frederick Dolsen. Following are several stories about this infamous mill pond. Perhaps the most detailed, dramatic, but authentic account of the events comes from an article written by Samuel Pelton for the *Warwick Valley Dispatch*, dated 29 July 1903:

> **EARLY DAY MEMORIES. _____ Matters of Historical Interest to Residents of the Warwick Valley, recalled by an octogenarian, SAMUEL PELTON. -- Being one of the few persons now living who can remember the circumstances, I have been requested by some of my friends to write down what I remember about the Dolson mill pond. I was quite young at the time, but I can remember the mill**

and the pond which was on the farm now owned by George Hyatt. The dam extended across the creek a hundred feet or more above the bridge now at the gate of the Driving Park, and caused the water to flow a number of acres, and backed up into the village. The power was used to run a grist mill, which stood near the bend in the lane that leads to the Driving Park, directly opposite the house formerly owned by Andrew Geraghty. The mill was owned and run by Isaac Dolson and afterwards by Frederick Dolson. For a number of years previous to 1829, chills and fever had been very prevalent in this valley, there being few families between Warwick and New Milford in which there was not some member who suffered from it, and caused a great many deaths. The people were discouraged. The place had a reputation of being unhealthy, and real estate would not sell. In the family of my grandfather, Jeremiah Morehouse, who lived between the residence of Pierson E. Sanford and the cemetery, there were four down with the fever at the same time. The wife of his son, George Morehouse, died while her husband was confined to his bed, unable to attend the funeral services, which were held at the home. My grandmother and a young girl that lived with them (Catherine Burroughs) were sick at the same time. My grandmother Morehouse died the next week. Mrs. John Pelton, my father's mother, who attended the funeral of her daughter, Mrs. George Morehouse, also took the fever and died the following week. The citizens became greatly alarmed and there were several meetings called and resolutions passed condemning the pond. A suit was brought against Mr. Dolson in the endeavor to have the pond declared a nuisance, but much to their disappointment the jury declared against them. During the following year, my father, Henry Pelton, was taken down with the fever and laid very low for some time, but afterwards recovered. A number of meetings of the inhabitants had been held and a proposition was made to Frederick Dolson, who then owned the mill, to buy the property. From a paper left by my father, I learn that Mr. Dolson, who lived near Middletown, attended one of the meetings with his attorney, Henry G. Wisner, but as the people considered Mr. Dolson's price too high, nothing was done. With breaking up of the ice in the following spring the dam was destroyed. It was rumored that some of the citizens helped to break the dam. Again I quote from my father … Thus matters rested until the dam went away. Another meeting was called and some strong resolutions were passed that we would not aid nor assist either by labor or with materials to build up the dam. By this time the owner seeing that the people were determined, thought proper to comply with their offers and a bargain was completed. A committee was appointed to circulate a subscription paper to raise money to pay the balance if there should be any lack in paying for the property at a sale at auction, which was cheerfully responded to … The bargain referred to was the sale of the farm containing about 50 acres, for $4,000 to the following men: Nathaniel Jones, Samuel Youmans, James Hoyt, Joseph Roe,

George Morehouse, Henry Pelton and Daniel Olmstead. The deed bears date April 20, 1829. The purchasers then sold the property at auction to John Ackerman for $2,902, and in the deed to him, dated May 6, 1829, the following clause was inserted: Excepting and reserving to the parties of the first part for themselves, their heirs as well as in behalf of the inhabitants of said vicinity, forever, the inalienable right to the said Warwick creek, that it freely pass uninterrupted by dam, for hydraulic use or other purposes, obstruction or obstructions of any artificial kind whatsoever, from or by him, the said party of the second part, his heirs, agents, attorneys, executors, administrators, assigns or any other person acting under or in pursuance of his or their attorneys to the intent that all the privileges or immunities heretofore held or enjoyed by the said Dolson, in or by the waters of the said creek for hydraulic machinery embraced within the above described premises, as well as connected therewith, shall all perpetually cease, also excepting and reserving the mill and flume upon the premises recently sold to Abram Van Valen. From the careful wording of the above reservations it would seem that the committee intended to finish the job for all time ... It was thought to be a great risk for Mr. Ackerman to buy the farm and live so close to the pond, but with the removal of the stagnant water the fever disappeared and the valley has been healthy ever since. I remember when the dam went down, I was in school in the old red school house, which stood near where the cemetery gate now stands. At noon we boys went down across the fields to see it. We saw a number of men gathering fish from the mud, but they were thought to be unfit to eat on account of the strong smell from the mud. The mill was afterwards sold to Abram Van Valen, who lived where Luther Buchanan now lives and owned the mill now owned by Conklin & Strong. The machinery was moved by Mr. Van Valen to his mill ...

William Benjamin Sayer, another well-known Warwick historian, related his version of the events in a diary published in 1927:

The old bridge stood a short distance below the present bridge, the road of which was down along the creek then across the bridge and intersecting the present road near the top of the hill above the new Brick Hotel (now 1927 the Dispatch building where that newspaper is published). The back water of the mill pond overflowed the meadows above for a considerable distance.

This occasioned law suits and trouble with the owners of the overflowed lands and the old mill was doomed to destruction. Some of the timbers are still to be seen in the creek. Charles Beardsley was a very industrious man, at time he worked on his farm by moonlight. He sold out to Stephen Rogers, who kept a tavern in the old stone house for some years, and it was a lively place where village statesmen smoked and "talked with looks profound", and was also the *dance house of the vicinity. Stephen Rogers held the property of 100 acres for sale at the price of 550 Pounds and finally sold for that price to John Cassidy, who removed to it from New Jersey. John Cassidy kept a store there for several years, enlarged the house and improved the farm, then sold to Isaac Dolson in 1806 for $4,000. This price was deemed so exorbitant they predicted the ruin of the purse holder as the consequence of his indiscreet bargain. In earlier days of the Warwick Valley settlement, the whole property had been offered for sale for 100 Pounds, but a man could not be found who was daring enough to risk the speculation* (Sayer, 1927).

Isaac Dolson, in about 1827, owned and ran a grist mill on the farm now owned by George W. Hyatt. He had a dam across the creek there which flooded the water back to the Main Street Bridge, forming a large pond. In dry weather he drew off the water in running the mill, leaving the mud in the bottom exposed to the hot summer sunshine, which caused a great amount of sickness. Finally, several citizens of Warwick, after the dam had been washed through by high water, bought the property and then resold it putting this provision in the deed—"that no obstruction should be placed in the creek while grass grew or water run." Since then this village has been very healthy (Sayer, 1898).

Following down the creek we come to the upper ford southeast from the Capt. Benedicts place. At our Main Street crossing there was a dam for the mill of Acel Chase, but below the village, a hundred feet or more above the bridge back of the John. Vail house on West Street, was a mill-dam that for years caused more trouble than anything else in town. It flowed the water of Isaac Dolson's shallow mill-pond almost up to the village of those days, as was very often the case, there was an epidemic of malaria or swamp fever, as it was called, of a most fatal type. Three members of the Pelton family, Mr. Sylvanus Francher and his wife and many others died with it. No family below the village escaped the sickness. At last the property was purchased by seven public-spirited citizens, the dam torn down and when resold a clause in the deed prohibited the building of a dam ever again on any part if the creek flowing through this farm.

Further downstream were important mills at Sandfordville. They were owned by the McCamlys and by the Wheelers at one time. General Hathorn ran a forge on the farm afterward owned by Edward Davis. This was later changed into a carding and fulling mill. At New Milford were more mills. The old machinery from the Isaac Dolsen mill below our village was taken to New Milford and is still there, I am told (Sayer, 1927).

Still another account of the mill pond story is provided by Hornby (1908):

The records of Orange County show that Mr. Frederick Dolson received deeds from the Master in Chancery, December 7th, 1826, 50 acres; July 8th, 1828, 17 acres. On this property he raised a dam and built a grist mill. This dam, it was declared, caused the waters to back up beyond the bridge, on the road leading toward Bellvale. From this Warwick was changed from a healthful locality to one scourged by agues, fevers and all their train of ills and accumulated woes. Numerous deaths occurred, not only in the village, but on its bordering lands, and far down the stream even into New Jersey. Property in Warwick became almost unsalable; in fact, the whole vicinity was affected. Showing the mortality it created, we append the deaths that took place in one limited family circle: Mrs. Sylvanus Fancher died July 19, 1828; her husband September 8, 1828; Mrs. John Pelton, a sister of Mrs. Fancher, January 18, 1829.

The citizens of Warwick were justly alarmed and indignant. They were relieved from their fears and trouble in this manner: While the greatest excitement prevailed, and they were discussing measures for relief, a thaw came, producing a freshet. The millpond was covered with thick ice, and in the night the dam gave way. Traditions of a particular family grievously afflicted by deaths, say that a young man was present at the dam at the beginning of the break, but that he made no outcry nor attempted in any manner to stop the flow.

Public-spirited citizens now arose and vigorously declared that it was the time to get rid of the nuisance. Edward Welling, Henry Pelton and others decided it would be best to call a public meeting. Mr. Pelton penned a notice promptly summoning the townsfolk to assemble; but before the time arrived he was smitten with the prevailing fever, and, though dangerously ill, and confined to his home a long time, his vigorous constitution triumphed, and he finally recovered. A committee was appointed to ascertain whether Mr. Dolson would dispose of the property, and for what sum. The result was that Frederick Dolson and Margaret, his wife, by deed dated April 20, 1829, conveyed to Nathaniel Jones, Samuel Youmans, James Hoyt, Joseph Roe, George Morehouse, Henry Pelton and Daniel Olmstead, described in the deed as a committee appointed by the inhabitants of the vicinity of Dolson's Mill Pond, by purchase the premises connected therewith.

The area of the land, as therein given, was 66 acres; the price paid $4,000...
In a very short time Warwick regained, in its village and vicinity, the reputation for perfect healthfulness aforetime held, and which it has maintained to the present day. At the time of the breaking up of the dam numbers congregated at the empty pond and gathered quantities of fine fish from the pools of water left in holes here and there, and a gentleman of Warwick, then a pupil at the "Red Schoolhouse," declares he went with a

companion to the empty pond, at the noon recess, and saw the fish carried away in large basketfuls.

These are the facts relating to the Dolson mill and pond, as accurately as could be gathered from data and remembrance of those living at the time. Among the lamented at this sad period was Miss Benedict, second daughter of William Benedict. She was a teacher in the district so long presided over (pp. 210-212).

One of the members of the committee which purchased the mill pond was Nathaniel Jones, who at the time was Warwick's Town Clerk. Nathaniel Jones was eventually elected as a member of Congress. This gentleman was highly regarded in the region. His obituary appeared in the *New York Times* on 31 July 1866 (Hull, 2005).

There is no doubt that the mill pond incident made a lasting impression on Warwick. As late as 1936, The *Middletown Times Herald* published an article entitled Down by the Old Mill Stream (31 October 1936). Dolson's mill was featured in the article.

While the stories associated with the mill pond episode are intriguing in themselves, of special genealogical interest are two details embedded in the events. First, in addition to Isaac Dolson of Warwick, Frederick Dolsen and Margaret Moore of Minisink were enmeshed in the ownership of the mill property. The involvement of Dolsens from Minisink in matters of the Dolsons of Warwick suggests a strong bond between these two lines of the family---a bond perhaps related to the paternity of Isaac's father, Abraham Jr. [*Undetermined, Theunis, Jan*]. Secondly, a Pelton family member not only suffered death from the disease triggered by the mill pond episode but also a gentleman by the name of Henry Pelton, a very prominent citizen of Warwick, was involved centrally in the subsequent purchase of the troublesome property which would lead ultimately to resolution of the unfortunate matter. This incident and Henry Pelton's involvement must have left an enduring impression on the entire Dolson family. Frederick and Margaret's son, John C. Dolson, who migrated to California in 1850, gave his son, David, the middle name of Pelton in 1861. The name Pelton was afterwards passed on to David's son, grandson, and great grandson.

Appendix Summary

As is the case with other branches of Dolson genealogy, the historical accounts regarding the members of the family from Warwick contain information gaps, ambiguities, and paradoxes. Even if the problems related to the Identity of the various Abrahams, Isaacs, Matthews, Peters, and Jacobs have not been satisfactorily resolved, the research evidence that is available provides a chronicle of what turns out to be a tremendously interesting part of the Dolson family narrative.

References

Adams, John Wolcott. 1916. Redraft of the Castello Plan, New Amsterdam in 1660. No Publisher. New York Public Library. New York.

Albanese, Jeffrey. 2007. The Rededication of the 124th NYSV Monument in the Orange County Historical Society Journal. Vol. 36. Arden, New York.

Baird, Jim. 2001. Ledger of Francis Baird 1773-1774. Albert Wisner Public Library. Warwick, New York.

Baldwin, John D. 1993. De Long Family Manuscript. Published by author. Clove Heights, Ohio.

Barratt, Albert Gedney. 1928. Newburgh in the American Revolution. Publisher not Identified. New York.

Barns, Cheyrene Buis. 2016. From Holland to Forsyth County Georgia. Retrieved from http://buicefamilyreunion.com/ on 11 April 2016.

Beauchamp, William M. 1913. Revolutionary soldiers resident or dying in Onondaga County, NY: With supplemental possible veterans based on a pension list of Franklin H. Chase, Syracuse, NY. McDonnell Company. Syracuse, New York.

Beck, Henry Charlton. 1983. Tales and Towns of Northern New Jersey. Rutgers University Press. New Brunswick, New Jersey.

Benton, John Hogan. 1906. David Benton Jr. and Sarah Bingham: their ancestors and descendants and other ancestral lines. Press of D. Clapp and Son. Boston, Massachusetts.

Bergen, Teunis. 1881. Register in Alphabetical Order of the Early Settlers of Kings County. S.W. Green's Son Printer. New York.

Bergen, Teunis G. 1876. The Monfoort Family. The New York Genealogical and Biographical Record, Vol. VII, No. 4, October 1876, pp. 152-160.

Bergen, Tunis. 1915. Genealogies of the State of New York. Lewis Historical Publishing Company. New York.

Bilali, Kevin Barett. 1992. Guinea: An African American Settlement in the Town of Wallkill in the Orange County Historical Society Journal. Vol. 31. Arden, New York.

Biographical and General History of The City of Newark and Essex County, New Jersey. 1898. Lew Publishing Company. New York and Chicago.

Bolton, Reginald Pelham. 1916. Relics of the revolution: The story of the discovery of the buried remains of military life in forts and camps on Manhattan Island. Published by the author. New York.

Bolton, Reginald Pelham. 1924. Washington Heights, Manhattan, Its eventful past. Dyckman Institute. New York.

Bolton, Reginald Pelham. 2016. Washington's Headquarters, New York: A Sketch of the History of the Morris Mansion (or Jumel Mansion) in the City of New York, Used by Washington as His Headquarters in 1776. Forgotten Books. London.

Boyer, Carl. 1978. Ship passenger lists, New York and New Jersey, 1600-1825. Published by author. Newhall, California.

Bradsby, Henry (Editor). 1893. History of Luzerne County Pennsylvania. S. B. Nelson and Company Publishers. Chicago, Illinois.

Brennan, Robert. 2000. Wallkill Orange County, New York. Vols.1 and 2. Orange County Genealogical Society. Goshen, New York.

Brennan, Robert. 2001-2005. Genealogical History of Blacks in Orange County. Vols. 1-5. Orange County Genealogical Society. Goshen, New York.

Brinkerhoff, T. VanWyck. 1866. Historical sketch and directory of the town of Fishkill. Dean and Spaight Publishers. Fishkill Landing, New York.

Burt, Roonie and Gary Burt. 1997. DeLong Family History. Manuscript published by the authors. Copy available at Family History Library, Salt Lake City, Utah.

Calendar of historical manuscripts, relating to the war of the revolution in the office of the Secretary of State. 1868. Weed, Parsons, and Company Printers. Albany, New York.

Carnochan, Janet. No Date. Names Only But Much More in Niagara Historical Society No. 27. Niagara Historical Museum. Retrieved at *www.niagarahistorical.museum* on 9 January 2018.

Carpenter, Amos B. 1898. A Genealogical History of the Rehoboth Branch of the Carpenter Family in America. Press of Carpenter and Morehouse. Amherst, Massachusetts.

Carpenter, David H. 1996. History and Genealogy of the Carpenter Family in America: The Settlement at Providence, Rhode Island (1637-1690). Acme Publishers. Charlestown, Massachusetts.

Cassidy, Henry. 1985. The Rombout Patent. Dutchess County Historical Society Collections. Vol. XI. Poughkeepsie, New York.

Chrysler, Walter and Boyden Sparkes. 2011. Life of an American Workman (Second Edition). Oxford City Press. Oxford, England.

Clark, Donald. 1972. Joseph Brant and the Battle of Minisink, 22nd July 1779 in the Orange County Historical Society Journal. Vol. I. Arden, New York.

Clark, Donald. 1974. Orange County New York in the Orange County Historical Society Journal. Vol. 3. Arden, New York.

Clark, Donald. 1975. A Challenge in Quantitative History in the Orange County Historical Society Journal. Vol. 4. Arden, New York.

Clark, Robert Gordon. 2015. Early New Netherland Setters. Posted at rootsweb.ancestry.com. Retrieved on 12 December 2017.

Cochrane, Charles H. 1887. The History of the Town of Marlborough. W. F. Bashart, Printers. Poughkeepsie, New York.

Coleman, Charles C. 1989. The Early Records of the First Presbyterian Church at Goshen, New York. Heritage Books. Bowie, Maryland.

Colonial Records of Pennsylvania, Minutes of the Provincial Council of Pennsylvania. 1852. Vol. IX, p. 49. Severns and Company. Philadelphia.

Colton, Julia M. 1901. Annals of Old Manhattan, 1609-1664. Heintzemann Press. Boston, Massachusetts.

Coulter, William. 1938. Van Dolsen Family Data. The Wantage Recorder. 18 February 1930. Sussex, New Jersey.

Cregier, Ellsworth B. 1959. One Line of the Cregier Family in America. Private Printing. Chicago, Illinois.

Davis, Norman. 2009. Westchester Patriarchs: A Genealogical Dictionary of Westchester County, New York, Families Prior To 1755. Heritage Books. Westminster, Maryland.

Davis, Winfield. J. 1890. An Illustrated History of Sacramento County, California. Transcribed by Karen Pratt, pp. 511-512. Lewis Publishing Company. Chicago, Illinois.

Deubler, Vernon A. (Editor). 2003. San Francisco California Columbarium Records 1847-1980. California Genealogical Society. San Francisco, California.

Disturnell, J. 1843. A Gazetteer of the State of New York, Second Edition. C. Van Benthuysen and Company, Albany, New York.

Doherty, Frank. 1990. The Settlers of the Beekman Patent (Vol. I). Series with multiple volumes. Volumes I through XIII available as of February 2018. The chapter on the Dolson family is contained in Volume IV, 1997. Series published by author. Orlando, Florida.

Doherty, Frank. 1990. The History of the Clove Valley 1697-1740 in The Dutchess County Historical Society Yearbook, Vol. 75, pp. 28-39, Poughkeepsie, New York.

Dolsen, Donald. 1992. What We Know about the DOLSEN Family. Manuscript published by the author. Copy on file at the Orange County Genealogical Society. Goshen, New York.

Dolson, Samuel D. 1932. The Dolson Family. Manuscript compiled and arranged by author. Original copy furnished by Maude Dolson MacGlasson. Beacon, New York.

Dutchess County Historical Society. 2004. Manuscript entitled Silver Ribbon House Tour Presented by Dutchess County Historical Society, June 12, 2004. Poughkeepsie, New York.

Eager, Samuel. 1846. An Outline History of Orange County. S.T. Callahan Publisher. Newburgh, New York.

Eberlien, Harold D. and Cortlandt Van Dyke. 1990. Historic Houses of The Hudson Valley. Dover Publishers. Mineola, New York.

Eastchester Historical Society. 1975. Records of the Combined Parish of Westchester (Bronx), Eastchester, New Rochelle, Yonkers, Pelham, Morrisania 1702-1720. Eastchester, New York.

Eastchester Historical Society. 1969. Records of the Town of Eastchester, New York. Eastchester, New York.

Ehrlich, Morris William. 1912. Historic Traces on Upper Manhattan or The Town of "Nieuw Haerlem" including Modern Harlem and Washington Heights: With the Present Lines of City Streets. No Publisher. New York Historical Society, New York.

Ellsworth, John La Coste. 1992. The Family History of Donald Joseph La Coste and Ellsworth John La Coste. Published by Author. Retrieved from Genealogy.Com on 19 July 2017.

Ewins, Donna G. 1999. Pieter Pieterse Lassen of Dutchess County and His Descendants in the New York Genealogical and Biographical Record, Vol. 130, No. 2, p.135.

Feagles, Carrie Timlow. 1949. History of the Amity Presbyterian Church. Reprinted 1994. Orange County Genealogical Society. Goshen, New York.

Felner, Royal. 2012. History of the American Automobile Industry, 1891-1929. Posted at *www.earlyamericanautomobiles.com*. Retrieved on 8 October 2012.

Fernow, Berthold (Editor). 1976. The Records of New Amsterdam from 1653 to 1774 Anno Domini, Vols. 1-7. Genealogical Publishing Company. Baltimore, Maryland.

Fernow, Berthold. 1887. New York in the Revolution. Weed, Parsons, and Company. Albany, New York.

Fernow, Berthold (Editor). 1887. Documents Relating to the Colonial History of the State of New York. New York State Archives. Albany, New York.

Fernow, Berthold. 1898. New Amsterdam Family Names and Their Origin. Putnam's and Son. New York.

Figliomeni, Michelle P. 1997. The Flickering Flame: Treachery and Loyalty in the Mid-Hudson during the Revolution. Spear Printing. Washingtonville, New York.

Florida, New York, Orange County: An early look at its faces, places and winding staircases. 2002. The Society. Warwick, New York.

Foley, Janet Wethy. 1993. Early Settlers of New York State, Vols. I and II. Genealogy Publishing Company. Baltimore, Maryland.

Francis Baird Account Book 1773-1774. 1981. Orange County Genealogical Society Quarterly, Vol. 10, Issue 4, pp. 27-28.

French, J.H. 1860. Gazetteer of the State of New York. Published by R. Pearsall Smith. Syracuse, New York.

Gardner, Susan. 2008. Compiled Service Records for Col. Hathorn's Militia Regiment - Compiled Service Records of Soldiers Who Served in the American Army during the Revolutionary War: 1775-1783. National Archives and Records Administration Number: NARA M881. Albert Wisner Library. Warwick, New York.

Gibson, James Jr. 1889. James Riker in the New York Genealogical and Biological Society Record. Vol. 20, No. 4, pp. 175-176.

Griffin, Walter Kenneth. 1909. The Dutcher Family. New York Genealogical and Biographical Record. Vol. 40, pp. 149-157.

Guide to the Archives of the Government of the United States in Washington, Second Edition. 1907. Peter Dolson Orderly Book. Carnegie Institute. Washington, D.C.

Gumaer, Harry T. 1981. A Minisink fragment: Early American frontier life in southeastern New York, with a brief Gumaer family history. Minisink Valley Historical Society. New York.

Hains, A.A. 1889. John Hathorn in the New York Genealogical and Biographical Record. Vol. 20, No. 4, p. 169.

Hall, Dennis Jay. 1999. The Journals of Sir William Johnson's Scouts 1755- & 1756. Essence of Vermont Publishers. Panton, Vermont

Hall, William K. No Date. The Bussing Family: Descendants of Arent Harmans Bussing. Manuscript on file at the New York Genealogical and Biographical Society. New York.

Hall, William Kearney. 1992. Genealogy of the Bussing family: Descendants of Arent Harman Bussing who came from Bentheim in Westphalia to New York City in 1639, settling at Harlem: With special attention given to the descendants of his great grandson, Timothy Bussing, born 1739, New York City, died 1831, Bethlehem, Albany County, New York. Available on WorldCat.

Hallam, Keith. 2009. Hallam-Dolson History. Vol. I. Published by author. Posted at *www.okhallam.com.*

Hamil, Fred Coyne. 1951. The Valley of the Lower Thames, 1640 to 1850. University of Toronto Press, Toronto.

Hamilton, William L. 1997. House Proud; To Get the Doorway, Buy the House. New York Times, 30 October 1997.

Hamlin, Belle. 1905. The Dolson family: Dealing mainly with the family in Fishkill, Dutchess County, Orange County, and Ulster County (New York). Report commissioned by Jacob Dolson Cox. Edited by Kenneth E. Hasbrouck. Manuscript on film at the Family History Library. Salt Lake City, Utah.

Hasbrouck, Frank. 1909. The History of Dutchess County New York. S.A. Matthieu Publisher. Poughkeepsie, New York.

Hasbrouck, Kenneth E. 1958. German Reformed Church of Montgomery, Orange County, New York. Vol. 1. New Paltz, New York. Posted at Ancestery.com.

Haxtun, Annie Arnoux. 1903. Early Settlers of New Amsterdam, New York. No Publisher. New York Historical Society. New York.

Heedley, Russel. 1908. The History of Orange County, New York. Van Deusen and Elms. Middletown, New York.

Heidgerd, Ruth. 1977. Ulster County in the Revolution. Huguenot Historical Society. New Paltz, New York.

Heidgerd, William. 1977. Mills Family Compiled. New Paltz, New York. Manuscript archived at Thrall Library, Middletown, New York.

Hendrickson, Mark, Jon Inners, and Peter Osborn. 2010. So Many Brave Men: A History of the Battle of Minisink Ford. Pienpeck Company. Easton, Pennsylvania.

Holbert, Grace Pelton. 1953. Members of the Old School Baptist Church, Warwick, NY 1765-1830. Published in The Warwick Advertiser, 26 February 1953. Transcribed March 2003 by Susan Gardner. Warwick Historical Society. Warwick, New York.

Holland, Emma F. 1931. History of the Sloat Family of the Nobility of Holland. Manuscript at Family History Library. Salt Lake City, Utah.

Holland Society (Editor). 1901. Baptisms from 1639 to 1730 in the Reformed Dutch Church of New York. The Gregg Press. Upper Saddle River, New Jersey.

Holland Society (Editor). 1901. Marriages from 1639 to 1730 in the Reformed Dutch Church of New York. The Gregg Press. Upper Saddle River, New Jersey.

Hornby, Eliza Benedict. 1908. Under Old Roof Trees. Cornell University Library Press. Ithaca, New York.

Horton, Elizabeth. No Date. Elizabeth Horton Collection of Genealogical Notes. Orange County Genealogical Society. Goshen, New York.

Hull, Richard W. 1975. People of the Valleys. Warwick Historical Society. Warwick, New York.

Hull, Richard W. 1996. History of Warwick New York: Three Centuries of a Community, 1696-1996. Warwick Historical Society. Warwick, New York.

Hull, Richard W. 2002. John Hathorn: American Patriot in the Orange County Historical Society Journal, Vol. 31. Arden, New York.

Hull, Richard W. 2005. People of the Valleys Revisited: History of Warwick, NY 1700-2005. Warwick Historical Society. Warwick, New York.

Hull, Richard. 2007. The Story of The Old-School Baptist Meeting House. Warwick Historical Society. Posted at _http://warwickvillagewedding.com_. Retrieved on 29 March 2011.

Joslyn, Roger D. Indentures of the Poor Children of Orange County, 1829-1847, 1871, 1884, and 1885, in The New York Genealogical and Biographical Record. Vol. 137, No. 4 (October 2006), pp. 294-303; Vol. 138, No. 2 (April 2007), pp. 138-143; Vol. 138, No. 3 (July 2007), pp. 227-231.

Kelley, Arthur C.M. 2000. Names, names, and more names: locating your Dutch ancestors in Colonial America. Ancestery.com. Lehi, Utah.

Kelley, Arthur C.M. 1974. Baptismal Record of the Zion Evangelical Lutheran Church of Athens, NY 1704-1899. Kinship Books, Rhinebeck, New York.

Kelly, Arthur and Nancy Kelley. 2007. Early Dutchess County Lists--Colonial Military. Colonial Archives (Vol. LX) in the Dutchess. Vol. 34, No. 4, Summer 2007. Dutchess County Genealogical Society. Wappinger Falls, New York.

Klett, Joseph R. 1996. Genealogies of New Jersey Families. Genealogical Publishing Company. Baltimore, Maryland.

La Lune, James. 2016. Adrien's Descendants, Part 2. Posted at Genealogy.com. Retrieved on 15 June 2016.

Lincoln, James Minor. 1925. The Nagle-Dyckman-Vermilye Cemetery. Manuscript on Film [No. 1016870, Item 1]. Family History Library, Salt Lake City, Utah.

Macy, Harry Jr. 1985. Gerritsen-Garrison, Van Wicklen, Hardenbergh, Wiltsie: Decedents of Gerrit Lubbertsen of Jamaica, LI in the New York Genealogical and Biographical Society Record. Vol. 116, No. 3, pp. 155-163.

Magee, Joan. 1984. Loyalist Mosaic, A Multi-ethnic Heritage, Dundurn Press. Toronto and Charlottetown, Canada.

MoDermott, William P. 1982. Land Grants in Dutchess County, 1683-1733 in Dutchess County Historical Society Yearbook, 1982. Poughkeepsie, New York.

Meeker Family Bible, 2002. Record [1753-1852] of the Family of David L. Meeker, son of the Revolutionary Soldier, David Nathanial Meeker, 3rd Bible. Copy taken from Daughters of the American Revolution. Family History Library Film [No. 317359], Salt Lake City, Utah.

Meeker, Leroy J. 1973. The Meeker Family of Early New Jersey. Capitol Printing Company. Charleston, West Virginia.

Military Minutes of the Council of Appointment of the State of New York, 1783-1821. 1901. State of New York. Albany.

Minisink – A Bicentennial History. 1988. Bicentennial Commission of the Town of Minisink. Minisink, New York.

Minutes of the Common Council of the City of New York, 1784-1831. 1917. Vol. 1. City of New York, New York.

Moore, James. 1903. Rev. John Moore of Newtown, Long Island, and some of his descendants. Chemical Publishers. Easton, Pennsylvania.

Monfoort, Monfort, Montfort Family. No Date. Typescript [LH 929.2]. Adriance Memorial Library. Poughkeepsie, New York.

Morris, Rod. 2011. The Morris Clan. Posted at *http://www.themorrisclan.com*. Retrieved on 29 March 2011.

Municipalities. Orange County Genealogical Society Quarterly. 1974. Vol. 4, Issue 3, p. 20.

Munsell, Joel. 1865. Collections on the History of Albany: From its discovery to the present time with notices of its public institutions and biographical sketches of citizens deceased. Published by Joel Munsell. Albany, New York.

Nash, Carolyn. 2010. Small Burghers of New Amsterdam: New Document, New Names. The New York Genealogical and Biographical Record. Vol. 141, No. 1, pp. 25-38.

National Bank of Orange County. 2014. Orange County A History. Goshen, New York.

Native Daughters of the Golden West. No Date. Index to the Roster of California Pioneers. Retrieved at ndgw.org on 8 January 2018.

New York in the Revolution as Colony and State. 1904. A Compilation of Documents and Records from the State Comptroller. Vol. I. J. B. Lyon Company Printers. Albany, New York.

O'Callaghan, E.B. 1850. The Documentary History of the State of New York. Weed, Parsons, and Company. Albany, New York.

O'Callaghan, E.B. 1865. The Register of New Netherland, 1626-1674. J. Munsell Publisher. Albany, New York.

Old Miscellaneous Records of Dutchess County - The Second Book of the Supervisors and Assessors. 1909. Vassar Brother's Institute. Poughkeepsie, New York.

Old Miscellaneous Records of Dutchess County - The Third Book of the Supervisors and Assessors. 1911. Vassar Brother's Institute. Poughkeepsie, New York.

Old School Baptist Church, Slate Hill. 1977. Orange County Genealogical Society Quarterly. Vol. 6, Issue 4, p.26.

Parker, Mildred Seese. 1941. Old Orange Houses. Albert Wisner Public Library. Book Mill. Middletown, New York.

Parker, Mildred Seese. 1945. A Tower of the Lord. First Presbyterian Church of Goshen New York, 1720-1945. Book Mill. Goshen, New York.

Parker, Mildred Seese. 1990. A Tower of the Lord in the Land of Goshen. Windy Hill Book Mill. Goshen, New York.

Pelton, Henry. Recollections of the Early History of Warwick. 1872. Advertiser Steam Job Printing Establishment. Albert Wisner Public Library. Warwick, New York.

Penross, Mary B. 1987. New York Law Book Patrons in 1792 in the New York Genealogical and Biographical Society Record. Vol. 118, No. 2, p. 85.

Plimley, Ronald. 2011. Dalfsens to Van Dolsons. A Collection of Dolson Genealogy Records. Revised Third Edition. Original published in 2003 by the author. Wappingers Falls, New York. Copy on file at Orange County Genealogical Society. Goshen, New York.

Pirsson, John W. 1889. The Dutch Grants, Harlem Patents, and Tidal Creeks. L.K. Strouse and Company, New York.

Portrait and Biographical Record of Orange County New York. 1895. Chapman Publishing Company. New York.

Poucher, J. Wilson and Helen Wilkinson Reynolds. 1976. Old Gravestones of Dutchess County New York. Richwood Publishing. Merrick, New York.

Proceedings of the Grand Lodge of Free and Accepted Masons of the State of New York. 1900. Press of J.J. Little and Company. New York.

Privitar, Ginny. 2012. What is in a Name? The Chronicle. Chester, New York. June 29, 2012.

Public Papers of George Clinton, First Governor of New York, 1777-1795, 1801-1804. 1973. Vols. II, III, IV, VI, VIII. Published by the State of New York. Albany, New York.

Pumpelly, Josiah Collins. 1903. The Old Morris House, Afterwards The Jumel Mansion: Its History and Traditions. The New York Genealogical and Biographical Society Record. Vol. 34, No. 2.

Purple, Edwin R. 1881. History of Ancient Families of New Amsterdam and New York. New England Historic Genealogical Society, Boston, Massachusetts.

Reaman, G. Elmore. 1993 (Reprinted). The Trail of the Black Walnut. Genealogical Publishing Company. Baltimore, Maryland.

Reamy, Martha and Bill Reamy. 2003. Pioneer Families of Orange County, New York. Heritage Books. Westminster, Maryland.

Reese, William Willis. 1938. Eighteenth Century Records of the portion of Dutchess County New York that was included in Rombout Precinct and the original Town of Fishkill. Helen Wilkinson Reynolds, Editor. Dutchess County Historical Society. Poughkeepsie, New York.

Reynolds, Helen Wilkinson. 1931. Dutchess County Doorways and Other Examples of Period Work in Wood 1730-1830 with Accounts of Houses, Places and People. William Farquhar Payson. New York.

Reynolds, Helen Wilkinson. 1940. First Settlers on Great Nine Partners Patent in the Dutchess County Historical Society Year Book, 1940. Dutchess County Historical Society. Poughkeepsie, New York.

Riker, David. 1999. Genealogical and Biographical Directory of Persons in New Netherland from 1613 to 1674. Five Volumes. Higgison Book Company. Salem, Massachusetts.

Riker, James. 1881. Harlem, City of New York: Its Origin and Early Annals. Reprinted by Kessinger Publishing. New York.

Riker, James. 1904. Revised History of Harlem: Its Origin and Early Annals. New Harlem Publishing Company. New York.

Ritterman, Saul. 1996. A Survey of Orange County Mills in the Orange County Historical Society Journal. Vol. 25. Arden, New York.

Roecker, Femi. No Date. Store Ledger 1785-1786 Baird's Tavern. Historical Society of the Town of Warwick. Albert Wisner Public Library. Warwick, New York.

Romney, Susannah Shaw. 2014. New Netherlands Connections. University of North Carolina Press. Chapel Hill, North Carolina.

Romer, H. Dorothea and Helen B. Hartman. 1981. Jan Dyckman of Harlem and His Descendants. J.A. Thompson Publisher. New York.

Roosa, Laura. 1906. A Grave Matter. The Compiler. Fishkill-on-Hudson, New York.

Ross, John F. 2009. War on the run: the epic story of Robert Rogers and the conquest of America's first frontier. Bantam Books. New York.

Ruttenber, Eduard Manning. History of the Town of Newbugh. 1859. E.M. Ruttenber Publisher. Newbugh, New York.

Ruttenber, E.M. and L.H. Clark. 1881. History of Orange County. Everts and Peck Publishers. Philadelphia, Pennsylvania.

Sabine, Lorenzo. 1864. Biographical Sketches of Loyalists in the American Revolution. Vols. I and II. Little Brown and Company. Boston, Massachusetts.

Samson, Fred B. 2011. Grant Samson Burton Genealogy and Family History. Posted at *http://sites.google.com/sites/grantsafamily/*. Retrieved 28 March 2011.

Saterfied, Lawrence Mackenzie. 2002. Ancestors of Lawrence Mackenzie Saterfield Sr. Rootsweb.com. Retrieved on 9 January 2018.

Sayer, W.B. 1898. Early Days in Warwick. Series originally published in the Warwick Advertiser between 31 March and 12 May,1898. Warwick, New York.

Scott, Kenneth. 1983 Minutes of the Mayor's Court of New York, 1674-1675. Genealogical Publishing. Baltimore, Maryland.

Scott, Kenneth and Kenn Stryker-Rodda. 2009. Denizations, naturalizations, and oaths of allegiance in colonial New York. Revised Edition. Clearfield Company. Baltimore, Maryland.

Seward, Augustus. 1866. An extract from a discourse delivered Sabbath evening, March 25, 1866: On occasion of the last public service held in the old house of worship of the First Presbyterian Church, Middletown. J.W. Hasbrouck Printer. Middletown, New York.

Skye, Stephen. 2015. Why the Goshen Militia Rushed to the Rescue and Was Devastated at the Battle of Minisink in the Orange County Historical Society Journal. Vol. 44. Arden, New York.

Slipper, James Henry. 1910. Resolved Waldron's Descendants: Vanderpoel Branch. Macgowen and Slipper. New York.

Sloat, Francis W. 1996. 300 Years of The Sloat Family, Denmark to Orange County, NY (and Beyond). Presentation to the Orange County Genealogical Society on 1 June 1996. Goshen, New York.

Sly Family History. 2016. Orange County Genealogical Society Quarterly. May 2016, Vol. 46, No. 1, pp. 2-4.

Sly, John T. 2010. Conrad Sly Home Page. Retrieved on 20 July 2017 from (http://familytreemaker.genealogy.com/users/s/l/y/John-T-Sly/Index.html.

Smith, James H. 1882. History of Dutchess County, NY with Illustrations and Biographical Sketches. D. Mason and Company. Syracuse, New York.

Stickney, Charles E. 1867. History of the Minisink Region. Coe, Finch, and I.F. Guiwits, Publishers. Middletown, New York.

Stoetzel, Donald I. 2008. Encyclopedia of the French and Indian War in North America, 1754-1763. Heritage Books. Westminster, Maryland.

Stokes, I.N. Phelps. 1918. The Iconography of Manhattan Island. Vol. III. Series of six volumes published between 1915 and 1928. R.H. Dodd Publisher. New York.

Storm, Raymond William. 1949. Old Dirck's Book: A Brief Account of the Life and Times of Dirck Storm of Holland, His Antecedents, and the Family He Founded in America in 1662. Published by author. Retrieved from the HATHI TRUST Digital Library.

Stressin-Cohn, Susan and Ashley Hurlburt-Biagini. 2016. In Defiance: Runaways from Slavery in New York's Hudson River Valley 1735-1831. Black Dome Press. Delmar, New York.

Tallmadge, Samuel. 1932. Orderly Books of the Fourth New York Regiment, 1778-1780, The Second New York Regiment, 1780-1783 and the Diaries of Samuel Tallmadge, 1780-1782 and John Barr, 1779-1782. Published by the University of the State of New York. Albany.

Tharp, Peter. 1801. An Elegy on the Death of Captain Annanias Valentine… No Publisher. New York Historical Society. New York.

The Port Jervis Evening Gazette. 10 May 1879. The Slain and the saved: Names of all who participated in the Minisink Battle. Port Jervis, New York.

The Record of a Century of Church Life of the Reformed Church, Warwick, 1804-1904. 2015. Forgotten Books. London.

Tilton, Edgar Jr. 1910. The Reformed Low Dutch Church of Harlem. The Consistory. New York.

Toedteberg, Emma. 1907. Inscriptions from the Montfort Buying Ground on the Farm of George Brown, Sprout Creek, Wappinger's Falls, Dutchess County, New York. N.P. New York Historical Society. New York.

Toler, Henry Pennington. 1903. The New Harlem Register: A genealogy of the descendants of the twenty-three original patentees of the town of New Harlem, containing proofs of births, baptisms and marriages from the year 1630 to date. New Harlem Publishing Company. New York.

Totten, John Reynolds. 1935. Jan Cornelis Buys (alias Jan Damen) in the New York Genealogical and Biographical Record, July 1935. Vol. 66, No. 3, pp. 225-237.

Totten, Sherman and Mary O'Connor English. 1979. Early Town Records of Mamaroneck, 1697-1881. Harbor Hill Publishers. Harrison, New York.

Town and City Registers of Men Who Served in the Civil War, 1861-1865. New York State Archives. Albany, New York.

Transcripts of Harlem Indentures, 1666-1855. No Publisher. New York Historical Society. New York.

Townsend, Robert. 2010. The Slots from Wall Street to Pompton. Retrieved from *www.northjersey.com* on 5 March 2011.

Vail, Henry Hobart. 1902. Genealogy of some of the Vail Family Descended from Jeremiah Vail at Salem Mass, 1639. Divinnie Press. New York.

Van Curen, D.G. No Date. Van Keulen/Van Keuren/Van Kuren/Van Curen?: A Family History. Published by author. Boise, Idaho.

Van Deusen, A.H. 1900. Butler's Rangers in the New York Genealogical and Biographical Society Record. P. 15.

Van Duzer, Elizabeth C. 1923. Elder James Benedict – The Pioneer Preacher of the Warwick and Wyoming Valleys. Manuscript from the original records of the Baptist Church in Warwick, New York and Wilkes-Barre, PA. Published on the Internet with permission of the Wyoming Valley Historical Society by the Albert Wisner Public Library. Warwick, New York.

Van Duzer, Genevieve. 1917. Old Landmarks About Warwick Town. Published in three parts in the Warwick Valley Dispatch on 7 March, 14 March, and 21 March 1917. Warwick, New York.

Van Glieson, Aomon P. 1893. Anniversary Discourse and History of the First Reformed Church of Poughkeepsie. The Consistory. Poughkeepsie, New York.

Van Loon, Hendrik Willem. 1930. The Life and Times of Rembrandt. Kessinger Legacy Reprints. Garden City Publishing Company. Garden City, New York.

Van Voorhis, Elias William. 1900. Dutch Church of Fishkill Village, Dutchess County, NY. G.P. Putnam. New York.

Wallace, John Hakins. 1877. The Hickorys in Orange County. Wallace's Monthly. Vol. III, No. I, February 1877, p. 249.

Warwick Historical Papers: 1914, 1933, and 1950. Historical Society of the Town of Warwick. Orange County Genealogical Society. Goshen, New York.

Weygant, Charles H. 1877. History of the One Hundred and Twenty-Fourth Regiment, N.Y.S.V. Journal Printing House. Newburgh, New York.

Wheat, Silas Cami. 1903. Wheat Genealogy. Reprinted in 1960 by Shkore Line Times Publishers. Guilford, Connecticut.

Williams, Franklin B. 1928. Middletown: A Biography. Lawrence A. Toepp Publisher. Middletown, New York.

Winslow, Mary Isabel. 1955. Dolson Family Manuscript. Family History Library. Salt Lake City, Utah.

Winslow, Mary Isabel. 1978. Henry Bush Revolutionary War Soldier – 1760-1839 in Historical Wyoming. Vol. XXV, No. 2, October 1978.

Wisner, G. Franklin. 2015. The Wisners in America and Their Kindred. Scholar's Choice Book Marketing. Rochester, New York.

Wolf, William III. 2000. First Reformed Protestant Dutch Church of Fishkill Town Dutchess County New York. Manuscript published by author. Adriance Memorial Library. Poughkeepsie, New York.

Woolsey, C.M. 1908. History of the Town of Marlborough, Ulster County, New York From Its Earliest Discovery. J.B. Lyon Company. Albany, New York.

Year Book 1947 Dutchess County Historical Society. 1947. Vol. 32. Dutchess County Historical Society. Poughkeepsie, New York.

Made in the USA
Monee, IL
23 April 2021